The Old Testament: An Introduction

Rolf Rendtorff

The Old Testament
An Introduction

Fortress Press   Philadelphia

Translated by John Bowden from the German
Das Alte Testament: Eine Einführung

© Neukirchener Verlag 1983

Translation © John Bowden 1985

First Fortress Press Edition 1986

First paperback edition 1991

Library of Congress Cataloging in Publication Data
Rendtorff, Rolf, 1925-
    The Old Testament

    "Translated by John Bowden from the German: Das Alte
Testament"—T.p. verso
        Bibliography: p.
        Includes indexes.
        1. Bible. O.T.—Introductions. I. Title.
BS1140.2.R3913 1985   221.6′1   85-47728
    ISBN 0-8006-0750-3 (cloth)
    ISBN 0-8006-2544-7 (paper)

Printed in the United States   1-2544
95   94   93   92   91   1   2   3   4   5   6   7   8   9   10

Contents

84625

Introduction

The Old Testament is a collection of writings which came into being over a period of more than a thousand years in the history of the people of Israel and which reflect the life of the people in this period. Therefore there is a reciprocal relationship between the writings or 'books' of the Old Testament and the life of Israel in its history. The understanding of the texts presupposes insights into the historical context and the development of the life of Israelite society, while at the same time the texts themselves are the most important, indeed for the most part the only, source for it.

This 'Introduction' attempts to take account of this reciprocal relationship. The first part deals with the history of Israel. However, its approach differs from most accounts of this history. It takes the Old Testament texts themselves as a starting point and first of all outlines the picture of historical developments and associations which the texts present. An attempt is then made, on this basis, to reconstruct historical developments by introducing material from outside the Bible. This method of working leads to close connections between the second and third parts, because it has to take account of the nature and original purpose of the texts and their function within the biblical books as they are now.

The second part attempts to present the texts collected in the Old Testament as expressions of the life of Israel. In so doing it follows the approach founded by Hermann Gunkel, which regards the Old Testament literature as 'part of the life of the people', to be understood on that basis. Here, more consistently than in most previous accounts, the starting point is the life of Israel and its institutions, and the texts are explained in terms of their particular 'Sitz im Leben'. This makes the formal characteristics of the genres understandable as an expression of the function of the texts. At the end of this second part there is a sketch of the way in which what were originally individual texts became 'literature'.

The third part discusses the books of the Old Testament in their present form. Here the main emphasis is a concern to understand the structure, composition and purpose of the final form of the individual books. This approach thus takes up the most important results of the critical analysis which now largely holds the field. However, the question of the composition of the books as they now are introduces another perspective, which attempts to go beyond the questions raised so far. As a result, the third part of the book at the same time refers back to the first, because the structure of a series of Old Testament books is based on a particular outline of history, and because in other respects, too, the history of the origin of the books often reflects historical associations and developments.

I should make it quite clear that in the framework of this introduction it is impossible to discuss the details of the religion of the Israel of the Old Testament. Of course religion and its phenomena are often mentioned in all three parts, but an extended and consecutive account would call for a book on its own and therefore must be reserved for a 'Theology of the Old Testament'.

The book is arranged as a working tool. The key words which appear in the margin serve several functions. First of all, they are meant to divide up the text and make it easy to follow, and also to make it easier to find particular themes or biblical texts. Then they form part of a reference system within the book. Page numbers at the side preceded by an arrow (→) refer to particular sections in which the reader will find further supplementary information. Here the arrows often indicate key words in the margin, but in addition they also point to other remarks or biblical references on the page in question.

Here is an example. At the beginning of the section on the patriarchs (I.3.1, p.7) there is a mention of the 'patriarchal history' in Gen.12-50. The marginal reference (→134ff.) refers the reader to the corresponding keyword in Section III.1.1, which discusses the book of Genesis. The next sentence mentions 'sagas'. The marginal reference (→85ff.) refers to this keyword in Section II.2, where the narrative forms are discussed within the life of the Israelite community. (References within a particular section are indicated by 'see below' or 'see above').

Finally, the key words are also the basis for the index. In it, further references appear to the individual names, subjects or texts as well as the page numbers of the reference system. It is supplemented by the Table of Contents.

In the bibliographies which appear at the end of each section I have mentioned mainly the basic literature. In Part I this consists of the relevant parts of a selection of accounts of the history of Israel; in Parts II and III of a selection of Introductions to the Old Testament; in Part III of the most important commentaries. Here I have also mentioned earlier standard works (e.g. Steuernagel and Eissfeldt), which are meant to open up to the reader the earlier history of research. The bibliographical details of the accounts of the history of Israel only indicated by the name of the author are to be found in the Abbreviations.

Otherwise, I have usually only cited the literature which is specifically mentioned in a particular section. Here I have deliberately been eclectic, because completeness was impossible (and in my view not worth striving for). I have mentioned earlier basic works, but taken into account the history of research only in so far as it has seemed to me to be relevant today. I have mentioned more books, especially from outside the literature written in German, where new approaches can be seen or where lively discussions are being carried on. In general the reader is referred to the detailed bibliographies in Hayes/Miller for the history of Israel and Childs for introductory matters; also to Kaiser and Smend, who provide a more thorough discussion of the history of research.

I have not been entirely consistent in the writing of names; in some cases I have chosen the more familiar names rather than striving for strict accuracy. I have used a simple transliteration for Hebrew words which does not aim at philological accuracy but seeks to make the words recognizable and pronounceable. Anyone who knows Hebrew will in any case use the original text, and those who do not know Hebrew will hardly be helped by an exact transliteration. At points the numbering of the Hebrew text differs from that used in most English versions; here I have given the Hebrew reference, *in italics*; a table at the back of the book (303f.) indicates how the English differs.

A large number of people have been more or less directly involved in the writing of this book, and I am most grateful to them. I was able to have discussions over its earliest beginnings with my teacher Gerhard von Rad, and I am still grateful to him now for his most important stimulus to my work. Much of the discussions over many years with colleagues and friends in Heidelberg and Jerusalem has found its way into print here; I think particularly of those with Shemaryahu Talmon, Abraham Malamat, Moshe Greenberg, Christian Macholz, Frank Crüsemann, Konrad Rupprecht, Berndt Jörg Diebner, Hermann Schult, Ekkehard Stegemann and Erhard Blum, who also read the manuscript and suggested numerous additions and improvements. Günther Welker read the manuscript through carefully, checked the biblical references and bibliographies and worked out the system of marginal references. His work, along with the reading of the proofs, was continued by Thomas Dermann and Reinhard Mentz. Konrad Rupprecht also read the manuscript and the proofs. Erhard Blum and Thomas Dermann provided invaluable help at the proof stage, when the marginal references had to be inserted, and in making the index, Frau Anneliese Brecht typed, improved and expanded the manuscript at all its stages with untiring commitment and gave a great deal of other help. I am most grateful to Dr Christian Bartsch and Frau Ursula Münden of Neukirchener Verlag for their kind collaboration.

Finally, a word to the reader. A work-book must be tested in use by its readers. Therefore I shall be grateful for any comments, above all for critical comments and references, whether in connection with the content or with the layout and practical usefulness of the book. I would particularly encourage student readers to let me know their experiences in using the book, and especially to send suggestions and criticisms.

Heidelberg, Autumn 1982   Rolf Rendtorff

I The Old Testament as a Source of the History of Israel

1 The Nature of the Sources

The Old Testament grew out of the history of the people of Israel. It is evidence of this history and reflects it in a variety of ways. At the same time the Old Testament is the only source from which we know anything about the course and context of this history. The reciprocal relationship between these two aspects is a basic problem in the exegesis of the Old Testament.

The most important task of exegesis is to understand the intention of the text. Some of the Old Testament texts have the express aim of depicting historical events and situations, so that the exegete is in accord with the author's aim when he enquires into these. That is particularly the case with texts which one can count as historiography in the narrower →106ff. or the wider sense. However, the exegete soon comes up against the problem that the Old Testament historians do not primarily aim at an 'objective' account of events. Moreover, their work (like that of any historian) is produced in a quite specific context from which it emerges and for which it is intended. Exegetes must therefore be concerned to understand this context and give it a due place in their interpretation of the text. Only against this background can they ask what 'really' happened. Other texts which report the same historical events from different aspects often provide help here.

The work of the exegete is more difficult in the case of texts which deal with 'historical' developments and events, but are not really concerned to report what happened 'then', intending their account to give to hearers or readers in their own day a particular message for which the events reported provide the substance and the illustrations. That is particularly the case with sagas, which make up a good deal of →85ff. the narrative tradition about the beginnings and the early period of the history of Israel. Here the exegete must enquire especially carefully into the real intention of the text before attempting to evaluate it as a historical source. The same goes for comparable texts in a later period, like the 'Diaspora novels' in the books of Esther and Daniel.

This produces a picture of the history of Israel which often resembles a mosaic. It is supplemented by statements and references in other Old Testament texts, above all in prophetic narratives within the historical →113ff. books and in the prophetic books where there is further material which can contribute to a reconstruction of historical developments. Psalms →96ff. and other cultic texts add insights into events and developments in religious life; legal texts give insights into an important sphere of human →88ff. social life and indicate social structures and changes. This is also true

1

of the wisdom literature, the significance of which has been increasingly recognized in most recent times.

An account of the history of Israel can adopt various approaches. It can use the Old Testament texts along with texts from outside Israel and archaeological discoveries (see below) as historical sources to provide the material for a reconstruction of the course of history, the outline and presentation of which are determined by the insights of historical scholarship. The Old Testament texts are relevant here only in so far as in the view of a particular historian they can make a contribution to this reconstruction. This is the course usually adopted by the Histories of Israel.

Because of its character and purpose, this book will attempt another approach. Its account primarily begins from the picture of events and developments offered by the Old Testament texts. It is concerned with the intention of the texts and then attempts to relate this picture to the insights of contemporary historical scholarship. This approach should enable the reader to connect the account in the Part One with the two following Parts, in each of which the texts are treated from other perspectives (see the Introduction). At the same time this has its limitations. I have made no attempt to embark on an extensive reconstruction of the history of Israel and its environment at points where the Old Testament texts are themselves silent. Here the reader must consult one of the Histories of Israel; the relevant sections of them are regularly mentioned in the bibliographies.

This limitation also extents to the citation of non-Israelite sources. Numerous Egyptian, Hittite, Babylonian and Assyrian texts give insights into the history of the ancient Near East in the second and first millennia BC, the period within which the history of Israel took place. In many cases we can recognize from these texts the factors which determined this history. However, Israel itself is mentioned only very rarely and even then for the most part incidentally, so that in only a few cases can we find direct insights into the history of Israel. Consequently, in the following account these texts are only introduced in specific instances, and here too the reader is otherwise referred to the detailed books about the history of Israel. The most important collected works in which these texts are accessible are mentioned in the bibliography below.

Finally, archaeological discoveries are an important addition to our knowledge of the history of Israel. Here the intensive excavations of recent decades have increased considerably the material available and resulted in marked differences in evaluation. However, it is important to realize that archaeological discoveries can only supplement the insights gained from written accounts; otherwise they remain 'dumb', apart from the rare cases in which texts are also found in excavations (cf. Noth 1960). In more recent times, moreover, the significance of archaeology for research into social conditions has been recognized more clearly (cf. Crüsemann). However, we shall be going into that only in particular instances. Some introductions and surveys are mentioned in the bibliography (cf. especially the most recent discussion by Fritz).

For the whole question, Herrmann, 25-38.

For biblical archaeology and geography

Y.Aharoni, *The Archaeology of the Land of Israel*, 1982; Y.Aharoni/M.Avi-Yonah, *Macmillan Bible Atlas*, 1977; M.Avi-Yonah/E.Stern (eds.), *Encyclopaedia of Archaeological Excavations in the Holy Land*, I-IV, 1975-78; D.Baly, *The Geography of the Bible*, 1974; F.Crüsemann, 'Alttestamentliche Exegese und Archäologie. Erwägungen angesichts des gegenwärtigen Methodenstreits in der Archäologie Palästinas', *ZAW* 91, 1979, 177-93; H.Donner, *Einführung in die biblische Landes- und Altertumskunde*, 1976; V.Fritz, 'Bibelwissenschaft I.Altes Testament, I/1. Archäologie (alter Orient und Palästina)', *TRE* VI, 1980, 316-45; K.Galling (ed.), *Biblisches Reallexikon*, ²1977 (*BRL*); K.M.Kenyon, *Archaeology in the Holy Land*, 1960; M.Noth, 'Der Beitrag der Archäologie zur Geschichte Israels', *SVT* 7, 1960, 262-82 (= *ABLA* I, 34-51); id., *The Old Testament World*, ET 1966; A.Ohler, *Israel, Volk und Land. Zur Geschichte der wechselseitigen Beziehungen zwischen Israel und seinem Land in alttestamentlicher Zeit*, 1979; B.Reicke/L.Rost (eds.), *Biblisch-Historisches Handwörterbuch* I-IV, 1962-79 (*BHH*).

Editions and collections of texts

W.Beyerlin (ed.), *Near Eastern Religious Texts relating to the Old Testament*, 1978; H.Donner/W.Röllig, *Kanaanäische und aramäische Inschriften*, I 1962, II 1964, ³1973; III 1964, ³1976 (*KAI*); K.Galling, *Textbuch zur Geschichte Israels*, ³1979 (*TGI*); H.Gressmann (ed.), *Altorientalische Texte zum Alten Testament*, ²1926 (*AOT*); O.Kaiser (ed.), *Texte aus der Umwelt des Alten Testaments*, 1982ff. (*TUAT*); J.B.Pritchard (ed.), *Ancient Near Eastern Texts relating to the Old Testament*, ²1955 (*ANET*), id., *The Ancient Near East. Supplementary Texts and Pictures Relating to the Old Testament*, 1969; D.Winton Thomas (ed.), *Documents from Old Testament Times*, 1958 (*DOTT*).

2 The Periods of the History of Israel

The Old Testament presents an outline of the history of Israel divided into clear periods. The first great period, which is depicted in the books of the Pentateuch, deals with the time before the Israelite settlement in the land of Canaan. It is subdivided into the time of the 'patriarchs', who live in the land of Canaan with their families and herds but are not yet sedentary (Gen.12-50); the time of the stay in Egypt and the Exodus from there (Ex.1-15); the time of wandering around in the wilderness (Ex.16-18; Num.10.11-20.13), which is interrupted by the stay on Sinai (Ex.19.1-Num.10.10); and finally the occupation of Transjordan (Num.20.14-21.35), along with other events prior to the crossing of the Jordan (Num.22-36). Deuteronomy is presented as Moses' last instructions before entering the promised land.

After that begins the history of Israel in its land. The book of Joshua reports the occupation of the land and its division into tribes. The book of Judges depicts the first period after the settlement which is characterized by a loss of continuity in the leadership of the people after the death of Joshua, a gap which is bridged by the appearance of judges. Yet another new period begins with the books of Samuel, in that Saul is appointed king (I Sam.1-15). The monarchy passes over to David, to whom the greater part of the books of Samuel is devoted (I Sam.16-I Kings 1). The first period of the monarchy comes to an end with the death of Solomon (I Kings 1-11). The division of the kingdom into two parts opens the second phase of its history, comprising the independent existence of the states of Israel and Judah down to the time when the northern kingdom was destroyed by the Assyrians (I Kings 12-II Kings 17). The last stage of the history of the state of Judah ends with the capture of Jerusalem, the destruction of the temple and the deportation of part of the population to exile in Babylon (II Kings 18-25).

Here the account of this great historical development breaks off. The books of Chronicles deal with the history from the beginning of the monarchy to the destruction of Jerusalem all over again, from different perspectives. They end by reporting that Cyrus king of the Persians proclaimed the rebuilding of the temple in Jerusalem and allowed the Israelites to return to their own home (II Chron. 36.22f.). That is the way in which the book of Ezra begins. There is no account of the period of exile in Babylon. We no longer have a consecutive account for the following period, but only reports of the rebuilding of the temple (Ezra 3-6) and the comparatively brief periods of the activity of Ezra and Nehemiah (in the books which bear their names).

In essentials, the division into periods given here corresponds to the established results of historical research. The first great period in the history of Israel is formed by the settlement in the land of Canaan,

settlement (as opposed to conquest) being a neutral term, introduced by Albrecht Alt. Historical research into the period before the settlement is difficult, but scholarly accounts usually retain the subdivisions given in the Pentateuch, into the time of the 'patriarchs', the exodus from Egypt and the events on Sinai (sometimes the wandering in the wilderness is treated as a separate theme), though the sequence is partly changed. The settlement itself is usually regarded as a process which extended over a considerable period of time, so that it is often made a separate period. The period between the settlement and the formation of the state is also usually treated as an independent period, though the term 'time of the judges' is often avoided or put in quotation marks; by

preference this is described as 'the period before the formation of the state'. The origin of the kingdom along with the foundation of the state is regarded as a basically new beginning, which stamps the whole period up to the end of the kingdom of Judah. Here, for a period of four hundred years, Israel found a form of political independence.

Historians also have difficulty in filling the gaps in the account of Old Testament history which comes after this. Other parts of the Old Testament, especially the books of Jeremiah, Ezekiel and Isaiah (40-55), provide some information on the period of the Babylonian exile,

but they are insufficient for a complete reconstruction of this period.

The same is true of the period of Persian rule after the exile. For the first phase up to the rebuilding of the temple the books of Haggai and Zechariah provide supplementary and varied information. There is no further information on the period leading up to the appearance of Ezra or Nehemiah (or vice versa), or for the following period up to the beginning of the Hellenistic era. Only in the late stages of the Old Testament does light fall once again on Jewish history from other sources. However, there is not enough to reconstruct this period to any degree, especially as there are disputes as to precisely which texts in the Old Testament come from it. (This is connected above all with the use of pseudonymity, which means that texts can often be presented under names from earlier periods, so that their actual time of origin remains obscure.) This is also true of the period of the Maccabees: the completion of the Book of Daniel, the latest book in the Old Testament, is to be dated to this time, and some exegetes would want to add yet other texts.

Thus the Old Testament largely remains our only source for the history of Israel, and the periods into which it divides that history have been confirmed in all essential points. In many individual details, however, some of them basic, there are differences between the account in the Old Testament texts and historical reconstruction. We shall be discussing these in the following sections.

First of all, a few comments on terminology. For the earlier period the community of which the Old Testament speaks is referred to as Israel. After the division of the kingdom on the death of Solomon the term 'Israel' comes to take on two meanings. On the one hand it denotes the northern kingdom in a narrower political sense, contrasting it with the southern kingdom, Judah. On the other hand, 'Israel' remains the term used to denote all the people who formed a political and national unity under David and Solomon. This applies above all in religious terminology: the community which has a special relationship to YHWH is called Israel; here the question of boundaries and the political form in which Israel is embodied are irrelevant.

This double terminology also appears in the post-exilic period: the term Israel is reserved above all for the religious sphere; 'Judah' is used in the narrower political sense. The adjective y‍ehudi which goes with the name Judah means primarily 'Judaean', 'of Judah' (cf. II Kings 16.6; 25.25). In post-exilic terminology it then takes on a wider meaning as a designation of members of the people (Esther 3: Ezra 4-6); here the religious aspect can even come into the foreground (cf.Zech.8.2,3). Here the word y‍ehudi has come to mean 'Jew', 'Jewish' in a comprehensive sense, including membership both of a people and of a religious community. The book of Esther uses only this designation, while the word Israel is absent. In the post-biblical period, in both Hebrew/Aramaic and in Greek, the terms Israel(ite) and Jew become largely synonymous and are used as equivalents. This terminological development shows that there was a gradual shift in terminology and not a break which can be said to have begun at a particular point (cf. Zobel, *TWAT* 3, 1008ff.).

It is customary to use the terms 'Israel' and 'Israelite' as descriptions in the pre-exilic period, above all in a religious sense; the terms 'Jew' and 'Judaism' are then used in the post-exilic period. This terminology makes a good deal of sense, provided that the continuity between the two terms is remembered. It becomes even clearer if one also uses the word 'people': the people of Israel and the Jewish people denote one and the same community which has a historical continuity with changing political and social forms. So it is wrong to mark out a clear division between Israel and Judaism or even to speak at a particular point of the 'end' of the history of Israel (cf. R.Rentorff, 'Das "Ende" der Geschichte Israels', *GS*, 267-76).

3 Israel before the Settlement

The different traditions of the Pentateuch have one thing in common: Israel's ancestors, of whom they tell, are not yet settled in the land in which the greater part of Old Testament history takes place.In their present context in the Pentateuch these traditions are connected by a continuous narrative thread: the patriarchs already live in the land but have not yet settled in it; their descendants, the sons of Jacob, have to leave the land in times of famine and go to Egypt, where they are oppressed, being able to escape again under the leadership of Moses. After that they spend a long time wandering in the wilderness, during which time their God YHWH makes himself known to them and proclaims his commandments to them on Sinai; finally their way takes them, after many battles, to the eastern frontier of the land which their God has promised them. Here Moses again communicates the divine commands to them as his last will and testament: these are the commands which in future they are to obey in their land.

On closer examination it is evident that this narrative thread binds together very different traditions. The clearest difference is that between the patriarchal traditions in Genesis and the subsequent narratives. The patriarchs are depicted as peaceful nomads who move up and down in small, compact family groups within the land of Canaan (making occasional forays outside). The situation is very different at the beginning of the book of Exodus. Here the Israelites are a 'people' of a considerable size, living in an uncertain social and legal position among a foreign people, and oppressed and exploited by them through forced labour and in other ways. The narrative link is that the twelve sons of Jacob become a great people (Ex.1.1-7), but there is still a fundamental difference in the nature of the traditions and in their specific presuppositions.

The next section is dominated by the account of the stay at Sinai (Ex.19-Num.10.10); this again is a distinctive block of material. It is concerned with the manifestation of God and the communication of his commands; to this have been added extensive texts about the making of the portable sanctuary (the tabernacle) and the elements of the cult. The central theme of the rest of the traditions in the books of Exodus (16-18) and Numbers (from 10.11) is the way through the wilderness with its countless dangers. Here the individual narratives are often associated with particular localities in the wilderness.

Literary and historical research into these different complexes of tradition has demonstrated even more clearly that they were originally independent. There is important evidence in this connection in the way in which this early period of Israel is reflected in the rest of the Old Testament. The deliverance from slavery in Egypt, the exodus, is often depicted in a great variety of ways as the basic saving act of YHWH to Israel (cf. e.g. Ex.20.2; Deut.6.20ff.; Hos.*12.10*; 13.4; Isa.51.9f.; Ps.136.10ff., etc.). By contrast, the patriarchs are mentioned very rarely. The oldest datable mention of Abraham outside the Pentateuch appears in the book of Ezekiel (33.24; cf. also Ps.105.6,9,42; Isa.51.2; for Jacob see Hos.*12.3-5, 13*). The patriarchs were evidently less deeply rooted in Israel's understanding of its 'salvation history'. It is particularly striking that they are only rarely connected with the exodus (there is a hint of this in Deut.26.5ff.; cf. I Sam.12.8; Josh.24.2ff.; Ps.105; Neh.9.6ff.); thus the latter is a tradition independent of this.

→7ff.

Sinai, too, is only mentioned rarely outside the Pentateuch (Judg.5.5; Ps.*68.9,18*; cf. Deut.33.2), and only in Neh.9.13 is there any mention of proclaiming the commandments. This is also the only place in which Sinai is spoken of in connection with the exodus and the subsequent settlement (cf. von Rad). Here too we clearly have an independent tradition which was only connected with the other traditions of the early period in a narrative during the course of the history of the tradition. Finally, the period in the wilderness, too, is often mentioned outside the Pentateuch as a forty-year period of wandering (e.g. Josh.5.6; Amos 2.10; 5.25; Psa.95.10), partly with a very positive view of YHWH's attitude to Israel (Hos.*2.16f.*; 9.10; Jer.2.2,6).

→10ff.
→14ff.

→17f.

So in the Pentateuch various traditions have been combined into an overall picture of the history of Israel before the settlement. Each of these traditions raises particular questions, so in the sections which follow they will first have to be discussed separately.

Bibliography

G.von Rad, 'The Form-Critical Problem of the Hexateuch', in *The Problem of the Hexateuch*, ET 1966, 1-78; M.Noth, *A History of Pentateuchal Traditions*, ET 1972, §7; R.Rendtorff, *Das überlieferungsgeschichtliche Problem des Pentateuch*, 1977, esp.19-29; 151-8.
  Kaiser, §7.

3.1 The Patriarchs

In its present form, the patriarchal history in Gen.12-50 is the result of a long process of tradition and composition. The earliest stratum is made up of sagas about the individual patriarchs which clearly indicate

→134ff.
→85ff.

that they each had their own histories. This is particularly evident from the various local focal points of the tradition: for Abraham this is Mamre near Hebron in the centre of the southern hill-country (13.18; 18.1: 25.9, etc.), and then Beersheba on the edge of the Negeb (21.33; 22.19); for Isaac the southern localities of Gerar (26.1,6) and Beersheba (26.23-25); for Jacob Bethel (28.10-22; 35.1-15) and Shechem (33.18-20) in the northern hill-country and then Mahanaim (*32.2f.*) and Penuel (*32.32f.*) in Transjordan.

However, despite their connection with particular places, the patriarchs are depicted as tent-dwellers, who often move around with their herds, changing pastures; still, only exceptionally do they leave the land (e.g. 12.10-20; 27.43ff.), and on each occasion they return to it (13.1ff.; 31.3ff.). This is the starting point for the problem of the patriarchs as historical figures.

First of all we must keep quite clearly in mind the basic feature of the tradition, that the land did not yet belong to the patriarchs. However, we hardly see anything of the real inhabitants of the land. (They are mentioned explicitly in 12.6; 13.7, but evidently at a great remove from 'then'; elsewhere there are only occasional mentions: 14.17,21ff.; 14.18-20; 23; 34.) We get the impression from the narratives that they do not have any exact historical idea of the period of the patriarchs, but that they want to stress that the patriarchs were not sedentary by depicting their nomadic life-style. (One could also call this a transitional stage between nomadic and sedentary life, cf. de Vaux, 241ff.; Herrmann, 48.)

The tradition puts the patriarchs in a wider context. In the genealogies which preface the patriarchal narratives, the family of Abraham is said to come from the city of Ur Chasdim ('Ur of the Chaldaeans': 11.28,31; presumably this is meant to be the famous Sumerian city of Ur near the mouth of the Euphrates, 11.31f.). The city of Hebron on the northern Euphrates appears as an intermediate stage on the way to the land of Canaan (11.31f.). This detail is evidently meant to express an affinity between the patriarchs and the inhabitants of this

city, which is taken up again in the Jacob story (27.43; 28.10; 29.4; cf. 24.10). However, this produces a tension between the origin of the patriarchs in a city and their nomadic life-style in the Genesis narratives. (For the genealogical connections in Genesis see Herrmann, 41ff.)

More recent scholarship has undertaken a new interpretation of the patriarchal traditions from two quite different perspectives. A. Alt began by noting that the patriarchal narratives often have the phrase

'God of my/your father' or 'God of Abraham', etc. (Gen.26.24; 28.13; 31.5,29,42,53; *32.10*; 43.23; 46.1,3; cf. Ex.3.6,13,15, etc.). He saw this as the characteristic of a specific patriarchal religion in which a particular nomadic group worships a god who has no other name but is given the name of the ancestor to whom he first appeared. He is primarily a leader god who goes with the group on its wanderings, but also makes it

promises (e.g. of countless descendants and the possession of land). This led Alt to see the patriarchs in Genesis as the ancestors of particular groups of worshippers of such patriarchal deities. On the basis of comparative material from outside Israel he declared that the patriarchs were historical figures whose memory was preserved and handed down in the individual groups. He regarded the places connected with individual patriarchs (see above) as the focal points of tradition in which the various groups established themselves after the settlement, taking over local Canaanite sanctuaries and transferring them to their patriarchal deities. This hypothesis was very widely accepted and at the same time served as an important key to the reconstruction of the early history of Israel.

American, French and Israeli scholars in particular have adopted another approach. They attempt to understand the 'patriarchs' in the context of the ancient Near Eastern world of the second millennium BC, which has become increasingly well known since the 1920s through a variety of archaeological discoveries, above all through new texts. They believe that they can find there names, legal customs, ways of life and so on which also appear or are presupposed in the patriarchal narratives, and as a result that they can clearly define a patriarchal period within the second millennium BC (cf. Albright, de Vaux, Kenyon, Bright). Here, however, the dates vary between about 2000 and 1200 BC (cf. Westermann, 71ff.), so that some representatives of this view often refrain from a specific dating (e.g. Malamat in Ben-Sasson I,40).

However, fundamental objections have been made to both approaches.

The basic weakness of the theory of the 'God of the Fathers' is that the comparative material adduced by Alt comes from a very late period. His theory has been undermined above all by the demonstration that the designation 'God of my father' also appears in other Near Eastern religions and is in no way the specific characteristic of a nomadic religion (cf. Vorländer, Albertz). Within the Old Testament it transpired that this designation of God appears predominantly in the later textual strata of Genesis (as also the divine promises which Alt thought to be part of patriarchal religion) and that it often appears outside Genesis (Ex.15.2; 18.4; Deut.1.11; 4.1; II Kings 20.5, etc.), where it can have nothing to do with a specific patriarchal religion (cf. also Van Seters 1980). Therefore Alt's theory can no longer be sustained (cf. also Diebner).

The archaeological approach always had to be content with drawing analogies and demonstrating possible backgrounds without being able to produce specific evidence for the existence and dating of the patriarchs. This led to great uncertainties and differences of opinion even among scholars who were convinced that this approach was basically right. In the meantime the value of the comparative material as evidence has been fundamentally challenged (cf. Thompson, Van Seters 1975, Leineweber). Moreover, we also have the problem here that the texts adduced quite often belong to later strata – quite apart from the question whether historical conclusions can be drawn from the texts at all, seeing that they are sagas. What we are left with, at any rate, is the insight that the patriarchal narratives (like the rest of the texts of the Old Testament) have a great many points of contact and affinities with other texts from the world of the Ancient Near East, to which they belong.

So we have to content ourseves with noting that the patriarchal narratives retain the memory of an early nomadic period in the history of Israel, without being able to reconstruct either a patriarchal period or a patriarchal religion from them. We shall discuss the many other aims and functions of these texts in II.2 and III 1.1.

Bibliography

R.Albertz, *Persönliche Frömmigkeit und offizielle Religion. Religionsinterner Pluralismus in Israel und Babylon*, 1978; W.F.Albright, *From the Stone Age to Christianity*, ²1957; id., *Archaeology and the Religion of Israel*, ⁵1968; A.Alt, 'The God of the Fathers', in *Essays in Old Testament Religion*, 1966, 3-77; B.Diebner, 'Die Götter des Vaters. Eine Kritik der "Vätergott"-Hypothese Albrecht Alts', *DBAT* 9, 1975, 21-51; K.M.Kenyon, *Archaeology in the Holy Land*, 1960; W.Leineweber, *Die Patriarchen im Licht der archäologischen Entdeckungen. Die kritische Darstellung einer Forschungsrichtung*, 1980; E.Ruprecht, 'Die Religion der Väter. Hauptlinien der Forschungsgeschichte', *DBAT* 11, 1976, 2-29; J.Scharbert, 'Patriarchentradition und Patriarchenreligion', *VF* 19.2, 1972, 2-22 (account of research); T.L.Thompson, *The Historicity of the Patriarchal Narratives*, 1974; J.Van Seters, *Abraham in History and Tradition*, 1975; id,. 'The Religion of the Patriarchs in Genesis', *Bib* 61, 1980, 220-33; R.de Vaux, 'Les Patriarchs hébreux et les découvertes modernes', *RB* 53, 1946, 321-48; 55, 1948, 321-47; 56, 1949, 5-36; id., 'The Hebrew Patriarchs and History', *Theology Digest* 12, 227-40; H.Vorländer, *Mein Gott. Die Vorstellungen vom persönlichen Gott im Alten Orient und im Alten Testament*, 1975; H.Weidmann, *Die Patriarchen und ihre Religion im Licht der Forschung seit Julius Wellhausen*, 1968; C.Westermann, *Genesis 12-50*, 1975 (account of research).

Noth, §10; Bright, ch.2; Mazar, II, chs.VIII, XI, XII; de Vaux, I, Part 1; Gunneweg, II, 1; Herrmann, I, 1; Hayes/Miller, II; Ben-Sasson, I,3.

Cf.also the bibliography on III.1.1.

3.2 The Exodus from Egypt

→139ff.

At the beginning of the book of Exodus, 'Israel', which appears here for the first time as a 'people' (1.9), is in Egypt. The drift of the story shows clearly that it is leading up to deliverance from Egypt, i.e. that the time there is not regarded as an independent period in the history of Israel. This is the time of servitude, and it culminates in liberation. Moses Therefore at the centre stands the figure of the saviour Moses who is sent by God: the perils surrounding his birth and deliverance (2.1-10), his intervention on behalf of his oppressed compatriots and his flight to Midian (2.11-22), his call and commissioning to lead out the people, supported by Aaron (chs.3f.). From here on everything moves towards the realization of this divine promise; the arguments with the Pharaoh (ch.5) and the intensification of the plagues on the Egyptians (chs.7ff.), leading up to the last plague, the killing of the firstborn, from which the Israelites are protected by the blood of the passover lambs, so that they can eventually leave the country (chs.11f.). The account comes to a last

Moses

10

dramatic climax with the pursuit of the Israelites by the Egyptians and their deliverance at the Sea of Reeds (ch.14).

Any attempt at a historical reconstruction must again keep in mind the character and intention of the texts. The predominant theme is the deliverance of Israel by the liberator sent by God. The historical presuppositions and circumstances are not an independent point of interest, so care must always be taken in working out what historical conclusions can be drawn from the narrative as a whole or from particular details.

That Israel was in Egypt is a basic feature of the tradition which has found expression in many places in the Old Testament. However, when we attempt to give this reminiscence a more specific historical form we are confronted with the question 'Who was in Egypt?' The present narrative context of the Pentateuch combines the various narrative traditions into an overall picture so that in Ex.1.1-7 Israel appears as the people of twelve tribes which is directly continuous with the patriarchs. However, our knowledge of the way in which the Pentateuch →160ff. was composed shows us that the patriarchal tradition and the tradition of the deliverance from Egypt were not originally connected. They were therefore presumably introduced into the tradition of all Israel by various groups, though we cannot identify these groups more precisely.

We have help from non-Israelite sources over the question of the historical circumstances of the stay in Egypt. First of all, Egyptian sources mention the names of the two cities Pithom and Raamses, which Pithom and according to Ex.1.11 the Israelites were set to build. The sources also Raamses cast light on the fact that they are mentioned together and designated 'store cities' (cf. Herrmann, 58f.), so we may regard this as a historical recollection. It fits with the fact that groups of Semitic nomads are mentioned in Egyptian texts as having been allowed across the frontier into Egypt (cf. *TGI*, 40f.) and that such Semitic groups were put to work at forced labour (cf. Herrmann, 58).

The designation *habiru* or *hapiru* (Egyptian ʿpr with unknown vowels) is used *habiru* often in ancient Near Eastern texts from the second millennium BC to denote particular foreign groups. This designation used to be connected with the Hebrew word *ʿibri*, 'Hebrew', which is also used often in Ex.1ff. (1.15ff; 2.6f.,11,13; 3.18, etc.). However, this association is disputed (cf. Borger), especially as the meaning of the word is still uncertain (cf. Koch; Herrmann, 54; Weippert, 63ff.).

So we can say that Ex.1 contains elements of tradition which can be well explained in an Egyptian context and therefore could indeed be regarded as historical reminiscence. That is all that Egyptian sources can tell us. In particular, they say nothing about the exodus (or the flight, cf. Ex.14.5) of the Israelites and their pursuit by the Egyptians (according to 14.6ff. even by the Pharaoh himself). The chronological Date of the context of these elements of the tradition is provided by the names of exodus the cities of Pithom and Raamses, which are connected with the Pharaoh Ramses II (1290-1224).

According to biblical chronology the Israelite stay in Egypt lasted 430 years (Ex.12.40f.; cf. Gen.15.13: 400 years). This conflicts with other information, which speaks of four generations (Gen.15.16; cf. Ex.6.14ff.: four generations between Levi the son of Jacob and Aaron and Moses). Unfortunately, it is impossible to be clear about the concept behind the chronology; the 430 years up to the exodus are presumably connected with the 480 years between the exodus and the beginning of the building of the temple in Jerusalem (I Kings 6.1).

Passover
→ 95, 140

The tradition of the deliverance from Egypt is bound up in the narrative with the passover, which was originally a specifically nomadic tradition. The exodus narrative proper ends at Ex.12.37ff. (The regulations for the feast of unleavened bread and the firstfruits in 13.1-16 are not part of the narrative.) The next dramatic climax in the narrative is the pursuit by the Egyptians and the deliverance at the Sea of Reeds (13.17-14.31). (Perhaps this narrative element was originally connected with the wilderness tradition, cf. Coats, Childs.) The obscure geographical details in 13.17f., 20; 14.2f. are connected with this and

Location of the crossing

perhaps represent the earliest attempt to locate the 'scene of the miracle at the sea' (cf. Noth 1947). We cannot get further than describing the biblical attempts at locating the miracle. It remains uncertain whether this tradition goes back to a 'historical' event.

The scene of the crossing of the 'Sea of Reeds' is usually assumed to be in the area of the Bitter Lakes (in the present-day Suez Canal zone). Two other conjectures appear in the literature: the 'Sea of Reeds' has been identified 1. with the Gulf of Eilath (or Aqaba, e.g. Gressmann, 414ff.); 2. with the Sirbonian Sea, a shallow lagoon on the Mediterranean coast east of the Nile delta (Eissfeldt).

Moses

The central figure in all the traditions in the books of Exodus-Deuteronomy is Moses. Moses is introduced in Ex.2.1-10 with the story of his birth, which has miraculous features. There are many other occurrences of the theme of the exposure and deliverance of a child who later becomes an important man. The most striking parallel is the story of the birth of King Sargon of Accad, who lived towards the end of the third millennium BC (cf. Gressmann, 8f.; *AOT*, 234f.; *RTAT*, 123f.). That Moses grew up in the Egyptian court is part of these legendary traditions about his childhood and youth; it is not mentioned anywhere in the Old Testament outside Ex.2. The fact that he has an Egyptian name may be the starting point for the formation of the legends which surround him.

Name

The name *moshe* corresponds to an element which often occurs in theophorous Egyptian names (i.e. names which include a divine name), like Thutmoses and Raamses: it indicates that the god gave birth to or begat the person bearing his or her name. Without the name of the god it is an abbreviated form, of a kind for which there is also evidence in Egyptian (cf. Herrmann ET 1973, 43f.; *History*, 61).

The character of the texts requires us to be as restrained over the question of the 'historical' Moses as over the reconstruction of the stay in Egypt and the exodus. We can trace the way in which he is connected **Exodus** with various complexes of tradition, but it is impossible to write his biography. It is important in this connection to note that very different traditions are held together by the person of Moses. Ex.2.15ff. reports Midian his flight to Midian. There he becomes closely associated with the priest of Midian (called Reuel in 2.18 and Jethro in 3.1, etc), whose daughter he marries. While tending his father-in-law's flock he arrives at Horeb, →14 the mountain of God (3.1), where the God of Abraham, Isaac and Jacob addresses him from a burning bush (vv.4-6) and commands him to bring the Israelites up out of Egypt (vv.7-10); he finally also makes his name YHWH known to him (vv.13-15). The mountain of God and →17 the making known of the divine name already point forward to what happens on Sinai (chs.19ff.). The connection between Moses and the Midianite priest raises the question whether there is an underlying tradition of a particular religious connection between the Israelites and the Midianites.

It has often been argued that the Israelites took over the cult of YHWH from Kenite the Midianites with Moses as an intermediary. The key passage here is Ex.18.1- hypothesis 12, where Jethro expressly confesses his faith in YHWH (vv.10f.) and then invides the Israelites to a sacrificial meal (v.12). As the Midianites and the Kenites are often identified in the Old Testament, this theory has come to be known as the Kenite hypothesis (cf. Gressmann, 161ff., 436ff.; Rowley; Schmidt, 60ff. De Vaux, 330ff., is critical). However, in my view here we have at most a reminiscence of religious connections or associations, perhaps because the site of the 'mountain of God' lay in the area where the Midianites tended their flocks (Ex.3.1f.). There is no indication that any cult was taken over (on the contrary, Ex.18.11 sounds more like a 'conversion' of Jethro, cf. II Kings 5.15).

Thus the figure of Moses is the factor which holds together all the traditions from the exodus from Egypt onwards. In all probability he only gradually assumed this central role. However, it is no longer possible to detach him from any particular traditions (cf. Rendtorff). Many people have tried to write his biography, and still do so (cf. Smend, Osswald, Schmidt), but this calls for a considerable degree of hypothetical reconstruction. On the other hand, to suppose that he is completely secondary (thus Noth ET 1972, 156, who only leaves the tradition about his tomb) is just as hypothetical.

Bibliography

R.Borger, 'Das Problem der 'apîru ("Ḥapiru")', *ZDPV* 74, 1958, 121-32; B.S.Childs, 'A Traditio-Historical Study of the Reed Sea Tradition', *VT* 20, 1970, 406-18; G.W.Coats, 'The Traditio-Historical Character of the Reed Sea Motif', *VT* 17, 1967, 253-65; O.Eissfeldt, *Baal Zaphon, Zeus Kasios und der Durchzug der Israeliten durchs Meer*, 1932; H.Gressmann, *Mose und seine Zeit. Ein Kommentar zu den Mose-Sagen*, 1913; S.Herrmann, *Israel in Egypt*, ET 1973; K.Koch, 'Die Hebräer vom Auszug aus Ägypten bis zum Grossreich

Before Settlement
Davids', *VT* 19, 1969, 37-81; M.Noth, 'Der Schauplatz des Meereswunders', *FS O.Eissfeldt*, 1947, 181-90 (= *ABLA* I, 102-10); id., *A History of Pentateuchal Traditions*, ET 1972; E.Osswald, *Das Bild des Mose in der kritischen alttestamentlichen Wissenschaft seit Julius Wellhausen*, 1962; R.Rendtorff, 'Mose als Religionsstifter', *GS*, 152-71; H.H.Rowley, 'Moses and Monotheism', in *From Moses to Qumran*, 1963, 35-63; H.Schmid, 'Der Stand der Moseforschung', *Jud* 21, 1965, 194-221; W.H.Schmidt, *The Faith of the Old Testament*, ET 1983; R,Smend, *Das Mosebild von Heinrich Ewald bis Martin Noth*, 1959; P.Weimar/ E.Zenger, *Exodus. Geschichten und Geschichte der Befreiung Israels*, 1975; M.Weippert, *The Settlement of the Israelite Tribes in Palestine*, ET 1971.

Noth, §9; Bright, ch.3 B1; Mazar, III, ch.V; de Vaux, I, chs. 12f.; Gunneweg, II,2; Herrmann, I,2; Hayes/Miller, III.1; Ben-Sasson, I,3.

Cf. also the bibliography on III.1.2.

3.3 Israel at Sinai

→140f.

A section of the narrative begins at Ex.15.22 which could be given the overall title 'Israel in the Wilderness'. Only with Num.20.14 do the Israelites begin to enter settled land. The dominant feature of this narrative complex is the group of traditions about Israel's stay at Sinai

→141ff.

(Ex.19.1-Num.10.10), which is a major independent section. Exegetical tradition tends to see it as an independent unit, and in accounts of the history of Israel before the settlement a whole chapter is usually devoted to these events. That is doubtless justified, and we shall do the same thing here. Nevertheless, it must be noted that there is a narrative link between the account of the stay on Sinai and what precedes it and what comes after it, though the transition is not marked particularly clearly. The note of the arrival in Ex.19.1f is not essentially different from other notes of itineraries (cf.15.22; 16.1; 17.1, etc.), and the notice of the departure in Num.10.12 (for vv.11,13 cf. Ex.40.36f.; Num.9.17-23) also fits into this context (cf. 10.33; 11.35; 12.16 etc.).

Mountain of God

→13

There was also mention earlier of the 'mountain of God' (*har ha-'elohim*: Ex.3.1; 4.27; 18.5), and in the present narrative context this can only be what is referred to as 'the mountain' (*ha-har*) in 19.2f. (cf. also 3.12!).

Horeb

The name of the mountain presents problems. In addition to the designation 'mountain of God' (Ex.3.1; 4.27; 18.5; 24.13; cf.I Kings 19.8; Ps.*68.16*), in Ex.3.1 (and I Kings 19.8) we find the name Horeb, whereas in Ex.19 the expression 'the mountain' (vv.2,3,12,14,16) alternates with the name 'Mount Sinai' (vv.11,18,20,23). Both names also appear in other books of the Old Testament; the name Horeb is particularly frequent in Deuteronomy (1.2,6,19; 4.1,15, etc.). It is usually assumed that there are two different traditions about the name of the same mountain, but recently the theory has also been proposed that there were two 'covenant' traditions which were originally separated (Cazelles). By contrast, Perlitt (1977) has conjectured that the name Sinai was replaced by the name Horeb because of its original connection with Edom (cf.Judg.5.4f; Deut.33.2), which for a time was regarded as Israel's particular enemy.

The exodus tradition and the tradition about the mountain of God are thus intertwined in the present narrative context. However, what happens at the mountain of God is something quite new. At the centre we have the account of a theophany, an appearance of God which is accompanied with violent natural phenomena: thunder, lightning, dense cloud and loud trumpetings (Ex.19.16, etc.), smoke, fire and severe earthquakes (e.g. vv.18f.). (Some exegetes seek to identify various literary strata here, in one of which the theophany is depicted as a storm and in another as a volcanic eruption.) The decisive aim of the divine epiphany is the solemn proclamation of the divine will in the form of the Decalogue (Ex.20.1-17). Here Moses plays a central role: he alone is allowed to come to God on the mountain (19.3,20), and God speaks only to him (v.9), while the people listens 'from afar' (20.18,21; cf.19.9). Thus Moses receives further divine commandments in order to hand them on to the people (20.22-23.33). Finally the whole event is sealed by a solemn conclusion of the covenant (ch.24).

A historical reconstruction of the underlying events is particularly difficult here because the texts have hardly any specific narrative features which make an evaluation possible. First of all one can say that the passage is one of those recollections by Israel of the early period of its history, that the decisive foundations of its religious life were given it by a proclamation of the divine will in the wilderness. For the great significance of the Sinai tradition for Israel's understanding of itself is clear from the way in which a wealth of religious and cultic legal traditions has been added to the nucleus of the narrative in Ex 19-24 and also from the way in which the further summary of the religious commandments in Deuteronomy is explicitly bound up with that (Deut.5.2ff.). Secondly, it can be said that here Moses takes on a central significance, for the whole legal tradition relating to religion and the cult has been associated with his name in all literary strata, and conversely we can find no tradition of this kind associated with any other name.

One can approach this complex of traditions with very different questions. Many generations of scholars have been concerned with the question of the location of Sinai (or Horeb or the mountain of God) without arriving at a consensus.

Up to the beginnings of modern critical scholarship there was no doubt that Sinai lay on the peninsula of the same name; local tradition took this to be *jebel Musa* (the mount of Moses). This is also thought to be an appropriate place by many modern scholars. However, a number of other theories have been put forward: other mountains on the Sinai peninsula, various mountains east of the Gulf of Eilath (where there are said to be extinct volcanoes) or further north in the area of Edom, a mountain near Kadesh, and so on. From time to time new arguments are added, but no agreement is in sight (cf. Davies, 63ff.). Evidently this question is something which lies outside the concerns of the text.

The question of the original content of the manifestation of the divine will on Sinai gets closer to the centre of the tradition. It is also difficult

Sinai

Theophany

→141

→141f.

→151

Location of
Sinai

**Before
Settlement**
Content of
the Sinai
command-
ments
to answer this question, since the present form of the commandments handed down here doubtless comes from a much later period. The Decalogue in particular, which is the nucleus of the proclamation of the commandments, is only the result of a lengthy process of tradition and reflection (cf. Childs, *Exodus*, 385ff.).

→92ff.

→156

Alt saw 'apodeictic law', in which he also included the Decalogue, as a tradition from the wilderness period which thus came close to the Sinai tradition. However, this theory has largely been abandoned. Baltzer, Beyerlin and others saw the Decalogue and other texts in the Sinai pericope as a covenant formulary which has its parallels in Hittite state treaties, and argued from this that they were extremely old and came from the wilderness period. Nowadays the tendency is to think, rather, of a late imitation of these formularies (cf. Perlitt 1969, Nicholson).

First and
second
commandment

→43

However, the Decalogue itself contains some elements which are particularly characteristic of Israelite religion. This is particularly true of the requirement for worship of YHWH (Ex.20.3) to be exclusive, which comes first in the Decalogue, and for his cult to be aniconic (v.4). In a religious environment in which polytheism, i.e. the worship of a number of gods with different functions, is taken for granted and in which images are the most widespread form of depicting the gods and above all making it possible to call on them, these two demands are particularly striking. As there is in fact no reference anywhere to the presence of images of YHWH, we can see here basic elements of Israelite religion which left their stamp on it from its earliest days. That is not to say that they originated in this form 'on Sinai', but they stand in such striking contrast to all the religions known to us from the civilizations of the ancient Near East that it seems as if they can only come from the nomadic early history of Israel. That does not exclude the possibility that they perhaps took their present form only in the controversy with Canaanite religion after the settlement; however, that in itself would confirm that the fundamental characteristics of the Israelites, as they settled, were understood as the specific features which they brought with them and had to be distinguished from and defended against the religion of the Canaanite inhabitants of the land (cf. Schmidt, 69ff.)

So we could say that the Sinai tradition is a concentration of reminiscences about the beginnings and foundations of Israelite religion, though it is impossible to paint a clear historical picture from it. One thing, though, is quite clear: that the God with whom these Sinai traditions deal is YHWH. However, in the present narrative complex the name of YHWH is already made known to Moses at his first divine encounter on the mountain of God (Ex.3.13-15; cf.6. 2-9), and Moses is told to hand this on to the Israelites (3.15; cf. 6.9). The name can therefore be presumed to be known in Ex.19ff. This again shows the significance of the way in which the complexes of tradition have been interwoven in the narrative.

Many attempts have been made to explain the name YHWH (cf. Schmidt, 53ff.; Fohrer, 75ff.). It is most probably derived from the root *hyh* (Aramaic *hwh*) 'be, become, happen'. Whether and how long the name still had a meaning which could be derived from the etymology is uncertain. In the Old Testament, only in 3.14 is an 'explanation' given, in the form of a word-play. There is no tradition of the pronunciation of the name and it can only be inferred approximately from extra-biblical texts. The form Yahweh, which has become very common, remains uncertain, and is not used in this book.

Bibliography

K.Baltzer, *The Covenant Formulary*, ET 1971; W.Beyerlin, *The Origins and History of the Earliest Sinaitic Traditions*, ET 1965; H.Cazelles, 'Alliance de l'Horeb et Renouvellement de l'Alliance', in *Beiträge zur alttestamenticher Theologie, FS W.Zimmerli*, 1977, 69-79; G.A.Davies, *The Way of the Wilderness*, 1979; G.Fohrer, *History of Israelite Religion*, ET 1973; E.W.Nicholson, *Exodus and Sinai in History and Tradition*, 1973; L.Perlitt, *Bundestheologie im Alten Testament*, 1969; id., 'Sinai und Horeb', in *FS Zimmerli* (cf. Cazelles), 302-22; W.H.Schmidt, *The Faith of the Old Testament*, ET 1983, §5 and 6.

Noth, §11; Bright, ch.3 B2; ch.4A; Mazar, III, ch.V; de Vaux I, chs.14f.; Gunneweg, II.4; Herrmann, I.3; Ben-Sasson, I.3.

Cf.also the bibliography on III.1.2.

3.4 Israel in the Wilderness

According to the account in the Pentateuch (Ex.13.17ff.), the Israelite stay in the wilderness begins immediately after the departure from Egypt (the word *midbar*, 'wilderness', appears in vv.18,20; 14.3,11f.) and ends forty years later (cf. Ex.16.35; Num.14.33f.; 32.13; Deut.1.3) with the entry into the promised land. Leaving aside the Sinai complex, a common theme connects together the narratives about the stay in the wilderness: the 'murmuring' against Moses (and Aaron). Some commentators conjecture that this is an overall interpretation of the wilderness period at a later stage of the tradition (cf. Coats, de Vries, Fritz; Childs, *Exodus*, 254ff., differs). This raises the question whether these narratives contain elements of tradition which make possible a historical reconstruction of the time in the wilderness.

Noth gave a forthright negative answer to this question. The whole theme of 'guidance in the wilderness' had only come into being after the settlement of the Israelite tribes and is a purely narrative bridging of the gap between the themes of 'deliverance from Egypt' and 'entry into arable land' (Noth, 123f., cf. Fritz, 135f.). Thus the texts could not be used as a source for the time of the stay in the wilderness.

A completely different view was put forward above all by Gressmann (following Eduard Meyer). In his view the designations of places in these texts all point to the area of Kadesh (cf.Num.13.26; 20.1,14), where according to Deut. 1.46 the Israelites spent an indeterminate period. This was where the founding of the religion took place.

→140f.

Gressmann constructed a bold hypothesis here. In his view Moses learned the YHWH cult as a priest in training from Jethro and in Kadesh founded a 'branch sanctuary' of the God by bringing the ark of YHWH, his main sanctuary, from Sinai to Kadesh (431ff.). Others have varied the theory by positing two different groups of Israelites, one of which one was on Sinai and the other at Kadesh (Rowley, 106ff.; de Vaux, 419ff.), whereas Beyerlin (145ff.) conjectures a pilgrimage from Kadesh to Sinai.

Both approaches have their problems. The first explains the texts as purely fictional narratives, without being able to explain why; the other makes the place names bear the burden of unverifiable hypotheses, some of which go against what is said in the text. In my view the two extremes reflect the same problem: the texts do not contain

→85ff.

historiography but sagas; from this some scholars draw the conclusion that they are simply to be declared unhistorical, while others attempt a coherent historical reconstruction at any price (Herrmann, 70ff., has a more judicious method). We should content ourselves with assuming the possibility of historical reminiscences from the time before the settlement without mistaking the character of the texts.

Bibliography

W.Beyerlin, *The Origins and History of the Earliest Sinaitic Traditions*, ET 1965; G.W.Coats, *Rebellion in the Wilderness. The Murmuring Motif in the Wilderness Traditions of the Old Testament*, 1968; V.Fritz, *Israel in der Wüste*, 1970; H.Gressmann, *Mose und seine Zeit. Ein Kommentar zu den Mose-Sagen*, 1913; E.Meyer, *Die Israeliten und ihre Nachbarstämme*, 1906 (1967); M.Noth, *A History of Pentateuchal Traditions*, ET 1972; H.H.Rowley, *From Joseph to Joshua: Biblical Traditions in the Light of Archaeology*, 1950; S.de Vries, 'The Origins of the Murmuring Tradition', *JBL* 87, 1968, 51-8.
Mazar III, ch.V; de Vaux I, ch.14, III; Gunneweg, II.3; Herrmann, I.3; Ben-Sasson, I.3.

3.5 Israel before the Settlement (Summary)

It is impossible to reconstruct a coherent picture of the history of Israel in the period before the settlement from the Old Testament texts. When considering the traditions as a whole it is necessary once again to remember their different characteristics. Apart from the impression of a nomadic life-style, the patriarchal narratives offer hardly any material for a historical reconstruction. By contrast, in the traditions about the stay in Egypt, the exodus, the time in the wilderness and on Sinai, there are historical references, geographical details and religious and cultic traditions which seem as though they may be references to earlier times. We have the impression that more historical reminiscences have been retained here.

This picture has been changed in more recent scholarship by the use of a good many traditions from outside Israel in a reconstruction of the patriarchal period. Above all, they take up the geographical details outside the patriarchal narratives proper, which suggest that the patriarchs came from Ur Chasdim (Gen.11.28, 31) and spent some time in Harran (11.31f.). Consequently many scholars think that the story of the patriarchs can be presented within the framework of the history of the ancient Near East; here the Genesis narratives, which describe the nomadic life of the patriarchs in the land of Canaan, are not of much consequence. At most, individual details (e.g. legal practices) are compared with remote parallels, but this does not get us very far with producing a historical reconstruction. So the extensive material from outside Israel, rather than the Old Testament texts, plays the decisive role.

By contrast, in the context of the traditions of the books of Exodus to Numbers, only a few references from sources outside Israel can be utilized. They do make it possible to connect the information in Ex.1 with Egyptian history, giving us clearer historical contours here. Otherwise the texts contain a mass of geographical information which is apparently available for attempts at reconstruction. However, arguments to and fro between a hypothetically reconstructed picture of this period and evaluations of detailed information lead to such different results, that here too it hardly seems possible to arrive at an acceptable reconstruction of the historical situation.

Still, these 'southern' traditions also contain a great many religious and cultic elements which deserve attention. Their focal point is the tradition of the divine epiphany and the giving of the commandments on Sinai, which can hardly be separated from the making known of the name YHWH on the mountain of God. Even on a careful assessment of these traditions, in my view we must conclude from them that decisive basic elements of Israelite religion are rooted in nomadic traditions from the area south of the land of Israel.

The same is also true of some individual cultic traditions of Israelite religion. The passover festival presumably derives from this nomadic sphere (cf. Rost), as is also evident from its association with the beginning of the wandering in the wilderness in Ex.12. The ark is also mentioned in the context of the wilderness wandering (Num.10.33-36; Num.14.14) and later in the settlement (Josh.3f.); and in my view it in fact belongs in this nomadic sphere. This is already suggested by its character as a portable sanctuary, though its exact significance remains uncertain (cf. Schmitt). The tent of meeting ('ohel mo'ed, Ex.33.7-11; Num.11.16; 12.4, etc.) probably originally had nothing to do with the ark, but was an independent nomadic sanctuary which among other things served for giving oracles (cf. Ex.33.7 and the comments by Schmitt); only later tradition made it into a projection of the temple of Jerusalem back into the wilderness period in the form of the great portable sanctuary of the 'tabernacle' (cf. Schmitt, Fritz). Finally, there are good reasons for supposing that the communion sacrifice (zebaḥ) is

**Before
Settlement**
→9

→8

→8

→11

→13f.

→12, 95f.

Ark

Tent of Meeting

→142
→95f., 98
19

to be explained from a nomadic way of life, so that it too belongs with the cultic traditions that were brought into the land.

However, all this by no means gives a full and coherent picture of the religion and worship of the 'Israelites' before the settlement. Rather, it shows that various and sometimes independent traditions from the nomadic sphere were introduced into the later cult of all Israel. Here it becomes clear that the image of the wilderness wandering as now presented by the texts is based on an overall view and unification of the traditions. At the same time, we can also see that these traditions contain valuable elements from the time before the settlement.

Bibliography

V.Fritz, *Tempel und Zelt*, 1977; L.Rost, 'Weidewechsel und altisraelitischer Festkalender', *ZDPV* 66, 1943, 205-15 (= *Das kleine Credo und andere Studien zum Alten Testament*, 1965, 101-12); R.Schmitt, *Zelt und Lade als Thema alttestamentlicher Wissenschaft*, 1972.

4 Israel between the Settlement and the Formation of the State

4.1 The Settlement

According to the Old Testament account, the Israelites travelled purposefully to the land promised them by God, in order to take
→148
possession of it. Numbers 13.1ff. reports that according to a divine command Moses sent out representatives of the twelve tribes to spy out the land. There was a dispute and finally an unsuccessful attempt to capture the land from the south (Num.13f.). Then began a further period of wandering, lasting forty years (14.33f.), until the generation responsible for this interlude had died (cf.26.64f.). Meanwhile the Israelites had approached the land by making a wide sweep to the east, and after fighting with a number of kings in Transjordan took possession
→149
of their territory (21.21ff.). This was subsequently assigned to the tribes of Reuben and Gad (32.33-38). After the death of Moses the Israelites then crossed the Jordan under the leadership of Joshua (Josh.3f.), again after sending out scouts in advance (Josh.2), and began to capture the country (chs.6ff.). Finally the land was divided among the remaining ten tribes with great exactness (chs.13-19).

Overall picture
However, on closer inspection the overall account of the occupation of the land proves to be very uneven. In particular it is evident that it contains only a very limited number of narratives about the occupation of the land. Apart from the brief narratives from Transjordan
→149
(Num.21.21ff.), the first report is of the capture of the cities of Jericho
(Josh.6) and Ai (Josh.7f.), and the subjugation of the inhabitants of

Gibeon without a fight (ch.9) – all in a narrow strip west of the Settlement Jordan crossing at Gilgal. Then the narrative goes further south with stereotyped reports about the capture of five further cities (10.28-43), finally moving in a great leap northwards (ch.11), where there is explicit mention only of the capture of the city of Hazor (chs.10f.). In 11.16-12.24 there are further summaries and lists of kings of conquered cities without any narrative detail. It is quite evident that Josh.1-12 sets out → 165 to be an overall account of the occupation of the country, but that very little specific material for it was available.

The problem is further complicated by the fact that Judg.1 contains →168f traditions some of which present a completely different picture of events. Two things are especially striking here. First, there are accounts of individual actions on the part of various tribes without any mention of Joshua, who in the book of Joshua is the sole protagonist. Further-more, we are explicitly told which cities the Israelites were unable to capture (vv.19.21,27, etc.). This 'negative list of possessions' clearly 'Negative list of possessions' contradicts the summary statements in Joshua about the occupation of the whole country. (For the sources, cf. in detail Hayes/Miller, 213ff.)

There are two different schools in connection with this question of Hypotheses about the settlement assessing the different traditions. In numerous publications Alt and Noth put forward the view that the settlement of the Israelite tribes was Peaceful an essentially peaceful process, a gradual infiltration by ways where there was least resistance, i.e. to begin with in the sparsely settled areas, above all the hill-country of central Palestine. There will have been warlike encounters at most in an advanced stage of the settlement of a particular area. One important argument in favour of this is the character of the texts in the book of Joshua, the focal point of which is provided by aetiological narratives which cannot be taken as historical accounts: →165 according to the archaeological evidence, the destruction of Jericho (Josh. 6) and Ai (Josh. 8) took place long before the Israelite invasion.

By contrast, Albright in particular has emphatically put forward the traditional view of a concentrated invasion and a warlike occupation of Warlike the country, and has sought to support his view with archaeological arguments. He advances external evidence (above all archaeological) for the historical accuracy of the biblical texts as opposed to their interpretation as aetiologies (for the whole question see Weippert, Hayes/Miller, 262ff.).

The views of Alt and Noth have largely prevailed in German-speaking scholar-ship (cf. Gunneweg, Herrmann). By contrast, Albright's view has been accepted by American (cf. Bright) and Israeli (cf. Mazar, Malamat, in Ben-Sasson; Aharoni differs) scholars; de Vaux takes a judicious intermediary position. In the meantime, however, things have again become fluid. Three aspects of the new development may be mentioned. First, scholars are increasingly sure that the process of settlement differed in different parts of the land (thus already de Vaux, Herrmann, etc.), with the result that the picture has become much more sophisticated and allows more than the alternatives sketched out above. Secondly, archaeological investigation of the country has led to important new insights: above all the question of the destruction of the Canaanite cities at the time of the Israelite settlement proves to be much more complex than the biblical texts suggest (cf. Hayes/Miller, 252ff.; Fritz, *TRE*, 330). According to Fritz (1980, 1982), however, Alt's model too needs to be corrected, as the cultural evidence in early iron-age settlements (1200-1000 BC) points to an intensive and protracted contact between the Israelite tribes and the inhabitants of cultivated Canaan. Finally, increasing attention is being paid to the theory that the conflicts between the 'Israelite' tribes and the Canaanites were not (or not just) the consequence of a penetration from outside, but that they reflect Social revolts social conflicts between the leading class of the country and socially disadvantaged groups rebelling against them, in which 'Yahwism' played a decisive role (Mendenhall; Gottwald; cf. Weippert, 55ff.; Gunneweg; Hayes/Miller, 277ff.); this strengthens and clarifies the view that the groups which later formed 'Israel' were heterogeneous. (The earliest mention by name of an ethnic group 'Israel' appears in a victory hymn of Pharaoh Merneptah [the 'Israel stele', of about 1219 BC, cf. *TGI*, 39f.; *DOTT*, 137ff.]. However, this piece of evidence is isolated and indeterminate.)

So it is only possible to make a historical reconstruction of the settlement in the form of hypothetical models. Each of the models is based on particular presuppositions which often seem more important in the discussion than the reconstruction itself, since they involve methodological, historical and theological questions of principle, all at the same time. Above all, it is evident that the settlement is only a transitional stage and that important decisions have to be made about the periods preceding and following it. Anyone who assumes that the Israelites already formed a religious or national community before the exile will also be inclined to regard the settlement as a more or less coherent process, the subject of which was the community as a whole. If, however, only different individual groups are thought to have been in existence in the period before the settlement, with little or no connections between them, the settlement too must be regarded as a complex and varied process. (Finally, anyone who thinks in terms of revolutionary activity within the country will only want to talk of a 'settlement' with reservations.) The same thing is true of the period after the settlement: assessments of the situation and organization of Israel after the settlement have a reciprocal relationship with conceptions about the settlement itself (see 4.2,3).

Bibliography

Y.Aharoni, *The Land of the Bible*, ²1980; A.Alt, 'The Settlement of the Israelites in Palestine' (1925), in *Essays on the History and Religion of Israel*, ET 1966, 133-69; id., 'Erwägungen über die Landnahme der Israeliten in Palästina', *PJB* 35, 1939, 8-63 (= KS I, 126-75); A.G.Auld, 'Judges I and History: A Reconsideration', *VT* 25, 1975, 261-85; V.Fritz, 'Bibelwissenschaft I. Altes Testament, I/I, Archäologie (Alter Orient und Palästina)', *TRE* VI, 1980, 316-45; id., 'Die kulturhistorische Bedeutung der früheisenzeitlichen Siedlung auf der Ḥirbet el-Msas und das Problem der Landnahme', *ZDPV* 96, 1980, 121-35; id., 'The Conquest in the Light of Archaeology', in *Proceedings of the Eighth World Congress of Jewish Studies. Division A. The Period of the*

Bible, 1982, 15-22; N.K.Gottwald, 'Domain Assumptions and Societal Models in the Study of Pre-Monarchic Israel', *VT* 28, 1975, 89-100; id., *The Tribes of Yahweh*, 1979; G.Mendenhall, 'The Hebrew Conquest of Palestine', *BA* 25, 1962, 66-87 (*BAR* 3, 1970, 100-26); M.Weinfeld, 'The Period of the Conquest and of the Judges as Seen by the Earlier and the Later Sources', *VT* 17, 1967, 93-113; M.Weippert, *The Settlement of the Israelite Tribes in Palestine*, ET 1971; M.Wüst, *Untersuchungen zu den siedlungsgeographischen Texten des Alten Testaments, I.Ostjordanland*, 1975; S.Yeivin, *The Israelite Conquest of Canaan*, 1971.

Noth, §6; Bright, ch.3, B3, C; Mazar, III, ch.V; de Vaux, II, Part 3; Gunneweg, III; Herrmann, I.4; Hayes/Miller, IV; Ben-Sasson, I.4.

Cf.also the bibliography on III.1.4 and III.2.1.

4.2 Where the Tribes Settled

The 'land of Canaan' (Gen.12.5, etc.) or 'land of Israel' (I Sam.13.19, etc.) has great variety and comprises many different kinds of country. From north to south it is marked out clearly by the Mediterranean and the deep cleft of the Jordan valley (which on the north shore of the Dead Sea sinks to more than 1200 feet below sea level). Between the two rises the central hill-country with heights up to 300 feet; to the west it falls away to the coastal plain, whereas in the south the transition is formed by a flatter hill-country, the Shephelah. If we add to this the hills of Transjordan, we get a fourfold division: coastal plain, hill-country of west Jordan, Jordan valley, hill-country of Transjordan. The division of the land

The hill-country west of the Jordan, the central area settled by the Israelite tribes, has two clear focal points, Hebron in the south and Shechem in the north; this naturally divides the land into two, a factor which was also highly significant in the history of its settlement and its political history. Given the later history, we can call these two areas the hill-country of Judah in the south and the hill-country of Ephraim (or Samaria) in the north. Further north the latter runs unto the Galilean hill-country, though separated from it by the wide plain of Jezreel. (For details cf. Noth 1966, Part 1; Ohler; Aharoni.)

We can reconstruct the process by which the Israelite tribes settled only hypothetically and with considerable qualifications. It is, however, easier to see in which locations the individual tribes settled. While the detailed description of areas in Josh.13-19 presents ideal, and sometimes only theoretical, information from different periods, it is confirmed, supplemented or corrected by a great many other texts. →165

The whole southern part of the hill-country was occupied by the tribe of Judah (cf. Josh.15). However, this remark must be qualified. First of all, according to Josh.19.1-9, the area of the tribe of Simeon also lies within the territory of Judah (see below). Furthermore, other texts show that groups lived in the southern part of this area whose names do not appear among the twelve tribes: above all Caleb (Josh.15.13f.; cf.14.13) and Othniel (Josh.15.15-19), and also the Jerahmeelites and the Kenites (cf. I Sam.27.10; 30.29). Here it becomes clear that the pattern of the twelve tribes cannot be seen directly as a reflection of historical and geographical facts. In the case of Judah the question Judah\nSimeon arises as to whether this is an individual 'tribe' or a larger grouping, to which the designation 'house of Judah' (II Sam.2.4,10f.) could also refer.

Joseph
Ephraim
Manasseh

The northern part of the hill-country is occupied by a larger group, the house of Joseph. This designation comprises two tribes, Ephraim and Manasseh (cf. Josh.17.17). However, the 'house of Joseph' itself repeatedly enters the action (e.g. Judg.1.22f.,35), and in Josh. 18.5 'Judah' is contrasted with it. Here too the changing names present a problem in the twelve-tribe scheme: sometimes Joseph appears as the real son of Jacob (Gen.30.22-24; 35.22b-26; 49.22-26; Deut.33.13-17), and sometimes his sons Ephraim and Manasseh (Num.1.32-35, in the reverse order in Num.26.28-37; in Judg.5.14, Ephraim and Machir, see below), who according to Gen.48 were adopted by Jacob.

Benjamin
→26

Between these two great blocks is the tribal territory of Benjamin (Josh.18.11-28). Benjamin was regarded as the youngest of Jacob's sons (Gen.35.16f.) and in fact seems to have been a smaller and politically weaker tribe between its great neighbours. Galilee in the north was the area of the settlement of the tribes of Zebulun (Josh.19.10-16), Issachar

Northern tribes

(19.17-23), Asher (19.24-31) and Naphtali (19.32-39). The tribe of Dan is said to have had a special fate: according to Josh. 19.40-46 it settled in the western hill-country, about on a level with Jerusalem. However, in Judg.1.34 we are told that the Amorites (here the designation of a group of the earlier inhabitants of the land) had forced the Danites back into the hills; this seems to be the reason why they looked for a new area to settle in, far to the north (cf. Josh.19.47; Judg.18).

Reuben, Gad

The areas settled by Reuben (Josh.13.15-23) and Gad (13.24-28) are said to have been in Transjordan. However, it is striking that we have no indication of a border between these two territories, so that essentially there was just one area. Finally, the area settled in by the 'half tribe of Manasseh' is mentioned only in very general terms (13.29-31). We may probably connect this with the information given in

Machir

Num.32.29f., where it is reported that Machir, the son of Manasseh, settled in Transjordan: this is probably an extension of the area in which Manasseh settled eastwards beyond the Jordan. (The exact relationship between the name of Manasseh and Machir remains uncertain, cf. also Judg.5.14.)

The areas in which the tribes settled are an important starting point for attempts at reconstructing the process of the settlement (therefore Noth discusses them before the settlement, cf. §5,6; cf. also Mowinckel, Kaiser, Schunck, Zobel). The extent of the division of the land and the

→23

very different sizes of the areas assigned to the tribes suggests that the settlement took very different courses in individual areas; however, the biblical texts do not give us any specific indications. A further problem is that the areas in which the tribes settled are very difficult to harmonize

→26f.
→139f.

with the scheme of twelve tribes, which is presupposed from the beginning of the book of Exodus on. This is also one of the main problems over the historical reconstruction of the 'period of the judges'

(see 4.3).

Bibliography

Y.Aharoni, *The Land of the Bible*, ²1980; O.Kaiser, 'Stammesgeschichtliche
Hintergründe der Josephsgeschichte', *VT* 10, 1960, 1-15: S.Mowinckel,
' "Rachelstamme" und "Leastamme"', in *Von Ugarit nach Qumran, FS
O.Eissfeldt*, 1958 (²1961), 129-50; M.Noth, *The Old Testament World*, ET
1966; A.Ohler, *Israel, Volk und Land. Zur Geschichte der wechselseitigen
Beziehungen zwischen Israel und seinem Land in alttestamentlicher Zeit*, 1979;
K.-D.Schunck, *Benjamin. Untersuchungen zur Entstehung und Geschichte eines
israelitischen Stammes*, 1963; H.J.Zobel, *Stammesspruch und Geschichte. Die
Angaben der Stammessprüche von Gen.49, Deut.33 und Jdc 5 über die politischen
und kultischen Zustände des damaligen 'Israel'*, 1965.

Noth, §5; Mazar, III, ch.5; de Vaux, II, Part 3; Herrmann, I.4; Ben-Sasson,
I.4.

Cf. also the bibliography on III.1.4 and III.2.1.

4.3 Israel in the Time of the Judges

There is mention at the beginning of the book of Judges of a break in
the continuity of the history of Israel: after the death of Joshua, a new
generation arose which knew nothing of YHWH's mighty acts towards
Israel (Judg.2.10). This reflects a significant change in the presentation
of the account and above all in the traditional material which it uses.
→167f.
For the time from the exodus to the settlement, the figures of Moses
and Joshua served as a unifying bond which kept together the great
variety of traditions. This approach also resulted in a completely
coherent picture of the history of 'Israel'. For the period which now
follows there is no such figure. At the same time, another kind of
tradition begins here, the heroic saga, at the heart of which we always
→87f.
have a particular individual whose acts – indeed, often just a single act
– are reported. Thus while the picture becomes less uniform, at the
same time the historical ground on which we are treading becomes
gradually firmer.

In the book of Judges, the retrospective verdict on this period is
negative: the unifying power of the monarchy was absent, so that each
person did what he wanted (17.6; 21.25). This judgment is based on the
presupposition that 'Israel' was a unity which only lacked leadership.
→167f.
However, the traditions show clearly enough that this unity never
existed. Granted, the Deuteronomistic framework of the book of Judges
regularly speaks of the 'Israelites' (*bene yiśrael*, 2.11; 3.7,12, etc.), or
simply of 'Israel' (2.14; 3.8,12b etc), but the narratives always move in
a very limited area.

At the centre of the account are individual figures who can be
described as 'deliverers' (*mošiaʿ*, 3.9,15; the verb also appears at 3.31;
6.14f.,36; 8.22; 10.1; 13.5, cf. Grether). They always appear when
'Israel' is in trouble. However, the narratives show that what we have
are predominantly limited local conflicts.

The Benjaminite Ehud (Judg.3.12-30) murders the Moabite king Eglon and then from the 'hill-country of Ephraim' declares war on the Moabites (v.27); the battle essentially takes place at the fords over the Jordan. According to the account no one takes part in it other than the Benjaminites and their northern neighbours, the Ephraimites. Shamgar is said to have carried out a one-man action against the Philistines (3.31).

Gideon's expedition against the Midianites (Judg.6-8) involves only his clan of Abiezrites to begin with (6.34), and is then extended to the tribe of Manasseh and the neighbouring northern tribes of Asher, Zebulun and Naphtali (v.35; Zebulun is missing from 7.23); finally, the Ephraimites are also summoned for the last act (7.24), complaining about their late inclusion (8.1).

Jephthah's battle against the Ammonites (10.6-12.6) is a purely Transjordanian affair (11.29: Gilead and Manasseh, i.e. the part east of the Jordan), and again the Ephraimites complain about not having been involved (12.1ff.); this is perhaps an expression of Ephraim's claim to leadership.

Only on one occasion is a larger number of tribes mentioned. In Judg.4;5 there are two descriptions of a battle on the plain of Jezreel

under the leadership of Deborah (and Barak, the commander appointed by her, cf. 4.6ff.). This time the enemy does not come from outside. The real opponent is Sisera from Harosheth-goyim (4.2b) on the north-west slope of the plain of Jezreel. (Moreover, in 4.2a there is mention of King Jabin of Hazor, who is even called 'King of Canaan' [cf. vv.23f.]; this is probably meant to indicate the basic importance of the battle in the struggle against the Canaanites; Jabin himself evidently has nothing to do with the battle.) In Judg.4 only Zebulun and Naphtali are

mentioned as tribes involved in the battle (vv.6,10). In Judg.5.14f., however, the circle is extended. Ephraim, Benjamin, Machir, Zebulun, Issachar (and Naphtali, cf. v.18) are involved, i.e. the whole of the northern tribes. It is significant that tribes are also mentioned and criticized which did not take part: the Transjordanian tribes of Reuben and Gilead along with the remaining northern tribes, Dan and Asher (vv.15b-17). Here we can recognize the view that all the tribes should

really have taken part in the battle. This unfulfilled postulate of unity, however, shows at the same time that this unity did not exist. Besides, the southern tribes of Judah and Simeon are not mentioned, so that the passage clearly does not envisage a people of twelve tribes. Nor do we find anywhere else in the traditions about the period of the judges a reference to there being twelve tribes, or to a sense of being all Israel, which would embrace this.

This point must also be made against the hypothesis that there was an 'amphictyony' of the twelve tribes, put forward by M.Noth (1930). Noth interpreted Israel in the period before the state on the basis of Greek analogies as a sacral association of twelve tribes which had its focal point in a central

sanctuary (the ark) at a cultic centre (according to Josh 24, this was Shechem) and which possessed a binding amphictyonic law. Later (1940, ET 1966) Noth, following Alt, associated this with 'apodeictic law', for which perhaps the 'minor

judges' (see below) were responsible. At all events they were supposed to have held an amphictyonic office (Noth 1950). This hypothesis had very wide influence and for decades occupied an important place not only in German but also in international scholarship (cf. Bright). In the meantime, however, considerable doubts have been cast on it, and therefore it has been largely abandoned (cf. Herrmann, 1962; Fohrer; de Vaux; Hayes/Miller, 304ff.). The question of the twelve-tribe scheme has had an important role to play here.

The deliverer figures appear spontaneously, always in situations of extreme need. It is evident that they do not hold any 'office' in the institutional sense and that there is no continuity between the individual deliverers. They are therefore often described as 'charismatic military leaders'. This primarily denotes that their function was essentially military, namely to summon and lead the 'army', i.e. all-able bodied men capable of bearing arms (cf. 3.27; 4.10; 6.34f.; 11.29). The use of the term 'charismatic' is particularly connected with the 'spirit' (ru^ah) of YHWH, which takes hold of the 'deliverer' (3.10; 6.34; 11.29). (However, Max Weber, who coined the phrase, understood it in a wider sense as a form of rule which rests only on personal authority, in contrast to other forms of leadership which are based either on the rational rules of an institution or on tradition, cf. above all 1922, ch.IX, and on it Malamat 1981.)

Charismatic military leaders

Von Rad used the term 'holy war' to describe the wars which are reported here. They have a variety of religious elements, and it is particularly significant that they are not really waged by Israel itself but by YHWH for Israel. It is therefore better to describe them as YHWH wars (Smend). Von Rad saw these wars as an important feature of the amphictyony. However, their connection with the alliance of twelve tribes has also been put in question (Smend, Stolz), as has the specifically Israelite character of such wars, waged by a god for his followers, since they also occur elsewhere in the ancient Near East (Weippert). The accounts of the wars in the Old Testament have a marked theological and literary stamp, so that there must be doubts about their use for historical reconstruction (cf. also Jones).

YHWH war

The deliverer figures are usually termed major judges. The book of Judges mentions a whole series of men (twelve in all) who are summed up in 2.16-19 as 'judges' (*šopᵉtim*). In addition to the figures of the 'deliverers', in 10.1-5; 12.7-15 we have a list of minor judges of whom it is regularly said that the person concerned 'judged Israel' (10.2,3; 12.8,11,13). Here a continuous office seems to be meant, as is indicated by the explicit stress on succession ('after him', 10.3; 12.8,11,13). Noth thought that this was a central amphictyonic office (see below, see also Schunck). In the meantime, however, the 'judges' have been supposed to have a more limited function relating only to a city and the district around it; the list was then perhaps later formulated by analogy with lists in royal annals (cf. Richter; Hayes/Miller, 320). What the specific function of the office was remains unknown. The verb 'judge' (*šapat*) suggests activities to do with legislation and the administration of law (thus Alt, 102f.), and perhaps also, more generally, administrative tasks (cf. Richter). However, in other Semitic languages the word can also

Major judges

Minor judges
→105f., 168f.

mean 'rule', etc.; in particular the title 'suffetes', from the Phoenician, as used for the supreme officials in Carthage, provides an interesting parallel (cf. Richter; Herrmann, 113), so that e.g. de Vaux, 770ff., thinks of an office over all Israel.

Thus the texts of the book of Judges provide a varied picture of this time, with numerous individual historical figures, but cannot be organized into a coherent overall account. Evidently this is a reflection of the actual character of this period, when 'Israel'was not yet a unity.

Recently, sociological models have been introduced into the interpretation of Israelite society in this period. Max Weber had introduced the concept of 'federation by oath', which he could also describe as 'regulated anarchy' (cf.

Schäfer). Crüsemann (201f.) and Schafer have taken over the term 'segmentary society' from ethnology; the essential characteristic of this society is the political equality of the individual sub-groups (clans, tribes) and the lack of a superior central authority. The temporary charismatic leadership of individual leaders provides an element of stability. In my view this approach could contribute to a better understanding of the time of the judges and should be developed further.

Bibliography

A.Alt, 'The Origins of Israelite Law' (1934), in *Essays on Old Testament History and Religion*, ET 1966, 79-132; F.Crüsemann, *Der Widerstand gegen das Königtum. Die antiköniglichen Texte des Alten Testamentes und der Kampf um den frühen israelitischen Staat*, 1978; G.Fohrer, 'Altes Testament – Amphiktyonie und Bund', *TLZ* 91, 801-16, 893-904 (= *Studien zur alttestamentlichen Theologie und Geschichte*, 84-119); O.Grether, 'Die Bezeichnung Richter für die charismatischen Helden der vorstaatlichen Zeit', *ZAW* 57, 1939, 110-21; S.Herrmann, 'Das Werden Israels', *TLZ* 87, 1962, 561-74; G.H.Jones, ' "Holy War" or "Yahweh War"?', *VT* 25, 1975, 642-58; A.Malamat, 'Charismatische Führung im Buch der Richter', in W.Schluchter (ed.), *Max Webers Studie über das antike Judentum. Interpretation und Kritik*, 1981, 110-33; M.Noth, *Das System der zwölf Stämme Israels*, 1930 (1966/1980); id., 'The Laws in the Pentateuch', in *The Laws in the Pentateuch*, ET 1966, ²1984; id., 'Das Amt des "Richters Israels"', in *FS A.Bertholet*, 1950, 404-17 (= *GS* II, 71-85); G.von Rad, *Der heilige Krieg im alten Israel*, 1951 (⁵1969); W.Richter, 'Zu den "Richtern Israels"', *ZAW* 77, 1965, 40-72; C.Schäfer, *Stadt und Eidgenossenschaft im Alten Testament. Eine Auseinandersetzung mit Max Webers Studie 'Das Antike Judentum'*, Heidelberg 1979; id., 'Stadtstaat und Eidgenossencaft. Max Webers Analyse der vorexilischen Gesellschaft', in W.Schluchter (see Malamat), 78-109; K.-D.Schunck, 'Die Richter Israels und ihr Amt', *SVT* 15, 1966, 252-62; R.Smend, *Jahwekrieg und Stämmebund*, ²1966; F.Stolz, *Jahwes und Israels Kriege. Kriegstheorien und Kriegserfahrungen im Glauben des alten Israel*, 1972; M.Weber, *Ancient Judaism* (1932), ET 1952; id., *Wirtschaft und Gesellschaft*, 1922 (⁵1972); M.Weippert, ' "Heiliger Krieg" in Israel und Assyrien', *ZAW* 84, 1972, 460-93.

Noth, §12,13; Bright, ch.4 B,C; Mazar, III, chs.VII, VIII; de Vaux, II, Part 4; Gunneweg, IV; Herrmann, I.5; Hayes/Miller, V §1-3; Ben-Sasson, I.5. Cf. also the bibliography on III.2.2.

5.1 Samuel and the Kingdom of Saul

I Samuel begins with a birth narrative (ch.1). This marks a change in period. However, Samuel, whose birth is reported here, does not himself mark the change. He is a transitional figure. The tradition gives him a varied role: he grows up at the sanctuary in Shiloh (I Sam.1.24-28), where he 'ministers' (2.18; 3.1). Later, though, there is nowhere any explicit mention of priestly ministry; rather, we are told that the word of YHWH is 'revealed' to him (3.7) and that 'all Israel' recognizes him as a prophet appointed by YHWH (vv.19f.). This prophetic function takes on decisive significance where we next hear of a word of YHWH: in the secret anointing of Saul as YHWH's 'prince' (*nagid*, 9.15ff.; cf.10.1). Here Samuel appears in the role of the kingmaker commissioned by God.

Samuel as prophet 170

Alongside this we find another feature of the tradition: Samuel 'judged Israel' (7.15-17; cf.v.6). Here he is included in the series of minor judges, and his activity in administering justice is vividly described. In the same chapter he is connected with a victory over the Philistines (7.2-14), which is attributed to the miraculous intervention of YHWH (v.10); this brings him nearer to the major judges.

Samuel as judge →27f.

→25ff.

There is dispute as to which of these roles Samuel in fact had or performed, and clarification is probably no longer possible (cf. Macholz, Langlamet, Miller). However, the tradition clearly wants to bring out two things: Samuel is in continuity with the 'judges' before him – and at the same time he opens a new era in the history of Israel by anointing at YHWH's behest the one chosen for the new office of king. That this is his decisive function also emerges from the fact that after the failure of Saul, Samuel is again commissioned to anoint the next (and now the rightful) holder of this new office (I Sam.16.1-13).

→112

With Saul, too, at first there is an evident element of continuity. He emerges as the 'deliverer', who, in the face of a threat from external enemies is seized by the 'spirit of YHWH' and conquers the enemy (11.1-13). The new development is that 'the whole people' makes Saul king immediately after this victory (v.15). Most exegetes see this as an accurate historical tradition: Saul is made king spontaneously after the victory over the Ammonites. The reason for this was probably the threatening situation in which the Israelites found themselves as a result of the military superiority of the Philistines (cf. ch.4; 13.19ff.). They could no longer cope with this danger through a temporary 'charismatic' leadership which was only exercised from time to time. It called for continuous leadership.

Saul as deliverer

Philistines

Here, however, we are already moving into the sphere of historical reconstruction, for such considerations are not reported in the texts themselves. Other problems are in the foreground. First of all, there is the question how the newly developing monarchy related to the will of

Saul as king 29

YHWH. Here we find a striking contradiction. On the one hand we are told of Saul's secret designation by Samuel (9.1-10.16), while on the other the demand for a king seems to be apostasy from YHWH (ch.8). This is a reflection of an ambivalent verdict on the monarchy which was probably there from the beginning. The resistance against the monarchy obviously had political as well as religious (cf. also Judg.8.22f.) elements (cf.Crüsemann).

The religious problems of Saul's reign are further accentuated by the fact that he is not personally up to the demands of the office, and this leads to sharp conflicts with Samuel and finally to Saul's rejection by YHWH (13.11-14; 15.10ff.). Here we have a prime example of the conflict between king and prophet. which was always to be a prominent feature in the subsequent history of the monarchy (cf. Rendtorff).

Saul's realm

The account of Saul's reign is so dominated by these problems that it is hardly possible to reconstruct the historical events (cf. Wildberger, Schunck, Wallis). The very nature of Saul's kingship and his sphere of influence remain unclear. The texts report only military conflicts; in 14.52 we have a reference to the institution of an army of professional soldiers as an innovation in comparison to the previous force. There is no indication of whether Saul exercised rule in more than military matters or even attempted to do so. In particular, the extent of the area which Saul either controlled or laid claim to is also unclear. The term 'Israel', which is regularly used, is nowhere defined more closely.

→32

As one step towards a reconstruction one could adduce the information in II Sam.2.8f., where the following places are mentioned as within the sphere of influence of Saul's son Eshbaal after Saul's death: Gilead (i.e. areas in Transjordan, cf. I Sam.11), Jezreel (really the name of a place but here meant as a general designation for the plain of Jezreel or for the tribal territory of Issachar?), Ephraim, Benjamin (why is Manasseh missing?) and ha-'ašuri (usually emended to 'the people of Asher', cf. Judg.1.32). This would cover essential parts of the northern and Transjordanian territories of the Israelite tribes (cf. Wallis, 63f.; Herrmann, 147f.). Judah is missing; while the narratives about David's flight from Saul indicate that David did not feel safe even in Judah (e.g. I Sam.24), in my view the beginnings of the kingdom of David do not suggest that Judah was an established part of the area ruled over by Saul.

Length of reign

The length of Saul's reign is given in I Sam.13.1 as two years. (Some commentators regard this number as problematical, but in my view there is no reason for any change.) They are dominated by conflict with the Philistines. After an initial victory by Saul, which however was only of limited significance (ch.13f.; cf. von Rad), it ended with an annihilating defeat of the Israelites and the death of Saul (ch.31).

The reign of Saul is regarded as a transitional period. That is already clear from the fact that Saul is predominantly depicted as a contrasting figure, on the one hand to Samuel, who represents the tradition of the 'judges' and at the same time the prophetic conflict with the new monarchy; and on the other hand to David, who even during Saul's lifetime becomes the dominant figure in the account (from I Sam.16

on). Therefore there was probably little interest in outlining the features **Samuel and**
of his reign more clearly. However, at his death it transpired that the **Saul**
institution of the monarchy had found a footing in Israel, so that in spite
of everything Saul is the first in the line of kings of Israel.

F.Crüsemann, *Der Widerstand gegen das Königtum. Die antiköniglichen Texte
des Alten Testamentes und der Kampf um den frühen israelitischen Staat*, 1978;
F.Langlamet, 'Les récits de l'institution de la Royauté (I Sam.VII-XII).
De Wellhausen aux travaux récents', *RB* 77, 1970, 161-200; G.C.Macholz,
Untersuchungen zur Geschichte der Samuel-Überlieferungen, Diss.Heidelberg
1966; J.M.Miller, 'Saul's Rise to Power. Some Observations Concerning 1
Sam.9:11-10:16; 10:26-11:15 and 13:2-14:36', *CBQ* 36, 1974, 157-74; G. von
Rad, 'Zwei Überlieferungen von König Saul', in *GS* II, 199-211; R.Rendtorff,
'Erwägungen zur Frühgeschichte des Prophetentums in Israel', *ZTK* 59, 1962,
145-67 (= *GS*, 220-42); K.-D.Schunck, *Geschichte und Überlieferung. Gedanken
über alttestamentliche Darstellungen der Frühgeschichte Israels und der Anfänge
seines Königtums*, 1968; A.Weiser, *Samuel. Seine geschichtliche Aufgabe und
religiöse Bedeutung. Traditionsgeschichtliche Untersuchungen zu I Samuel 7-12*,
1962; H.Wildberger, 'Samuel und die Entstehung des israelitischen Königtums',
TZ 13, 1957, 442-69 (= *Jahwe und sein Volk*, 1980, 28-55).
    Noth, §14; Bright, ch.5 A; Malamat, IV.1, IV; Gunneweg, V; Herrmann, II,
1; Hayes/Miller, V.§4; Ben-Sasson, I.7.
    Cf. also the bibliography on III.2.3.

5.2 David's Rise to be King over Judah and Israel

We have more detailed reports about David than about any other king.
They are essentially contained in two great literary complexes: in the
History of the Rise of David to the Throne (I Sam.16-II Sam.5)) and in
the Succession Narrative (II Sam.9 – I Kings 2). The designations of →107, 171ff.
these two works indicate the interests of the authors or collectors. In
the first instance they were dealing with the prelude to David's reign,
which is essentially a history of his conflict with Saul, and in the second
with the question of his succession, which at the same time reflects the
struggles for power at his court. David's activity as king, the measures
that he took and his successes in both internal and external politics, are
often mentioned in this context, but there are only a very few passages
of whch they are the real theme.
    David's way to the throne begins at the court of Saul (about which Rivalry
we have a number of accounts). The rivalry between the two and Saul's between Saul
jealousy of David are reported in detail (I Sam.18.1-16, etc.); this and David
eventually leads to Saul's desire to kill David (19.1). At that point David
flees (vv.12,18ff.). In the following narratives David is emphatically
presented as the innocent victim of persecution who nevertheless spares
the life of his persecutor (esp. chs 24-26), because Saul is the 'anointed

of YHWH' (24.7,11; 26.9,11 etc). At the same time, however, it is clear that he is playing a double game in that he falls in with Israel's most dangerous enemies, the Philistines. As a vassal of Achish of Gath, the Philistine king, he is even given the city of Ziklag for himself (27.1-7). This ambivalence does not seem untypical of David and of the picture which the tradition has preserved of him.

David's conduct after Saul's death also has this double aspect. He laments Saul's death in moving words (II Sam.1.1ff., 17ff.), but he embarks immediately and purposefully on preparations to take over the succession.

Abner and
Eshbaal
→30 In II Sam.2-4 we have very detailed narratives about the events following the death of Saul. In Hebron David allows himself to be anointed king of Judah (2.1-4), while Abner, Saul's commander, has Saul's son Eshbaal made king of Israel in Mahanaim in Transjordan (2.8f.). There follows in 2.12-32 a broad and very vivid historical account of the conflict between the military leaders on the two sides, Abner and Joab. This is followed in 3.6-4.12 by a passage which already marks the transition from historical narrative to history proper: over a long period, with changing persons and scenes, it depicts the events which lead to Abner's changing sides, to his assassination by Joab and finally to the death of Eshbaal, which clears the way for David to rule over Israel. This section could be called the 'Abner history' (cf. Rendtorff, 432, 439; Soggin).

After Eshbaal's assassination, the representative of the northern tribes made David king over Israel and concluded a treaty with him
King of Judah
and Israel (5.1-3). This meant that David was king over Judah and Israel. The distinction is explicitly maintained in a note from the annals in 5.4f.: David was king 'over all Israel and Judah'. (The note about his death in I Kings 2.10f. differs; there we are told that David had been king 'over Israel' for forty years.) We can regard the terminology which draws a distinction as being more accurate and legally more appropriate,
→5 though it also alternates with the more comprehensive use of Israel (cf. Alt 1950, 43ff.). That the unity of the two kingdoms was hardly something that could be taken for granted was clear at the latest after the death of Solomon. (For criticism of this view of Alt's cf. Buccellati, 146ff.; Hayes/Miller, 354ff.).

Two important events are reported in II Sam.5: the capture of Jerusalem (vv.6-9) and the decisive battle against the Philistines (vv.17-25). Perhaps these things happened the other way round (cf. v.17, cf.
→29 Noth, *History*, 189ff.); at all events David's victory over the Philistines was the decisive presupposition for the stabilizing and later expansion
Jerusalem as
capital of his rule. The capture of Jerusalem, which previously had still been in the hands of the Jebusites, was similarly of great political significance; with it David made himself an independent capital (the 'city of David', v.9), which on the one hand was central and on the other did not belong to any of the Israelite tribes (cf. Alt 1925).

There is no evidence in the Old Testament to support Alt's conjecture that to his twofold kingship over Judah and Israel David added a third, that over
Jerusalem (1930, ET 217f.). However, it is clear that to some degree Jerusalem

had a special status from the fact that in the Old Testament we often find the double expression 'Judah and Jerusalem' (II Kings 23.1; Isa.1.1; 2.1; Jer.29.2; 30.3, etc.; cf. Hayes/Miller, 355; Noth 1950. Buccellati, 160ff., is critical). **Judah and Israel**

According to II Sam.6, David gave the city of Jerusalem further significance by having the ark brought there. According to the account in the ark narratives, the ark had been lost in the wars against the Philistines; it had then been recovered, but since then had been forgotten (cf. I Sam.7.2a). We might see this as a particularly astute measure by David, which was to make Jerusalem also the religious and cultic centre of all the Israelite tribes. If we dismiss the idea of a central sanctuary of an alliance of twelve tribes existing before the state, there had previously been no such centre. Nor was the ark immediately predestined to perform this function; it probably only attained its central significance when it was set up in Jerusalem. This action on the part of David was commemorated by a cultic repetition of the introduction of the ark into the temple (cf.Ps.132). Transfer of the ark
→170

→26f.

→19

→99, 108

At this point, where for the moment the domestic political consolidation of David's empire had come to a conclusion, we are given a brief resumé (probably based on official documents) of his successes in foreign policy (II Sam.8.1-14). After the victory over the Philistines (v.1), he subjugated the neighbouring states of Moab (v.2), Ammon (see the detailed account in 10.1-11.1; 12.26-31) and Edom (vv.13f.) in Transjordan and also extended his power northwards by subjugating the Aramaean states of Zobah (vv.3f.) and Damascus (vv.5f.) and accepting tribute from the king of Hamath (vv.9f.). Thus his power extended 'from the River (Euphrates) to the frontier of Egypt' (cf. I Kings 5.1), and thus comprised a greater empire than ever existed in this area beforehand or afterwards (cf. Alt 1950, 66ff.). Still, it is striking that the Old Testament account notes this side of David's activity only in passing. We are told even less about internal organization. However, it emerges from the lists of officials in 8.16-18 and 20.23-26 that David built up an administration for his empire in which he took Egyptian patterns as his model in both organization and the official functions needed in it (cf. Begrich; Mettinger; Herrmann, 160ff.; Hayes/Miller, 356ff.). Successes in foreign policy
→106

Internal organization
→105f.

The account of the struggle over the succession to the throne of David takes up a good deal of room. First of all, it is a struggle among the sons of David, of whom Amnon (II Sam.13) and Absalom (ch.18) are killed, so that it finally comes to a power struggle between Adonijah and Solomon (I Kings 1). This is at the same time a struggle between rival groups at court which is carried on with a great many intrigues. However, more deep-seated problems can be seen behind Absalom's rebellion (II Sam.15-19). Absalom evidently exploited a widespread dissatisfaction with the rule of David (15.1ff., cf. Crüsemann, 94ff.). His rebellion affected the whole area ruled over by David, so that the latter could only rely on the mercenary troops; however, with them David was ultimately able to defeat the army raised against him 'from Dan to Beersheba' (17.11). On his return a new problem arose as a result of Struggle for the succession

Absalom's rebellion

the rivalry between the people of Judah and the members of the northern tribes over the restoration of the king; this led to a sharp conflict (19.9b-16, 42-44), from which a new rebellion of the northern tribes developed (ch.20). Here we can see deep-seated tensions between the north and south towards the end of David's reign. (Perhaps a fundamental rejection of the monarchy even underlies the rebellious words of Sheba, cf. Crüsemann, 104ff.).

Bibliography

A.Alt, 'Die Formation of the Israelite State in Palestine' (1930), in *Essays in Old Testament History and Religion*, ET 1966, 171-237; id., 'Das Grossreich Davids', *TLZ* 75, 1950, 213-20 (= *KS* II, 66-75); id, 'Jerusalems Aufstieg', *ZDMG* 79, 1925, 1-19 (= *KS* III, 243-57); J.Begrich, 'Sofer und Mazkir. Ein Beitrag zur inneren Geschichte des davidisch-salomonischen Grossreiches und des Königreiches Juda', *ZAW* 58, 1940/41, 1-29 (= *GS*, 67-98); G.Buccellati, *Cities and Nations of Ancient Syria*, 1967; F.Crüsemann, *Der Widerstand gegen das Königtum. Die antiköniglichen Texte des Alten Testaments und der Kampf um den frühen israelitischen Staat*, 1978; T.N.D.Mettinger, *Salomonic State Officials. A Study of the Civil Government Officials of the Israelite Monarchy*, 1971; M.Noth, 'Jerusalem and the Israelite Tradition' (1950), in *The Laws in the Pentateuch*, ET 1966, 132-44; R.Rendtorff, 'Beobachtungen zur altisraelitischen Geschichtsschreibung anhand der Geschichte vom Aufstieg Davids', in *Probleme biblischer Theologie, FS G.von Rad*, 1971, 428-39; J.A.Soggin, 'The Reign of *'Ešba'al, Son of Saul'*, in *Old Testament and Oriental Studies*, 1975, 31-49.

Noth, §15; Bright, ch.5 B; Malamat, IV.1, V, VI; Gunneweg, VI; Herrmann, II.2; Hayes/Miller, VI §1-3; Ben-Sasson, I.7.

Cf. also the bibliography on III.2,3,4.

5.3 The Reign of Solomon

→174ff.

The traditions about Solomon are of a very different kind from those about David. They are collected together in I Kings 1-11 in a 'History of Solomon', which has a clear Deuteronomistic stamp. That means that the picture of Solomon offered to us by these texts is retrospective and was composed a long time after the events. It is the picture of a wise, just and pious king of peace.

→107, 172f.

However, right at the start this picture is considerably disturbed by the conclusion of the Succession Narrative, which at the same time marks the beginning of the history of Solomon. I Kings 2 records how Solomon inexorably, often cruelly, and on unconvincing pretexts eliminated his political opponents, beginning with his older brother Adonijah (vv.13,25). Thus the closing sentence 'And the kingdom was secure in the hand of Solomon' has a macabre ring (cf. Delekat; Crüsemann, 180ff.).

Something quite different then begins with ch.3. The godfearing young king Solomon asks in a nocturnal vision for an 'attentive heart' (v.9) and as a response to this exemplary petition is promised all the things he did not wish for himself: riches and honour and a long life (vv.13f.). These are the key words in terms of which the history of Solomon is depicted.

Within chs.3-11 there is a variety of material which makes possible a historical reconstruction of the reign of Solomon. The most striking thing here is that there is no mention of any wars. Evidently the time of Solomon was a period of peace abroad. His activity in foreign policy is essentially reflected in the diplomatic sphere, with a clear predominance of mercantile interests.

With Hiram, king of the Phoenician coastal city of Tyre, Solomon made a mercantile treaty (*5.15-26*, cf. Fensham), by which Hiram delivered wood from the Lebanon and in exchange Solomon supplied grain and oil. 9.10-14 mentions a somewhat obscure deal in which Solomon ceded twenty cities in Galilee to Hiram in exchange for the deliveries of wood and gold which he had received. In addition, with the help of the Phoenicians Solomon built a trading fleet on the Gulf of Elath (9.26-28) which carried gold, silver and other precious commodities (cf.10.11,22). Diplomatic relationships with Egypt were expressed in Solomon's marriage with a 'daughter of Pharaoh', who occupied a prominent position in his harem (3.1; 7.8, etc.); however, it is difficult to tell which Pharaoh this will have been (cf. Noth, *Könige*, 49). Trade relationships with Egypt consisted, among other things, in the purchase of horses and chariots which Solomon sold on to kings of the 'Hitittes' and 'Aramaeans', probably smaller states in Syria (10.28f.). The presence of other foreign wives whom Solomon is said to have had in his harem (11.1) suggests diplomatic and trade relationships with the countries concerned.

Within his kingdom Solomon considerably developed the adminis- tration and made it more sophisticated (cf. I Kings 4, and Mettinger). The need for this arose not least from the expensive style of the court and costly building works. Thus the division of the country into twelve districts (4.7-19, cf. Alt, Wright) predominantly had the function of ensuring provsions for the royal court, in that each district had this responsibility for a month (v.7, cf. also *5.2f.*). The building activity could only be carried out with forced labour, i.e. with a conscripted, unpaid work force. (9.15-23 mentions only non-Israelites, but *5.27-32* mentions 'all Israel'; perhaps the latter refers only to the work on the temple and possibly also on the royal palace [Mettinger, 134ff.], or what we have here are later 'corrective additions' to the 'Account of the Building of the Temple' [Rupprecht, 36f.]). All this paints all too clearly the picture of a ruler who exploits his subjects to make it possible for him to develop his power and demonstrate it brilliantly.

Among the many and extensive building works of Solomon, the fortresses, store cities, and so on are given only summary mention (9.15-19). Interest is wholly concentrated on the royal buildings in Jerusalem: the temple and the royal palace, which consists of a whole series of buildings. In the extensive complex made up of *5.15*-8.66, first mention is made of the building of the temple (ch.6) and the palace buildings (7.13-51), and then of the equipping of the temple (7.13-51); here, above all in the last section, there is a clear indication of the adoption of Canaanite models, especially in the religious symbolism of the equipment. (Elsewhere, too, in the Old Testament there are numerous indications that in Jerusalem there were various connections between Israelite and Canaanite religious traditions, cf. Schmidt § 13.) This whole work is crowned with the dedication of the temple (ch.8).

The analysis of the 'account of building the temple' in I Kings 6 and other related texts shows that what we have here is not a new building but a rebuilding of the temple. This was probably a Jebusite temple, the cultic aetiology of which we have in II Sam.24, and which David had already put into use, as is evident e.g. from II Sam.12.20 and Ps.132. As it now stands, the account is presumably meant to erase memories of the Jebusite prehistory, which is why it represents Solomon's measures in rebuilding the temple as the building of a new one. (For the whole question, see Rupprecht.)

→96f.

Solomon's
wisdom

→108ff.

The last basic feature brought out by the story of Solomon is the king's wisdom. It is granted to him right at the beginning by God (I Kings 3.12) and is soon confirmed in a wise judgment (3.16-28); it shows its world-wide superiority (*5.9-14*; 10.1-13) and is finally stressed once again as a special characteristic of Solomon's rule (11.41). In particular, the comparison with the wisdom of other peoples suggests that at the court of Solomon, as at other royal courts of the time, 'wisdom' was cultivated in a variety of ways. An essential part of the wisdom traditions of the Old Testament have their origin here.

Weaknesses
in foreign policy

Towards the end, the account of Solomon reports a decline in his power. In two directions he came up against adversaries who reduced his empire. In the north Damascus regained its independence (11.23-25; cf. II Sam.8.5f.); in the south an Edomite prince succeeded in again ruling over his own land (11.14-22). Both these developments took place during Solomon's reign (vv.21,25); this shows that Solomon could not hold the territory ruled over by David, especially as he took no steps in that direction. Here one could also recall the loss of twenty cities in Galilee (9.10-14, see above).

Tensions in
domestic
politics

Finally, there were domestic tensions: in 11.26-28,40 we hear of a rebellion which was sparked off by a royal official called Jeroboam, connected with the system of forced labour. We are not told more here, but it is enough for the reader to know that it was this Jeroboam who became king of the northern tribes after Solomon's death. Thus the end of the empire created by David and administered by Solomon comes into sight.

Chronology of
the period of
the monarchy

The death of Solomon is the first date in the history of Israel which can be ascertained with any degree of certainty. The chronological details about the kings of Judah and Israel give a relative chronology for the following period; in detail it presents many problems, but generally speaking it offers a reliable framework. At some points it can be synchronized with events outside Israel which can serve as fixed points for an absolute chronology. This gives us a

chronological framework for the period of the monarchy which begins with the
death of Solomon (unless we want to include the round figures of forty years
each for David [II Sam.5.4; I Kings 2.11] and Solomon [I Kings 11.42]; according
to this Solomon's death falls in the year 926, according to other calculations
some years earlier or later. (For the whole question see Jepsen in *BHH* 3,221ff.
and Hayes/Miller, 678ff., with alternative tables.)

Bibliography

A.Alt, 'Israels Gaue unter Salomo', in *Alttestamentliche Studien, FS R.Kittel*,
1913, 1-19 (= *KS* II, 76-89); F.Crüsemann, *Der Widerstand gegen das Königtum.
Die antikönigliche Texte des Alten Testamentes und der Kampf um den frühen
israelitischen Staat*, 1978; L.Delekat, 'Tendenz und Theologie der David-
Salomo-Erzählung', in *Das ferne und nahe Wort, FS L.Rost*, 1967, 26-36;
F.C.Fensham, 'The Treaty between the Israelites and Tyrians', *SVT* 17,
1969, 71-87; T.N.D.Mettinger, *Solomonic State Officials. A Study in the Civil
Government Officials of the Israelite Monarchy*, 1971; K.Rupprecht, *Der
Tempel von Jerusalem. Gründung Salomos oder jebusitisches Erbe?*, 1977;
W.H.Schmidt, *The Faith of the Old Testament*, ET 1983; G.E.Wright, 'The
Provinces of Solomon', *Eretz-Israel* 8, 1967, 58-68.
  Noth, §16; Bright, ch.5 C; Malamat, IV.1, V and VI; Gunneweg, VII;
Herrmann, II.3; Hayes/Miller, VI.§4; Ben-Sasson, I.7.
  Cf.also the bibliography on II.5; III.2.4.

6 Israel and Judah in the Time of the Monarchy

With the death of Solomon the nature of the traditions again changes
fundamentally. The books of Kings provide an overall account of the
whole period of the monarchy (I Kings 12 – II Kings 25), which is →176f.
moulded by a framework in which in each case the chronological details
about the reign of the king concerned are connected with a religious
assessment of his rule and a reference to the 'Chronicles of the kings of →106
Israel or Judah' as a source of further information. Here the mode of
working and the interests of this account become clear. It is wholly
orientated on the person of the king in question. However, it relates
only the bare essentials about him and otherwise refers the reader to
the sources indicated. The religious assessment is particularly important
in the account as a whole; this is orientated on the demand of
Deuteronomy for the purity of the cult of YHWH and a single place of →151f.
worship.
  At very few points within this framework are there detailed narrative
accounts of particular events or situations: there are some shorter
historical narratives (I Kings 12.1-19; II Kings 11) and a number of →106f., 114
prophetic narratives which have partly been brought together into larger
complexes (I Kings 17 – II Kings 9; II Kings 18.13-20.19), in some of
which it is impossible to make a clear distinction between prophetic
narrative and historical narrative (e.g. II Kings 9f. on Jeroboam,

see below). The prophetic narratives contain many reports on and references to historical and political conditions, but these are determined by the specific interest of these narratives.

The historical reconstruction of the history of the period of the monarchy has to be based almost exclusively on the Old Testament sources. Only from the middle of the eighth century are there cross-references to and from events recorded in the sources of the Assyrian empire, which round about this time rose to become the leading power in the Near East. The same is true at the end of the period of the monarchy for the Babylonian empire, which forced the Assyrians out of their position of dominance.

6.1 The Split in the Empire of David and Solomon

→106f.

Rehoboam

Northern tribes

→32

→34

The historical narrative in I Kings 12.1-19 gives a vivid picture of events after the death of Solomon. At the beginning we have a surprising piece of information: 'Rehoboam (the son of Solomon) went to Shechem; for all Israel had come there to make him king' (v.1). The change in the situation is fundamental: the representatives of the northern tribes had come to David at Hebron to offer him the kingship over Israel (II Sam.5.1-3); Solomon was appointed king in Jerusalem without there being any special indication that the northern tribes were involved (I Kings 1); now Rehoboam himself had to go to Shechem. We can conclude from this that the tensions between north and south which had already become visible during David's reign had now become so acute that the efforts of the northern tribes towards separation from the south had received a new impetus (cf. Crüsemann, 111ff.).

Jeroboam

→36

In Shechem Rehoboam was confronted with clear demands from the northern tribes: easing of the 'yoke' which Solomon had laid on them (v.4). Here we can see a connection with the rebellion launched by Jeroboam against Solomon (cf.11.26ff.; Jeroboam did not originally appear in the narrative in ch.12; vv.2,3a are an anticipation of v.20). The narrative gives a vivid account of the differences betwen two groups of advisers, the 'old' and the 'young' (this is hardly to be understood in terms of a 'system of two houses', thus Malamat 1965); the old are for wise compromise, the young for uncompromising harshness. Rehoboam follows the advice of the young 'who had grown up with him' (v.10), with the result that the northern tribes refuse to follow him. The separatist call which already rang out in Sheba's rebellion against David (II Sam.20.1) is now intensified: 'Look after your own house, David!' (v.16). Verse 18 reports a sequel in which Adoniram, the official in charge of forced labour, is killed and Rehoboam is lucky to get away with his life.

That brought an epoch to an end. I Kings 12.19 speaks from the perspective of Judah about a 'rebellion' of Israel from the house of David (cf. also Isa.7.17). In view of II Sam.5.3, it would be historically more appropriate to speak of a failure to renew the treaty between the northern tribes and the representatives of the Davidic dynasty. (The term 'division of the kingdom' which is often used is misleading, since under David and Solomon there was no integrated 'kingdom'.) In Judah, on the other hand, the Davidic dynasty was evidently so firmly rooted that there were no problems for Rehoboam here. The note in I Kings 11.43 simply registers the fact that he became king in place of his father Solomon, whereas in 12.20b it is expressly stated that only the tribe of Judah remained faithful to the house of David.

The loyalties of the tribe of Benjamin pose a problem. In I Kings 12.21-24 a brief prophetic narrative reports an attempt by Rehoboam to win back rule over Israel by force of arms. Here 'the house of Judah and the tribe of Benjamin' are mentioned as a military unit (v.21, cf.v.23), which is in contradiction to v.20. A similar problem arises in 11.30-32: the prophet Ahijah of Shiloh tears his cloak into twelve pieces; he gives ten of them to Jeroboam, and only one tribe is to be left for Solomon – the twelfth remains unnamed. Here we have a fluctuation in the tradition which reflects a change in the loyalties of Benjamin. Underlying this we perhaps have frontier struggles as a consequence of which the greater part of the territory of Benjamin finally fell to Judah (cf. I Kings 15.17-22). Schunck (139ff.) even conjectures that the tribe of Benjamin voluntarily followed Rehoboam after Solomon's death (cf. also Grønbaek, Seebass).

Immediately after the report of the 'apostasy' of Israel there follows in I Kings 12.20a the account of the appointment of Jeroboam as king over 'all Israel'. It takes up the narrative of Jeroboam's rebellion against Solomon (I Kings 11.26ff.), which mentions first his flight (v.40) and then his return. The account of the revolt thus proves to be a prelude to the reign of Jeroboam. However, another element is not taken up again: the designation of Jeroboam as king over Israel by the prophet Ahijah of Shiloh (11.29-39). The situation is the same as that with Saul and David: both are secretly anointed by Samuel (I Sam.10.1; 16.13), but their appointment then appears as a purely political act (I Sam.11.15; II Sam.2.4; 5.1-3 [however, this recalls the designation in v.2b]). In all three instances the divine designation by a prophet is clearly part of the picture painted by the tradition of the king in question; here, in all three, we have a new beginning, in which the king did not already have credentials in the form of royal birth and the dynastic claim which that implied.

Alt put forward the theory that designation by a prophet was a characteristic of the monarchy in the northern kingdom of Israel, which was understood as a 'charismatic' monarchy, in contrast to the dynastic monarchy in Judah. However, this theory is based on a generalization from the rare mentions of designation by a prophet. Apart from the case of Jeroboam, this is mentioned only in the case of Jehu (II Kings 9.1ff.), and only there (in contrast to Jeroboam) is a direct connection made between the designation and the accession to the throne which is effected immediately afterwards (by force). Moreover, the formations of dynasties which came about in the northern kingdom (see below) are never criticized as being against the divine will - on the contrary, Jehu is promised in the name of YHWH that his family will rule for four generations (II Kings 10.30)! The instability of the monarchy in Israel can be explained far more clearly from political factors than from the religious idea of a 'charismatic' kingdom (cf. Thornton).

With the enthronement of Jeroboam as king, for the first time there were now two independent kingdoms of Israel and Judah. We are told of two steps which Jeroboam took after his accession to establish and consolidate his newly-won throne. First of all he developed Shechem and 'lived there' (I Kings 12.25), in other words he made the city his capital. Strikingly enough, we are told in the same verse that he moved from there to Penuel in Transjordan. This is often connected with the campaign by Pharaoh Shoshenk (Hebrew Shishak), who according to Egyptian sources is said to have conquered numerous places in Palestine at this time (cf. also 11.25ff., and Herrmann, 193). This could have caused Jeroboam to move over the Jordan. However, it remains very obscure why he did not return to Shechem, but later resided in Tirzah (14.17; cf.15.33; 16.8, etc.).

Jeroboam's capitals

Policy over worship

The second measure had far greater consequences: Jeroboam established central sanctuaries in Bethel and Dan, i.e. in the south and in the extreme north of his kingdom. The account of this in I Kings 12.26-33 portrays it from the perspective of Judah as apostasy from the legitimate cult in Jerusalem. The relevant feature of the account is doubtless the point that the independence of the state inevitably had also to entail cultic independence (vv.26f.). Thus Jeroboam founded his own sanctuaries with a priesthood to go with them (v.31), feasts (vv.32f.), etc.

Bethel and Dan
→87
→96f.

Bull images
→142

Bethel had an ancient cultic tradition (cf. Gen.28.10-22; 35.1-7) and was later explicitly designated a state sanctuary (Amos 7.13). There was also an aetiological tradition about the cult at the sanctuary of Dan (Judg.18). Difficulties are presented by the statement that Jeroboam made 'golden calves' and had them set up in the sanctuaries (vv.28f.). There is evidently a connection with the narrative in Ex.32, which many commentators regard as a projection of the 'sin of Jeroboam' back on to the early history of Israel. There is some dispute over the religious significance of the 'calves', i.e. the bull images. Eissfeldt wanted to understand them as portable nomadic sanctuaries; they are often regarded as the pedestals, in the form of animals, on which an invisible divinity was believed to stand (cf. Weippert, 103; *BRL*, plates 30.2,11). However, it is easy to see the danger of identifying the bull with the deity itself and of syncretism with Canaanite conceptions of God. (For the many problems presented by this text cf. further Aberbach/Smolar, Donner, Motzki and the commentaries.)

We are not given any more information about the reigns of Jeroboam and Rehoboam. We hear nothing of the disentanglement of the domestic administration of the two states, which previously had been directed from one centre. Only a few later references throw any more light on foreign affairs after Solomon: the king of Moab rebelled from Israel after the death of Ahab, i.e. about seventy years later (II Kings 1.1; 3.5) and was therefore up to that point still a vassal of Israel; rather

→45

later we have a report of the rebellion of Edom from Judah (8.20-22). The final note about Jeroboam, however, is content with the general comment that 'how he waged war and how he ruled' can be read in the 'annals' (I Kings 14.19). This comment can be connected with that about Rehoboam, to the effect that throughout his reign there was war between him and Jeroboam (v.30). In connection with Rehoboam we are also told of the invasion by Pharaoh Shoshenk (14.25-28), but the perspective is so limited that it is hardly possible to recognize the events. (According to a special tradition in II Chron. 11.5-12, Rehoboam built fortified cities, which were probably meant to serve as protection against the Philistines as well as against the Egyptians.)

Otherwise the tradition has a predominantly negative interest in Jeroboam. With him began what is later referred to by the stereotyped phrase the 'sin of Jeroboam': the cultic revolt from Jerusalem which is also already described explicitly here as 'sin' (12.30). This is matched by the 'rejection' of Jeroboam by the prophet Ahijah (14.1-18), who earlier had designated him king of Israel (11.29-39). Thus the Deuteronomistic history understands the history of the northern kingdom essentially in negative terms (cf. Debus; Hoffmann, 59ff.).

David and Solomon

→106

→286

The 'sin of Jeroboam'

→176ff.

Bibliography

M.Aberbach/L.Smolar, 'Aaron, Jeroboam and the Golden Calves', *JBL* 86, 1967, 129-40; A.Alt, 'Das Königtum in den Reichen Israel und Juda', *VT* 1, 1951, 2-22 (= *KS* II, 116-34); F.Crüsemann, *Der Widerstand gegen das Königtum. Die antiköniglichen Texte des Alten Testamentes und der Kampf um den frühen israelitischen Staat*, 1978; J.Debus, *Die Sünde Jerobeams*, 1967; H.Donner, ' "Hier sind deine Götter, Israel"', in *Wort und Geschichte, FS K.Elliger*, 45-50; O.Eissfeldt, 'Lade und Stierbild', *ZAW* 58, 1940/41, 190-215 (= *KS* II, 282-305); J.H.Grønbaek, 'Benjamin und Judah. Erwägungen zu I Kön. xii 21-24', *VT* 15, 1965, 421-36; H.-D.Hoffmann, *Reform und Reformen. Untersuchungen zu einem Grundthema der deuteronomistischen Geschichtsschreibung*, 1980; A.Malamat, 'Organs of Statecraft in the Israelite Monarchy', *BA* 28, 1965, 34-65 (= *BAR* 3, 1970, 163-98); H.Motzki, 'Ein Beitrag zum Problem des Stierkultes in der Religionsgeschichte Israels', *VT* 25, 1975, 470-585; K.-D.Schunk, *Benjamin*, 1964; H.Seebass, 'Zur Königserhebung Jerobeams I', *VT* 17, 1967, 325-33; T.C.G.Thornton, 'Charismatic Kingship in Israel and Judah', *JTS* 14, 1963, 1-11; M.Weippert, 'Gott und Stier', *ZDPV* 77, 1961, 93-117.

Noth, §18; Bright, ch.6 A; Malamat, IV.1, VII; Gunneweg, VIII.1; Herrmann, II.4; Hayes/Miller VII § 1; Ben-Sasson, I.7.

Cf. also the bibliography on III.2.4.

6.2 Israel and Judah Side by Side

For the following barely two centuries down to the end of the northern kingdom the account in the books of Kings is essentially limited to the

Monarchy

→176ff.

→178f.

War between
Israel and
Judah

The dynasty of
Omri

→45f.

Samaria as
capital

→32f.

Alt's theory

Religious
policy of the
Omrids

42

stereotyped information in the framework about the individual kings, into which only brief supplementary information has been inserted. There is no kind of division or accentuation within this history, so that all kings are treated in essentially the same way, whether they are significant or unsignificant, whether their reigns were long or short. Only at one point does the account become broader: in the inclusion of extensive prophetic narratives at the time of king Ahab of Israel and his sons Ahaziah and Jehoram (I Kings 17 – II Kings 9).

The brief notes about the individual kings give some basic indication of political developments. First of all there was a constant state of war between the two states (I Kings 14.30; 15.7,16), which was probably expressed above all in frontier clashes (cf. 15.17-22). The comments about this state of war end with the death of Baasha of Israel (15.16); nothing is said about Omri, but his son Ahab lived at peace with Jehoshaphat of Judah (22.45). This is an indication of changed relationships between the two states.

There is certainly a connection here with the most basic change in the northern kingdom. Omri who (like Baasha before him, 15.27ff.) had come to power through a military revolt (16.15-22) succeeded in founding a dynasty which ruled for three generations (Omri, Ahab, Ahaziah/Joram). True, it was removed by a military coup (II Kings 9f.), but the usurper Jehu in turn succeeded in making his rule so secure that his dynasty even lasted for almost a century (Jehu, Jehoahaz, Joash, Jeroboam II). Thus after initial confusion the monarchy in Israel attained long-term stability until in the last decades before its end it was again involved in new confusion.

Omri founded a new capital. He bought a hill (still not settled on?) from a man called Shemer and called the city which he built on it *šomron* after him (I Kings 16.24). The more usual name Samaria goes back to the form of the name used by the Assyrians, *samerina*). We are not told the reason for the move from Tirzah (v.23) to Samaria. However, the geographical situation of Samaria, strategically and in terms of trade, was so superior that no further reason need be sought. Perhaps Omri also followed David's example and wanted to create an independent capital. At all events, the excavations there show the construction of a very impressive fortified residence at the time of Omri and his son Ahab (cf.Parrot).

Alt (1954) put particular emphasis on the comparison between Jerusalem and Samaria and argued that Samaria had been an independent city state modelled on Jerusalem. It had Canaanite features, to meet the desires of the Canaanite part of the population, which was still present and influential. Alt explained this above all in terms of the Baal cult which was offically practised in Samaria (cf. I Kings 16.32; II Kings 10.18ff.; however, there are reports of prophets of YHWH in Samaria, cf. I Kings 22; II Kings 5.3ff., etc.) (For criticism of Alt's theory, cf. Buccellati, 181ff., 228ff.)

Beyond question Omri left his stamp on his age (cf. Timm). The Old Testament tradition, however, only devotes a few verses to him (I Kings

16.16f., 21-28). The religious judgment notes that his actions were worse than those of all his predecessors (v.25), without making it clear what this means. This emerges more clearly in the case of his son and successor Ahab (16.29ff.). 'He took to wife Jezebel the daughter of Ethbaal, king of the Sidonians, and went and served Baal, and worshipped him' (v.31). Here two things are connected: political marriage with a Phoenician princess and the Baal cult. The two things were evidently indeed closely associated. In contrast to the numerous foreign princesses in Solomon's harem, Jezebel was a central figure at the court of Ahab, and the tradition makes her responsible for the perseuction and extermination of the prophets of YHWH (18.4; 19.2), while the prophets of Baal 'ate at her table' (18.19). Thus domestic policy at the time of Ahab and his sons was shaped by the controversy between YHWH religion and Baal religion.

Here we can see a gap in the Old Testament tradition. We learn almost nothing about the way in which relationships between Canaanites and Israelites developed in the centuries after the settlement. Therefore it is uncertain right from the beginning whether and to what extent there were portions of the population in Israel at the time of Omri and Ahab who understood themselves as Canaanites (cf. Bucellati, 213ff., 228ff.). We learn even less about religious developments. Only once in the time of the judges is there mention of a local conflict between supporters of Baal and supporters of YHWH (Judg.6.25-32; the narrative has a striking similarity to I Kings 18, see below); here, however, the supporters of Baal are not Canaanites but Israelites. Moreover, in Deutero-nomistic passages there are complaints about the mixing of the population and its religious consequences (e.g. Judg.3.5f.). We do not know what the real situation was. Alt's theory about the Canaanite character of Samaria and whole areas of the state of Israel (see below) is a hypotheses with no concrete support in the text. On the other hand the assumption that the population was purely Israelite, practising a 'pure' religion of YHWH, is most improbable. (Cf. e.g. the names of the sons of Saul and Jonathan with Baal as an element in their names: Eshbaal [I Chron.8.33] and Merib-baal [v.34]).

Rather, we must suppose that Jezebel could find a point of contact in more or less strong elements of Baal religion among the Israelite population; however, we cannot get beyond hypotheses.

We have further details about the reign of Ahab in the prophetic →114, 178f. narratives in I Kings 17ff. In chs.17-19, differences over religious policy are focussed on the confrontation between Elijah and Ahab or Jezebel. At the centre is the great scene on Carmel (ch.18) in which the question is who is really God: YHWH or Baal. We must put this in the context of the tradition according to which a temple to Baal had been built in the capital Samaria (16.32) and Elijah could even say that 'the Israelites' had torn down the altars of YHWH and killed his prophets (19.10,14). The manifestation of the superiority of YHWH on Carmel does not change the religious situation in any way. Elijah has to flee again in order to escape from Jezebel (ch.19).

The problem of relationships between Israelite and Canaanite traditions also perhaps underlies the narrative of Naboth's vineyard. Ahab wants to buy a piece of land which the owner refuses to sell because it is the *naḥalah* of his family (v.3), i.e. the heritage assigned to it, which may not be sold (cf. Lev.25.23f.). Jezebel argues against this from a standpoint according to which there are no restrictions to the right of the king (v.7). She finally secures Ahab his 'rights' by the judicial murder of Naboth (vv.8-16). (For the whole question cf. Welten; Miller 1967 and Steck, 32ff. differ. For the legal questions cf. Baltzer, Andersen.)

The prophetic narratives also report various battles with the Aramaeans. However, they are less orientated on political and military events than on the conflict between kings and prophets. Chapter 20 mentions anonymous prophets whose designations change (vv.13,22,38 etc., *nabi'*; v.28, man of God; v.35, one of the 'sons of the prophets'); in ch.22 the king is confronted with both a group of prophets faithful to him (v.6) and the individual Micaiah ben Imlah (v.7). Ahab is mentioned in both chapters (20.2,13f.; 22.20); however, alongside him there is often only 'the king of Israel' (20.4,7,11 etc.; 22.2ff.). Therefore many commentators regard it is as questionable whether this was originally an account of Ahab's struggles with the Aramaeans.

The fact that he is mentioned in an inscription of the Assyrian king Shalmaneser III in a coalition with the Aramaeans against the Assyrians in the year 853 (cf. *TGI*, 49f.; Herrmann, 213) could tell against this; however, relationships with the Aramaeans could have changed during the reign of Ahab, which lasted for more than twenty years, so that in my view this argument does not carry much weight. A further problem is thought to be that in 22.34f. we are told that Ahab fell in a battle against the Aramaeans in Transjordan (which he undertook against the advice of the prophet Micaiah), whereas in v.40 we are told that he 'slept with his fathers', which indicates a peaceful death. (As a counter-question: if that were felt to be a contradiction, why did not the final redactors eliminate it? Cf. also, in the case of Josiah, II Kings 22.20 with 23.29f.)

At all events, the references to the battles with the Aramaeans are too sporadic to allow us to make any exact reconstruction. That also applies to the corresponding reports about battles in the time of the prophet Elisha. Here in II Kings 6.8-7.20 there is only mention of the 'king of Israel'. Joram is meant in the present context; in the framework to the story, at 8.28f.; 9.14f., he is also said to have fought against the Aramaeans in Transjordan. Finally, there are also reports of battles with the Aramaeans in the time of Jehoahaz, i.e. more than thirty years later (13.3ff.). Some commentators try to reconstruct other historical contexts by transposing and reinterpreting the texts (cf. Whitley, Miller 1966, Schmitt), but everything here remains very hypothetical and is dependent on the literary-critical presuppositions of the exegetes.

In the light of all these reports there can hardly be any doubt that there were conflicts with the Aramaeans in the second half of the ninth

century. It is hard to say what the power-relationships and the military

successes were. There are several reports of the besieging of the capital Samaria by the Aramaeans (I Kings 20.1f.; II Kings 6.24ff.), then of Israelite victories and a personal surrender by the Aramaean king Benhadad (I Kings 20.31ff.), and finally even of offensive wars by the Israelites against the Aramaeans in northern Transjordan (I Kings 22). Then again we hear of conquests by the Aramaeans in Transjordan (II Kings 10.32f.) and of an almost complete annihilation of Israelite forces by the Aramaeans (13.7), and later of a reconquest of Israelite cities (v.25). The character of the texts is so varied that they cannot be brought together into an overall picture. However, it is clear that in this period there was a constant threat to Israel from the north. Even Judah was affected by it (cf. 12.18f.). **Israel and Judah**
Siege of Samaria

There is also mention of battles with the Moabites (II Kings 3). Some light is shed on this by the inscription of king Mesha of Moab (cf. v.4), which was found in Transjordan (cf. *TGI* 51f., and Herrmann, 215f.). The texts show clearly that the Israelites could no longer prevent the 'rebellion' of the Moabites (cf. 1.1; 3.5f.). Nor could Judah keep control of the Edomites, who according to 3.9ff. were still their partners in a coalition in battles against the Moabites (8.20-22). So now, about seventy years after the death of Solomon, the last remnants of what was once a great empire were lost. Israel and Judah were now only two small states, who were soon to be the playthings of the great powers. Israel-Moab

Judah-Edom

The situation in the northern kingdom changed yet again as a result of Jehu's revolution (II Kings 9f.). The report of this is completely dominated by the religious aspect of the abolition of the Baal cult. The direct prophetic involvement in Jehu's military coup is itself unusual and strange (9.1-10). When Jehu meets king Joram, the narrator makes him say that the only reason for his intervention is 'the harlotries and sorceries of your mother Jezebel' (9.22). The occupation of the capital Samaria comes to a dramatic and gruesome climax with the murder of the assembled Baal worshippers in their temple and the destruction of the temple and the symbols of the cult (10.18-28). In the tradition the real aim of the revolt seems to be 'wiping out Baal from Israel' (v.28). It remains quite unclear what political motives were at work here. (Cf. also the negative verdict in Hos.1.4.) Jehu's revolution

→178f.

Jehu's revolution had effects on the situation in Judah. Ahaziah king of Judah was similarly killed there (9.27). Thereupon in Jerusalem, Athaliah, Ahab's daughter (8.18, according to v.26 the daughter [granddaughter?] of Omri), seized power and tried to exterminate the whole royal house (11.1f.). However, one prince was rescued, and after six years (vv.3f.) he was made king in a coup. Athaliah was assassinated, and this brought to an end the only interruption to the continuous rule of the Davidic dynasty between David's accession and the Babylonian exile. Athaliah as usurper
→179

The *'am ha-'ares* (literally 'people of the land') played an important role in overcoming this crisis (cf.11.14, 18-20). They also appear in other crises of the dynasty (14.21, 'people of Judah'; 15.5; 21.23f.), and their close connection 'am ha-'areṣ

45

with the king is also expressed in the fact that sixty members of the ʿam ha-ʾareṣ were executed by the Babylonians along with Zedekiah, the last king of Judah (25.19-21). Evidently this was a phenomenon peculiar to Judah, since they are never mentioned in the texts from the northern kingdom. Whether and how they were organized and the specific nature of their role remains obscure. The texts cited show that the preservation of the continuity of the Davidic dynasty was their decisive contribution to history (cf. Würthwein, Nicholson, Soggin, Talmon).

For almost a century – from the middle of the ninth to the middle of the eighth century – the books of Kings give us only sparse information. I have already mentioned the clashes with the Aramaeans. There is one report of a hostile encounter between Judah and Israel (14.8-14), albeit in almost anecdotal form, which makes the whole matter seem a very isolated event. The long reigns of Jeroboam II in Israel (14.23-29: forty-one years) and Azariah in Judah (15.1-7: fifty-two years; in 15.13, 30, 32, 34 the same king is called Uzziah) were probably a time of relative tranquillity for both states. Apparently Jeroboam also had successes in foreign politics (cf. 14.25, 28, and the comments by Haran). However, it is certainly no coincidence that it was in the reign of Jeroboam II that the prophet Amos appeared on the scene with his sharp accusations of social injustice. The prophetic texts of the eighth century, and archaeological evidence (cf. de Geus), indicate that this phase of political stability was at the same time a period of economic boom and heightened social tensions. However, our insights into social and economic conditions and developments in this period are not enough to give further details (cf. Alt, Donner, Fendler, Herrmann, 239f.).

With the death of Jeroboam II, the long-drawn-out period of stability and continuity in the northern kingdom under the dynasties of Omri and Jehu came to an end. A series of military coups followed in swift succession (II Kings 15.8-12, 13-16, 17-22), reminiscent of the time before the beginning of the dynasty of Omri (cf. I Kings 16.8-22). Finally, Menahem was able to assert himself as king (II Kings 15.17-22). The first expedition of the Assyrian king Tiglath-pileser III to Syria in 738 (vv.19f., here he is designated by his throne-name Pul) falls in his time. Menahem paid a substantial tribute in order to forestall an attack by the Assyrians (v.20). This is also mentioned in several Assyrian inscriptions, where 'Menahem of Samaria' appears alongside other kings of this region as having paid tribute (cf. *TGI* 55, Weippert). He raised the money for the tribute by a very high poll tax.

The appearance of the Assyrians signals a development which had meanwhile taken place in Mesopotamia. There the Assyrians had established their power, and they now set about taking over the whole of the Near East. This brought to an end an era in which the small states in Syria and Palestine could more or less sort out among themselves power relationships in their region. In this period the empire of David had come into being and fallen again; however, so far no foreign power had appeared from outside the region and laid claim to empire. The Assyrians now did just this, thus ushering in the long series of foreign

Margin notes:
Jeroboam II
Azariah
(Uzziah)

Amos
→232f.

Social tensions

The Assyrian advance

→31ff.

powers who sought to dominate this strategically important area of the Near East (like the Egyptians and Hittites as early as the second millennium).

The Old Testament accounts of the last years of the northern kingdom are again very brief. After Menahem's death his son Pekahiah fell victim to a coup, and Pekah made himself king in his stead (II Kings 15.23-26). A second campaign by Tiglath-pileser in 733 falls in his reign; this time it had serious consequences for Israel. In 15.29 we are told that Tiglath-pileser advanced, captured a series of places and territories, and deported their inhabitants to Assyria. This brief account is the summary of a very disturbed and momentous period for Israel and Judah. Two further pieces of information broaden the perspective from the side of Judah. In 15.37 we are told, in connection with the reign of king Jotham of Judah, that Rezin the king of Aram and Pekah the son of Remaliah (the king of Israel) advanced against Judah. There is a more detailed account of this attack on Judah by its northern neighbours in 16.5-9, this time for the period of King Ahaz, who was Jotham's successor. This conflict is traditionally known as the Syro-Ephraimite war.

Here 'Syria' is the once customary designation of Aram, while 'Ephraim', perhaps taking up Isa.7.9, is used for the northern kingdom of Israel. The expedition of the Aramaeans and Israelites against Jerusalem was presumably only a subsidiary aspect of a larger anti-Assyrian coalition which was formed in this period among the states of Syria and Palestine under the leadership of Damascus. Evidently Judah did not take part in this coalition. So the purpose of this thrust against Jerusalem seems to have been to put a king on the throne there who was ready for a coalition (cf. Isa.7.6). Ahaz attempted to avert the threat by sending tribute to Tiglath-pileser and asking him for help (II Kings 16.7-9). Whether Tiglath-pileser felt this a reason to intervene or whether he intended to do so in any case is an open question. Be this as it may, in 733/32 he captured Damascus and Samaria (the chronological details are disputed). At this particular point there was evidently a revolution in Samaria and the new king Hoshea (II Kings 15.30) paid homage to the Assyrians and in this way at any rate saved the nucleus of his territory. (An Assyrian text even tells us that Tiglath-pileser himself appointed Hoshea king, cf. Herrmann, 249; *TGI*,58f.) According to II Kings 15.29 Galilee in the north and the regions of Transjordan ('Gilead') were cut off and made Assyrian provinces. (For the whole question cf. Herrmann, 248ff.; Hayes/Miller, 412ff.; Kaiser, *Isaiah 1-12*, OTL 1983, 148ff.)

After the events of 733/32, Israel and Judah were vassals of the Assyrians. Moreover, Israel had lost substantial parts of its kingdom. Its history was not to continue for much longer. II Kings 17.1-6 reports that Hoshea, the last king of Israel, again took part in an anti-Assyrian coalition, which also entered into negotiations with Egypt, and that he defaulted on his tribute payments. Shalmaneser V, the Assyrian king, thereupon undertook, in 722, a campaign in this region. He captured Samaria, deported part of the population, and now made the whole of Israel into an Assyrian province. The implementation of these measures

Monarchy	already took place during the rule of Sargon II, Shalmaneser's successor (cf. *TGI*, 60f.).
→55ff.	This brought the history of the northern kingdom, Israel, to an end. How profound a break this was is evident from a comparison with the situation at the end of the state of Judah more than a century later. The
Deportation	Assyrians deported part of the population (probably in essentials the upper class, craftsmen, etc.) into other parts of their empire where they disappeared from sight, whereas the Babylonians later settled the deported people of Judah together, so that they were able to maintain
Resettlement	their traditions and later to return. Moreover the Assyrians resettled groups of the populations of other conquered territories in Israel (II
→179f.	Kings 17.24), so this produced a mixed population whose character was determined by the traditions of the upper class who had newly been settled there. The Babylonians did not do this, so that those who returned could pick up the earlier traditions more easily. The tradition therefore interprets the political end of the state of Israel as essentially the end of the history of this northern part of Israel, because it was no longer possible to continue the religious and cultural traditions of Israel
→73f.	there. (These were later continued to a limited degree in the history of the Samaritans.)

Bibliography

A.Alt, *Der Stadtstaat Samaria*, 1954 (= *KS* III, 258-302); id., 'Der Anteil des Königtums an der sozialen Entwicklung in den Reichen Israel und Judah', *KS* III, 348-72; F.I.Andersen, 'The Socio-Juridical Background of the Naboth Incident', *JBL* 85, 1966, 46-57; K.Baltzer, 'Naboths Weinberg (1.Kön 21). Der Konflikt zwischen israelitischen und kanaanäischen Bodenrecht', *WuD* 8, 1965, 73-88; G.Buccellati, *Cities and Nations of Ancient Syria*, 1967; H.Donner, 'Die soziale Botschaft der Propheten im Licht der Gesellschaftsordnung in Israel', *OrAnt* 2, 1963, 229-45; M. Fender, 'Zur Sozialkritik des Amos', *EvTh* 33, 1973, 32-53; C.H.J.de Geus, 'Die Gesellschaftskritik der Propheten und die Archäologie', *ZDPV* 98, 1982, 50-7; M.Haran, 'The Rise and Decline of the Empire of Jeroboam ben Joash', *VT* 17, 1967. 266-97; J.M.Miller, 'The Fall of the House of Ahab', *VT* 17, 1967, 307-24; id., 'The Elisha Cycle and the Accounts of the Omride War', *VT* 85, 1966, 441-54; E.W.Nicholson, 'The Meaning of the Expression ʿam ha-ʾareṣ in the Old Testament', *JSS* 10, 1965, 59-66; A.Parrot, *Samaria*, ET 1958; H.-C.Schmitt, *Elisa. Traditionsgeschichtliche Untersuchungen zur vorklassischen nordisraelitischen Prophetie*, 1972; J.A.Soggin, 'Der judäische ʿam ha-ʾareṣ und das Königtum in Juda', *VT* 13, 1963, 187-95; O.H.Steck, *Überlieferung und Zeitgeschichte in den Elia-Erzählungen*, 1968; S.Talmon, 'The Judaean ʿam ha-ʾareṣ in Historical Perspective', in *Fourth World Congress of Jewish Studies*, 1967, 71-6; S.Timm, *Die Dynastie Omri, Quellen und Untersuchungen zur Geschichte Israels im 9. Jahrhundert vor Christus*, 1982; M.Weippert, 'Menahem von Israel und seine Zeitgenossen in einer Steleninschrift des assyrischen Königs Tiglathpileser III. aus dem Iran', *ZDPV* 89, 1973, 26-53; P.Welten, 'Naboths Weinberg (I Könige 21)', *EvTh* 33,

1973, 180-61; C.F.Whitley, 'The Deuteronomic Presentation of the House of
Omri', *VT* 2, 1952, 137-52; E.Würthwein, *Der 'am ha-'areṣ im Alten Testament,*
1936.
   Noth, §19-21; Bright, ch.6,7A; Malamat, IV.1, VII, VIII; Gunneweg, VIII.2-
4; Herrmann, II.5-7; Hayes/Miller, VII. §2-5; Ben-Sasson, I.8-9.
   Cf. also the bibliography on III.2.4.

6.3 Judah to the Babylonian Exile

We know nothing of the effect of the decline of the northern kingdom
on Judah. Perhaps the Assyrians regarded Judah as a loyal vassal since
King Ahaz had paid tribute.

II Kings 16.10-18 reports that after his meeting with Tiglath-pileser, Ahaz had
set up in the temple in Jerusalem an altar for which 'the altar in Damascus' had
served as a model. It is often supposed here that the Assyrian state cult was
installed in the temple in Jerusalem, and this is seen as a political gesture on the
part of Ahaz. However, the details given about the cult point to Canaanite
rather than Assyrian analogies (cf. McKay, 5ff.). Moreover, the historicity of
this section is doubtful (cf. Hoffmann, 141ff.), so at all events it cannot serve as
an example of cultic concessions to the Assyrians.

   Three things in particular are reported of Hezekiah, the son and
successor of King Ahaz, in II Kings 18.1-8: a reform of the cult (v.4),
defection from the Assyrians (v.7) and a victory over the Philistines
(v.8). The second point is the easiest to deal with. Hezekiah's defection
occurred in a wider political context about which Assyrian sources also
inform us. After the death of the Assyrian king Sargon II in 705, there
was much unrest in the Assyrian empire; Egypt and Babylon, for
example, which had formerly been subject to the Assyrians, again
achieved independence. Hezekiah evidently took part in negotiations
against Assyria, as is shown by the visits of Egyptian (cf.Isa.18; also
30.2; 31.1) and Babylonian (II Kings 20.12f.) delegations to Jerusalem.

Presumably the war against the Philistines (II Kings 18.8) is also to be seen in
this connection. This was probably primarily a reconquest of the cities of Judah
said to have been captured from the Philistines in II Chron.28.18; at the same
time it was also the formation of an anti-Assyrian coalition, since the city of
Gaza, contested by Hezekiah, appears in the account of Sennacherib's campaign
(see below) with the cities among which the territories of Judah were later
divided, presumably because they had not turned against the Assyrians (cf.
Hayes/Miller, 444ff.).

   In the year 701 Sennacherib, the successor of Sargon II, undertook
a campaign in this region to restore his rule (cf. *TGI*, 67f.). He conquered
an Egyptian army which opposed him, and occupied the rebellious cities
of the Philistines. Then he turned against Judah, took 'forty-six of its
fortified cities and countless small cities in its territory' (*TGI*, 68, cf. II

Kings 18.13), and shut up Hezekiah himself in Jerusalem 'like a bird in a cage' (*TGI* 69, cf. Isa.1.7f.). Nothing is said about the end of the

siege in Sennacherib's account. It is simply reported that Sennacherib removed the conquered cities from Hezekiah's sphere of influence, giving them to the kings of Ashdod, Ekron and Gaza, and that he laid heavy tribute on Hezekiah. This latter note agrees with the reports in

→180

the first four verses of the Isaiah narratives (II Kings 18.13-20.19), but a new section (which itself has many strata) begins in 18.17. This reports a siege of Jerusalem with an invitation to surrender and the miraculous deliverance of the city (18.17-19.37). There is dispute as to what historical consequences can be drawn from the conflicting reports (cf. Childs, 11f.; Herrmann, 258f.; Hayes/Miller, 449ff.); however, it is clear that Hezekiah retained his throne, though with a much reduced territory to rule over and on condition that he paid heavy tribute. (Apparently the areas he lost were later wholly or partially restored to Judaean rule, but we are told no more about them.)

Two different elements can be distinguished in the note about Hezekiah's 'reform of the cult' (18.4). First we hear of the removal of the high places (*bamot*) and the cultic symbols of stone (*mazzebot*) and wood (*'ašera*): this is very much within the framework of the

→176ff.

Deuteronomistic composition of the books of Kings, and repeats I Kings 14.23 word for word. There, at the beginning of the history of Judah, we find criticism directed against the institution of these cultic

objects. However, the following note about the removal of the 'brazen serpent' named Nehushtan has no parallel in the Deuteronomistic history. It is evidently the historical nucleus of the reports about the reform of the cult. According to it, Hezekiah removed a theriomorphic cultic symbol from the temple in Jerusalem which according to tradition came from the time of Moses (cf. Num.21.4-9). We can see the influence

→97

of the prophetic movement here (Hoffmann, 153). There is no support in the text for the often-repeated assumption that Hezekiah also removed Assyrian cult symbols and that the reform therefore had a political character. Rather, in its report on the last phase of the history of Judah, the Deuteronomistic account has a constant alternation of negative and positive reforms of the cult (Ahaz-Hezekiah-Manasseh-Josiah). Therefore it is probable that in the context of this conception, the note about the removal of the 'brazen serpent' was reshaped into a report of 'a reform of the cult' (but cf. Conrad).

Reports about Manasseh, the son and succesor of Hezekiah, are exclusively concerned with cultic matters and are completely negative (II Kings 21.1-18). He is depicted as the great 'heretic king'. Here all that is said about him serves in every detail as a negative foil for the

→180f.

subsequent reform by Josiah (cf. Hoffmann, 164f.). It is hardly possible to make a historical evaluation of this information. The texts do not indicate that Manasseh's cultic policy was an expression of a very special deference towards the Assyrians, as is often suggested (cf. McKay, 20ff.; Hoffmann, 16). So the only historical statement we are left with

is that Manasseh had an unusually long reign (fifty-five years!) and evidently had no competition either abroad or at home. However, in retrospect his reign could be seen as a time of cultic apostasy from the legitimate religion of YHWH.

II Chron.33.11ff. reports the deportation of Manasseh to Babylon; this moves him to repent, so that after his return he instigates a restoration of the legitimate YHWH cult. This narrative is probably to be understood as a midrashic explanation of the fact that so sinful a king could have such a long and untroubled reign (cf. Ehrlich). It is improbable that there is a historical background to it (cf. Nielsen; Hayes/Miller, 454ff.).

Manasseh's son Amon (II Kings 21.19-26) became the victim of a palace intrigue (v.23). It was again the *'am ha-'ares* which secured the continuity of the Davidic dynasty. Thus at the age of eight Josiah came to the throne (22.1). With him began the last phase of the history of the state of Judah.

→45f.
Josiah

At the centre of the detailed report about Josiah (II Kings 22.1-23.30) stands the great cultic reform which according to 22.8 began in the eighteenth year of Josiah, i.e. in 622 BC. According to the account it was sparked off by the discovery of 'the book of the Torah' (v.8) in the renovation work on the temple. The reference here is without doubt to Deuteronomy (whether in its present form or an earlier one). However, there is considerable doubt as to whether this account is historical or has a historical nucleus. In its present form the report has a thoroughly Deuteronomistic stamp, so that it is hardly possible to make a historical reconstruction of the details of the cultic reform and its context. (According to II Chron.34 the cultic reform [vv.3ff.] began six years before the discovery of the book [vv.8ff.], but this is hardly likely to be an independent tradition, cf. Hoffmann, 254ff.) It has often been said that there are differences between Deuteronomy and the account of the reform of the cult (e.g. in the rights of priests from the country sanctuaries which are done away with, cf. Deut.18.6-8 with II Kings 23.8f.), so that at all events Deuteronomy cannot be regarded as the direct model for the reform; however, the basic agreements are substantially greater than the differences. So we must accept as the historical basis of the tradition a reform of the cult by Josiah along the lines of Deuteronomy or the movement standing behind it (cf. Hoffmann, 264ff.).

Reform of the cult 622 BC

→155f.

→180f.

Josiah's reform stood in a wider political context. It took place at a time when the Assyrian empire was collapsing. As early as 625 Babylon had regained its independence under king Nabopolassar. In 612 the capital Nineveh was destroyed; the last Assyrian king, Asshur-uballit, withdrew to Harran in Western Mesopotamia and attempted to defend his empire from there with the help of the Egyptians.

Collapse of the Assyrian empire

Josiah evidently exploited this power vacuum to consolidate and extend his rule. (The widespread assumption that the reform of the cult was also or primarily concerned to remove elements of the Assyrian state cult cannot, however, be sustained, cf. McKay, 28ff.). The action against the altar in Bethel, the former state sanctuary of the northern

Josiah builds up his power

kingdom (II Kings 23.15-18), could be seen in the context of an extension of the sphere of rule of the king of Judah over parts of what used to be the northern kingdom. (Alt has even conjectured that Josh.15; 18f. contains a list of 'districts' of Josiah's kingdom which included parts of what was once the northern kingdom.) Above all, the circumstances of Josiah's death indicate his political ambitions. He opposed the Egyptian Pharaoh Necho, who moved north to support the Assyrian king (not to oppose him, as the translation of II Kings 23.29 usually reads, cf. Herrmann, 271f.). Perhaps he wanted to prevent Assyrian power being strengthened with the help of the Egyptians, or he feared an Egyptian domination in the wake of that of Assyria; the texts (cf. also II Chron.35.20ff.), however, are silent about his purposes.

After the death of Josiah, Judah was drawn into the struggles of the great powers for control of this area. To begin with, the *'am ha-'areṣ* appointed Josiah's younger son Jehoahaz king (II Kings 23.30; for his age cf. v.31 with v.36) – a very unusual step. Probably this had something to do with foreign policy (cf. Malamat 1975, 126), since only three months later Pharaoh Necho again deposed him and deported him to Egypt. Necho appointed Jehoahaz' brother Eliakim in his place. Eliakim was evidently more acceptable to Necho; Necho changed his name to Jehoiakim – as a demonstration of Egyptian superiority. Moreover Necho imposed a heavy tribute on the country (II Kings 23.31-35). However, power relationships soon changed in favour of the Babylonians, once they had defeated the Egyptians in 605 at Carchemish on the Euphrates (cf.Jer.46.2; *TGI*, 73; Herrmann, 275f.). The Egyptians therefore had to give up their claims to the area 'from the brook of Egypt to the river Euphrates', i.e. to Syria and Palestine (cf. II Kings 24.7), and Jehoiakim became a vassal of the Babylonians (v.1). However, three years later he again defected from the Babylonians, probably as a reaction to a defeat which the Babylonians suffered in the winter of 601/600 in a campaign against Egypt (cf. Herrmann, 277f.; Malamat 1975, 131f.). Still, Nebuchadnezzar, who had been king of Babylon since 605, soon undertook another campaign in this region and at the beginning of 597 appeared before Jerusalem, where immediately beforehand Jehoiachin had succeeded his father as king. Jehoiachin seems to have handed over the city voluntarily (24.11f.); he was taken prisoner and deported. Nebuchadnezzar appointed his uncle (i.e. another son of Josiah) Mattaniah king; again he changed his name (as Necho had done in an earlier case), to Zedekiah (v.17).

Parts of the population were deported along with Jehoiachin (24.14ff.). Those mentioned are the officials (*śarim*), the well-to-do tax-paying citizens (*gibbore-ḥayil*, cf.15.20 and *TWAT* II, 906), and also particular groups of craftsmen (*ḥaraš* = armourer; *masger* = fortress builder, etc., cf. Malamat 1975, 133); only the poorer stratum of the population (*dallat 'am-ha-'areṣ*) remained behind.

The numbers pose a problem: in II Kings 24.14 there is mention of 10,000 deportees; then in v.16 of 7000, and 1000 craftsmen; by contrast Jer.52.28 gives

Jehoahaz

Jehoiakim

Battle of
Carchemish

Nebuchad-
nezzar
597 BC
Jehoiachin

Zedekiah
First
deportation

52

the number 3023. These are possibly two groups of deportees, since Jer.52.28 speaks of the seventh year of Nebuchadnezzar, while II Kings 24.12 speaks of the eighth year. Thus the figure 10,000 could be understood as a round number for the 3000 deportees of the first group, directly after the capture of the city, and the second group of about 7000, which followed some time later (cf. Malamat 1975, 133f.).

One last time there was a repetition of events which had happened Defection from Babylon so often before: the defection of the king of Judah from foreign rule and a subsequent penal expedition against Jerusalem. These are both reported very briefly in II Kings 24.20b; 25.1. Perhaps we can infer from Jer.27.3 an anti-Babylonian 'conference' in Jerusalem in which delegates from the Transjordanian cities of Edom, Moab and Ammon took part, along with others from the Phoenician coastal cities of Tyre and Sidon (Malamat 1975, 135ff.). Evidently there was public debate in Jerusalem over the right policy, as can be seen from Jeremiah's warnings against a defection from the Babylonians (Jer.27), and from his controversy with the prophet Hananiah (Jer.28). In a letter to those who had been deported to Babylon, Jeremiah also warned them to prepare for a long time in exile (Jer.29). →204

Finally, at the beginning of 588 a Babylonian army approached Jerusalem and laid siege to the city (II Kings 25.1ff.; for the dating cf. Siege of Jerusalem Malamat 1968, 150ff.). Apparently the siege was interrupted for a time because of the approach of an Egyptian army (Jer.37.5,11; cf. the dates in Ezek.29.1; 30.20, and the chronological table in Malamat 1975, 144f.). In summer 586 the Babylonians first made a breach in the city 586 BC wall; then finally, about a month later, they completely occupied the city, burnt the temple (which they had earlier plundered, vv.13-17), the royal palace and the rest of the city, and destroyed the city walls (cf. II Kings 25.3f., 8 [Jer.52.6f., 12]).

We can discover some interesting details about the situation during the siege from the ostraca (inscribed pottery fragments) which were discovered at the excavation of the city of Lachish (cf. *TGI*, 75-8 and Herrmann, 282f.).

Zedekiah attempted to escape from the city (II Kings 25.4; for the The fate of Zedekiah text cf. Jer.39.4), but was overtaken by the Babylonians in Jericho (i.e. before he could cross the Jordan to safety), taken prisoner and brought to Nebuchadnezzar's headquarters at Riblah. There he was cruelly punished for his defection. His sons were killed before his eyes, and he himself was blinded and brought in chains to Babylon (v.7). We hear nothing further of his fate.

Of the inhabitants of Jerusalem some military, court and temple Second deportation officials and sixty members of the upper class ('am ha-'ares, perhaps the remainder) were also brought to Nebuchadnezzar at Riblah and executed there (25.18-21). Moreover, 25.11f. states sweepingly that the surviving remnant of the population was deported, along with those who had defected to the king of Babylon and (according to the text of Jer.52.15) the remainder of the craftsmen, while parts of the poorer stratum of the population (*dallat ha-'areṣ*) were left behind to work in the vineyards and the fields.

Jer.52.29 gives the number of 832 deportees 'from Jerusalem' for the eighteenth year of Nebuchadnezzar, i.e. before the capture of Jerusalem, which according to 25.8 fell in the nineteenth year; these could be the turncoats mentioned above (Malamat 1975, 145). Verse 30 mentions 745 further 'Judaeans' for the twenty-third year of Nebuchadnezzar, i.e. only four years after the capture of Jerusalem. According to this, the deportation after 586 will have been substantially smaller than that of 597. However, the application of the figures in Jer.52.28-30 produces a discrepancy from II Kings 24f., because the 7000 deportees of the second group of 597 (see above) are absent in this listing. (For the number of the deportees cf. also Schottroff, 49.)

The fall of Jerusalem marks a great division in the history of Israel. With it the rule of the Davidic dynasty, which had lasted more than four hundred years, came to an end, as did the history of the monarchy in Israel and the existence of Israel as an independent state. For the next four centuries down to the completion of the last books of the Old Testament, Israel (or Judah) lived under the rule of different super-powers, and only during the second century BC did it once again achieve its own monarchy and temporary national independence in completely different circumstances, as a result of the collapse of these super-powers.

There are two further brief sections in II Kings, which serve as a kind of appendix to the history of the monarchy. The first (25.22-26) deals with the brief activity of Gedaliah, whom the Babylonians had appointed 'over the people who remained in the land of Judah' (v.22; it is impossible to discover his precise status). From Mizpah, where he presumably had his residence, he attempted to pursue a policy of submission to Babylonian rule (v.24). However, after only a short time he was murdered by one of the 'captains of the forces' (who had perhaps kept hidden from the Babylonians with their followers, cf. Jer.40.7), named Ishmael (v.25). The report ends with the information that thereupon 'all the people' and the captains of the forces fled to Egypt for fear of the Babylonians (v.26).

This episode is dealt with at greater length in Jer.40-44. According to this, after the murder of Gedaliah, Ishmael tried to escape to the Ammonites in Transjordan (41.10), but was pursued by the other captains of the forces under the leadership of a man called Johanan and only managed to escape with a handful of his people (vv.11-15). Johanan and the rest of the captains now planned to go to Egypt with their followers and those whom Ishmael had forced to go with him (vv.16-18). They asked Jeremiah for a message from God (42.1-7), and he gave them one, but it was not what they had hoped for: Jeremiah →205f. told them in God's name that they should remain in the land (vv.8-22). However, they disregarded this, set off for Egypt, and even took Jeremiah and Baruch with them by force (43.1-7). Jeremiah's activity ends there (43.8-45.5). Still, we might guess that one of this group of fugitives, perhaps Baruch himself, returned to Judah, since otherwise it is hard to explain how this last chapter came to be handed on and could be integrated into the book of Jeremiah.

The last section of II Kings (25.27-30) describes Jehoiachin's fate. In contrast to Zedekiah, the last king of Judah, we do not completely lose track of Jehoiachin in exile. After an imprisonment of thirty-seven years (i.e. in about 560) he was released from prison by the Babylonian king Evil-merodach and was allowed to eat at the king's table 'all the days of his life' (cf. also the Babylonian text in *TGI*, 78f.). This is the last information we have about a king of Judah. The question whether this is also meant to be the last word about the Davidic monarchy depends on how one understands the Deuteronomistic history.

Judah to Exile

Pardon for Jehoiachin

→187

Bibliography

A.Alt, *Judas Gaue unter Josia* (1925, = *KS* II, 276-88); B.S.Childs, *Isaiah and the Assyrian Crisis*, 1967; D.Conrad, 'Einige (archäologische) Miszellen zur Kultgeschichte Judas in der Konigszeit', in *Textgemäss. FS E.Würthwein*, 1979, 28-32; E.L.Ehrlich, 'Der Aufenhalt des Königs Manasse in Babylon', *TZ* 21, 1965, 281-8; H.-D.Hoffmann, *Reform und Reformen. Untersuchungen zu einem Grundthema der deuteronomistischen Geschichtsschreibung*, 1980; A.Malamat, 'The Last Kings of Judah and the Fall of Jerusalem', *IEJ* 18, 1968, 137-56; id., 'The Twilight of Judah: In the Egyptian-Babylonian Maelstrom', *SVT* 28, 1975, 121-45; J.McKay, *Religion in Judah under the Assyrians*, 1973; E.Nielsen, 'Political Conditions and Cultural Developments in Israel and Judah during the Reign of Manasseh', in *Fourth World Congress of Jewish Studies* I, 1967, 103-6; W.Schottroff, 'Zur Sozialgeschichte Israels in der Perserzeit', *VF* 27, 1982, I, 46-68.

Noth, §21-23; Bright, ch.7B, 8; Malamat, IV.1, IX and X; Gunneweg, IX; Herrmann, II.8-11; Hayes/Miller, VIII §1-5; Ben-Sasson, I.10.

Cf. also the bibliography on III.2.4.

7 Judah after the Babylonian Exile

7.1 The Babylonian Exile

The Old Testament contains no consecutive account of the period of the Babylonian exile. The books of Kings give us details of the deportations; in 24.15f. 'Babylon' is mentioned several times as the destination, whereas in 25.11 (cf.21b) there is mention only of the fact of deportation. The narrative texts give us no information about the subsequent fate of the exiles or about the situation in the homeland. Only with the decree of the Persian king Cyrus relating to the rebuilding of the temple in Jerusalem, from the year 538, does a new section of narrative begin (Ezra 1.1ff.; cf. II Chron.36.22ff.)

→52f.

Chronicles explicitly states that the land was uninhabited for seventy years and lay fallow (II Chron.26.20f.). This is interpreted as the fulfilment of a prophecy by Jeremiah (cf. Jer.29.10). At the same time such a view made it possible to associate those who returned with the pre-exilic traditions, without a break (vv.22f.) and with no conflict with those who had remained behind in the land. This may suit a particular post-exilic concept of history, but it does not correspond to historical reality (cf. Janssen, Ackroyd).

Sources

Reconstruction of the exilic period is largely dependent on references in the books of Jeremiah, Ezekiel and Isaiah (40-55); in addition, Lamentations and some psalms contain important material relating to the religious and cultural situation. In other respects, it may be assumed that the exile was a 'creative period' (Ackroyd), in which many traditions were collected and worked over. Therefore texts which have undergone such revision can also be used, though with great care, as there are rarely explicit or clear references to the time of the revision.

A first, fundamental approach to an assessment of the situation after 597 or 586 emerges from the accounts in II Kings. They explicitly state Deportation of that the deportation specifically affected the upper classes, while the the upper class poorer stratum of the population was left behind, above all (in contrast to II Chron.36.21!) to till the land (II Kings 24.14-16; 25.11f.). Some conclusions can be drawn from this which are supported by other texts.

First of all, these texts show that after the deportation, the history of Land of Israel Israel (or Judah) had two focal points: the land of Israel and the and Diaspora Babylonian Diaspora (for the Egyptian Diaspora see below). The different developments in these two groups and their relationship, during the exile and above all afterwards, are a central theme in the understanding of the exilic and post-exilic period. There is evidence of lively interchange for the time between 597 and 586. Thus Jeremiah wrote a letter to the exiles (Jer.29.1ff.); in reaction to this a letter came back to Jerusalem from another prophet (vv.24-28), to which Jeremiah in turn replied (vv.29-32). The news of the fall of Jerusalem was brought by a refugee (Ezek.33.21) who evidently knew where to find the exiled Judaeans.

Rivalries

There were also rivalries between the two groups, concerned with the question which of them was the better Israel and the legitimate heir to the traditions of salvation history. Although he was still in Jerusalem, Jeremiah resolved this question clearly, and in a marked antithesis, in favour of the Diaspora, in the imagery of the two baskets of figs (Jer.24). Ezekiel countered the arguments of those who had remained in the →210 land, who said of the exiles: 'They are far from YHWH; to us this land is given for a possession' (Ezek.11.15), and: 'Abraham was only one man, yet he got possession of the land; but we are many; the land is surely given us to possess' (33.24); he also challenged this claim, with the repudiation of idolatry playing a decisive role (11.16ff., esp.21; 33.25ff.).

After 586 there is no further evidence of any direct contacts between the two groups. This may be the result of a fortuitous absence of information, but the reason may also be that after the end of the monarchy (and the death of the governor Gedaliah, appointed by the Babylonians), Jerusalem was no longer the seat of an independent administration, so that there was no longer an official courier service to Babylon.

Lamentations paints a comfortless picture of the situation in the land itself. Famine prevailed in the destroyed city of Jerusalem (1.11; 2.12; 4.9; 5.4 etc.) and violent deeds endangered life (5.9,11-13); there was nothing left but to lament. Other places presented more hopeful aspects. Thus at Gedaliah's bidding, those who emerged from hiding or had been left behind in the land began to gather in the harvest (Jer.40.9-12), and with great success (v.12). There are also indications here of a redistribution of land. In Jer.39.10 we are told (in contrast to II Kings 25.12) that Nebuchadnezzar left behind 'the poor who had nothing' and gave them vineyards and fields. These will have probably been not only publicly owned lands but also lands of owners who had been deported. Moreover, we should not put too much stress on the statement that only members of the lowest social strata remained behind, since evidently many people were able to evade deportation and emerged again later (see below). At all events there were people who could write texts like Lamentations and similar psalms (e.g.Pss.74; 79), which were probably actually composed in Jerusalem.

The situation in the land →267ff.

The question of land-ownership

What we can see of the religious situation in the country presents an ambivalent picture. On the one hand Lamentations and Psalms (see below) show a marked awareness of guilt, and readiness to accept the fate of the people and the land as a divine judgment, while at the same time specifically preserving the traditions of salvation history (e.g. Ps.74.12,20); these texts were presumably also used at religious festivals, whether in the destroyed temple or elsewhere. Secondly, there is mention of foreign cults (Ezek.8; 11.21; 33.25; cf. Jer.44); here we might perhaps distinguish between a return to earlier cults (cf. Jer.44.17ff.) and the adoption of the religion of the conquerors (Ackroyd, 40ff.). Evidently both these reactions to the catastrophe emerged.

The religious situation

The main feature of the situation of the exiles from Judah in Palestine was that the Babylonians settled them all together. Evidently, too, they were able to some extent to order their common life and thus maintain the traditions they had brought with them. Thus there is often mention of 'elders' who seek out the prophet Ezekiel in their capacity as representatives of the community (Ezek.8.1; 14.1; 20.1). Jeremiah, too, addresses his letter to the 'elders among the exiles' (Jer.29.1). Here the word *gola* (literally 'exiling') appears as a stereotyped term for the group of Jews living in exile in Babylon (cf. also Ezek.1.1; 3.11,15; 11.24f.). When Jeremiah calls on the exiles to build houses, make gardens and have families (Jer.29.5f.), his words suggest that these things were possible for them and that they took advantage of the possibilities. Tel-Aviv on the river Chebar is mentioned as the place where they live (Ezek.3.15). Otherwise we hear nothing about their circumstances, their activity, and so on. (It has been conjectured that the Babylonians set them to reconstructing ravaged areas, as we learn

The situation in exile

→67

Judah after **the Exile**	from earlier Assyrian sources, cf. *ANET*, 284f., lines 10-17, 72-76, etc.; however, there is no specific indication of this.)

Religious life   There is no clear information about the religious life of the exiles. Ps.137 reflects the situation of mourning in a foreign land when thinking about Jerusalem. However, it remains uncertain whether there was worship in the exile and what form it might have taken. Perhaps one
→121f.   can conclude from the 'oracles of salvation' in Deutero-Isaiah that there were services of lamentation (von Waldow). It is often also assumed
Liturgy   that the liturgy of the word, without a sacrifice, had its origin in the time
of the word   of the exile, which then led to the foundation of the synagogue; however, here we cannot get beyond conjectures (cf. Hruby; *EJ* 15, 579ff.)

The words of the prophets Ezekiel and Deutero-Isaiah are an
Ezekiel   important element in the traditions of the exile. In Ezekiel, who was one of those deported in 597, we find a fundamental shift from preaching
→214   of judgment to preaching of salvation with the fall of Jerusalem in 586. There is constant talk of bringing together and leading back the Israelites who have been scattered among the nations (11.17ff.; 20.41f.; 34.12ff., etc). The aim of this is the purification (36.24ff.) and revival of Israel (37.1-14) and ultimately a new combination of the separated portions of Judah and Israel under the Davidic monarchy (37.15-28). This created the basis for the rebuilding of the temple and the restoration of its cult (40-48, cf. Ackroyd, 110ff.). The announcement of an imminent
Deutero-Isaiah   return is expressed even more strongly in Deutero-Isaiah (Isa.40-55).
→194f.   Here, too, the aim is the restoration and revival of Jerusalem (49.14ff.; 52.1-10; 54, etc.). So eschatological features emerge more markedly (e.g. the transformation of the wilderness into fertile land [41.18f.; 43.20, etc.], the levelling of the hills [40.4; 42.16; 49.11], a new exodus [43.16ff.; 51.9ff. etc.]), whereas there is no explicit mention of the temple and worship (but see 52.11).

Formation of   It is impossible to establish the reaction of the exiles to this prophetic
tradition   proclamation or to know how widespread among them were such ideas and hopes. It is very probable, though, that in this period there was an intensive concern with the religious traditions and perhaps with revising them and reinterpreting them in a creative way (cf. Ackroyd). This is
→243ff.   particularly true of the revision and formation of the prophetic books, and presumably also of those cultic traditions which we find in the Pentateuch and in Ezek.40-48. However, this theological work should not be limited too strictly to the period of the exile, since on the one hand
→183ff.   there are reasons for assuming that, for example, the Deuteronomistic history had in essentials already come into being before the exile, and
→198ff.   on the other hand that particular prophetic books (e.g. the book of Isaiah) were certainly given their final form only after the exile.

Diaspora in   The Diaspora in Egypt presents a particular problem. We learn from
Egypt   II Kings 25.26 and Jer.40.16-44.13 that a group from Judah fled to
→54   Egypt. Their first halt is given as Tahpanhes (Jer.43.7f.; Greek Daphne), a frontier fortress on the eastern side of the Nile delta (cf. *BHH* 3,

1963); later, in 44.1, there is mention not only of neighbouring Migdol (cf. *BHH* 2,1215) but also of Memphis on the lower Nile (about twelve miles south of modern Cairo) and the 'land of Pathros', i.e. Upper Egypt. This last place, in particular, cannot be connected with the group mentioned above; it probably presupposes that at the time when this text was written there were also Jews in Upper Egypt. When and how they arrived there is unclear. It is often pointed out that Manasseh put troops from Judah at the disposal of the Assyrians for a campaign against Egypt (cf. Hayes/Miller 487); others conclude from Deut.17.16 that mercenaries from Israel (or Judah) came to Egypt in exchange for horses. Be this as it may, in the fifth century there was a Jewish military colony on Elephantine, an island in the Nile in Upper Egypt, as is Elephantine →73 indicated by a number of letters written in Aramaic (cf. *AOT*, 450-62; *TGI*, 84-88; Porten; Herrmann, 323f.). This group had a temple of its own and a distinctive, syncretistic-type cult, in which two further deities emerge alongside *yhw* (the short form of YHWH), one of them apparently feminine and called ʿnt-yhw (Anat-yahu, in other passages also Anat-bethel). It remains unclear whether these two groups were related and whether Jews were still living in other places in Egypt at this time. Nor do we hear anything about people returning from Egypt, so that this branch of the Diaspora remains almost without significance for Jewish history in the first centuries after the exile. (Only in the Hellenistic period does the Egyptian Diaspora again have a role.)

Bibliography

P.R.Ackroyd, *Exile and Restoration* 1968; H.Hruby, *Die Synagoge. Geschichtliche Entwicklung einer Institution*, 1971; E.Janssen, *Juda in der Exilszeit*. 1956; B.Porten, *Archives from Elephantine. The Life of an Ancient Jewish Military Colony*, 1968; H.E.v. Waldow, *Anlass und Hintergrund der Verkündigung Deuterojesajas*, Bonn dissertation 1953.

Noth, §24; Bright, ch.9 A; Gunneweg, X; Herrmann, III.1; Hayes/Miller, VIII §6-7; Ben-Sasson, I.11.

7.2 Return and Restoration

The end of the period which we usually call the 'Babylonian exile' is connected with the person of the Persian king Cyrus, who in the middle Cyrus of the sixth century rose within a decade to become ruler over large areas of the Near East. After the subjection of Media in the East (550) and Lydia, ruled over by the fabulous king Croesus, in the extreme Conquest of Babylon north-west of Asia Minor (547), he turned against Babylonia, which was now in a decadent state, and in 539 occupied its capital Babylon. Thus Cyrus came to rule over the biggest empire there had ever been in this part of the world. (His son and successor Cambyses also conquered Egypt in 525 and added further to this kingdom.)

The sources at our disposal for the post-exilic period are the books of Ezra and Nehemiah. In their account they limit themselves to two focal points: the time from the 'edict of Cyrus' (538) to the conclusion of the building of the temple (515), and the activity of Ezra and Nehemiah (from 458 or 445). The books of Haggai and Zechariah are supplementary sources for the first phase. All in all, however, the picture is very fragmentary.

Edict of Cyrus
538 BC

At the beginning of the book of Ezra (and similarly at the end of II Chronicles) we are told that in the first year of his rule (i.e. probably in his first full regnal year, 538) Cyrus publicly proclaimed that he had been commissioned by YHWH, the God of heaven, to build him a house in Jerusalem (Ezra 1.1-3; II Chron 36.22f.); at the same time he had invited the Jews to go up to Jerusalem and build this house for their God (thus the full wording in Ezra 1.3). There is another version of this decree in Aramaic in Ezra 6.3-5. In that passage there is more detailed mention of the building of the temple: the size (v.3) and the method of building (v.4a) are given; and it is decreed that the costs are to be paid from the royal purse (v.4b); the return of the temple vessels is ordered (v.5). However, there is no mention of a return of the exiles.

→278

Most exegetes see Ezra 6.3-5 as a reliable historical source which may even have preserved the original wording of the 'Cyrus edict' of 538 (thus already Meyer, 46ff.: de Vaux, etc.). This is indicated e.g. by the use of Aramaic, since Aramaic was introduced by the Persians as an official language. (This form of Aramaic is therefore designated 'imperial Aramaic'.) In contrast, Ezra 1.1ff. is usually seen as a free formulation by the author of Ezra. (Cf. Galling, 61ff.; Bickerman differs, regarding both documents as authentic: he says that 6.3-5 was intended for the royal administration and 1.2-4 for the Hebrew-speaking Jewish exiles.) Galling (78ff.) sees 1.8-11 as the Hebrew translation of an authentic list of temple vessels which were handed over to Sheshbazzar (cf.5.13-15).

Rebuilding of
the temple

Thus the sources agree that immediately after his accession, Cyrus ordered the rebuilding of the temple in Jerusalem. This was in accord with his policy towards the regions he had conquered, which emerges from an official text by Cyrus himself about his accession (the 'Cyrus cylinder'). Here he reports the return of divine images and the restoration of sanctuaries in various parts of his empire (*TGI*, 82ff., lines 30ff.). However, it is disputed whether at the same time Cyrus also gave

Return of the
exiles

permission for the exiles to return. It is often assumed that the report about this in Ezra 1.3 and the account of its implementation in v.5 is governed by the view of the Chronicler that the land was empty during the exile, so that the return was the indispensable presupposition for the rebuilding in Jerusalem. However, it can be argued that in the inscription on the 'Cyrus cylinder' (see above) there is also mention of the return of former inhabitants to other regions, so that immediate permission to return seems quite possible.

This question is bound up with another one, namely under whose

Sheshbazzar

leadership the return took place. According to Ezra 1.8 the temple vessels were handed over by the Persian treasurer to Sheshbazzar, who is designated *naśi'* (prince) of Judah (on this, cf. Japhet 96ff.). In the Aramaic text of 5.13-16 a remark by the 'elders' of Jerusalem (cf. v.9) is quoted; according to this he not only brought the temple vessels to Jerusalem (cf. 1.11) but was appointed governor (*peḥah*) by Cyrus (v.14) and laid the foundations of the temple (v.16).

Since E.Meyer (77), Sheshbazzar has often been identified with Shenazzar (I Chron. 3.18) and thus made a member of the Davidic line, but cf. Berger.

Otherwise another name is in the foreground: Zerubbabel. The list   Zerubbabel
of those who returned (Ezra 2.2; cf. Neh.7.7) begins with him, and
there is a detailed report of the beginnings of his activity after his arrival
in Jerusalem: the beginning of sacrificial worship on a provisional altar
(Ezra 1.3), the celebration of the feast of tabernacles (v.4) and the
continuation of regular sacrificial worship (v.5). Above all we are then
told that the building of the temple was begun and continued (chs.4f.)   Beginning of
under his leadership (which he shared with the priest Joshua, vv.8-13).   the building of
There are close connections here with the accounts by the prophets   the temple
Haggai (1.14; 2.2ff.) and Zechariah (4.8ff.), who are also mentioned in
Ezra 5.1; 6.14. The title *peḥah* (governor) is also repeatedly used for   Haggai and
Zerubbabel, in the form 'governor of Judah' (Hag.1.1,14; 2.2,21).   Zechariah

There is a dispute over the exact administrative and legal status of the   Province of
'province' (*mᵉdina*) of Judah (Ezra 2.1; Neh.7.6). Evidently the 'governor of   Judah
Transeuphrates' (Ezra 5.3,6; 6.6,13), who perhaps had his base in Damascus,
was superior to the 'governor of the Jews' (6.7). (Alt conjectured that Judah
was part of the province of Samaria, but cf. Smith, 193ff.; Hayes/Miller, 509ff.;
Japhet, 80ff., 97f.).

So the relationship between the activity of Sheshbazzar and that of
Zerubbabel in the tradition is unclear. We get the impression that
Zerubbabel has been put in the foreground at the expense of Shesbazzar.
This is also suggested by the fact that in 4.1-5 Zerubbabel's activity is   →278
put as early as the time of Cyrus (cf. vv.3,5), whereas elsewhere it is
very closely connected with Haggai and Zechariah, i.e. with the time
of Darius (cf. also 4.24). So it seems likely that here too the remarks
in the Aramaic text (5.13-16) should be taken seriously and that
Sheshbazzar should be seen as the predecessor of Zerubbabel, who
began on the works for the temple but was not able to carry them
through. (Cf. Japhet; Talmon. *IDB Suppl*, 319, differs.)

It emerges clearly from the text that Zerubbabel, along with the   Joshua
(high) priest Joshua, had a decisive share in the eventual completion of
the temple building. It is all the more surprising that neither of them is
mentioned in the report of the completion and dedication of the temple
(Ezra 6.14ff.).

The disappearance of Zerubbabel could be connected with the explicit messianic
expectations which are associated with them in the prophets Haggai and
Zechariah because they are members of the Davidic dynasty (cf. esp.   →236f., 238f.
Hag.2.20ff.; Zech. 4.6ff.; 6.9ff.), but are not fulfilled. Zechariah 3 suggests that

Joshua was exposed to hostile attacks (cf. also 6.9-14). However, the book of Ezra says nothing of any of this. Japhet sees the failure to mention the leading figures as a deliberate 'democratization' of the tradition (85f.).

Ezra 4-6 reports opposition to the building of the temple. According to 4.1f. the 'enemies of Judah and Benjamin' want to share in building the temple. The formulation suggests inhabitants of the northern territories, i.e the former state of Israel. They claimed to have been YHWH worshippers since the days of king Esarhaddon of Assyria (681-669), who had brought them there (v.2). Otherwise we hear nothing of any settlement of foreign groups of population in this period. This report is evidently meant above all to disqualify the people making the offer by associating them closely with the groups of the population mentioned in II Kings 17.24ff. who according to the account there practised a syncretistic cult (cf. Talmon 1981, 67f.). So this is evidently a way of dissociating those who rebuilt the temple from other groups, the purity of whose religion seemed questionable (see below). Verse 4 speaks in summary terms of the 'people of the land' (ʿam ha-ʾareṣ) in contrast to the 'people (of) Judah' who wanted to build the temple. This is developed in 5.3ff., where there is mention of further resistance which comes from the governor of 'Transeuphrates'. Those building the temple in Jerusalem are again designated 'Jews' (or 'Judaeans', 5.5; 6.7f., 14; cf. 5.1). Finally, 6.13ff. describes the completion and dedi-

cation of the temple. The beginning of the building is dated in Hag.1.15 in the sixth month of the second year of King Darius (autumn 520); its completion in Ezra 6.15 in the month of Adar (the twelfth month) of the eighth year (early in 515).

We can see in Ezra 4.1ff. a concern for the purity of the Jewish religion and its delimitation, as opposed to mixing with foreigners. This is a characteristic of the post-exilic period, occasioned by the situation, which had changed in many respects. In the time of the exile the two main parts of the people lived in very different circumstances. The group in exile saw themselves confronted with a completely different population with which they had nothing at all in common, above all in respect of religion. This evidently reinforced their awareness of the independence of their own religious and ethnic allegiance and constantly encouraged reflection on their special character and a concern to maintain their purity. In contrast to this, those who had been left behind in the land lived in a largely 'open' situation. There was no temple as a centre to set its mark on the cult, no vital contribution from the intellectual and religious upper class, but rather a variety of alien groups: the Babylonian soldiers with their colourful camp-followers, people from neighbouring countries who had seeped into the vacuum left by the deportations, and so on. Thus those who returned came back to their country with very explicit and strict ideas about the purity of the Jewish religion and found there quite the opposite situation. Of necessity this resulted first in segregation from the inhabitants of the northern provinces, which had undergone their own religious development since as early as 722. However, clarifications and demarcations were necessary even in Judah. This is already reflected in Hag.2.10ff., where the people of Judah is designated an 'unclean people' (v.14). It is expressed even more clearly in the time of Ezra and Nehemiah. **Return and Restoration** →237 →67, 70f., 281f.

However, this is only one aspect. In the case of Haggai and Zechariah we can see not only a marked interest in the temple and in cultic and religious purity but at the same time an intensive eschatological Eschatological expectations expectation. This is primarily directed towards the imminent future and is connected with the person of Zerubbabel, who comes from the house of David. However, it is extremely significant that it was preserved, handed down and transmitted after the 'imminent expectation' failed to come about. This is particularly clear with Zechariah, whose own proclamation in the book which bears his name has been expanded until it is almost twice the length. It is evident here how lively the prophetic →74f., 243ff. tradition was at this time and how intensively it was continued, right up to the transition to apocalyptic. Other prophetic books, too, only received their final form in the post-exilic period, as e.g. the book of Isaiah, in which apocalyptic elements are similarly unmistakable. Thus the final formation of the prophetic books and their collection into the 'prophetic canon' took place at this time. That presupposes an involved interest in the prophetic tradition, which evidently went along with the concern for cultic and religious purity. (For piety associated with the Torah see below under Ezra.)

Here we can see that the exilic and post-exilic period not only brought Continuity with it characteristic changes in the Israelite religious tradition but at the same time was moulded by a strong and evidently very conscious continuity with the pre-exilic period. We might even call it a time of renewal and rebirth, whereas other peoples of the ancient Near East disappeared from the scene after the loss of their political independence (Thomas).

Finally, an essential element in completing the picture is that the 'Babylonian exile' in no way came to an end with the events of the years after 538. We do not know the numerical ratio between the number of those who returned and the number of those who remained in Babylon. But it is clear that the situation which had existed since the beginning of the exile continued, and that the history of Israel (or of Judah or Judaism) now had two focal points: the mother country and the Motherland and Diaspora Diaspora. The following decades show that there was an intimate relationship between the two, indeed that the Jews living in the Diaspora felt a degree of responsibility for conditions in the mother country and that they exercised an important influence. So we cannot in any way approach the history of Israel in the next centuries solely from the perspective of the 'Jerusalem cult community' (Noth).

An archive in clay tablets from the second half of the fifth century BC found in the Babylonian mercantile city of Nippur gives us an interesting insight into the life of the Jewish Diaspora. It contains the business records of the banking Life in the Diaspora 63

Judah after the Exile

house of Murashu (*AOT*, 434ff.). Here, among the names of the multinational clientele, there are also numerous Jewish names, the bearers of which were obviously intensively occupied in the trading and commercial life of their locality; in some cases they also occupied leading positions in commerce or public life (cf. Coogan 1974). The names show that the bearers preserved their Jewish identity, which is expressed e.g. in the preservation of names with the theophorous element *yahu* or *yaw* (= YHWH: cf. Coogan 1976, 49ff., 119f.; Zadok, 7ff.).

Situation in Judah

The biblical texts give us no direct information about the social and economic situation in Judah. So we do not discover the effect of the change in the ownership of property after the deportation and what arrangements were made between those who returned and those who remained in the country. There are no reports of conflicts over this question. In 'Trito-Isaiah' marked social contracts become evident (Isa 58, etc.), of a kind which we also find later in Nehemiah (ch.5), though the basis and reasons for them are not evident. (Cf. the attempt at reconstruction made by Kreissig; also Kippenberg, 42ff.; Schottroff, 59ff.).

Bibliography

P.R.Ackroyd, *Exile and Restoration*, 1968; A.Alt, 'Die Rolle Samarias bei der Entstehung des Judentums', 1934 (= *KS* II, 316-37); P.-R.Berger, 'Zu den Namen *ššbṣr* and *šn'ṣr*', *ZAW* 83, 1971, 98-100; E.Bickerman, 'The Edict of Cyrus in Ezra I', *JBL* 65, 1946, 249-75 (= *Studies in Jewish and Christian History* I, 1976, 72-108); M.D.Coogan. 'Life in the Diaspora. Jews at Nippur in the Fifth Century BC', *BA* 37, 1974, 6-12; id., *West Semitic Personal Names in the Murašu Documents*, 1976; K.Galling, *Studien zur Geschichte Israels im persischen Zeitalter*, 1964; D.E.Gowan, *Bridge Between the Testaments. A Reappraisal of Judaism from the Exile to the Birth of Christianity*, 1976; S.Japhet, 'Shesbazzar and Zerubbabel - Against the Background of the Historical and Religious Tendencies of Ezra-Nehemiah', *ZAW* 94, 1982, 66-98; H.G.Kippenberg, *Religion und Klassenbildung im antiken Judäa*, 1978; K.Kreissig, *Die sozialökonomische Situation in Juda zur Achämenidenzeit*, 1973; E.Meyer, *Die Entstehung des Judentums*, 1896 (1965); W.Schottroff, 'Zur Sozialgeschichte Israels in der Perserzeit', *VF* 27, 1982, H.1, 46-68; M.Smith, *Palestinian Parties and Politics That Shaped the Old Testament*, 1971; S.Talmon, 'Ezra and Nehemiah', *IDB Suppl*, 317-28; id., 'Polemics and Apology in Biblical Historiography – 2 Kings 17:24-41', in R.E.Friedman (ed.), *The Creation of Sacred Literature. Composition and Redaction of the Biblical Text*, 1981; D.W.Thomas, 'The Sixth Century BC: A Creative Epoch in the History of Israel', *JSS* 6, 1961, 33-46; R.de Vaux, 'Les décrets de Cyrus et de Darius sur la reconstruction du temple', *RB* 46, 1937, 29-57 (= *Bible et Orient*, 1967, 83-113); R.Zadok, *The Jews in Babylonia during the Chaldean and Achaemenian Periods according to the Babylonian Sources*, 1979.

Noth, §25,27; Bright, ch.9B; Gunneweg, XI.1; Herrmann, III.2; Hayes/Miller, IX; Ben-Sasson, I.11.

Cf. also the bibliography on III.3.4.10 and 11; III.4.6.

7.3 The Time of Ezra and Nehemiah

The sources are silent over the decades after the dedication of the rebuilt temple. Scholars therefore often talk of a 'dark' period. However, the same thing is true for lengthy periods of the monarchy, so we should not put too much stress on this. The impression of darkness and obscurity is produced, among other things, by the fact that we have no clear information on the political and administrative structures under which Judah lived in this period. So we do not know whether Zerubbabel had a successor as 'governor of Judah', who this was, and what authority he had.

→46, 50f.

It also remains unclear what function the 'high priest' had. The title is occasionally used in accounts about the pre-exilic period (II Kings *12.11*; 22.4,8; 23.4). In Haggai and Zechariah it is used for Joshua (Hag.1.1,12,14; 2.2,4; Zech.3.1,8; 6.11), but not in the book of Ezra. (Chronicles also avoids the title, cf. Japhet, 343f.) It then appears again in Nehemiah (3.1,20; 13.28). With the exception of the prophetic announcement of the 'coronation' of Joshua in Zech.6.11, there are no obvious circumstances in which the high priest has a prominent posiiton. In particular, there is no evidence in the Old Testament for the claim of the Jewish historian Flavius Josephus (first century AD) that since the Babylonian exile the high priest had been head of the Jewish state in place of the king (*Antiquitates* XI,4,8). It was probably only in the Hellenistic period that the high priest became the main representative of the Jewish community (for the whole question cf. Koch).

High priest

→239

Among our sources for this period are the books of Ezra (from ch.7 on) and Nehemiah. They report the activity of the two men after whom the books are named. A basic difficulty for historical reconstruction lies in the fact that in the account of these books the activities of Ezra and Nehemiah are linked, although the two men apparently did not work together and at the same time. This has produced chronological discrepancies which remain unresolved.

Sources

First of all, however, Ezra and Nehemiah have one important thing in common. Both come from the circles of the Jewish exiles. It is said of Ezra that he set out from 'Babylon', i.e. from Babylonia, where the centre of the Jewish exiles had been since 597/586. Nehemiah, on the other hand, had an exalted position as cupbearer at the Persian court in the capital, Susa (Neh.1.1). (The Book of Esther, later, also presupposes the presence of Jews in Susa and their activity in the service of the court, cf. also Dan.8.2.) Both figures are connected with the Jewish homeland, though in quite different ways. In his professional capacity Ezra was evidently concerned with Jewish questions. His title 'scribe of the law of the God of heaven' (Ezra 7.12,21) is probably to be understood as an official Persian title (secretary or the like), and 'law of the God of heaven' as an official Aramaic designation for the Jewish religion, whose God is revered as creator of the world and thus as 'God of heaven'. So Ezra was secretary (or recorder) for matters relating to the Jewish religion (Schaeder, but cf. Mowinckel 1965, 121ff.). Accordingly, he too travelled to Jerusalem on an official mission.

Origin in the
Diaspora

Ezra the scribe

Nehemiah's connections with his mother country of Judah at first seem to be more of a 'private' nature. On the basis of reports from relatives about the situation in Jerusalem (Neh.1.2f.) he asked permission from the king to rebuild 'the place of my fathers' sepulchres' (Neh.2.3,5). Thereupon he received permission from the king and the relevant papers, along with a military escort (2.7-9). However, later on in the narrative he appears as 'governor' (5.14).

So the common feature is that Ezra and Nehemiah come to Jerusalem as two men from the Babylonian-Persian Diaspora and intervene in affairs there with appropriate authority. This indicates the close connection between the mother country and the Diaspora, where people evidently felt a responsibility for conditions in Palestine. Moreover, the fact that their activity is the only one reported in the extant sources about the period after the time of the rebuilding of the temple shows the great significance which was attached to it.

According to Ezra 7.7f., Ezra came to Jerusalem in the seventh year of king Artaxerxes, and according to Neh.1.1; 2.1, Nehemiah came in the twentieth year of Artaxerxes. The sequence of the two, and the mention of the king without any further addition, leave hardly any doubt that in the present context the same king is meant both times. It can be regarded as certain that Nehemiah's activity took place in the time of Artaxerxes I (465-424). (In a letter from Elephantine from the year 407 there is mention of the sons of Sanballat, the governor of Samaria; this Sanballat is evidently identical with Nehemiah's opponent [cf. Neh.2.10,19 etc.], cf. Rowley, 155ff.) Accordingly, Ezra would have come to Jerusalem in 458, Nehemiah in 445. However, this dating is often doubted (for the reasons see Kellermann 1968, 55ff.), and Ezra is put after Nehemiah or in the period mentioned in Neh.13.6, in Nehemiah's absence from Jerusalem (though there is no indication of its duration). For this, however, either the date in Ezra 7.7 must be changed or the king in Ezra 7 must be Artaxerxes II (404-359). Although an overhelming amount of literature has appeared on this question (cf. Rowley, Kellermann 1968), so far no generally convincing answer has been found. It therefore seems best, especially in view of the difficult literary problems of the books of Ezra and Nehemiah, to leave the text unchanged and to be content with noting that the activities of Ezra and Nehemiah seem to be independent of each other.

→73

Ezra's commission is described in the credentials given him by King Artaxerxes (Ezra 7.12-26), which have been handed down in Aramaic. First of all, any Israelites wanting to return home may join him (v.13). From the list of those returning in 8.1-14 a total of five thousand people (including members of families) has been calculated (cf. Rudolph, Commentary, 81); in addition to this are the Levites and temple servants (8.18-20). As well as taking money and temple vessels (7.15-23), Ezra's commission consists above all in 'inquiries about Judah and Jerusalem according to the law of your God which is in your hand' (v.14). We are later told that on the basis of this law (which here is designated 'wisdom', *ḥokma*) Ezra is to appoint judges and experts in the law in order to instruct those who know the law to judge by it and teach it to others (v.25). In addition there are penalties against those who do not follow 'the law of your God and the law of the king' (v.26).

The matter in question here is clearly seeing to the observation and implementation of the Jewish law among the subjects of the Persian empire in so far as they belong to the Jewish people and Jewish faith. In addition, 'supplementary instruction' is to be given to those who do not know the law (but hardly to non-Jews). The interest of the Persian king is expressed very clearly in v.26; the law is primarily regarded as law of the king. Accordingly one could suppose that the real purpose of Ezra's mission was a 'visitation', and inspection of legal observances; here the existing Jewish law was to serve as a basis (cf. Mowinckel 1965, 124ff.).

The first and only area in which there is any mention of the implementation of Ezra's commission is the question of mixed marriages (Ezra 9f.). The report of this appears as the implementation of the 'visitation': the leaders of the people tell Ezra about a problematical state of affairs which represents a violation of religious obligations (*ma'al*, 9.2,4; 10.2,6). (This is evidently also something of which those making the report are aware.) At the next investigation of the situation (ch.10) we are told of a great readiness to cooperate on the part of all concerned (vv.1-4, 12-14) which finally leads to the appointment of a commission (vv.16f.; judges are also mentioned in v.14, cf. 7.25); and the listing of all those involved. (It is not explicitly reported that mixed marriages were broken up; the reason for this omission is probably the combination of the accounts about Ezra and Nehemiah.) Here we can again see the concern for the purity of the Jewish community which is already evident in the accounts from the first phase after the exile (see above on Ezra 4.1ff.). In both passages the 'peoples of the lands' (or 'the peoples [or people] of the land') are the opposition, partly as enemies (Ezra 3.3; 4.4; cf. Neh.9.30), but above all as those from whom the Israelites are to separate themselves (Ezra 9.1,2,11,14; 10.2.11, cf. Neh.*10.29,31,32*).

The shift in the meaning of the word *gola* is very illuminating for the self-understanding of the Jewish community which appears in these texts. In Jer.29.1 (cf. Ezek.1.1, etc.) it appears as a stereotyped term for the group of Judaeans living in the Babylonian exile. The word is also used in this sense in Ezra 1.11; 2.1 [= Neh.7.6]. Elsewhere, though, those who return are called *b^ene ha-gola*, 'members of the *gola*' (Ezra 4.1; 6.19f.; 8.35; 10.7,16), *q^ehal ha-gola*, 'community of the *gola*' (10.8) or simply 'the *gola*' (9.4; 10.6; cf. also Zech.6.10). The question of mixed marriages (Ezra 9f.) involves those who had returned from the exile some time before (there are already children of these marriages). In Neh.10 we get the impression that the assembled community of the people as a whole is termed *gola* (for this whole question cf. Vogt, 22ff.).

However, it would be wrong to seek to draw any conclusions from this terminology for the actual relationship with the Diaspora. Presumably people continued to be aware in Jerusalem and Judah of the existence of the Diaspora and cultivated relationships with it, as is also evident from Nehemiah's temporary return there (cf. Neh.13.6). Ezra is mentioned again in Neh.8. It is reported here that he read from the 'book of the Torah of Moses' (v.1) in a solemn liturgical setting

Question of mixed marriages →279f.

The designation *gola*

→57

Reading of the Torah

(v.1). Most exegetes identify (usually implicitly) this Torah with the 'law' which, according to Ezra 7.14,25, was 'in the hand of' Ezra. It is usually concluded from this that Ezra's task was to bring this law to Jerusalem to 'proclaim', 'promulgate', 'implement' it there and thus make it the legal basis for the Jewish community in Jerusalem. Many commentators therefore assume that Neh.8 originally came directly after Ezra 8, so that this proclamation of the law will have been the first and most important task that Ezra will have fulfilled immediately after his arrival. However, in my opinion this view is untenable.

Problem of the
'Law'
The Aramaic word *dat*, which stands for 'law' in 7.14,25, usually denotes royal decrees and laws (cf. Ezra 8.36; Esther 1.19; 2.8; 3.14f.,etc.; Dan. 2.13; *6.9,16* etc.). It cannot be regarded as a translation of *tora*; in Ezra 7.11 the Hebrew expressions *miṣwot* and *ḥukkim* are used for this (in the translation of the Aramaic title which follows in v.12); these can also denote 'secular' law, e.g. ordinances decreed by a king or a ruler (e.g. I Kings 2.43; II Kings 18.36 [= Isa.36.21]; Neh. 11.23 or Gen.47.26; Ex.5.14). The designation of Ezra in Ezra 7.6 as 'scribe of the Torah of Moses' is not to be understood as a translation of the Aramaic title but as a reference forward to Neh.8.1. Thus the Hebrew text which serves as a framework has a completely different view of the 'law' of Ezra from the Aramaic document contained in 7.12-26. Moreover, it is also striking that nowhere in the Old Testament is there a Hebrew rendering of the Aramaic expression 'law of the God of heaven'; it probably derives from the language of the Persian court and cannot in any way be identified with the 'Torah of Moses' (Neh.8.1).

This means that it is impossible to produce any direct link between the 'law' (Aramaic *dat*) which according to Ezra 7.12-26 Ezra is commissioned to implement, and the 'Torah of Moses', which according to Neh.8, Ezra reads out in a solemn liturgy. Each has a completely different function. Another thing that tells against the widespread conception that Ezra brought a new 'Law' to Jerusalem is the fact that in both cases it is presupposed that the law in question is already known. According to Ezra 7.25, those who know it are to be judged by it; and in Neh.8.1, Ezra is asked by the assembly 'to bring the book of the Torah of Moses' (v.1) in order to read from it, without so much as a hint that this book was new to the assembly and first brought by him. This conjecture only arises through an inappropriate association with Ezra 7 and a rearrangement of the text (see below).

Ezra as visitor
So there are two sides to the picture of Ezra. First, he is the 'visitor' appointed by the Persian king, who is to implement the Jewish law sanctioned by the king in his own interest among the subjects of Persia who are adherents of the Jewish religion. Secondly, he is the pious

As teacher of
the Law
→281
scholar and teacher of the Torah (Ezra 7.10), who performs the first synagogal reading of the law recorded in the tradition. These two aspects must be clearly distinguished. However, that does not mean that they are exclusive. Ezra could easily have performed his official function and at the same time have played an important religious role in the consolidation and further development of post-exilic Jewish

religion. The tradition has put the second perspective in the foreground by introducing Ezra right at the beginning as a scholar and teacher of the law. This, along with Neh.8, shows a quite specific interest in his activity in connection with the 'Torah of YHWH' (Ezra 7.10). This is specified more closely as the 'Torah of Moses, which YHWH, the God of Israel, has given' (v.6), or 'which YHWH commanded Israel' (Neh.8.1). Here we can recognize a line of tradition which clearly derives from Deuteronomy (cf. Deut.4.44, etc.). The public reading of the Torah at the feast of Tabernacles is prescribed in Deut. 31.9-13; Neh. 8 appears as the implementation of this ordinance (though that is not explicitly said to be the case; cf. Mowinckel, 1965, 133f.).

It is hardly possible to distinguish the historical process which underlies Nehemiah 8 and its interpretation by the authors of the books of Ezra and Nehemiah. However, the description of Ezra's activity shows an important feature of post-exilic religious development. The Torah, its reading and exposition, forms the centre around which the Jewish community assembled in Jerusalem and throughout Judah. Here we can see a piety connected with the Torah of a kind which is already suggested in Deuteronomy (e.g. in the $\check{s}^ema^\circ yi\acute{s}ra'el$, 'Hear, Israel', of Deut. 6.4ff.). The temple with its sacrifical cult does not play a direct role in this piety; it is only hinted at in Neh. 8.18b. That certainly does not mean that the two are to be completely separated; in Ezra, too, there is explicit mention of the encouragement of temple worship as a result of his journey (Ezra 7.15-23, cf. v.27). However, a very marked and independent line in post-exilic religious development can be seen here.

The most prominent subject in Nehemiah's autobiographical 'memoirs' is the rebuilding of the walls of the city and the difficulties which have to be overcome in connection with this (Neh.1-6). The opposition comes above all from Samaria. In the foreground we have a man by the name of Sanballat (2.10,19; 3.33f.; 4.1f.; 6.1-14); his title is not given, but he may probably be seen as the governor of Samaria. So here we can see rivalry between Jerusalem and Samaria. Possibly Jerusalem did not have a governor of its own before the arrival of Nehemiah, and perhaps Nehemiah was only nominated governor at a later stage (the title first appears in 5.14,18; cf. 12.26), so that people in Samaria feared a limitation of their own sphere of influence through Nehemiah's activity. Moreover, Nehemiah's position was made more difficult and endangered by a group in the upper classes of Jerusalem who conspired with his opponents in Samaria (cf. 6.17-19). However, despite all opposition he succeeded in winning over the great majority of the inhabitants of Jerusalem and Judah to his plans, so that the rebuilding of the city wall was completed with great involvement on all sides (3.1-32; 4.9-17) in a period of only fifty-two days (6.15f.).

The Aramaic section Ezra 4.7-23 mentions an attempt to rebuild the city wall in Jerusalem which was prohibited by King Artaxerxes because of an intervention by the people of Samaria and thereafter hindered by the people of Samaria with force of arms. The more exact dating of these events is uncertain.

However, it seems likely that they should be assumed to have begun before the appearance of Nehemiah; perhaps they should be connected with the report which according to Neh.1.3 was the occasion for Nehemiah's journey. This failure to rebuild the walls is often associated with Ezra, and support for this could be found in the reference to those who returned from exile (Ezra 4.12; cf. Rudolph, Commentary, 44f.; Kellermann, 1967, 184f.). However, the texts themselves do not make any references to the matter, so that in my view a tolerable historical reconstruction is impossible.

Synoikismos

In direct conjunction with the building of the walls there is a report that Nehemiah increased the inadequate population of Jerusalem (Neh.7.4) by having a tenth of the inhabitants of other places in Judah transferred to Jerusalem (11.1). This 'synoikismos', of a kind known to us from ancient Greece, is meant on the one hand to make the city of Jerusalem viable and on the other to provide a closer link between the capital and the rest of the country. This at the same time indicates that life was in no way concentrated on Jerusalem, but that the majority of the population lived outside Jerusalem. (Possibly the area of the province of Judah was increased with the appointment of Nehemiah as governor; this emerges from a comparison of the lists in Ezra 2 and Neh.3, cf. Kellermann 1967, 159ff.)

Social tensions

The social situation is illuminated at a stroke by the account in Neh.5 which reports far-reaching social tensions within the population of Judah. The population of the land complained about its increasing poverty, which led to situations of economic dependence and finally slavery for debt (vv.1-5). It was thought particularly scandalous that those who practised this exploitation were Jewish 'brothers' (vv.1,5). Unfortunately we do not discover the origin of this 'agrarian crisis' (Kippenberg 55ff.) in any detail. However, it is quite clear from vv.6ff. that the creditors were members of the upper class: 'nobles' (*ḥorim*), i.e. members of well-to-do families, and 'officials' (*śeganim*), i.e. those who held particular offices or performed special functions (v.7). So the crisis did not involve everyone in the same way; on the contrary, it heightened the social distinctions and led to tensions and unrest.

Remission of
debts

Nehemiah implemented a general remission of debts, the binding nature of which the creditors had to accept in a public assembly and through an additional religious oath (v.12).

Self-imposed
obligation

Whereas according to the account in the text this must have been a once-for-all measure aimed at surmounting an acute crisis, Neh.10 mentions a permanent obligation (vv.*1,30*) which was confirmed by the endorsement of all groups in the population (vv.*1b-29*). Several aspects of this obligation correspond to measures which according to ch.13 Nehemiah either arranged or carried through himself. So they are the expression of quite specific demands and necessities in the situation of the time.

This relationship to the situation is evident in the combination of very different kinds of themes which in no way embrace the whole sphere of the 'Torah of God' (the summary formula in v.*30*): 1. No marriage with those who belong to the 'people of the land' (v.*31*), in accordance with Deut.7.3 and the demands of Ezra (Ezra 9f.) and Nehemiah (Neh.13.23-30a; cf. 13.1-3). 2. No dealings with aliens on the sabbath and on feast days (v.*32a*), already presupposed in Amos 8.5 (cf. Jer.17.19ff.; Isa.58.13) as a consequence of the sabbath commandment (Ex.20.8ff.; Deut.5.12ff., etc.) and emphatically carried through by Nehemiah (Neh.13.15-22). 3. The land to lie fallow in the seventh year and loans (i.e. their equivalent value) to be written off by the creditor (v.*32b*); this corresponds verbatim to Deut.15.2, and in substance with Nehemiah's remission of debts (Neh.5). 4. Payment of a temple tax (vv.*33f.*), cf. Ex.30.11f. 5. Regulation of the provision of wood as fuel for the altar of sacrifice (v.*35*), implemented by Nehemiah himself (Neh.13.31). 6. Offering of the firstfruits (vv.*36-38a*) in accordance with Ex.23.19; 34.26; Deut.26.1ff., regulated by Nehemiah himself (Neh.13.31). 7. Payment of tithes to the levites (vv. *38a*β) in accordance with Num.18.21,24ff., carried through by Nehemiah in the face of resistance (Neh.13.10-13). (For the whole question, cf. Kippenberg, 69ff.)

This obligation imposed by Nehemiah and the measures which went with it combine a number of intentions: the demand for a demarcation of the Jewish community and for its purity, a concern for the regular observance of temple worship, and explicit social concern. This last feature also clearly comes to the fore in matters of the temple cult. This is the case with the fair distribution of sacrificial gifts and of tithes to the levites, who had been forced to fight for sustenance (cf. 13.10). The concern also appears, conversely, from the fact that it was again the upper class which sought to evade these obligations (cf.13.11).

If we attempt to form an overall picture of Nehemiah's activity, we can best understand it in terms of consolidation. By rebuilding the walls of Jerusalem and increasing the number of its inhabitants, he restored a political (and at the same time a spiritual) centre to the province of Judah. By regulating the offerings to the temple he guaranteed that sacrificial worship would be performed in an orderly way, so that Jerusalem could fulfil its role as a religious centre. By remitting debts and arranging a year of remission he helped to diminish social tensions and thus made the Jewish community more viable.

Consolidation

The nature of the sources has led other scholars to come to quite different estimates of Nehemiah's activity. Thus Kellermann (1967) sees Nehemiah as a member of the house of David (from an offshoot of the Davidic dynasty), who derived from this descent the right to intervene in political and cultic matters. He will then have been drawn into the wake of a 'Zionist-messianic party' which wanted to make him king (cf. the accusations of his opponents in Neh.6.6f.), finally failing because the Persian king withdrew his support from Nehemiah and recalled him from Jerusalem. Smith develops quite a different picture. In his view Nehemiah was a 'tyrant' in the Greek sense who waged a successful battle against the aristocracy with the aid of the lower classes and thus at the same time helped the 'YHWH-alone party' to victory over the syncretistic majority (including the priesthood, who tolerated syncretism). In this way he made a decisive mark on later Judaism. Both outlines are based on a wealth of conjectures which are unproven and for which there is no evidence in the text. In my view a historical reconstruction based on the picture presented by the Old Testament tradition deserves more trust.

Verdicts on Nehemiah

The report of Nehemiah's work brings to an end the narrative account of the history of Israel within the Old Testament. In the books of Ezra and Nehemiah, the period after the end of the Babylonian exile has been summarized into a unity with two focal points: the activity of Sheshbazzar and Zerubbabel, which comes to an end with the restoration of the temple, and the activity of Ezra and Nehemiah. This leads to a further internal and external consolidation and so creates the conditions for the life of the Jewish people over subsequent centuries.

Bibliography

S.Japhet, 'The Supposed Common Authorship of Chronicles and Ezra-Nehemia Investigated Anew', *VT* 18, 1968, 330-71; U.Kellermann, *Nehemia. Quellen, Überlieferung und Geschichte*, 1967; id., 'Erwägungen zum Problem der Esradatierung', *ZAW* 80, 1968, 55-87; H.G.Kippenberg, *Religion und Klassenbildung im antiken Judäa*, 1978; K.Koch, 'Hoherpriester', *BHH* II, 737-40; S.Mowinckel, *Studien zu dem Buche Ezra-Nehemia*, I and II 1964, III 1965; H.H.Rowley, 'The Chronological Order of Ezra and Nehemiah' (1948), in *The Servant of the Lord*, 1965, 137-68; H.H.Schaeder, *Esra der Schreiber*, 1930; M.Smith, *Palestinian Parties and Politics That Shaped the Old Testament*, 1971; H.C.M.Vogt, *Studie zur nachexilischen Gemeinde in Esra-Nehemiah*, 1966.
Noth, §26; Bright, ch.10; Gunneweg, XI.2,3; Herrmann, III,3; Hayes/Miller, IX; Ben-Sasson, I.11.
Cf. further the bibliography on III.4.6.

7.4 Israel at the End of the Old Testament Period

Nehemiah marks the end of the account of the history of Israel within the Old Testament. No event and no name from the period after his activity is explicitly mentioned in the Old Testament. This is hardly a coincidence. The books of Ezra and Nehemiah present the period from the Edict of Cyrus (538) to the end of the activity of Nehemiah (c.430) as a self-contained period of return, rebuilding and consolidation, in which the history of Israel, interrupted by the Babylonian exile, is again taken up and the cultic and national institutions, which were partially destroyed, are restored. Thus this period forms a supplement to the history of Israel up to the end of the monarchy, which has already become canonical, and at the same time brings to an end this history, which now, in its entirety, becomes the subject of tradition.

This gives us some pointers towards interpreting the history of Israel in the following centuries. Outwardly this history gave little occasion for further historiography. Judah remained under Persian rule for about a century; for this period there are almost no accounts at all which could give insight into conditions. Nor are there any references to important changes, so that the situation created by Ezra and Nehemiah evidently continued to exist (cf.Gowan, 61ff.)

However, particular stress should be put on two aspects. First of all, relations with the Jewish Diaspora: in this respect the traditions about Ezra and Nehemiah offer a remarkably ambivalent picture. On the one hand, the great significance of the Diaspora is recognizable from the fact that both Ezra and Nehemiah come from the Diaspora to Jerusalem and there intervene in the situation in a fundamental way. Moreover, they seem to have the authority of the Persian king behind them, though this does not explain their actual influence on domestic, and especially religious, affairs in Jerusalem and Judah. Rather, here they continue the line which had already become visible with Zerubbabel: the standards of purity in Jewish religion and its demarcation over against the outside world were set by those who returned from exile or from the Diaspora. However, Ezra and Nehemiah leave their positive stamp on religious, political and social life in Judah far beyond this. So clearly the authority of the Diaspora is recognized in these questions, whether tacitly or explicitly.

On the other hand the account of events gives the impression that the *gola* as a whole returned and was now identical with the community in Jerusalem and Judah. This is particularly remarkable in connection with Nehemiah, since (in contrast to Ezra) according to his own account he came to Jerusalem by himself, so that it is impossible to see him as the representative of the Jewish Diaspora (or a group of it). However, that should without doubt be presupposed. The Book of Esther also records the presence of a large number of Jews in the Persian empire and in the capital Susa; they kept in touch and were regarded as a closed ethnic and religious group (cf. Esther 3.8). However, there is no explicit mention here of their connections with the homeland. Still, the fact that the book of Esther was incorporated into the biblical canon suggests not only the presence of such connections but also the recognition of the Diaspora in Babylon and Persia as an ingredient of the Jewish people, not least – indeed especially – in religious terms.

Relations with the Egyptian Diaspora are less clear. The Jews on the island of Elephantine in the Nile evidently felt links with the homeland, since after their temple had been destroyed by Egyptian priests in about 410, they asked support from Bagoas, the governor of Jerusalem, towards its rebuilding (cf. *AOT*, 450ff.; *TGI*, 84ff.), because they had had no answer to a first letter to the priesthood in Jerusalem (lines 18f.). A temple outside Jerusalem must have been unacceptable to the priests in Jerusalem. However, a compromise seems to have been reached: the governor allowed the rebuilding on the express condition that only food offerings (*minha*) and incense offerings (*lebona*) could be made, and not burnt offerings (*'ola*). The people of Elephantine seem to have accepted this (cf. *AOT*, 452f.; *TGI*, 88; and Porten, 284ff.), so that the temple could be rebuilt. However, we have no information about other relationships between Jerusalem and Elephantine, and the further fate of the Jewish military colony remains unknown. The last of the texts that have been discovered dates from the year 399.

The second aspect concerns the relationship between Jerusalem and Samaria. The conflicts in the time of Zerubbabel and Nehemiah were not only political rivalries; they also had a religious side. The Jews would not allow the Samaritans to take part in the building of the temple (Ezra 4.1ff.) and the city (Neh.2.20). The Samaritans stressed that they were also worshippers of YHWH (Ezra 4.2). Here we can see the beginnings of the development of a distinctive Samarian (or Samaritan) religious community which later led an independent existence from that of Judah. The details are uncertain. According to the report by Josephus (*Antt.* XI,8,3ff.), the Samaritans received rights from Alexander the Great to build their own temple. At all events, it is certain that in the Persian or Hellenistic period they made themselves independent in religious terms (cf. Kippenberg) and in so doing claimed as their holy scripture the Pentateuch in the same complete version which we find in the Jewish Bible (with some characteristic deviations, cf. Würthwein, 42ff.). (A Samaritan Chronicle, only recently discovered, outlines an independent history of the temple on Gerizim, which is said already to have been built by Joshua. Moreover, substantial parts of the biblical books of Joshua, Judges, Samuel, Kings and Chronicles have been used for it, cf. Macdonald.)

However, none of this has left any recognizable mark on the books of the Old Testament. The same is true (leaving aside the books of Koheleth and Daniel) of the far-reaching changes which came about with the conquest of the Near East by Alexander the Great (after 333 BC) and the ensuing Hellenization (cf. Hengel). The collection and editing of the books was probably essentially completed in this period. However, this means that the literary and theological work to which the books of the Old Testament owe their final form was carried out to a greater or lesser degree in the first two centuries after the Babylonian exile.

This results in a very complex and differentiated picture of this period. According to the account in the books of Ezra and Nehemiah, the fight for the purity of Jewish religion stands in the foreground. This struggle is matched e.g. by the great significance attached to cultic regulations in the final shaping of the Pentaeuch. However, here we should not ignore another feature: the delight which is often expressed in the temple, in the services and festivals (Ezra 3.12f.; 6.11; Neh.8.12,17; 12.27,43f.). Here we can see an affinity with the hymnic tradition of the Psalms, which plays a major role in the final collection of the book of Psalms.

Alongside this, another line clearly emerges in which the Torah, set down in writing, has a central place, and becomes the basis of a new Torah piety. The statement that Ezra 'set his heart to study the law of the Lord, and to do it' (Ezra 7.10), comes close to the statements in the 'Torah Psalms' (Pss.1; *19.8ff.*; 119) which are a further influential element in the book of Psalms as we now have it. Both elements, the cultic-hymnic delight in festivals and Torah piety, are also part of the characteristic features of the historical account contained in the books of Chronicles.

Strikingly, another line is absent from the books of Ezra and

Nehemiah (though certainly not by chance): the prophetic line. Thus there is no trace in the book of Ezra of the messianic expectations that we find in Haggai and Zechariah. Nevertheless this tradition was continued in the editing of the book of Zechariah (cf. e.g. Zech 4.6; 9.9f.). That has a place in the wider context of the collection and editing of the prophetic books, which in their final form have a marked eschatological element. At the same time, however, the proclamation of judgment to be found in the pre-exilic prophets is preserved in them and often updated. This in turn provides us with another connecting link to Torah piety, which contains not only an invitation to practise the Torah, but also a warning against the consequences of not practising it. Here we can see a further direct connection with the Books of Chronicles, where the portrait of the prophets as those who admonish and warn is orientated on the portrait of Moses (cf. Deut.18.15,18), while the eschatological element is again completely absent. The figure of David also provides direct connections. He plays a central role in the books of Chronicles without being a messianic figure; his significance for the temple cult is also part of this. Again, the figure of David has left its mark on the Psalms in the collection that has come down to us because of the significance of his person for worship and its messianic function.

Finally, wisdom traditions play an important role in the final shaping of various books and collections. Moreover the books which express the 'crisis of wisdom' (Job, Koheleth) show the significance of wisdom thinking and the controversy associated with it in the centuries after the exile.

This short sketch should indicate the variety of theological and spiritual movements with which we have to reckon in the post-exilic period (cf. Steck). We do not know how far they were nurtured at particular times in specific groups or circles and how these related to one another (cf. Blenkinsopp). This also applies to the associations and direct connections indicated; some of them may in fact have existed, whereas others simply show that the same traditions could be taken up and developed further in quite different directions. Nevertheless in this case, too, the traditions themselves serve as a binding element. Above all, however, the existence of all these different aspects make it clear that we should not consider the post-exilic period in a one-sided way (e.g. along the lines suggested by the books of Ezra and Nehemiah). Rather, the collection, editing and interpretation of the many traditions which have found expression in the books of the Old Testament is an indication of a very intensive and varied religious and spiritual life and at the same time shows a marked awareness of the continuity of the history of Israel.

End of OT Period
Prophetic traditions
→236ff., 239f.
→256ff.

Figure of David

→248f.

Wisdom traditions
→252f., 265f.

Theological and spiritual variety

Bibliography

J. Blenkinsopp, 'Interpretation and the Tendency to Sectarianism: An Aspect of Second Temple History', in E.P. Sanders (ed.), *Jewish and Christian Self-Definition II. Two Aspects of Judaism in the Greco-Roman Period*, 1981, 1-26; D.E. Gowan, *Bridge between the Testaments. A Reappraisal of Judaism from the Exile to the Birth of Christianity*, 1976; M. Hengel, *Judaism and Hellenism*, ET 1974; H.G. Kippenberg, *Garizim und Synagoge*, 1971; J. Macdonald, *The Samaritan Chronicle No II*, 1969; B. Porten, *Archives from Elephantine. The Life of an Ancient Jewish Military Colony*, 1968; O.H. Steck, 'Das Problem theologischer Strömungen in nachexilischer Zeit', *EvTh* 28, 1968, 445-58; E. Würthwein, *The Text of the Old Testament*, ET 1980.

Noth, § 27,28; Bright, ch.11,12; Gunneweg, XI.4,5; XII.2; Herrmann, III.4; Hayes/Miller, XI; Ben-Sasson, I.11.

II The Literature of the Old Testament in the Life of Ancient Israel

1 Form Criticism and Social Structure in Israel

For the most part, the texts handed down in the Old Testament are not 'literature' in the sense that they were set down in writing from the beginning and intended for 'literary' use. Many texts were primarily composed for a particular occasion within the life of Israelite society — and also used there. Only in the course of time did they then grow together into the books that we now have, or were fitted together in the course of systematic work.

Hermann Gunkel was particularly insistent in drawing attention to this situation. In his view, in ancient Israel 'literature is part of the life of the people and must be understood from this life'. He therefore spoke of the 'setting in the life of the people', which the texts have, or simply of the 'setting in life' (Sitz im Leben, 3f.). These observations have fundamental consequences for any approach to the Old Testament (and of course not only there, nor only in ancient texts). If we see the texts as part of particular features of everyday life, it follows that – regardless of their individual expression and stylization – they display structures of content and expression which they have in common with other texts. Such constant textual structures are always already there for speakers or authors to use as rules for structuring what they have to say, even if they shape their texts on each specific occasion with a view to a particular audience, context, occasion, purpose and so on. Using a term from literary criticism, when talking about the structural rules which transcend the individual (the models for shaping a text), we speak of 'genres' (the specific individual texts which are a subordinate category to this are 'examples of genres', cf. Hardmeier). Gunkel's term 'Sitz im Leben' denotes a particular situation of communication with which a genre – or even several genres – may be connected. In a more comprehensive sense the term can therefore also denote the social context in question.

This reciprocal relationship of textual genre and *Sitz im Leben* is the basic insight of 'form criticism' or 'genre criticism', which goes back to Gunkel. 'Typical situations' and constant textual structures appear most strikingly where particular series of events are repeated with great regularity on the basis of fixed rules and in stereotyped forms. That is the case, e.g., with the cult in its varied forms: each cultic festival or form of worship needs a 'liturgy', i.e. a fixed sequence and form for specific sequences and actions and the texts to be spoken or sung with them. In many cases such a liturgy consists of fixed parts, which remain unchanged at every performance of the cultic action, and variable parts, which can be altered or changed from time to time. It goes without

Method

Forms

Cult
→94ff.

saying that the former have quite stereotyped forms. However, even the forms of the latter are not random; rather, here too the rules of the genre determine the themes and means of expression, so that for all the differences in details, the texts which are to be used at a particular part of the liturgy (e.g. psalms, hymns, prayers) have distinct characteristics in common.

In the Old Testament, as a rule we do not have the forms of service in which the course of a cultic action is laid down. It is also questionable to what degree these forms of service were in fact put down in writing, since this was part of the professional priestly knowledge that would be handed down by word of mouth. However, we can recognize the genres of liturgical texts which will have belonged to them (e.g. psalms) and draw conclusions from their themes and forms about the liturgy itself. Thus, an approach by means of forms or genres gives us insight into part of the religious life of ancient Israel. This means that interpretation of the Old Testament is involved in a reciprocal relationship: discovering a Sitz im Leben makes it possible to recognize a particular genre, to describe its function, and thence to derive criteria for the interpretation of the texts within that genre: conversely, comparative exegesis of the texts within a genre gives us insight into the sequences of events in which they have their setting.

What has been said here in connection with cultic texts also applies, *mutatis mutandis*, to other spheres of life. In the sphere of law, processes similarly need quite definite, stereotyped forms, in which they have to run their course, and specific texts which are to be spoken on particular occasions. Here, too, there are stereotyped parts which in some circumstances can simply consist in short formulas, bringing into being the legal body which summoned individual parties and asked them to present their arguments, and finally pronounced the verdict and its consequences. However, here too the number of variable parts must have been very much greater, since each case is different, and the important thing is to discover the special feature about the individual case and to pass judgment accordingly. However, these variable parts also obey the fixed laws of the genre in question. Therefore here too interpretation is involved in a reciprocal relationship: insights into the course of legal procedures make it possible to assign texts to particular genres from which in turn it is possible to gain new insights into the practice of Israelite law and the thought behind it.

There were also regularly recurring occasions at the royal court, e.g. the coronation of a king, the public proclamation of the birth of an heir to the throne, and perhaps coronation festivals repeated annually. Here there are close connections with cultic events, since all these happenings also had a religious significance and therefore were celebrated in the cult. However, the military and political spheres also impinged on the cult, e.g. in victory festivals or lamentations by the people after defeats, etc. The army and the government also needed permanent listings: annals of military and political events; treaties and agreements with other states; and also narrative or historical accounts of particular

Sphere of law
→88ff.

Royal court
→105ff.

events and situations. The cultural life of the court produced its own crop of forms, and the education of successors to court officials also called for fixed, traditional forms.

The emergence of prophets, too, did not come about without fixed forms. The genres of prophetic speech are stereotyped and are given specific content on each occasion by the individual prophets; this process introduces many changes. Finally, everyday life also provides a great many regularly recurring occasions on which stereotyped forms and genres of speech are used: marriage, birth and death and the way in which the community (family, clan, tribe, local community) reacts to them; the legal and economic relationships within society which need to be regulated by contracts and agreements, accounts and invoices, and so on (in cases of dispute what has already been said in connection with the laws applies); shared work can be the occasion for songs and sayings which become the common property of the community; the development and handing down of traditions from one generation to the next take place in constantly recurring forms; and finally, social celebrations provide many occasions for developing regular forms of entertainment in songs, proverbs, riddles, tales and so on.

Prophets
→112ff.
Everyday Life
→80ff.

This first survey of the various spheres of life and the literary genres which arise from them and have their roots in them should indicate the multiplicity of occasions and the variety of forms. At the same time it should bring out the fact that the laws of form which the texts obey have grown out of the life of society in its various spheres and have been determined and shaped by that. This already brings us to a further question: the relationship between oral and written tradition.

Oral/written tradition

A very lively and sometimes controversial discussion has been carried on among Old Testament scholars. Scandinavian scholars in particular have stressed very strongly the significance of oral tradition in the ancient Near East and have used it to attack a purely literary approach to the Old Testament, especially the literary-critical work of the 'Wellhausen school' (cf. Nielsen). This is beyond question the justification for such theories, which in this respect follow Gunkel's new approach and his view that the genres of Old Testament literature were handed down by word of mouth in their original Sitz im Leben.

However, in the meantime it has emerged that sometimes false alternatives have been introduced here. On the one hand we must certainly reckon with the fact that for a long period in ancient Israel a variety of texts, including more extended ones (e.g. sagas and tales, but also cultic and legal texts) were preserved and handed down by word of mouth and only set down in writing at a relatively late stage. On the other hand, we often hear in the Old Testament that particular things were written down: laws and commandments (Ex.24.4; 32.25; Josh.24.26), legal documents (Deut.24.1; Jer.32.10), cultic texts (Ex.17.14; Num.5.23); letters (II Sam.11.14; I Kings 21.8; II Kings 10.1) etc. There were also books like the 'Book of the Wars of YHWH' (Num.21.14): the 'Book of the Just' (Josh.10.13; II Sam.1.18), the 'Chronicles' of Solomon (I Kings 11.41) and the 'Chronicles' of the kings of Israel (I Kings 14.19, etc.) and Judah (I Kings 14.29, etc.).

Furthermore, the extensive textual finds from the ancient Near East show that long before the Israelite period there was a flourishing written culture there, so that there is no reason to suppose that Israel was part of a culture which was essentially illiterate. Still, as I have said, the objections against a purely literary consideration of the Old Testament texts remain. Many texts took on their distinctive stamp precisely because they were intended for oral presentation, and to begin with were also handed down by word of mouth.

The way towards literature →124ff.

This also directs our attention towards the further history of Old Testament literature. We must also consider the development from the original oral or written genres and their use in their original Sitz im Leben down to the final literary stage of the Old Testament as we now have it. Exegesis cannot be limited to a purely literary consideration of the text as it now is, nor can it be content to work out the original literary genres and leave out of account the further history of the tradition of the texts. Insight into the way in which Old Testament literature was originally rooted in specific situations of the life of Israelite society has made the task of the exegete more sophisticated and more extensive. The exegete must now be concerned to trace developments from the beginning of the formation of the tradition to the final form of the text as we have it today. Thus exegesis will be closely connected with the history of Israel, its traditions and its faith.

Bibliography

H.Gunkel, *Die israelitische Literatur*, 1925 (1963); C.Hardmeier, *Texttheorie und biblische Exegese*, 1978; E.Nielsen, *Oral Tradition*, 1954.
Eissfeldt, §2; Fohrer, §2-6; Soggin, 1.VI; Smend, §17; Koch, §3.7.

2 Family, Clan, Tribe, Local Community

The communities in which daily life runs its course offer many occasions for communication in more or less stereotyped forms. It is in the nature of things that most of these everyday expressions are never written down and therefore do not become literature. For members of a particular, more or less intimate, community, these forms are taken for granted, and for outsiders they have hardly any significance.

Family

In considering ancient Israel we must first look at structures of community life which are essentially determined by kinship (cf. de Vaux, 19ff.; Crüsemann, *Widerstand*, 204ff.; Kippenberg, 23ff.): the smallest unit is the family, in the Old Testament often described as the 'father's house' (*bet 'ab*) or simply as 'house' (*bayit*, e.g. 12.3); this can also refer to the wider family which includes not only the husband, his wife (or wives), his children, male and female slaves, but also married

sons and other dependent relatives (like Lot in Abraham's family **Family to**
according to Gen.12f.). In economic terms the large family was a unit **Community**
of production which could look after itself (cf. Crüsemann, *Mann und
Frau*, 43ff.).

The next larger unit is the clan (*mišpaḥah*), the group of blood   Clan
relations in the wider sense; among other things this has legal functions
(e.g. land ownership, the institution of 'redemption' [*ge'ulla*], cf.
Lev.25.24f.) and cultic functions (cf. Kippenberg, 25ff.). Finally, for
greater solidarity, several clans form a tribe (*šebet* or *matte*; both words   Tribe
also mean 'staff'). According to texts from the book of Judges the tribe
was particularly significant in the early period, especially under threats
of war (cf. Thiel, 109f.).

In Josh.7.14-18 we can see a tripartite division: tribe-clan-family. However, the
terminology fluctuates within the Old Testament, and the boundaries between
the individual elements are often fluid. There is some dispute as to how far the
Israelite tribes of which the Old Testament speaks had already come into being
in the nomadic period and whether they were only formed in the course of the
conquest or even later. At all events, we can clearly see that the organization
by tribes played an important role in the period after the settlement. This   →23ff.
organization covered specific areas of settlement and the Israelite places situated
in it.

As well as the division by descent we find daily life further ordered
in terms of the local community, primarily the city ('*ir*). Although life   Local
was predominantly determined by agriculture, people lived above all   community
in fortified cities which offered protection against attacks and marauding
wild animals; they went out to work in the fields in the morning and
returned in the evening. (Hence Ps.121.8: 'The Lord preserve your
going out and your coming in' – in that order!) The city was the most
important basis for community life in terms of law, politics and social
life. As the cities were built very tightly and did not have streets in the
real sense, let alone largish squares, the local community gathered 'in   →89
the gate', i.e. in the open space immediately before the city gate,
especially as the inhabitants passed this place any way, in the morning
and the evening (cf. the scene in Ruth 4.1f.).

Only a little from the everyday life of these limited communities has
found its way into the literature, and then only very much by chance.
Nevertheless, the Old Testament discloses a large number of stereotyped phrases from everyday language, like greetings (e.g. the many
different forms of the word *šalom*, peace), formulas to open conversations, requests and thanks, wishes, oaths and blessings (cf. Lande,
Fohrer, § 9).

The basic events of human life – marriage, birth and death – were
special occasions for the development of stereotyped forms of speech.
Before the marriage, the bride's family might send the bride on her way
with a blessing for fertility, of the kind echoed in Gen.24.60. Ruth 4.11f.   →261ff.
has also handed down blessings for the bride. A large number of love   Love songs
songs have been collected together in the Song of Songs; these were   81

possibly sung and performed on the occasion of a wedding feast lasting a number of days, and show the variety of this genre (cf. Horst). The phrase about the 'voice of the bridegroom and the bride', which recurs frequently in Jeremiah (Jer.7.34; 33.11, etc.), probably alludes to the singing of wedding songs.

We do not have any texts connected with the birth of a child; at most we might regard the phrase 'Fear not, for you have borne a son', which occurs twice (Gen.35.17; I Sam.4.20), as a stereotyped formula which was spoken to the mother after the birth. Giving a name was also a formal action with stereotyped phrases. Evidently it was usually done by the mother (cf.Gen.29.31ff.; I Sam.1.20, etc.), but there are also reports of namings by the father (Gen.16.15; 17.19; Ex.2.22 etc.).

Events connected with death are more clearly recognizable. The lament for the dead took specific stereotyped forms: tearing clothes, putting on mourning garments, weeping, fasting and raising a lament for the dead person (cf. Gen.37.34; II Sam.1.11; 3.31, etc.). One stereotyped element in the lament for the dead was the cry *hoy*, 'Woe' (cf. I Kings 13.30; Jer.22.18; 34.5, which also appears in the forms *'oy* and *ho*, cf. Amos 5.16), and the dirge, the *qina* (cf.Jahnow; this is one of the rare occasions in which we find a clear designation of genre within the Old Testament itself.)

According to Amos 5.16; Jer.*9.16*, the dirge was sung by a special 'professional group', probably mainly consisting of women. But it is also said that David himself composed and sang dirges (II Sam.2.27ff.; 3.33f.). The dirge evidently played a great part in public life and awareness, so that the prophets could adopt this genre and transform it within the framework of their prophetic proclamation (cf. Hardmeier).

Communal songs were certainly also sung on other occasions of daily life. Thus the 'Song of the well' quoted in Num.21.17f. was perhaps originally a work song which was sung at the digging of a well. A work song (of lamentation) can also be recognized in Neh.4.4. There were certainly also similar songs for other common forms of work, above all at the harvest, when a proverbial joy prevailed (cf. Isa.*9.2*; Ps.126.5), and especially at the wine harvest (cf. Judg.9.27; 21.21; Isa.16.10); however, we do not have any instances of them. Isaiah 5.11f. and Amos 6.4-6 indicate that there were drinking songs; in Isa.22.13 there is a quotation from a short song of this kind, and probably also in Isa.56.12 (cf. also Amos 4.1). There is a quotation from a taunt-song in Isa.23.15, and a boasting song in Gen.4.23f. The genre of the watchman's song, sung by a watchman standing on the wall by night, is reflected in the form of a word-play of question and answer in Isa. 21.11f.

The existential experiences acquired, exchanged, formulated and handed down in human society have often been expressed in the form of short sayings. Thus there are typical proverbs of the kind that we know from many cultures, e.g. 'What does the straw have in common with the wheat?' (Jer.23.28); 'A living dog is better than a dead lion' (Koh.9.4); 'Wickedness comes forth from the wicked' (I Sam. 24.14) etc. The last example is explicitly designated a *mašal*, which here **Family to Community** evidently means 'proverb'. (However, the word also denotes other forms of sayings, e.g. the wisdom saying, the taunt-song, etc.) The saying 'Is Saul also among the prophets' (I Sam.10.12) is also introduced as a *mašal*; the same saying is also introduced in I Sam.19.24 with the phrase, 'Therefore they say', in the same way as the saying 'A mighty hunter before the Lord like Nimrod' (Gen.10.9). The Israelite king Ahab provokes the Aramaean king Ben-hadad, by sending him a →44f. mocking proverb through messengers (I Kings 20.11), and the prophet Ezekiel takes up a *mašal* current among the people of Judah in exile (Ezek.18.1ff.).

Riddles in stereotyped form have also been handed on to us. Judges Riddles 14.12-18 shows us that on social occasions – in this case a wedding – Numerical riddles were asked to entertain the guests. According to I Kings 10.1, sayings the Queen of Sheba tested the wisdom of Solomon with riddles. Another variant of the proverb, which was perhaps also developed in the playful form of a question and answer game (Köhler, 104ff.), is the numerical saying, e.g. 'Three things are never satisfied; four never say "enough" ' (Prov.30.15f. cf. vv.18f., 21ff., 24ff., 29ff.). Finally, mention should →108 also be made here of the fable, which occurs in the Old Testament in the form of the plant fable (II Kings 14.9; Judg.9.8-15). →169

The last instances show clear connections with wisdom literature. Wisdom Here we can see that as well as wisdom at court there was also a popular →108ff. wisdom which initially developed its own forms of expression, but was later collected and handed down along with court wisdom. The division between the two is often hard to define, especially as the spheres of experience with which they are concerned often overlap. Moreover, the transitions from simple popular sayings to wisdom sayings with an artistic formulation are fluid (cf. Hermisson, 52ff.).

Like court wisdom, popular wisdom is also concerned with the upbringing and education of the younger generation. Thus there are many sayings which contain the rules of life for living together in the family, above all for the behaviour of children towards their parents; e.g. 'A wise son delights his father and a foolish son is the bane of his mother' (Prov.10.1; cf. 15.20; 17.21,25, etc.). This didactic character is also expressed in the address 'My son' (e.g. Prov.19.27; 23.26; 24.13,21) or in a saying like Prov.15.5: 'A fool despises the discipline of his father...'

Finally, advice and prohibitions which are meant to regulate and safeguard social life within the community also belong here. They have found expression above all in prohibitions which, with a form of address Prohibitions in the second person, forbid actions and forms of behaviour which could endanger communal life. These begin with the closest, most intimate realm of the family: sexual relationships with kindred or with the partners of kindred are forbidden, because they would destroy the common life within the wider family which is presupposed here (see above; cf. Lev.18). Advantage is not to be taken of groups in the community without legal privileges, like widows, orphans, aliens and so on (e.g. Ex.*22.20f.*; 23.9, etc.). This applies especially to legal proceedings; a particular concern of this prohibition is that these should be carried out unexceptionably 'without respect of person' (cf. Ex.23.1-3,6-9). Here the prohibitions have contacts with other texts which have their setting in the legal sphere.

→92ff.

Alt assigned the prohibitions to 'apodeictic law'. However, Gerstenberger has shown that they derive rather from the 'clan ethos' and have their setting there, particularly in the sphere of education. Consequently they are often collected in groups of two or three with a common theme so that they can be remembered

→141, 152f.

better; occasionally there are also longer series (as e.g. the Decalogue, Ex.20), though these reflect a later stage of the tradition. However, there is some argument as to whether one can speak of a specific form of 'clan wisdom' (cf. Hermisson, 81ff.).

Sayings have encapsulated not only experiences in the social life of human individuals but also relationships between a variety of human

Tribal sayings

communities, especially the individual tribes. The tribal sayings which

→136, 155, 26

have been collected above all in Gen.49; Deut.33; Judg.5 reflect the various relationships among the tribes. They often contain assessments and evaluations of the behaviour of individual tribes; from this it emerges that on occasion these sayings have been formulated from the viewpoint of other tribes. Comparisons and word-plays are employed here. Comparison with animals is particularly popular. Thus the tribe of Benjamin is compared with a wolf (Gen.49.27); Judah, Gad and Dan with a lion (Gen.49.9; Deut.33.20,22; cf. Num 23.24; 24.9); Naphtali with a hind (Gen.49.21), Issachar with an ass (Gen.49.21; cf. also Gen.16.12), Dan with a snake (Gen.49.17). So there are no fixed associations of particular animals with particular tribes; however, the comparisons with animals express patterns of behaviour which often show recognition and praise of power, bravery, speed, dangerousness and so on. They can also impute blame, as e.g. in the case of Issachar's idleness.

The tribal sayings often indicate specific historical relationships and situations as well as general characteristics. This is particularly clear in

→26

the tribal sayings within the song of Deborah in Judg.5. Here praise and blame for individual tribes are expressed in connection with their participation in (v.18) or absence from (vv.15b-17) the fight. Other sayings describe the circumstances of individual tribes (Gen.49.13,15,

→136f.

20),their particular functions (Deut.33.8-11) or claims within the tribal community (Gen.49.8-12, esp.v.10), special dangers (Deut.33.6; Gen.49.5-7, esp. v.7b), etc.

The relationships of the Israelites to other peoples or groups of peoples have also found expression in similar sayings, as e.g. their relationship with the Canaanites (Gen.9.25-27), Edomites (Gen.25.23; 27.27-29,39f.; cf.Num. 24.18), Moabites (Num.24.17), Amalekites (Num.24.20, cf. also the sayings with a cultic stamp in Ex.17.14,16), Kenites (Num.24.21f.) and Ishmaelites (Gen.16.12).

The life of the community finds expression not only in songs and
sayings but also in very varied kinds of narratives. The most important
basic forms of narratives (leaving aside myth, which belongs in the
religious sphere) are usually distinguished in terms of folk-tales, sagas
and legends; however, the boundaries between these genres cannot
always be defined clearly. The narratives were probably handed down
and recounted repeatedly within the circle of the family or the wider
family, and later also when the local community met in the evening
before the gate of the city. The artistic forms and length of some
narratives (cf. above all the Novelle, see below) suggest professional
narrators. The transition from oral to written transmission will similarly
have introduced changes.

No independent folk tales have been handed down in the Old Testament (cf.
Gunkel 1917). However, themes from folk tales appear, like the container of
grain (I Kings 17.16) or cruse of oil (II Kings 4.1ff.) which never fails; there are
talking animals like Balaam's ass (Num.22.28ff.), or creatures which bring
people food (I Kings 17.1-6, etc.). It is hard to say whether there were
independent, extended tales on such themes in Israel.

Sagas occupy a good deal of space in the Old Testament tradition.
The use of this term does not necessarily have the negative connotation
(frequent in current but vague terminology) that what is reported here
is not historically 'true'. Rather, the concept of saga denotes a different
way of dealing with things, another form of 'preoccupation with the
spirit' (Jolles) which is not historiography. The saga is not primarily
concerned to report what happened, although in many instances it is
concerned with historical events. However, it is not interested in one
specific event as such, but in the typical, universal human characteristic
to which it gives expression. The interest of the saga is not really directed
towards the past; rather, the saga is concerned that the present hearer
and reader should see himself, his own problems and experiences in it,
and gain knowledge and insight as a result. Moreover, the sagas of the
Old Testament are concerned with the awareness of the historical
continuity of the community which is handing them on, and the ancestors
of whom they tell; in this way the saga becomes part of their own history.
    That the saga describes typical events, on which it invites the hearer
to reflect for himself, is also expressed in the fact that events take place
within the narrowest of frameworks: the world is presented as a family.
The main characters are individuals who belong to a family; and even
when they are set over against, say, a 'king', he nevertheless appears as
an individual. As a rule only two or three people appear in the action
of a saga; if there are more than two, we only find two in each individual
scene. As a rule the action follows a straight line, and there is only one
continuous narrative thread. There is usually a tension at the beginning,
which leads to a climax and is finally resolved. However, on closer
inspection it becomes evident that even the short, terse sagas are often
more artistic and complex than appears at first sight.

Here is an example. The tale of the 'betrayal of the ancestral mother' in the version to be found in Gen.12.10-20 (cf. 20; 26.7-11) is rightly regarded as one of the 'classical' sagas of Genesis. A tension is generated at the beginning which is finally resolved in a way which satisfies and delights the audience. However, the narrative is on many levels. One tension (How will Abraham fare when he comes to Egypt with Sarah?, vv.11f.) is resolved: Abraham remains alive and all goes well with him (v.16). But that generates a new tension (What will become of Sarah?). So the resolution proves unsatisfactory, not just in narrative terms, but also from the perspective of the audience, who are themselves descendants of Abraham and Sarah. (Here at the same time we see the direct relationship of the narrative to the time of the audience!) Now YHWH himself intervenes and thus brings the problem to its final solution (cf. Culley, 35f.).

We can see a wide range of sagas. The 'classical' form of the saga is very brief; it concentrates on essentials and often does not run to more than ten verses in the Massoretic text (e.g. Gen.12.10-20; 16; 18.1-16; 28.11-19). However, there are also sagas in a broad, 'extended' narrative style (Gunkel, *Genesis* XXIII) with numerous repetitions, etc., like Gen.24 (64 verses!). The basic pattern of family relationships, with few people involved, and a straight-line course of action is also maintained here, but at the same time a completely different style of narration appears. Gunkel regarded these differences as points of reference for a development of Israelite sagas and took it that the brevity of the narratives was an indication of old tradition. In individual instances this judgment can be correct (moreover, the themes of the extended narrative in Gen.24 – the problem of mixed marriages, land, etc. – clearly belong in a post-exilic context). However, there is no basis for his generalization in empirical research. So we must also reckon with the possibility that the brief, polished sagas of Genesis represent artistic revisions of popular traditions focussed on particular topics.

Be this as it may, the sphere of 'popular' narrative may be transcended in a text like the Joseph narrative (Gen.37-50), which Gunkel described as a Novella (op.cit., LV). The Novella, too, depicts events in the narrowest of frameworks and only has a few individuals in the action, but it skilfully links together different sequences of action and narrative threads and continues them over long periods. One can hardly imagine such a complex composition in oral tradition.

The sagas discussed so far all presuppose that the characters in them have a nomadic life-style. Of course that is no indication that they themselves come from the nomadic period. However, in this respect they preserve a historical image of the ancestors of the Israelites and thus also a form of narration which can have had its roots in that time. In their present form the patriarchal narratives all tell of the beginning of the history of the people, e.g. in the peril to Sarah, the mother of the tribes, and her preservation (12.10-20) or of the miraculous circumstances of the birth of Isaac (18.1-16 with 21.1ff.; the topic here is also the paradigmatic behaviour of Abraham, as in Gen.22). Secondly, the sagas also explain the origin of the relationships existing between Israel and its neighbours at the time of the narrator: Gen.16 and 21.8-21 tell

→110, 136
Novellas

→8

Aetiological
elements

how the ancestor of the 'kindred' Ishmaelites got his name and his life-
style in the wilderness; 19.30-38 derive the origin of Moab and Ammon in
their land from unusual circumstances; the conflicts over primogeniture
and blessing between the brothers Jacob and Esau (25.21ff.; 27) lay the
basis for the superiority of Israel to Edom; 21.22-32 and 26.25-33 are
concerned with relationships with the Philistines. In so far as these texts
seek to explain why something is as it is, they have an aetiological intent
(from the Greek *aitia*, cause). In respect of their themes they can be
described in Gunkel's terms as ethnological sagas.

Family to Community →135

Other sagas can be described as local sagas, because they are primarily
interested in particular localities. Thus Gen.21.22-32 is interested (or
rather, also interested, see above) in the explanation of the name
'Beersheba' (cf. 26.25-33), and 26.18-22 in the names of other springs.
We can also describe such explanations of names as 'etymological
aetiologies'. Genesis 28.11-19 is also and above all concerned with the
holiness of a place which thus becomes a cult place (see below).

→40

Other aetiologies seek to explain particular customs, e.g. a food tabu
(Gen.*32.33*), or particular geological features like the 'pillar of salt' (Gen.19.26),
and so on. (Occasionally the aetiological intent of the narrative is stressed by
the phrase 'to this day', e.g. Gen.*32.33*; Josh.5.9.) In many cases these are
simply aetiological motifs which stand alongside other narrative elements:
however, a text can only be said to belong to the genre of 'aetiological saga' if
the aetiological element coincides with the scope of the text (Westermann, 40).

→165

The patriarchal sagas predominantly run their course in the family
realm. This corresponds to the Israelite view of the early days of the
people. (The material presented in the narrative is what might be
expected: jealousy among wives [16; 21.8ff.], childlessness [18.1-16],
disputes between brothers [25.20ff.; 27] etc.) The scenery changes
consistently in the sagas about the time of the judges and the beginning
of the monarchy. Here the wider community, the 'people', now clearly
emerges, to become a foil to the individual leading figures who stand at
the centre of the narrative. At this point we can therefore speak of hero
sagas, which in the mode of life that they depict probably reflect the
'nationalist' rural milieu of the narrators (cf. Koch, 186). This is true
above all of the sagas in the book of Judges and those about Saul and
David (I Sam.11 – II Sam 5). However, at this point we already have
signs of an approach to historiography, though we should see that as
originating more in the political institutions which were now developing.
Finally, among the hero sagas we also find some with braggart, almost
burlesque features, like the Samson stories (Judg.14-16); in addition
we also have anecdotes like that in I Sam.*21.11-16*.

→169, 170ff.

Hero sagas

→106f.

→169

Legends are usually distinguished from sagas. The criteria for this
distinction primarily relate to content: 'If the men or places or occasions
which are central to the narrative are of religious significance – priests
or prophets, sanctuaries or festivals – then we call such a narrative a
legend' (Eissfeldt, 34). Thus for example some prophetic narratives
could be described as legends, above all those which report exemplary

Legends

conduct prompting imitation, which are therefore 'edifying' in the same way as mediaeval legends about saints. However, the boundaries are difficult to draw, since there are also similar features in the Moses sagas and patriarchal sagas. The nearest examples to the type of the mediaeval →273f. legends are the martyr legends of Daniel and his friends (Dan.1-6). The aetiological narratives which explain the sanctity of particular cult places →96 can be described as cult legends (e.g. Gen.28.10-22). The term *hieros* *hieros logos* *logos* is also used here; this refers to the sacred narrative which was read within the context of the liturgy at the sanctuary in question or →170, 172 performed as cultic drama. In this sense e.g. the 'ark narrative' (I Sam.4-6; II Sam.6) is also to be understood as the cult legend of the sanctuary of the ark in Jerusalem, or the story of Jephthah's daughter (11.30-40) as the cult legend of a feast of lamentation held every year (cf. v.40).

Bibliography

A.Alt, 'The Origins of Israelite Law'(1934), ET in *Essays on Old Testament History and Religion*, 1966, 79-132; F.Crüsemann, *Der Widerstand gegen das Königtum. Die antiköniglichen Texte des Alten Testamentes und der Kampf um den frühen israelitischen Staat*, 1978; id./H.Thyen, *Als Mann und Frau geschaffen. Exegetische Studien zur Rolle der Frau*, 1978; R.C.Culley, *Studies in the Structure of Hebrew Narrative*, 1976; E.Gerstenberger, *Wesen und Herkunft des 'apodiktischen Rechts'*, 1965; H.Gunkel, *Das Märchen im Alten Testament*, 1917; id.,*Die Sagen der Genesis* (Introduction to the Genesis Commentary), ⁵1922 (⁹1977); C. Hardmeier, *Texttheorie und biblische Exegese. Zur rhetorischen Funktion der Trauermetaphorik in der Prophetie*, 1978; H.-J.Hermisson, *Studien zur israelitischen Spruchweisheit*, 1968; F.Horst, 'Die Formen des althebräischen Liebesliedes' (1935), in *Gottes Recht*, 1961, 176-87; H.Jahnow, *Das hebräische Leichenlied im Rahmen der Völkerdichtung*, 1923; A.Jolles, *Einfache Formen*, 1930 (= ²1958); H.G.Kippenberg, *Religion und Klassenbildung im antiken Judäa*, 1978 (²1982); L.Köhler, *Hebrew Man*, ET 1956; I.Lande, *Formelhafte Wendungen der Umgangssprache im Alten Testament*, 1949; W.Thiel, *Die soziale Entwicklung Israels in vorstaatlicher Zeit*, 1980; R.de Vaux, *Ancient Israel*, ET 1961; C.Westermann, 'Arten der Erzählung in der Genesis', in *Forschung am Alten Testament*, 1964, 9-91 (= *Die Verheissungen an die Väter*, 1976, 9-91).

Eissfeldt, §5,7,11-13; Fohrer, §8,9,12,40; Soggin, 1.V; Kaiser, §5; Schmidt, §5; Koch, §10,12-16.

3 The Legal Sphere

One of the most important functions of the community in which daily life runs its course is the preservation of the ordinances of social life. For that, every community needs specific principles and more or less detailed individual regulations to determine the pattern of social life, along with a clearly defined procedure to watch over and safeguard the
observance of these principles and rules and deter offences against

them. Both these features grow over the course of generations and centuries, but they can also continually undergo changes and transformations as a result of external or internal pressures. In this way a legal sphere comes into being which reflects the social and political structures and changes of a specific society while at the same time taking on an existence of its own.

In the social structure of the early period, in Israel, as in comparable cultures, the supreme head of a particular family, the 'father', was the sole legal authority in this sphere. This situation is still presupposed in some passages of the Old Testament, most clearly in Gen.16; in her dispute with the slave girl Hagar, Sarah appeals to Abraham with the words, 'May the wrong done to me be on you' (v.5); i.e., as *pater familias* he is responsible for removing the injustice and seeing that justice is done. He is accountable to no one, but has the sole power to decide, so that he can say to Sarah: 'Your maid is in your power' (v.6). It is also as head of the family that Judah exercises his jurisdiction in Gen.38 – in this case even by pronouncing the death penalty – alone and in an authoritarian way (v.24); moreover he is also the sole person to receive appeals and to pardon (vv.25f.).

We may assume that the clan had legal jurisdiction as a superior authority in those cases which concerned more than a single family. This authority was presumably exercised by the 'elders', i.e. by the heads of individual families who represented the clan in a common assembly. The Old Testament gives no examples of the exercise of judicial power by the clan. Presumably, however, clan organization is reflected in the institution of the 'elders'. This is evident, e.g., in Deut.21.18-21, where we are told that the 'elders of the city' are given a case to decide. (It is also evident here that in the circumstances, which had changed in the meantime, the *paterfamilias* no longer had any legal authority over his own son.)

The example just mentioned reflects the transition from family justice to local justice. The local community has become the basic legal authority and usually also the sole competent authority. It is also constituted as a 'legal assembly' (Köhler), by meeting 'in the gate' in order to decide cases put before it. Here, in accordance with a widespread but not undisputed view, not only the elders, but all the full citizens of the place, i.e. all the Israelite men who regularly lived there, had the right to speak and vote. (Women, children, slaves and 'strangers' [*gerim*], i.e. temporary residents or those who had settled but did not have full rights as citizens, were excluded. After the formation of the state, not only the legal community but also the king was the authority in particular legal issues, cf. e.g. II Sam.14; 15.2-6; I Kings 3.16-28; cf. Macholz.)

The cases presented to the local legal assembly could differ widely: accordingly the specific function of the legal assembly and the forms of discourse used there differed widely. Thus e.g. the legal assembly could merely serve to witness some legal business in which two citizens of a place had become involved, as e.g. in

Ruth 4.1-2. Here the legal question of the break up of family possessions in connection with the marriage of a widow is dealt with in a specially summoned legal assembly at the gate. The purchaser tells them, 'You are witnesses' (v.9f), and they explicitly confirm this fact (v.11).

Procedure

In many cases the legal assembly is brought in to settle a dispute or to pass judgment in a quarrel. The transition from dispute to legal process is marked by formulae which appear in a derivative form in prophetic sayings: 'Come now, let us reason together' (Isa.1.18), or, 'Let us together draw near for judgment' (Isa.41.1). Before the court the parties either continued their dispute and hoped for a settlement, or the injured party made an accusation. One example of this is the story of 'the judgment of Solomon' in I Kings 3.16-28, where one of the

Accusation

two women lays a charge against the other, presenting the case from her point of view. Further accusations appear in Deut.21.20 and perhaps in 22.14; in a transferred way the first part of the 'Song of the Vineyard'

→191

in Isaiah (Isa.5.1-7) is also an accusation which ends by calling on the audience to pronounce a legal verdict (v.3). In other cases the accusation is made through the statements of witnesses (I Kings 21.13) or introduced with a suggested verdict, e.g. 'This man is worthy of death'

→204

(Jer.26.10f.). (Jer.26 shows that towards the end of the monarchy royal officials exercised a form of justice of their own, cf. also II Chron. 19.5-11; it is hard to decide how this was related to local justice, cf. Macholz, 314ff.)

Defence

The accusation is matched by the speech for the defence, which can be recognized in the cases already mentioned (I Kings 3.22; Jer.26.12-15). In the latter instance, not only is there the defence made by the accused person himself but also one made by others who as it were act as defence counsel (vv.17-19; the verses probably belonged originally before v.16). However, there was no formal legal institution of the defence counsel; rather, each member of the legal assembly could speak in any function, so that the defendant could at the same time be a witness in favour of acquittal. Similarly, no clear distinction can be made between the prosecutor and the witness for the prosecution. – A variety of prophetic texts can be understood as adopting the genre of the speech for the defence, e.g. Jer.2.29-35 ('Why do you make this charge against me?', v.29) and Micah 6.1-5 ('What have I done to you?', v.3).

Confession

A confession by the accused evidently often consisted in a single word, *ḥattati*, 'I have sinned'. However, the Old Testament evidence of this derives not so much from formal legal processes as from disputes which are presented with forms taken from legal processes, e.g. the argument between Saul and David in I Sam. 26. Here David moves over from defence (v.18) to prosecution (v.20b), and Saul finally acknowledges his guilt (v.21); cf. also II Sam.12.13; 19.21.

Verdict

Similarly, the verdict probably also took the form of a short formula, e.g. 'You are innocent' (*ṣaddiq 'atta*), cf. Prov.24.24. In particular cases the other party in the trial also had to make a public declaration: 'She is innocent, and I am not' (Gen.38.26; cf. I Sam.24.16,18). The acquittal

in a fuller form might be, 'This man does not deserve death' (Jer.26.16); **Legal Sphere**
here the verdict called for by the prosecution (v.11, see above) is
explicitly rejected; or, 'He has no blood guilt' (Ex.*22.1*), or, with a view
to the consequences of the verdict: 'He must pay no compensation'
(Ex.*22.10,12,14*) or 'They shall not be killed' (Lev.29.20). The declaration of guilt was not made in general terms but indicated the nature
of the crime, similarly in a short formula, e.g. 'He is a murderer'
(Num.35.16-18,21), or perhaps 'He has shed blood' (Lev.17.4b; cf.
Ezek. 18.10; Gen.9.6). – In I Kings 3.27 we have a declaration, 'She is
the mother'.

Finally there is a statement of the consequences of the action, i.e. the Consequences
legal consequences which arise from the judgment, e.g. 'He shall pay
full compensation' (Ex.21.36; *22.2,5,13*), or compensation twofold
(Ex.*22.6,8*) or fourfold (II Sam.12.6). There is a similar short formula,
'He must be killed' (*mot yumat*), e.g. Num.35.16-18,21; Ex.21.12,15-
17, etc.). The manner of death can also be laid down, e.g. by burning
(Gen.38.24; Lev.20.14; 21.9) or stoning (Lev.20.2; Num.15.35). There
is a detailed ruling about consequences in I Kings 3.27: 'Give her the
child, do not kill it!'. Some scholars assume that in former times the
judgment in the gate was no more than an arbitration, in other words
that the 'verdict' was a suggestion to the parties and that the assembly
had no executive power to implement the legal consequences; however,
for a later period Deuteronomy presupposes that the verdict will be
carried out immediately (e.g. Deut.17.5; 22.21,23).

The basis for the decisions of the legal assembly was provided by Casuistic law
traditions which initially were handed down orally and later in writing.
These are above all 'casuistic' formulations of legal principle (Alt).
Their main characteristic is their conditional or 'casuistic' style: they
begin with a 'When', present a case and end by formulating the legal
consequences. Here, in the description of the case, the definition of the
situation, different possibilities are outlined; sometimes this results in
very complicated sentences. They often contain a main case, which in
Hebrew is introduced with *ki* (suppose that, when), and one or more
subsidiary cases, introduced by *'im* (if, suppose). For example, in
Ex.*22.6f.* the main case is posited like this: 'If (*ki*) a man delivers to his
neighbour money or goods to keep, and it is stolen out of the man's
house'; then follow two subsidiary cases, 'If (*'im*) the thief is found', and
'If the thief is not found'. The legal consequences of the two subordinate
cases are given: in the first instance the thief must restore what has been
stolen twofold, in the second case the person from whose house the
things have been stolen must proclaim his innocence by a solemn oath.
In other instances the subsidiary cases are divided further (e.g. Ex.21.7-
11: main case: v.7 subsidiary case 1a: v.8, 1b: v.10. 2b: v.11) or there
are not only two but three subsidiary cases (e.g. Ex.21.2-6: main case:
v.2; subsidiary case 1: v.3a; 2: v.3b; 3a: v.4; 3b: vv.5f.; see the tables in
Liedke, 31ff.)

Alt adduced Ex.21.18f. as an example of a very detailed individual case.

'When(*ki*) men quarrel and one strikes the other with a stone or with his fist and the man does not die but keeps his bed, then if (*'im*) the man rises again and was abroad with his staff, he that struck him shall be clear; only he shall pay for the loss of his time, and shall have him thoroughly healed.' Here the main case (in a quarrel, one person strikes another) is differentiated further: he has struck him with a stone or with his fist, i.e. not with a weapon, so that in principle he did not mean to wound or kill him. The person struck does not die (alternative: he dies) but is disabled (alternative: the blow has no serious consequences). The subsidiary case deals with the next phase. After some time the person who was struck can get up again and walk around (alternative: he remains bedridden and is unable to work). This is presumably the moment at which the case is presented for legal judgment. The differentiations in the main case show that the person who struck the blow did not act deliberately and that the person struck has not suffered any permanent harm. This produces the first legal consequence: the person who struck the blow pays no penalty. However, as the person struck has suffered damage and costs, there is a further consequence: the person who struck the blow must make good the material damage arising out of loss of work, and pay the costs of the doctor. We can easily see how similar cases with some differences (e.g. the alternatives indicated above) would have been treated, and this would have led to other legal consequences.

We can infer from the character of these legal maxims how a verdict was arrived at. The sentences do not present abstract norms of law, nor do they contain theoretical legal arguments; rather, these are specific individual cases which were taken as precedents because they were typical and were then used as the basis for later decisions in comparable cases.

Alt gave as the object of casuistic law 'those matters which we can see at once were within the competence of the local secular jurisdiction: the law of slavery, murder, compensation for bodily injuries, damage to stock and crops, the misappropriation of goods given in trust, and marriage laws' (92). He also conjectures that the Hebrew word *mišpat* denotes a legal statement with a casuistic form (cf. Ex.21.1); however, this conjecture is disputed (Liedke, 94ff.).

There are numerous parallels to the casuistic legal statements from the ancient Near East. The best known is the Babylonian Codex Hammurabi (eighteenth century BC). However, the common features do not arise from literary dependence, but from the fact that conditions of life and social structures partly correspond. Therefore comparisons are interesting and important, but we must keep in mind the independence of each individual legal sphere (cf. Boecker 1976).

Alt named law with an apodeictic formulation as the second main legal genre. It is distinguished from the casuistic if-style by the apodeictic and unconditioned way in which it is formulated. In Alt's view, its Sitz im Leben would seem to be not the balanced negotiations of a legal assembly but rather a solemn presentation by an authority endowed with supreme power. Moreover, in this sphere of law, as opposed to the casuistic sphere, Alt argued that there were no parallels from outside Israel; he regarded it as 'related exclusively to the Israelite nation and the religion of YHWH' (124); it was set forth at the sacral act of the renewal of the covenant between YHWH and Israel, which took place every seven years at the Feast of Tabernacles. **Legal Sphere**

Since then, scholars have discussed Alt's theory intensively. First, they have established that it is impossible to talk in terms of a uniform genre of apodeictic law. The legal formulations brought together by Alt differ widely in genre and Sitz im Leben. Some of the statements, the prohibitions, do not strictly belong in the sphere of law, but lie as it were just outside it, in instruction in the family or clan (Gerstenberger); here it is not a matter of making good a breach in legal order, but of preventing infringement of the law from the start, by education. So the statements are prohibitions, but do not give legal consequences. Behind these statements, as Alt rightly sensed, we can see an authority – here that of the father of the family (Liedke, 120ff.). Prohibitions →83f.

Other sentences belong completely in the legal sphere, so that we can speak of apodeictic legal statements. These give situations and the legal consequences. The basic difference from casuistic legal statements is that they do not analyse a case and lay down the legal consequences, but lay down the legal consequence for offences against a particular injunction even before a particular situation arises. Again an authority can be seen behind them. In the narrative Gen.26.7-11 it is the king who proclaims an apodeictic law: 'Anyone who touches this man or his wife must die' (v.11; cf. also II Kings 10.19,24); in other instances it is the commander of the army (I Sam.11.7; cf. II Kings 11.8,15) or the father of the family (Gen.31.32). Apodeictic legal statements also appear in narrative texts as a direct word from YHWH (Gen.4.15; Ex.19.13b; Josh.7.15).

In all the examples cited, the penalty announced is death. This also holds for numerous statements of apodeictic law which occur in the various collections of legal texts in the Old Testament. We find particularly often the stereotyped formula *mot yumat*, with the intensifying absolute infinitive: 'He shall surely die'. For example it appears in the statements adduced by Alt from Ex.21.12,15-17, etc. Here we can also see the formation of sequences of apodeictic clauses with a similar construction, which Alt also stresses. This is certainly connected with the fact that apodeictic law was 'proclaimed' solemnly by the authority in question, so that those affected by it were well aware of the limits which they were not to overstep. This again happened first of all in the most intimate circle of family or clan, as is evident, say, from the sequences in Ex.21.12ff. and Lev.20.11-13, dealing with situations predominantly related to this sphere. This also explains why the content is so close to the prohibitions (cf. Lev.18; 20.11-13). However, it remains questionable whether one can speak of an independent 'law of death' which grew out of prohibitions (Schulz). Law of death

→83

In addition to the series of crimes worthy of death, Alt also produced a series of crimes to be cursed, all of which are given with the same term *'arur*, 'be cursed' (Deut.27). However, there is an essential difference. The curse, unlike the death penalty, cannot be implemented by human Curse

→154f.

beings. This series is above all concerned with things which have happened in secret. In these instances the curse is pronounced and it 'seeks' the perpetrator. I Samuel 14 is an interesting example: the order not to eat is backed up by an apodeictic statement, to the effect that anyone who transgresses it is accursed (vv.24,28). The death penalty is then imposed, in just as formal a way, on the culprit, who is discovered by a process of lot (v.44). Here we can also see very clearly how close apodeictic law is to the sacral and cultic sphere: the pronouncement of the curse involves the deity, and conversely, it is cultic matters which have the weight of the curse behind them (e.g. Deut.27.15). This brings up the question of the relationship between the legal sphere in the narrower sense as discussed here and the sacral sphere (for the whole question cf. Schottroff).

However, apodeictic law also has connections with normal legal procedures. It seems likely that once apodeictic sentences existed and were known, they could also be brought into legal proceedings. This is probably the basis for the juxtaposition of casuistic and apodeictic

→141 sentences in the Book of the Covenant; we also find the same thing in other collections of law (cf. e.g. Lev.24.15,17,19 [casuistic] with v.16 [apodeictic] or Num.9.10-12.14 with v.13).

Bibliography

A.Alt, 'The Origins of Israelite Law' (1934), in *Essays on Old Testament History and Religion*, ET 1966, 79-132; H.J.Boecker, *Redeformen des Rechtslebens im Alten Testament*, ²1970; id., *Recht und Gesetz im Alten Testament und im Alten Orient*, 1976; L.Köhler, 'Justice in the Gate', in *Hebrew Man*, ET 1956, 149-76; G.Liedke, *Gestalt und Bezeichnung alttestamentlicher Rechtssätze*, 1971: G.C.Macholz, 'Die Stellung des Königs in der israelitischen Gerichtsverfassung', *ZAW* 84, 1972, 157-82; id., 'Zur Geschichte der Justizorganisation in Juda', ibid., 314-40; W.Schottroff, *Der altisraelitische Fluchspruch*, 1969; H.Schulz, *Das Todesrecht im Alten Testament*, 1969; I.L.Seeligmann, 'Zur Terminologie für das Gerichtsverfahren im Wortschatz des biblischen Hebräisch', in *Hebräische Wortforschung, FS W.Baumgartner*, SVT 16, 1967, 251-78.

Eissfeldt, §8; Fohrer, §8; Kaiser, §6; Schmidt, §9.

4 The Cult

Religion forms an important element in the life of any community in the ancient Near East – as in comparable societies of other cultural groups and periods. It is not primarily a matter for the individual, but for the community as a whole, so that its practice is one of the most important features of life.

The phenomena of religion and the cult in which it is practised are
conditioned by changes in the forms of life of the community in

question. The transition from a nomadic way of life to a sedentary state and cultivation of the land brought with it far reaching changes for Israelite society. One substantial difference already lay in the fact that the nomadic cult was not primarily associated with fixed places of worship but was practised wherever the nomads stopped. Therefore the sanctuaries and cult objects had to be 'portable'. We can assume that the ark and the 'tent of meeting' are part of the nomadic traditions of the Israelite tribes.

That does not exclude the possibility that particular holy places also play a role in the religion of nomadic groups. Thus Sinai was a nomadic place of pilgrimage. Other places of religious significance are mentioned in the traditions about the wilderness period, as for example the oasis sanctuaries of Massa and Meribah (Ex.17.7; Num.20.13) or an altar built in the wilderness (Ex.17.15). Even the 'burning bush' (Ex.3.2f.) was probably a holy place in the wilderness. The cultic usages and ceremonies were similarly determined by the nomadic way of life. Thus the communion sacrifice (*zebah*) was a nomadic custom: any slaughter of an animal from the herd, the most valuable possession of the nomads, had a religious character, in that a specific part of the animal, thought to be especially valuable, was handed over to the deity by burning it. The rest was eaten in a communal ceremony by which those who sacrificed entered into communion with the deity and with one another. So we also hear of the 'meal offering' or the 'fellowship offering'.

The passover festival also comes from the nomadic tradition. It was probably originally celebrated each year when the nomads changed the pastures of their flocks, as they set out at the beginning of the dry period from their pastures in the steppes to those within cultivated land (Rost). Smearing the entrances to their tents with the blood of a slaughtered lamb (cf. Ex.12.7,13) was intended to provide protection for men and animals from the demons of the wilderness during the dangerous journey.

Conditions underwent a fundamental change with the transition to a settled existence. Now the cult was practised essentially in certain fixed local sanctuaries. Here the Israelites partly took over already existing Canaanite sanctuaries with the traditions observed there (thus e.g. in Bethel, cf. Gen.28.10ff.; see below) and partly founded new sanctuaries (thus e.g. in Beersheba, cf. Gen.21.33). The festival cycle was also taken over. The three great annual feasts are marked by the agricultural year (cf. Ex.23.14-17; 34.18,22f.; Deut.16.16): the 'feast of unleavened bread' (*mazzot*) occurred at the beginning of the grain harvest (bread was baked from the new barley, which was the earliest grain to appear, without 'old leaven', cf. Ex.13.3-10); the 'harvest festival' (also 'feast of weeks', Ex.34.22; Deut.16.9,16) occurred at the end of the grain harvest (i.e the harvest of wheat, Ex.34.22). The 'feast of winegathering' (also the 'feast of tabernacles', Deut.16.13,16) came right at the end of the harvest year. The feast of *mazzot* was later combined with the passover into one feast and was 'historicized' with reference to the exodus from Egypt (cf. Ex.23.15; 34.18; Deut.16.1-8).

Cult
Nomadic traditions
→8

→19f.

→15

→143

Communion sacrifice
→19, 98

Passover
→19

Pilgrimage festivals

Moreover, the feast of tabernacles, which originally marked the change of year, was preceded by a special New Year's Day (Lev.23.24; Num.29.1) and the 'Day of Atonement' was inserted between the two (23.27; cf. Num.29.7). This produced a great festival cycle lasting three weeks, when taken with the seven-day celebration of the feast of tabernacles (Lev.23.24ff.; Num.29.12ff.).

The great annual feasts were pilgrimage feasts, and it was a religious obligation to take part in them. All the men (they were the only ones to be allowed to take part in the public cult) gathered at the sanctuaries (Ex.23.17; 34.23; Deut.16.16). First of all the festivals were celebrated at different local or regional sanctuaries. Thus we learn of a 'YHWH feast' in Shiloh which was connected with dancing in the vineyards (Judg.21.19ff.); this could be a reference to the grape harvest. I Samuel 1 describes a regular pilgrimage by Elkanah, Samuel's father, to Shiloh, to which many Israelites came for regular sacrifices (2.11f.); there was a temple there with the ark of God (3.3; cf.Ps.78.60; Jer.7.12,14). Amos and Hosea mention Bethel (Amos 4.4; 5.5; Hos.4.15; cf. Gen.28.10ff.; 35.1ff.; I Kings 12.26ff., etc.) and Gilgal (ibid.; cf. Josh.3-5, etc.), and Amos also mentions Beersheba (ibid., cf. Gen.21.33; 26.23-25, etc.) as pilgrimage sanctuaries. Mamre in the south, and Shechem, Ophrah and Dan in the north are mentioned as sanctuaries, as are Mizpah (I Sam 7.5f.; cf. I Macc.3.46), Gibeon (I Kings 3.4) and Mount Tabor (Deut.33.19). These traditions are quite random and of varying historical weight; however, they clearly demonstrate that there were also sanctuaries with more than local significance in all parts of the land outside the local 'high places'. Later, Jerusalem increasingly became the central sanctuary after David had brought the ark of YHWH there, and Solomon had given it its final resting place in the holy of holies in the temple.

Cult legends The holiness of particular places was explained by narratives which we may call cult legends. Thus the story of Jacob's dream in Bethel (Gen.28.10-22) explains why there was a sanctuary there: Jacob 'discovered' the holiness of the place by chance (cf. vv.16f.; we can therefore also call this a 'discovery saga'), erected a pillar there (vv.18,22), gave the place its cultic name *bet-'el*,'house of God', and finally also provided a basis for the payment of tithes to the sanctuary (v.22). This text was presumably retold and re-enacted ceremonially within the framework of some cultic occasion as a *hieros logos*; thus at the same time it formed part of the liturgy of the cult at the sanctuary of Bethel. (However, this complex narrative now also contains elements of the 'call' of Jacob, cf. esp.v.15; a cultic discovery saga and a call legend are similarly also combined in the narrative about the 'burning bush' in Ex.3.1ff.) In Gen.35.6f. a further note provides aetiological legitimation for the cult at the altar of Bethel.

The cult legend of the sanctuary of Shechem is given in Gen.33.18-20 in a very brief form which does not amount to an extended narrative. In Gen.16.13f. the element of the cult legend appears within an ethnological saga. The narrative of Gen.18 is also often understood as a cult legend of the sanctuary of Mamre, though this feature too has now been displaced by the announcement of the birth of Isaac. There are further sanctuary legends in Judg.6.11-24 (Ophrah) and Judg.17f. (Dan). Two sanctuary legends have come down to us in connection with Jerusalem: the narrative of David's building of the altar on the 'threshing floor of Araunah' in II Sam 24.16-25 perhaps goes back to an earlier pre-Israelite legend of the foundation of a cult (cf. Rupprecht, 5ff.): the 'ark narrative' in I Sam.4-6 and II Sam.6 contains the aetiology of the cult in the Israelite ark sanctuary in the Jerusalem temple.

In some texts the pattern of the cult legend is reduced to its most basic elements: the epiphany of the deity and the building of an altar (Gen.12.6f.; 26.24f.; in 12.8 there is not even an epiphany); here we probably have a later literary imitation of this genre.

Not only sacred places, but also festivals, cultic objects and cultic customs were also founded and legitimated by appropriate legends. Thus the instructions for the feast of the passover in Ex.12 are developed wholly out of the narrative of the oppression of the Israelites in Egypt and the plagues; even individual details of the passover rite are explained in these terms (cf.vv.11,13). The book of Esther is the festal legend of the feast of Purim (cf. Esther 9.20ff.). The 'brazen serpent' in the temple of Jerusalem (II Kings 18.4) is legitimated by the legend in Num.21.4-9 (in reality it was probably a Canaanite cult symbol). Sometimes there are just short aetiological comments: thus perhaps Lev.9.24 is intended to be grounds for the special holiness of the altar fire in Jerusalem; I Sam.5.5 contains a reference to a cultic practice in the Philistine temple of Dagon in Ashdod, and Gen.*32.33* to a food tabu.

The great annual feasts governed the yearly rhythm of cultic events. They have found expression in festal calendars (Lev.23; Num.28f.; Deut.16.1-17). These calendars show that sacrifices were an essential part of the feast. (However, this fades completely into the background in Deut.16 – though that is a special feature of Deuteronomistic theology, since Ex.32.5f.; Amos 5.21f., etc, clearly show that sacrifice and festival belong together.) One could properly call Num.28f. a sacrifical calendar; here we have not only sacrifices at the annual feasts, but also the sacrifices to be offered daily (28.3-8), together with additional sacrifices on the sabbath (v.9) and at new moon (vv.11-15), in accordance with sacrificial practice (for the daily sacrifice cf. II Kings 16.15; Ex.29.38ff.).

We are given little detailed information in the Old Testament about how the cult was carried on in detail. The procedures were certainly known to all who took part in them by being handed on from generation to generation, and for the priests in particular they were part of a professional knowledge which was taught and handed down by word of mouth. We have a ritual for only one feast, the 'Day of Atonement' (Lev.16; it is called *yom ha-kippurim* in Lev.23.27). However, this describes only the internal rites to be performed by the priest, at which otherwise no one might be present (v.17). Only rest from work and fasting is prescribed for the community (vv.29,31).

Other instructions for the cult have been preserved in rituals. The sacrificial rituals in Lev.1-7 display a strict form in which the individual phases of the sacrificial action are closely described, e.g. Lev.1.1-9: bringing of the sacrificial animal (v.3); laying hands on the head of the sacrificial animal (v.4); sacrifice (v.5a); sprinkling blood on the altar (v.5b); dividing up the sacrificial animal (v.6); burning it (vv.7-9). Verses 10-13 have the same structure as the individual sections of chs.3 and 4. The other chapters contain further different formal elements which reflect a long history in the development of these cultic regulations (cf. Rendtorff 1967; there are further regulations for sacrifices in Ex.29; Lev.8f.; Num.15; Ezek.45f.).

These texts also clearly indicate the history of the individual kinds of sacrifice and their relationship. The 'burnt offering' ('ola), in which the whole animal was assigned to YHWH through burning, comes first (Lev.1; 6.1-6). Then follows the 'meal offering' (minha, Lev.2; 6.7-16), consisting of milled grain; this was usually not a separate sacrifice, but was offered along with the animal sacrifices (cf. Num.15.1-16, where 'drink offerings' of wine are also mentioned as additional sacrifices). Third in Lev.3 is a sacrifice which came about through a combination of the 'communion sacrifice' (zebah), which was originally nomadic, with a 'treaty sacrifice' (šelamim), producing the zebah-šelamim; the rendering 'peace offering', which is often used, comes from the Septuagint, which has connected the term with the word šalom, 'peace, salvation'. However, the significance of this sacrifice evidently declined, since in Lev.6f. it is put at the end of the series (7.11f.). It has been displaced by another sacrifice: the 'sin offering' (hattat) has been moved forward from fourth (Lev.4) to third place (Lev.6.17-23). Its increasing significance can also seen from the fact that in the sacrificial calendar in Num.28f. it has been added to the new moon and other festal sacrifices (28.15,22,30; 29.5,11,16 etc.); in some lists of sacrifices it even comes first (e.g. Ex.29.10ff.; Lev.8.14ff.; 9.2,3f.). It is unclear how it differs from the 'guilt offering' ('ašam, Lev.5.14ff.; 7.1ff.).

The rituals do not say much about the significance of the sacrifices. That is not in fact their function, as they are above all meant to ensure that the sacrifice is offered properly. However, at some points particular formulas give us an insight into the understanding of the sacrifices. Thus at the end of the 'sin offering' it is said: 'the priest is to make atonement (kipper) for him, and so he will be forgiven' (Lev.4.20,26,31,35, etc.). Thus the priest makes atonement (above all through the blood rite) – but YHWH himself grants forgiveness. This understanding of atonement is also transferred to the 'burnt offering': according to Lev.1.4, laying hands on the head of the sacrificial animal effects atonement and makes the person sacrificing 'well-pleasing' to YHWH. That the sacrifice has been performed correctly is confirmed by a declaratory formula: 'ola hu', 'This is a burnt offering' (Lev.1.13,17; cf. 2.6,15; 4.21,24, etc.; cf. Rendtorff 1963).

Prescriptions for purity of various kinds (e.g. Lev.11-15; Num. 5f.; 9; 19) also belong in the cultic sphere, since the impurity from which they are meant to provide protection or purification is primarily

exclusion from the cult. 'Purity' and 'holiness' belong closely together Cult
(cf. Lev.10.10).

Regulations about piety and purity are often designated *tora*. Thus we regularly
find 'This is the *tora* of the burnt offering', etc., as a title in Lev.6f. (*6.2,7,18*;
7.1,11; cf. 7.37). The word *tora* appears in the closing section of each of the
prescriptions for purity (11.46; 12.7; 13.5; 14.32,54,57; 15.32; in 14.2 it also
appears in the title). So here, in addition to the further comprehensive
understanding of *tora*, we have a closer one, which reflects the cultic side of this →163
complex term.

We learn little from the Old Testament about the course of festivals
and cultic actions. Only rarely is the holding of a festival explicitly
mentioned, and it is always in special circumstances which are stressed:
the passover in Josh 5.10f. and in II Kings 23.21ff.; the feast of
tabernacles in Ezra 3.4 and in Neh.8.14ff. In I Kings 8 the date in v.2
implies the feast of tabernacles. Finally, the note in I Kings 9.25, that
Solomon offered sacrifices three times in the year, points to the
celebration of the three annual festivals.

Thus we can only discover details of what happened in the cult
indirectly. Our most important source for this is the Psalms. However, Psalms
they essentially reflect the cult only from the perspective of the
comunity. They are not orders of service for the priests, but are rather
to be understood as the 'hymn book' of the temple community of
Jerusalem. It is hardly possible now to establish whether the Psalter
also contains psalms which have their origin in other sanctuaries; in the
form which has come down to us, they were without doubt sung at the
temple in Jerusalem, and also collected there. Texts from very different
times clearly stand side by side, as also happens in our modern
hymnbooks.

Jerusalem, the 'city of God', with the temple, the 'abode' of YHWH, Hymns
is itself the theme of a number of psalms which can be described as
songs of Zion (Pss.46; 48; 76; 84; 87; 122, cf.137). They praise the city Songs of Zion
of God and the God who dwells in it and protects it; here we clearly
have echoes of Canaanite conceptions, which are familiar to us particularly from Ugaritic texts (cf. Schmidt, §13). These psalms also make
many references to specific cultic procedures: Ps.122 speaks of the
pilgrimage of the participants in the festival to Jerusalem, as does Ps.84.
Psalm 48.13 issues an invitation to a procession round the city. Perhaps
the invitation 'Behold and see the works of YHWH' (Ps.*46.9*; cf. 66.5)
also indicates a representation in a cultic drama of the events described
in the psalms.

Other psalms also suggest similar cultic proceedings: processions with the
ark underlie Ps.132 (cf. esp.vv.7f. and Num.10.35f.) and Ps.24.7ff. (YHWH →33, 108
enthroned invisibly on the ark will enter through the temple gates.) Ps.26.6
speaks of going round the altar, Ps.118.27 of a ring dance at which perhaps
ropes or garlands were thrown round the 'horns' of the altar. Psalm 100.2,4 is
an invitation to enter though the gates into the forecourts of the temple; Ps.132.7
an invitation to enter the 'abode' of YHWH (the temple) and to fall down before

his footstool (the ark); cf. also Ps.95.6 etc. In Pss.15; 24.3-6 we have entrance liturgies, with a question from the pilgrims about what is needed to take part in the temple cult, and the reply of the priests (these are also called 'gate liturgies' or '*tora* liturgies', the latter because of the answer given by the priests).

The songs of Zion belong to the wider genre of hymns. Since Gunkel, this term has been used to cover the large group of psalms whose essential content is the praise of God. (Westermann proposed the designation 'descriptive psalm of praise' for them – in contrast to the 'song of thanksgiving', which he designated the 'narrative psalm of praise'; however, the two genres can be distinguished clearly, cf. Crüsemann.) They show many affinities to the cultic hymns from the ancient Near Eastern world.

Pariticipial
hymns

This is particularly true of the 'participial hymn', which makes statements about God in the form of participial clauses. In them YHWH is praised above all as creator and sustainer of the world, as happens with other gods in many hymns from the Near Eastern world.

Crüsemann (153) has conjectured that the formula 'YHWH is his name', which often occurs in participial hymns, can be seen as an adoption of hymnic traditions from the ancient Near Eastern world, thus claiming them exclusively for YHWH. However, this formula does not appear in the hymns handed down in the book of Psalms – is this by chance? – but above all in the hymnic passages

→222
→194f., 202f.,
204f.

in the book of Amos (4.1; 5.8; 9.6), in Deutero-Isaiah (51.15; 54.5, etc.) and in the book of Jeremiah (10.16; 31.24; 33.2 etc.) (cf. Crüsemann, 95ff.).

Imperative
hymns

In the second basic form of the hymn, the 'imperative hymn', those taking part in the cult are called upon to praise YHWH. The 'Song of Miriam' in Ex.15.21 has the briefest form of this hymn. It also contains the basic elements of the form. The imperative invitation, 'Sing to YHWH', is followed by statements about YHWH and his mighty acts for Israel, introduced by a *ki* ('for' or 'indeed'): 'He raised himself up on high, horse and chariot he cast into the sea.' Psalm 117 shows the same short, pregnant form. However, the brief refrain, 'Praise YHWH! Indeed he is God, and his praise endures for ever', is also an independent hymn. This is evident above all from Ps.107.1, where from v.2 on there is a list of all those who are to sing this hymn. (Cf. also Ps.106.1; 118.1,29;136.1, etc.)

This basic form has been further developed in many ways, e.g. by expanding the invitation in the imperative (Ps.100), the statements about YHWH (in Ps.136, each of them is introduced by *le*), or by what is sometimes a very extended expansion of the content (Ps.105). Finally, both forms, the imperative and the participial hymn, are combined in a series of psalms, so that the invitation to praise YHWH and the celebration of his mighty acts in creation and the salvation history of Israel are fused together into a new unity (Ps.33; 113; 135; 136 [see above]; 147, etc.). They doubtless have their Sitz im Leben in the great feasts in the temple in Jerusalem, at which YHWH was worshipped as the God of Israel and as the creator and lord of the world.

The hymns to YHWH as king stand out as a special group (Ps.47; 93; 96-99). They celebrate YHWH as the king, usually with the stereotyped phrase *YHWH malak*, 'YHWH is king' (Ps.93.1; 96.10; 97.1; 99.1; in Ps.*47.9, malak 'elohim*, 'God is king'). Mowinckel translated the phrase 'YHWH *has become* king' and inferred from this an 'enthronement festival of YHWH' on the basis of Babylonian parallels. This enthronement was supposed to have been celebrated annually at the New Year festival. However, this theory has now been almost universally abandoned. Still, we might assume that the praise of YHWH as king had a special place in the festal liturgy, perhaps bound up with a processsion of the ark (cf. Ps.24.7ff., where YHWH entering on the ark is designated king).

(For the royal psalms see II.5 below.)

→108, 248

The majority of hymns are songs sung by the community assembled for worship. Alongside this we find the independent genre of the individual hymn, in which the worshipper speaks in the first person singular (Ps.8; 104; Ex.15.1-18). This genre was originally closely connected with particular lamentations. Its independent existence indicates a development in which the psalms were no longer composed and used as liturgical texts in the narrower sense, but were also religious poetry without a specific Sitz im Leben in the liturgy.

In addition to the regular cult at the great annual festivals, there were also services for special occasions. Services of lamentation and intercession were arranged above all in situations of distress which affected the people as a whole (cf. I Kings 8.33,35,37). They were probably associated with the public 'fasts' (*zom*) which were proclaimed on such occasions (cf.Jer.36.9f.; II Chron.20.1-13), and which also included other mourning rites like putting on a coarse mourning garment (*sak*), public weeping and lamentation, and so on (cf. Joel 1.13f.). However, such services are seldom mentioned explicitly, though they are already presupposed in the early period (cf. Judg.20.26; I Sam.7.5f.), and II Chron. 20 offers an example from a post-exilic perspective, cf. also Joel 2.15-17. It emerges from Zech.7.3,5; 8.19 that after the exile certain fast days were observed regularly in commemoration of the capture of Jerusalem by the Babylonians (in the fourth month, cf. Jer.39.2), the destruction of the temple (in the fifth month, cf. II Kings 25.8f.) and other events. Some of the examples of the lamentation of the people which have come down to us speak explicitly of the destruction of the temple (Pss.74.3-8; 79.1-3) and were therefore composed only in the exilic or post-exilic period. Others also give political and military threats or catastrophes as reasons for the lamentation (Ps.44; 60; 80; 83, cf. also Lamentations, esp. ch.5), though the connection with particular historical events often remains uncertain. However, it may well be that the popular lamentations which have come down to us also contain earlier elements, though in their present form they have been stamped by their use in exilic and post-exilic liturgies.

→267ff.

Bound up in these psalms with a description of distress we find the lament, often with the question 'Why?' (Ps.*44.24*; 74.1,11; 79.10; *80.13*), or 'How long?' (Ps.74.10; 79.5; *80.5*), and a petition for deliverance and restoration of the people and punishment of the enemy. There are often references back to earlier acts of YHWH which are formulated in hymnic style as an address to YHWH (Ps.*44.2-4*; 74.12-17; *80.9-12*); in Ps.*44.5-9* there follows an expression of trust, while Pss.79.13; *80.19* contain a vow constantly to thank and call on YHWH after the deliverance. This hardly refers to special songs of thanksgiving from the people (for which there is no evidence); the reference, rather, is to the usual liturgy with its varied hymns of praise.

Not only the people or the cultic community as a whole, but also an individual, could appear in the temple to pray. That probably did not happen within the regular liturgy of the community but either on feast days outside the official fasts (which we can infer from, e.g., the 'great congregation' in Ps.*22.26*) or quite independently. The lamentations could also be uttered outside the temple, if that was called for by the situation of the suppliant, whereas the thanksgivings had their fixed setting in the temple.

The lamentations of the individual are numerically by far the largest group in the psalms which have come down to us. However, only rarely do they indicate the situation of the suppliant. There is a remarkable tension between the descriptions of suffering, which often seem very personal, and the usually vague statements about what the suffering consists of. The reason for this is certainly that usually these are not individual poems, but cultic formulas which are used again and again and therefore are framed in such general terms that they can be used by quite different suppliants.

Two themes above all stand out as occasions for a lamentation: illness and enemies. Both are often connected, but there are a number of psalms which enable us to make a fundamental distinction. For example, Pss.38; 88 can clearly be seen as prayers by a sick person (cf. Seybold). It is also evident here that the enemies are the 'friends and kinsmen' (Ps.*38.12*; *88.19*) who spurn the sick person, as we also hear in the case of Job's friends. In some of these psalms enemies are mentioned at much greater length (e.g. Pss.22; 69). In Ps.*22.4-6*, the individual suffering of the suppliant is at the same time put in the wider context of the history of Israel since the time of the fathers, and in Ps.*77.6,12,15ff.* even in the history of the acts of YHWH 'from primal times'.

In another group of psalms, persecution by enemies is the dominant theme. These prayers of the persecuted can often be recognized from the fact that the suppliant has to defend himself against serious charges and that God himself is called on to decide his case (e.g. Pss.7; 17; 26, etc.). They perhaps belong in the context of a cultic legal procedure and are to be understood as prayers of a defendant who asks God to pass judgment (cf. Beyerlin). In some psalms the sin of the suppliant against God has become the dominant theme (above all Pss.51; 130; the church tradition recognizes seven 'penitential psalms': Pss.6; 32; 38; 51; 102; 130; 143). In yet others the theme of trust from the lamentations has become independent, so that these can be described as songs of trust (e.g. Pss. 16; 23; 62 etc.).

The lamentations often end with a vow that the suppliant will thank God for the help and deliverance that he hopes for. Sometimes there is express mention of the sacrifices that the suppliant will offer (Pss.27.6; 54.8; *56.13*; cf. *22.26f.*). However, the word *toda*, which in Ps.*56.13* also means 'thank-offering, can also denote a 'song', as is evident from the parallelism in Ps.*69.31*, and many lamentations explicitly promise a hymn of thanksgiving (Pss.*7.18; 13.6; 61.9*). Here the connection with the individual thanksgiving is clear. (It is another question whether this expresses a 'spiritualizing' of the sacrifice [Hermisson].)

Often the certainty of being heard is already expressed within the lamentation. This sudden 'change of mood' probably arises from the fact that the person lamenting is promised by a priest that his petition will be heard (cf. I Sam.1.17). This enables him to continue, 'YHWH *has* heard my loud weeping' (Ps.*6.9*; cf. 28.6; 54.9; *56.10*, etc.). This 'oracle of salvation' from the priest has not been handed down to us in the psalms, as they do not contain the full order of the liturgy but only the parts to be spoken or sung by the laity; Begrich has inferred its existence from the way in which the oracle is taken over in Deutero-Isaiah.

→121f.

Songs of thanksgiving

The individual thanksgiving was originally connected directly with the offering of a sacrifice of thanksgiving, which is explicitly designated as a 'thanksgiving sacrifice' (*zebaḥ-toda*) e.g. in Ps.116.17 (cf. Lev.7.12ff.). In offering the sacrifice to YHWH, the suppliant addresses him in the second person (e.g. Pss. *30.2ff.*; 66.13ff.; 116.8). However, the thanksgivings also contain passages in which the suppliant speaks of YHWH in the third person (e.g. *30.5f.*; 66.16ff.; 116.1f.); these are evidently addressed to those taking part in the sacrificial meal who are gathered around him, as a proclamation of YHWH's help. The thanksgivings are stamped by this way of speaking in two directions, in thanksgiving and proclamation, which sometimes alternate quite frequently. In both elements the indication of the distress and the deliverance of the suppliant is a basic element.

Thus the psalms give us a great many insights into Israelite worship. However, we must remember that here a good deal remains hypothetical because we can usually infer details of the cult only indirectly from the psalms, with the result that new exegetical insights constantly change our picture. Nor can we assign all the psalms which have come down to us in the Old Testament to a specific genre. That is partly because of our inadequate knowledge of the cult and partly also because changes have come about in the course of time, so that psalms were written with no relation to a specific cultic happening (e.g. the individual hymns), but as vehicles for theological reflections or to provide teaching (or both). This is particularly clear in a number of psalms in which wisdom thinking emerges, psalms which originally had no direct connections with the cult. Sometimes there are only indiviudal elements of wisdom within a psalm (e.g. Ps.25.8-10, 12-14; *39.5-7*; *40.5f.*), but sometimes this affects whole psalms, so that we can call them wisdom psalms (e.g.

→108ff.

Pss.1; 34, esp. vv.*12ff.*; 37; 49; 112; 128, and perhaps also 73; 139). The *tora* psalms *19.8ff.*; 119 (cf. Ps.1) are also close to the wisdom psalms.

The psalms have distinct poetic formal characteristics, of a kind which also occur in other genres in the Old Testament, e.g. in prophetic sayings and wisdom sayings. The basic, and dominant, stylistic means is parallelism: as a rule the verses are in two parts, and the two parts are related in a particular way. Two basic forms can be recognized.

In synonymous parallelism the content of the first half of the verse is repeated in a varied way in the second, e.g. 'But his delight is in the *tora* of YHWH/ and on his *tora* he meditates day and night' (Ps.1.2), where the central word *tora* is repeated; or, 'Why do the nations conspire/ and the peoples plot in vain?'(Ps.2.1) – here two synonymous nouns are used: *goyim*, peoples, and *l*ᵉ*ummim*, nations; or 'YHWH, rebuke me not in thy anger/ nor chasten me in thy wrath' (Ps.6.2) – here noun and verb are varied by a synonym in the same grammatical form. This indicates the variety which can be achieved by the form; it is helped by the large number of Hebrew words which can be used as synonyms in particular contexts (conversely, this poetic style also helped to produce synonyms).

In antithetical parallelism the two halves of the verse make opposite statements, e.g. 'For YHWH knows the way of the righteous/ but the way of the wicked will perish' (Ps.1.6). Here the word 'way' is repeated, but at the same time the fate of the righteous and of the wicked is contrasted; or 'For all the gods of the peoples are idols/ but YHWH has made the heavens' (Ps.96.5). This form of parallelism occurs above all in wisdom sayings, which are largely dominated by the contrast between the wise and the foolish or the righteous and the wicked.

→109

The two-membered verse structure is also used often without it being possible to recognize parallelism of content in either sense. This is then described as 'synthetic' parallelism, but the expression does not mean much. Often the thought runs on from the first to the second half of the verse without a break in content, or there is an intensification, a statement about cause and effect, or some other effect. Many different designations have been proposed for this, but they are far from covering all the phenomena. Occasionally the parallelism is also extended by two whole lines of verse being in parallelism. There are also frequent elements of parallelism in the artistic prose of the Old Testament.

The reason why the parallelism is not only (and perhaps not primarily) dictated by the content of the clauses lies above all in the metric structure of Hebrew poetry. However, it is not possible to define the laws of metre with certainty. There have been two different attempts to solve this problem (cf. Horst). The system of accentuation begins from the fact that the rhythm of the verse corresponds with the rhythm of the words, so that the accent on the individual words determines the rhythm of the clauses (or means that the words must be chosen by the poet in such a way that their accentuation fits in with the verse). As the words are of different length, there is a varied number of unstressed syllables (up to three) between two stressed syllables (stresses), and sometimes none at all. The alternating system counts on a regular change between stressed and unstressed syllables, so that the accent in the verse often does not correspond with the accent on the word.

Neither of these systems has become clearly established, though the majority of exegetes tend towards the system of accentuation, because it corresponds better to the natural rhythm of Hebrew. However, there is wide agreement on one basic feature; both halves of a verse usually have the same number of stressed syllables (accentuated predominantly 3:3, alternating 4:4). The dirge (*qina*) is a characteristic exception; here the second half of the verse is shorter (3:2 or 4:3), giving a dying (or limping) rhythm (cf. e.g. Amos 5.2).

→82

Bibliography

J.Begrich, 'Das priesterliche Heilsorakel', *ZAW* 52, 1934, 81-92 (= *GS*, 217-31); W.Beyerlin, *Die Rettung der Bedrängten in den Feindpsalmen der Einzelnen auf institutionelle Zusammenhänge untersucht*, 1970; F.Crüsemann, *Studien zur Formgeschichte von Hymnus und Danklied in Israel*, 1969; H.Gunkel/J.Begrich, *Einleitung in die Psalmen*, 1933 (³1975); H.-J.Hermisson, *Sprache und Ritus im altisraelitischen Kult. Zur 'Spiritualisierung' der Kultbegriffe im Alten Testament*, 1965; F.Horst, 'Die Kennzeichen der hebräischen Poesie', *TR* 21. 1953, 97-121; H.J.Kraus, *Worship in Israel*, ET 1966; id., *Psalmen* (BK), ⁵1978 (esp. Introduction); S.Mowinckel, *Psalmenstudien II. Das Thronbesteigungsfest Jahwäs und der Ursprung der Eschatologie*, 1922 (1961); R.Rendtorff, *Die Gesetze in der Priesterschrift*, ²1963; id., *Studien zur Geschichte des Opfers im Alten Israel*, 1967; L.Rost, 'Weidewechsel und altisraelitischer Festkalender', *ZDPV* 66, 1943, 205-15 (= *Das kleine Credo und andere Studien zum Alten Testament*, 1965, 101-12); K.Rupprecht, *Der Tempel von Jerusalem. Gründung Salomos oder jebusitisches Erbe?*, 1977; W.H.Schmidt, *The Faith of the Old Testament*, ET 1983; K.Seybold, *Das Gebet des Kranken im Alten Testament*, 1973; R.de Vaux, *Ancient Israel*, ET 1961; C.Westermann, *The Praise of God in the Psalms* (the later German edition is entitled *Lob und Klage in den Psalmen*, ⁵1977, 11-124).

Steuernagel, §30; Eissfeldt, §6, 15; Fohrer, §5, 39; Soggin, 5.1; Kaiser, §26,27; Koch, § 13,14.

5 Political Institutions. The Monarchy

The forms of organization among the Israelite tribes at the time before the rise of the monarchy remain largely obscure to us. So for this period we can hardly designate a particular Sitz im Leben for individual texts. In the case of some genres, however, we have to assume that their origin presupposes a more comprehensive organization.

→6ff.

This applies first to various kinds of lists. The collection and arrangement of particular things in a list presupposes an interest in listing them and preserving them; if such lists contain statements about a number of tribes, they indicate an interest going beyond the individual tribe. Thus in Judg.1.19,21,27ff. we find a list of territories which the Israelites could not conquer, arranged by tribes. It has also been conjectured that lists of boundary points from the period before the formation of the state are the basis of Josh.13-19; while the dating of these lists remains uncertain, they offer a further example of this genre. The list of 'minor judges' in Judg.10.1-5; 12.7-15 extends beyond the limits of an individual tribe.

Once the organization of the community has been achieved, the function of the lists becomes clearer. We have a list of supreme officials from the reign of David (II Sam.8.16-18; cf. 20.23-26) and a collection in a list of the 'heroes of David' (II Sam.23.8-39), though in its present form the first part has been elaborated by anecdotal narrative elements. From the time of Solomon we have not only a list of court officials (I Kings 4.2-6) but a list of the twelve administrative districts which Solomon formed to provide for the royal court, each of which was under a governor (vv.7-19).

Here the list reflects the new administrative structure; at the same time it forms the legal basis for the performance of administrative tasks and thus becomes an important document. The list of sanctuary cities into which those who have committed homicide can flee to avoid blood vengeance (Josh.20.7-9a) also has legal significance.

We again have official lists from the post-exilic period in the books of Ezra and Nehemiah: a list of those who returned from exile (Ezra 2; cf. Neh.7), those who accompanied Ezra on his journey to Jerusalem (Ezra 8.1-14), mixed marriages (Ezra 10.18-44), the inhabitants of Jerusalem (Neh.11.3-19), the extent of the territory of Judah and Benjamin (Neh.11.20,25-35), the priests and levites (12.1-26), etc.

With the rise of state institutions the official enumeration of important political and military events also begins. These are often designated annals. One example of such enumerations is the list of David's successes in foreign policy in II Sam.8.1-14; however, this is a comprehensive, retrospective account for which presumably current official chronicles were used. References to the 'Book of the History of Solomon' (I Kings 11.41) and the 'Chronicle of the Kings of Israel' (I Kings 14.19 etc.) and the 'Chronicle of the Kings of Judah' (I Kings 14.29 etc.) clearly show that there were such lists at the royal court. Presumably these books provide the information about Solomon's building activities (I Kings 6), his trade enterprises, his wealth and the development of his splendour (I Kings 9.26-28; 10.11f., 14-22, 26-29), together with specific details about the palace buildings (I Kings 12.25; 16.25) and other important building enterprises by individual kings (I Kings 22.39; II Kings 20.20), about particular events in war and their consequences (I Kings 14.25-28; II Kings 15.19f., 29; 18.9-11, 13-16), and about usurpations of the throne by violence (I Kings 15.27; 16.9f., 15-18, 21f.). They probably also contained the chronology, which is always given with reference to the king reigning in the neighbouring kingdom (I Kings 15.1,9,25-33, etc.).

The narrative tradition also undergoes clear changes as a result of the rise and establishment of state institutions. Alongside the heroic sagas we now find narratives whose main interest is no longer in an individual; rather, they describe historical developments involving changing figures and scenes (cf. von Rad 1944). These can be described as historical narrative. A first example of this genre is the narrative about the monarchy of Abimelech in Shechem (Judg.9). The transition within the David story is particularly clear; first of all we have individual narratives which belong to the genre of the heroic saga (I Sam.16ff.; for the composition see below). The struggles over the succession to Saul are then depicted in a wider context, in which places and people change and are held together by the narrative threads (II Sam.2-4). Here the narrative interest is in the institution of the monarchy and its fate. A further example of historical narrative is the account of the Ammonite war in II Sam.10.1-11.1; 12.16-31, which was perhaps composed as an official report for the royal archive (Rost).

Monarchy
→87

Historical
narratives
→169

→173

Finally, we now get larger narrative complexes which cover the individual phases of the beginnings of the monarchy. Here a clear development in the way in which the narrative is constructed is evident. The story of Samuel and Saul (I Sam.1-15) is dominated by the conflict between these two charismatic figures; from a literary point of view it appears as a relatively loose collection of different traditions in which it is difficult to see a dominant principle of arrangement. The history of the rise of David (I Sam.16-II Sam.5) also consists of originally independent individual traditions; as well as the narrative there are numerous short notes which cannot be described as narratives but have been added by the person who collected and edited the story of David's rise in order to complete the picture (e.g. I Sam.18.1,3f.,6-8,10f.,13; 22.1f.,3f.,5, cf. Rendtorff). The whole narrative complex is held together by statements that YHWH was with David (I Sam.16.13,18; 17.37; 18.5,12,14,28; II Sam.5.10,12) and that he had already handed the kingdom over to David in the lifetime of Saul – the latter statement is often made by people involved, and even Saul acknowledges the fact (I Sam.20.13ff., 31; 23.17; 24.21; 25.28,30; 26.25; II Sam.3.9f.). So here – in contrast to the story of Samuel and Saul – the element of planning in the composition is much clearer.

→29ff., 170ff.

Rise of David
→31ff., 172

The Succession Narrative (II Sam.9 – I Kings 2; Rost also includes II Sam.6f.) is of a different kind. It does not consist of what were originally individual narratives, but was conceived from the start as a unified narrative. Thus it is far removed from the genre of the saga, and its literary form is comparable with the Joseph Novella in Gen.37-50. It derives its tension from the question who will be David's successor, and from its account of the struggle and intrigues which finally lead to Solomon's victory over his rivals. A tendency to criticize Solomon is unmistakable; this probably suggests that the author was one of the wise men at court (see below; Crüsemann).

Succession to
the throne
→33f., 110,
173
→86, 136

The Succession Narrative is a high point of Israelite historiography which is not attained again. Further examples of the genre of historical narrative are: the narrative of the division of the kingdoms of Israel and

Judah (I Kings 12.1-19); Jehu's revolution (II Kings 9f.; for the prophetic element see II.6) and the fall of Queen Athaliah (II Kings 11).

The religious side of the monarchy was also of great significance for its self-understanding and consolidation. This is primarily evident in the cultic sphere, where it is reflected in a series of psalms which can be summarily described as royal psalms. Psalm 110 suggests an enthronment ceremony in which the king is appointed as a successor to the pre-Israelite priest-king Melchizedek (v.4). Psalm 2 belongs in the same cultic context; this celebrates the king as the world ruler appointed by YHWH on Zion and declares him 'Son of God' after the model of oriental kings (v.7). The prayer for the king in Ps.72 also depicts him as world-ruler; here in addition to the stress on his significance for the maintenance of justice and righteousness, there are also features which elevate the king above the human sphere (vv.5-7,16f.; cf. Ps.*89.37f.*), of a kind which often occur in texts from the Ancient Near East (cf. Schmidt, § 12).

The king's vow to preserve justice (Ps.101) and the thanksgiving for the king (Ps.21) probably also belong in the context of an enthronement festival (or perhaps a royal festival repeated regularly). Ps.132 has another cultic aspect: in the setting of a procession with the ark, it probably celebrates David as founder of the ark sanctuary on Zion and combines with this the divine promise that his dynasty will endure; this possibly reflects another aspect of the same cultic festival.

The cultic situation of Ps.89 is harder to define, in that it combines a hymn (vv.*1-19*), a quotation from a divine oracle for David and his descendants (vv.20-28), and a lamentation over the decline of the monarchy (vv.*39-52*). In the light of this last part, we must at any rate think in terms of a cultic celebration at a time of distress; it must remain open whether this is the celebration of a regular royal festival or a festival on a special occasion. – Psalm 20 is a prayer for the king before he goes out to war, Ps.144 (vv.1-11) a psalm in the mouth of the king himself, Ps.18 a thanksgiving after victory; the exact cultic setting for this psalm remains uncertain, as does the question whether the present texts are later revisions. Ps.45 is a song at a royal marriage.

Finally, in Jerusalem too a court life developed on the model of other royal courts in the ancient Near East. This was expressed especially in the adoption of wisdom traditions. In I Kings *5.9-14* the wisdom of Solomon is explicitly connected with that of the 'East' and of Egypt. Plants and animals are mentioned as objects with which Solomon's wisdom was concerned (v.*13*). This recalls the enumerative 'list science' of the ancient Near East, which was concerned to collect and arrange systematically all known natural phenomena. The special feature stressed here is that Solomon expressed this wisdom in sayings (*mašal*) and songs (*sir*, v.*12*). In this connection Alt referred to the numerical sayings in Prov.30.15f., 18-20, 24-28, 39-31 in which natural phenomena are collected together under an overriding perspective which goes beyond mere ordering.

However, otherwise we have hardly any instances of nature wisdom in ancient Israel. The Old Testament wisdom traditions offer primarily experiential wisdom. The parallels in the ancient Near East, and especially in Egypt, suggest that this too originated in the court, specifically in schools to educate the children of officials. There is much to suggest that for Israel in the time of the monarchy, too, there were schools for officials and scribes; for the ability to write, combined with a knowledge of foreign languages, was a necessary qualification for holding office at court and in the royal administration (cf. Hermisson, 113ff.; Lemaire. Whybray, 33ff. is critical).

Monarchy
→256

Among the wisdom sayings collected in the book of Proverbs there are many which clearly come from court circles. Thus e.g. there are rules and advice for behaviour in the presence of the king (Prov.14.35; 16.12-15; 19.12; 20.2; 22.11,29; 24.21; 25.6f. etc.) or other superiors (23.1-3; 24.21; 25.13,15, etc.). Here knowing when to speak and when to keep silent plays an important role (16.13; 22.11; 25.15); as this is a frequent theme of wisdom sayings elsewhere, too (e.g. 17.27f.; 18.20f.; 21.23; 25.11ff.; 29.20, etc.) we may regard this as a basic element of training in the wisdom schools. The embodiment of this education is the 'wise man' (*ḥakam*), i.e. the one who has knowledge and insight, who behaves accordingly and teaches others (13.14,20; 16.21,23; 18.15; 24.5; 25.12, etc.). His counterpart is the 'fool', the one with no insight (12.23; 13.20; 14.33; 15.2; 17.10,16,24, etc.), the blockhead (10.14; 11.29; 12.15; 14.2; 29.9, etc.).

Wisdom sayings

However, by no means all the sayings which reflect this ideal of education belong to the court sphere. Rather, we must imagine that there were broader strata in which such traditions were cherished and handed down, and served to educate the rising generation. Here on the one hand we might think of an extension of the training of officials to a wider stratum; on the other hand we might also posit the independent development of a popular wisdom, above all a peasant wisdom, which also served as education. It is hardly possible to draw a clear line between the two, especially as the Old Testament does not give us any details of educational patterns and institutions (but cf. Lang, 1979). The two seem to have fused in the collections of sayings that we have. (The address 'my son' can be used of the father, but also of the wisdom teacher.)

→83

First of all, two basic forms can be distinguished in wisdom sayings: statements and admonitions (cf. Zimmerli). The admonition shows most clearly its origin in instruction (e.g. Prov.19.20; 22.17; 23.19,22,26; 27.11, etc.). More often than not it is formulated in the negative (e.g. 22.22,24,26,28, etc.; this form is often designated 'vetitive'); it is thus closely related to the prohibition (cf. Richter). However, in terms of content it is impossible to recognize any basic differences between admonitions and statements, as the latter often necessarily result in admonitions; moreover the admonitions are often connected with a statement on which they are based (e.g. 22.23,25,27).

Admonitions

→83f.

Among the statements, the collections of wisdom sayings also include genuine proverbs, many of which are especially concerned with the connection between action and outcome (e.g. Prov.16.18;22.8a;26.27

Proverbs
→82f.

etc.). Contrasts are also popular elsewhere; the Hebraic style with parallelism almost asks for them.

Thus there are contrasts with 'better...than' (*tob...min*, e.g. 15.16f.; 16.8,16,19,32; 17.1 etc.), comparative sayings which usually consider human conduct in analogy to behaviour in another sphere (e.g. 10.26; 11.22; 25.22-15, 18,20; 26.11,14, etc), the contrast between the wise and the fool (e.g. 10.1,14; 12.15,23, etc., see below) or even without these terms the contrast between correct, wise behaviour and wrong, stupid behaviour (according to Skladny, in Prov.10-15 no less than 89.1% of sayings are in antithetical parallelism, and in chs. 28-29, 61.8%). The didactic element is clear everywhere, since correct, or better, conduct is presented to the hearer or reader so that he can orientate himself on it and act accordingly.

Didactic
discourses
→255

In addition to individual sayings, loosely juxtaposed, in Prov.1-9 we find larger units which can be designated didactic discourses (Lang). Each time they are introduced with the address 'My son' (1.8; 2.1; 3.1,21; 4.1,10,20; 5.1; 6.20; 7.1), followed by an invitation to hear and observe the teaching, which is then developed in various ways. Here the warning against seduction plays a major role, whether this is seduction by 'sinners' (1.10; cf. 2.12ff.), or above all by the 'strange woman', to whom three whole discourses are devoted (5.1-23; 6.20-35; 7.1-27).

→86, 136
Didactic
narrative

Wisdom thinking has also found expression in narrative genres. Thus the Joseph story (Gen.37-50) can be described as a didactic wisdom narrative. It portrays Joseph as the ideal embodiment of the wise man who knows when to speak and when to keep silent, who does not allow himself to be seduced by the strange woman. who patiently bears his fate, then consummately shows his skill as an advisor in the presence of the king, while at the same time remaining modest and humble. He describes this art as a divine gift, and is finally singled out for the highest offices at court. Everything that happens here is seen as the hidden guidance of God (Gen.45.5-8; 50.20). Here the court milieu is most evident, and in addition the narrative probably also has a specific

→107, 125

political aim (Crüsemann, Blum). The Succession Narrative (II Sam.9 – I Kings 2) also has features from wisdom and in addition has the similar trait of interpreting events as divine action (II Sam.11.27b; 12.24b; 17.14). Its critical attitude to Solomon again suggests a political aim in court circles of wise men, among whom we should probably look for its author.

Didactic narratives with a wisdom stamp can also be found outside the sphere of the court (cf. Müller). These may be taken to include the narrative frameworks

→250f.

of the Book of Job (1f.; 42.7-17), the narratives of the books of Ruth and Esther (and the apocryphal book of Tobit) and the legends of Daniel and his friends

→273f.

(Dan.1-6). However, a comparison of these narratives shows that the tradition of such didactic wisdom narratives could combine shifting presuppositions with very varied intentions.

103f., 125f.

These last examples cannot be assigned either to court circles or to the popular sphere. Rather, they show that wisdom thinking was influential beyond these areas. This becomes clear, e.g., also in the wisdom psalms, which have found a way into the collection of cultic songs. Their affinity to the *tora* psalms raises the question of the relationship of wisdom to the Deuteronomic-Deuteronomistic tradition in which the *tora* has a central role.

Monarchy

The wisdom texts are often concerned with acquiring, finding (Prov.3.13), attaining (4.5,7) etc. 'wisdom'. Here the term 'wisdom' is itself used as a comprehensive designation of the aim of wisdom teaching. This view is developed particularly impressively in Job 28: people look for wisdom in the depths of the earth, on the highest mountains, in the deepest seas; but they cannot find it, nor can they buy it with the costliest treasures in the world – only God knows where it is to be found (v.23).

→253

This independent and almost absolute use of the word 'wisdom' is the basis for the portrayal of wisdom as a person. In Prov.9 she is spoken of as a woman who invites guests to a meal by which they are to obtain insight; she is contrasted with 'folly' (v.13ff.), who also tries to entice guests into her house. In Prov.1.20ff.; 8.1ff., wisdom also calls people to her in public; here at the same time it is said that rejecting the invitation has serious consequences (1.24ff.), but accepting it leads to riches, renown and power (8.15ff.). Finally, Prov.8.22f. speaks of the wisdom which YHWH made the 'firstborn of his creation', 'from earliest times' (vv.22f.). She was there at creation and 'played' before YHWH (vv.30f.). Here conceptions from the world of the ancient Near East are transferred to wisdom in order to express its incomparable position: it is the 'primal order' of the world (von Rad 1970). Here again the question of the relationship between wisdom and *tora* arises.

Wisdom as person →255

Bibliography

A.Alt, 'Die Weisheit Salomos', *TLZ* 76, 1951, 139-44 (= *KS* II, 90-9); E.Blum, *Die Komposition der Vätergeschichte*, Heidelberg dissertation 1982; F.Crüsemann, *Der Widerstand gegen das Königtum. Die antiköniglichen Texte des Alten Testamentes und der Kampf um den frühen israelitischen Staat*, 1978; H.-J.Hermisson, *Studien zur israelitischen Spruchweisheit*, 1968; C.Kayatz, *Studien zu Proverbien 1-9*, 1966; B.Lang, *Die weisheitliche Lehrrede*, 1972; id., 'Schule und Unterricht im alten Israel', in M.Gilbert (ed.), *La Sagesse de l'Ancien Testament*, 1979, 186-201; A.Lemaire, *Les écoles et la formation de la Bible dans l'Ancien Israel*, 1981; H.-P.Müller, 'Die weisheitliche Lehrerzählung im Alten Testament und seiner Umwelt', *WO* 9, 1977/78, 77-98; G.von Rad, 'The Beginning of Historical Writing in Ancient Israel' (1944), in *The Problem of the Hexateuch*, ET 1966, 166-204; id., *Wisdom in Israel*, ET 1972; R.Rendtorff, 'Beobachtungen zur altisraelitischen Geschichtsschreibung anhand der Geschichte vom Aufstieg Davids', in *Probleme biblischer Theologie. FS G. von Rad*, 1971, 428-39; W.Richter, *Recht und Ethos. Versuch einer Ortung des weisheitlichen Mahnspruchs*, 1966; L.Rost, *Die Überlieferung von der Thronnachfolge Davids*, 1926 (= *Das kleine Credo und andere Studien zum Alten Testament*, 1965, 119-253); W.H.Schmidt, *The Faith of the Old Testament*, ET 1983; U.Skladny, *Die ältesten Spruchsammlungen Israels*, 1962; R.N.Whybray, *The Intellectual Tradition in the Old Testament*, 1974; W.Zimmerli, 'Zur Struktur der alttestamentlichen Weisheit', *ZAW* 51, 1933, 177-204.

Eissfeldt, §4,16; Fohrer, §12, 13, 47; Soggin, 5. II; Kaiser, §32.

6 Prophecy

The emergence of prophets is a particularly characteristic feature of the life of ancient Israel. The phenomenon of prophecy is certainly not limited to Israel, but also occurs in other spheres of the ancient Near East; however, as far as the sources indicate, nowhere did prophets become as significant as they were in Israel.

Nevertheless, the picture of prophecy which emerges from the Old Testament is very disparate. Right at the beginnning of its history we find two quite different kinds of prophets. I Samuel 10.5f., 10-13; 19.18-24 report groups of prophets whose most striking characteristic is ecstasy, which is infectious. By contrast, Samuel (in I Sam.3.7ff.) is portrayed as an individual prophet and clearly differentiated from the ecstatic group (19.18ff.). We hear nothing of ecstasy in connection with him; rather, his main characteristics are religious political action and speaking in the name of YHWH, and we are told that he was expressly called by God (I Sam.3). The designation 'prophet' (*nabi'*) is used both for members of the ecstatic groups (I Sam.10.5,10f., etc) and for Samuel; in addition, Samuel is described with the terms 'man of God' (*'is-'elohim*, 9.6,10) and 'seer' (*ro'e*, 9.11,18f.); the latter is identified with *nabi'* in 9.9. (Some scholars want to infer from this that there was an ancient office of 'seer', who could also be called *hoṣe*, cf. II Sam.24.11; Amos 7.12, but this remains uncertain.)

In Kings 22 a group of prophets (v.6, 400 men!) who are summoned by the king and go into action 'before him' (v.10), so that they can be called 'his' prophets (vv.22f.), are contrasted antithetically with an individual prophet (Micaiah ben Imlah, vv.8ff.). Both are 'asked for' (vv.5,7f.) a word of YHWH about the military plans of the king and both give one (vv.6,10f.; or 14ff.). The difference here lies above all in the dependence on or independence from the king.

Finally, a further group is mentioned whose members are called *bᵉne ha-nᵉbi'im* ('disciples of the prophets, members of a prophetic guild'). This group is especially associated with Elisha (II Kings 2.3ff.; 4.1,38; 6.1; 9.1; cf. I Kings 20.35ff.). They 'sit before him' in a special assembly room (II Kings 6.1; cf. 4.38) and turn to him in personal distress (4.1ff., 38ff.; 6.1ff.). He sends out individuals in order to give a politically effective word of YHWH (9.1ff.; cf. I Kings 20.35ff.). However, he himself usually appears alone (see below).

Thus the relationship between prophetic groups and individual prophetic figures varies considerably. Samuel and Elisha are connected with the prophetic groups which are mentioned at the same time but are clearly distinct from them; by contrast, Micaiah ben Imlah is shown to be a firm opponent of the group of prophets. The latter group has a close institutional bond with the court, whereaas Micah seems to be in solitary opposition. However, this distinction cannot be generalized, since on the one hand the groups around Samuel and Elisha have no connection with the royal court (which did not in fact exist in the time of Samuel); on the other hand, in the time of David, Nathan (II Sam.7;

Margin notes:
Groups of prophets
→29
Individual figure

→44

bᵉne ha-nᵉbi'im

112

12; I Kings 1) and Gad (I Sam.22.5; II Sam.24.11, 'David's seer') appear as two 'court prophets' without any connection with a group. At the same time it is evident here that institutional membership of the court by no means excludes a critical attitude, or even sharp accusations against the king (II Sam.12; 24).

The question of relationships with the court is therefore no criterion for a closer definition of the nature of prophecy. It is in the nature of the Old Testament tradition that prophets often appear in opposition to the kings. However, e.g. in the case of Elijah, it is evident that the prophet only finds himself in the role of an outsider in opposition as a result of the religious politics of Queen Jezebel (I Kings 19.10,14). The king asks Elisha for advice (II Kings 3.11f.) or makes suggestions to him without being asked (6.8ff.), and visits him on his death bed (13.14ff.). Kings also seek advice of Isaiah (II Kings 19.2ff. = Isa.37.2ff.) and Jeremiah (Jer.21.1ff.; 37.3ff.; 38.14ff.; 42.1ff). However, all these prophets also approach the king with complaints and announcements of judgment.

Relationship to the king

→43, 179

→114, 179f.

The fact that the prophets mostly appear as individuals is also connected above all with the nature of the tradition, which had a special interest in these individual figures. However, Elijah sees himself as the representative of a larger number of prophets whom Jezebel has killed (I Kings 18.4.13; 19.10,14). In the prophetic books, each of which has collected the sayings of an individual prophet, there is often, of course, derogatory mention of 'prophets' in the plural (e.g. Micah 3.5; Jer. 2.8; 5.31, etc.; Ezek.13.2ff. etc.); however, the opponents can also be individual prophets (e.g. Jer.28; 29.24ff.). Conversely, Jeremiah can chide his contemporaries for failing to understand what 'the prophets' say (5.13). Finally, the statements in Jeremiah with a Deuteronomistic formulation, to the effect that YHWH has spoken to Israel through 'his servants, the prophets' (7.25; 25.4; 26.5, etc.), certainly have some connections with the genuine Jeremiah tradition.

→201f.

All this shows that we cannot posit any fundamental distinction between groups of prophets who are dependent on the royal court and therefore are not 'true' prophets, and individual prophetic figures who are independent and always in opposition. Granted, detailed issues in connection with the question of an institutional development of the prophetic 'office' remain unclear. (This is also true of the existence of cultic prophets, which is often conjectured.) However, it is quite evident that the Old Testament tradition principally reports situations of conflict between prophets and kings, and later between prophets and all Israel, and that the picture of the prophets is stamped by this. Still, it is evident that proclamation of salvation and disaster cannot be divided out between different kinds of prophets; both are to be found among the majority of Old Testament prophets.

Prophetic 'office'

Finally, it also emerges that the prophets can only be understood in the general context of Israelite religion. They do not develop any independent theology, but stand within the religious traditions of Israel, which they presuppose and to which they often refer. This in no way precludes the possibility that in particular questions one or more prophets introduce new theological accents or express ideas which had not been formulated before them; however, that is also true of other 'theologies' in the Old Testament. So it is wrong, as often happens, to regard the proclamation of the prophets as a kind of norm for the whole of the Old Testament, because this means that the specific relationship of their proclamation to their situation becomes lost.

Narratives about prophets

The traditions about the prophets of the earlier period take the form of narratives. They can be described as prophetic narratives. Some of them are at the same time concerned with the persons and fates of the kings against whom the prophets appear; thus the Samuel stories are at the same time often concerned with Saul (e.g. I Sam.9f.; 15.28) or David (16.1-13); those about Nathan (II Sam.7.12) and Gad (II Sam.24) at the same time with David; those about Ahijah in Shiloh at the same time with Jeroboam I (I Kings 11.29-39; 14.1-18).

In other narratives, interest is directed more strongly towards the person of the prophet. Leaving aside I Kings 13, which is unique and stands quite on its own, this is true of the prophetic traditions which are collected in I Kings 20, of the narrative about Micaiah ben Imlah (I Kings 22.1-28) and the three great complexes of narratives about Elijah

→178f.

(I Kings 17-19; 21; II Kings 1), Elisha (II Kings 2 [a link between the Elijah and Elisha narratives, cf. also I Kings 19.19-21]; 3.4-8.15; 9.1-10

→179f.

[connected with the narrative about Jehu's revolution in 9.11ff.]; 13.14-21) and Isaiah (II Kings 18.13-20.19 [= Isa.36-39]).

Some of the Elisha narratives are miracle stories which concentrate on an individual miracle which takes place in a very restricted setting; its effect remains limited to that setting (II Kings 2.19-22, 23f.; 4.1-7, 38-41, 42-44; 6.1-7; 13.20f.). Magical means are also used here (e.g.

→87f.

2.21, 24; 4.41; 6.6). These narratives can be designated legends in the narrower sense (Rofé). Alongside such narratives, which are always very short, we find the more developed genres of the 'literary' legend (II Kings 4.8-37), the biographical legend (II Kings 2.1-18) and the didactic legend (I Kings 17.8-16, 17-24; II Kings 5; 20.1-11); in the latter case the presentation of the miracle is less magical, and a clear religious and didactic intent can be recognized. (Rofé finds the genre of the parable in Jonah and in I Kings 13.)

There are also narrative sections in the prophetic books, though they are isolated. Some of them are reports which speak of the prophet in the third person. These often describe conflicts with priests (Amos 7.10-17), kings (Isa. 7.1-16; Jer.36-44), other prophets (Jer.28) or the whole people (Jer.7; 26). Others speak of sign-actions performed by the

Sign-actions

prophets (often less appropriately called 'symbolic actions') in which they depict through a sign an impending action by YHWH (e.g. Isa. 8.1-4; 20; Jer.13.1-11; 19; 27f.; 32.1-15 etc.; Ezek.4f.; 12; cf. also I

→204, 208

Kings 11.29-39; 22.11; II Kings 13.14-19); in some cases the personal

→215f., 212

life of a prophet becomes a sign-action (Hos.1; 3; Jer.16.1-9; Ezek. 24.15-24).

Other narrative texts are formulated as the prophet's own account;

i.e., in them the prophet speaks of himself in the first person (e.g. Hos.3). This is also particularly true of the accounts of visions which have been handed down in a number of prophetic books (and in I Kings 22.17,19-22). They often begin with the words 'I saw' (e.g. I Kings 22.17,19; Isa.6.1; Zech. 1.8); 'YHWH showed me' (e.g. Amos 7.1,4,7; 8.1; Jer.24.1; Zech.3.1), with the question to the prophet 'What do you see?' (Jer.1.11,13; Zech.4.2; also Amos 7.8; 8.2; Jer.24.3) or with other phrases which speak of the prophet's 'seeing' (e.g. Ezek. 1.1,4; 8.1f.; Zech.2.1,5; Dan.8.1-3).

Sometimes the prophet only sees objects, e.g. a basket of fruit (Amos 8.1), the branch of an almond tree (Jer.1.11), a steaming cauldron (Jer.1.13), two baskets of figs (Jer.24.1f.). Mostly, however, he sees particular events, though these can be very varied. Sometimes they are only hinted at ('all Israel scattered', I Kings 22.17; 'a man riding on a red horse', Zech. 1.8, 'a flying scroll' (Zech 5.2; cf. Amos 7.1,4, etc), but they are often developed at length: e.g. scenes in the heavenly throne-room (I Kings 22.19ff.; Isa.6.1ff.; Zech.3.1ff.) or other divine epiphanies (Ezek.1-3; 43.1ff.); mysterious events in the future: a field full of dead bones which come alive (Ezek.37.1ff.), a spring which flows from under the threshold of the temple (Ezek.47.1ff.), and finally, in the apocalyptic visions of Daniel, eschatological battles (Dan.7f.).

The prophet can understand some visions without further explanation, e.g. as the portrayal of an imminent judgment by YHWH on Israel (Amos 7.1ff.; Ezek.8); here the prophet himself speaks (see below). In other cases, above all when the prophet is only shown objects, he is asked, 'What do you see?' (see above); when he replies, he is told the significance of what he has seen. With the later prophets Zechariah and Daniel there is also a further question to see if the prophet has understood (Zech.2.2,4,6; 4.4,11,12; 5.6,10; 6.4; Dan.7.16; 12.8; cf. 8.13f., 15ff.; 12.6f.).

So here, in addition to the vision, there is always a word to the prophet by which he is drawn into the visionary event. However, the word serves only to help the prophet understand the event and contains no command to hand it on. In the cases in which the prophet himself speaks, he turns to YHWH in intercession (Amos 7.2b,5; Ezek.9.8); here, too, the conversation is limited to the prophet and YHWH.

There are other ways in which the prophet can be drawn into the visionary event or be affected by it. The 'hand of YHWH' seizes him (Ezek.1.3b; 8.1; 37.1; 40.1); he is taken to another place (Ezek.8.7,14,16; 37.2; 40.17 etc.; cf. Dan.8.2), aroused from sleep (Zech.4.1) or affected in other physical ways (Isa. 6.7; Ezek.1.28; 3.14f.; Dan.7.27; 8.27; 10.8ff.). He is often also drawn into the happenings within the vision. He has to say a prophetic word over the dead bones and to the 'spirit' (Ezek.37.4,9) or wade through the water from the temple spring to demonstrate the depth of the water (Ezek.47.3f.); according to the Hebrew text (which is emended by many exegetes), in Amos 9.1 he has to strike the capitals of the pillars; in Zech.3.5 he intervenes in the vision with a command.

Finally, sometimes within the vision the prophet is called on to speak to others. This is particularly the case with the reports of visions which at the same time contain the prophet's call and thus the legitimation of his prophetic activity. In Isa.6, in the temple vision the prophet has his unclean lips cleansed (v.7) and then at Yahweh's request offers himself as a messenger (v.8); he is bidden to make a proclamation (v.9f.), and this leads him to ask another question (v.11); all this brings out the personal qualification, the commissioning and the legitimation of the prophet. In Ezek.1-3 the vision also culminates in the sending of the prophet (2.3; 3.4); he is entrusted with uttering the word of God (2.4.7; 3.1,11) and is accredited to the people of Israel (2.5f.; 3.8f.). (In Jer.1.4-10 the call does not take place in a vision; a direct visionary element appears only in v.9.)

→212

Outside the call visions there is often a commission to the prophets to make a proclamation. In Ezek.37, after the prophet has spoken prophetic words over the dead bones and to the 'spirit', he also has to speak to the Israelites (v.12) and announce to them that YHWH will again raise them to life and restore them to their land. In Ezek.40.4b; 43.10f. the prophet is charged to tell the Israelites what he has been shown in the great temple vision. Zechariah is charged to proclaim YHWH's zeal for Jerusalem and his wrath against the peoples (Zech.1.14f.). The element of the word which all the accounts of visions contain in one form or another is therefore only exceptionally presented as an explicit commission to make a proclamation. That probably means that the account of the vision as such was handed down by the prophet and thus made an element of his prophetic proclamation. (For the accounts of visions generally, cf. Heinzmann.)

In other respects, the prophetic word is the characteristic and essential element of the prophet's apearance. It is often introduced by the phrase,

'Thus says YHWH' (*ko 'amar yhwh*). This messenger formula also appears in the secular sphere when messengers are sent, above all in diplomatic communications (cf. e.g. I Kings 20.3,5; II Kings 1.11; 18.19, 28f., 31). The fact that it is taken over by the prophets gives an important insight into the way in which they understand their role: they are sent by YHWH to communicate a particular word of YHWH. The prophetic narratives often explicitly report the sending of prophets (e.g. II Sam.7.4f.; 12.1; 24.11f.; I Kings 21.17; II Kings 1.3; 20.4f.), and this self-understanding is also often expressed in the accounts of their call (Isa.6.8; Jer.1.7; Ezek.2.3ff.; 3.4ff.; cf. Amos 7.14f.). However, in the prophetic tradition the formula is not limited to the function of introducing the prophet's message. Thus e.g. it can stand as the introduction to a word through which a miracle is done (I Kings 17.14; II Kings 2.21; 3.16f.; 4.43; cf. 7.1); in Ezek.2.4f.; 3.11,27 it is used as a summary of the prophetic proclamation, without being followed by a word of God.

The formula 'The word of YHWH came...' is often used to preface a prophetic saying (this is known as the 'word-event' formula, e.g. I Sam.15.10; I.Kings 16.1), above all in the books of Jeremiah (1.4,11,13; 2.¹; 7.1; 13.8, etc.) and Ezekiel (6.1; 7.1; 11.13; 12.8 etc.). The formula *ne'um yhwh* ('saying of YHWH', etc., the exact meaning is uncertain) occurs at the end of a prophetic saying

(e.g. Amos 3.15; Hos.2.15; Isa.3.15; Jer.8.3), and more frequently within it, **Prophecy**
often in conjunction with formulas like the oath formula *ḥay 'ani* (= 'as I live',
e.g. Jer.22.24; Ezek.5.11; 14.16, 18,20, etc.) or with eschatological formulas
like 'on that day', etc. (e.g. Amos 2.16; 8.3,9; Jer.4.9; 7.32; 8.2,etc.). (Cf. →119
Rendtorff 1954 and Baumgärtel.)

In the earlier narrative tradition the prophetic word is always
addressed to an individual, usually the king or someone elected to be
king. Here the content and form of the prophetic word are usually
determined by the occasion in question. A divine designation to be king
is often expressed by a prophet (I Sam.10.1; I Kings 11.31; II Kings
9.1ff.); David is promised by Nathan (albeit in a text with a marked
Deuteronomistic stamp) that his dynasty will last for ever (II
Sam.7.8ff.); an anonymous prophet promises Ahab victory over the
Syrians (I Kings 20.13,28). These words can be summed up as words of
salvation. This genre includes the words which sometimes appear as
oracles within the miracle stories (I Kings 17.14; II Kings 2.21; 3.16-19; →114
4.43). It is impossible to identify clear characteristics of genres.

The majority of prophetic sayings in the narrative texts are words of disaster. Words of
The prophet usually approaches the king with an accusation relating to a disaster
particular crime. The form of this accusation can vary: Nathan presents David
with a fictitious case, and by his reaction to it David pronounces judgment on
himself (II Sam.12.1-7). We have the same sort of thing in I Kings 20.35ff.,
though here in v.42a the accusation is again formulated explicitly with an
introductory 'because you...'. Elijah accuses Ahab in the form of a rhetorical
question (I Kings 21.19a; similarly II Kings 1.3).

At the same time the accusation contains the grounds for the
announcement of judgment which now follows; it is the culmination of Announcement
the prophetic saying (e.g. I Kings 20.42b; 21.19b; II Kings 1.4). Thus of judgment
we have a two-part statement, giving an announcement of YHWH's
action and the reason for it. Here there is often a direct reciprocal
relationshp between the two, e.g. I Kings 21.19b: 'In the place where
dogs licked up the blood of Naboth shall dogs lick your own blood' (cf.
also I Kings 20.42a and b; II Sam.12.9-10).

Gunkel designated these two parts 'rebuke' and 'threat'. Wolff in
particular drew attention to the function of the first part as a motivation
(though it can also come second), and Westermann (1960) has suggested
the designations 'accusation' and 'announcement'. However, the motivation does not always take the form of an accusation (Koch calls it
'reference to the situation'), so that it would be better not to use a single
term, and choose designations which match a particular function.

In II Kings 1.4 the messenger formula, prefaced by a 'therefore' (*laken*), only
comes before the second half of the prophetic saying, and this is also often the
case with prophets in the following period (e.g. Amos 7.16f.). It has been argued
from this that only the announcement of the divine action is a 'word of God in
the real sense' (Westermann, 1960, 94), with the prophet himself prefacing the
reason (cf. Wolff, 6f. [15f.], von Rad, 37f.). However, the use of the formula is
far too disparate to justify such an assertion; moreover, this would presuppose

an insight into the psychological process of 'receiving' the word of God by the prophet of which we have no knowledge.

From the middle of the eighth century the picture changes. This first affects the form of the tradition. Virtually the only prophetic words to be handed down are collected together in independent 'books', each under the name of an individual prophet. Only occasionally are there narrative traditions, so that the circumstances in which a prophetic word was spoken are largely passed over; nor can they often be discovered clearly from the words themselves. This evidently indicates a different interest in the prophets: the word which the prophet spoke at the behest and in the name of YHWH stands in the foreground; his person and the situation in which he came forward fade away.

However, we must distinguish clearly between the prophets themselves and those who collected their words and handed them on. Evidently the prophets themselves usually spoke in connection with a particular situation. Their words often suggest underlying controversies which not infrequently put the prophets themselves in personal danger, as we are occasionally told (e.g. Amos 7.10-17; Jer.26; 32.3ff; 37ff.; according to Jewish tradition Isaiah died a martyr death under Manasseh). Their words were then preserved and handed on – either orally or in writing. Isaiah 8.16f.; 30.8 mentions the writing down and preservation of the prophet's words for a future time (cf. Hab.2.2f.), and Jer.36 (cf. 30.2) reports that Jeremiah saw to it that 'all the words of YHWH which he had spoken to him' were written down (v.4); Ezek.2.9f. also presupposes the existence of scrolls with prophetic sayings. The present prophetic books stand at the end of this process of tradition; most of them probably arrived at their final form only long after the time of the prophet concerned. Here the theological understanding of prophecy and of the word of God spoken by the prophets has played an important role for particular editors. The usual designation 'writing prophets' for the prophets after the eighth century must not be taken to mean that the prophets themselves wrote these books.

A further basic change can be seen in the audience to which the prophetic sayings are addressed. Whereas the earlier prophets always address their words to individuals, usually to the king, the prophets after the eighth century BC usually address Israel as a whole; alternatively particular authorities are mentioned (priests, prophets, high officials, etc.). Similarly, the announcements of disaster are addressed to Israel as a whole, with a forecast of imminent judgment. This gives the announcement of judgment a much more fundamental character, as is evident, for example, from Amos 8.2: 'The end is come upon my people Israel.' The words of salvation also indicate the destiny of the whole people (e.g. Hos.2.16ff.). The judgment and salvation of Israel are determined by YHWH's future action. This can therefore be described as the 'eschatologizing of historical thought by the prophets' (von Rad, 112ff.).

Despite these changes, a remarkable continuity is evident in the genres of prophetic sayings. In the prophetic books, too, above all in those of the pre-exilic prophets, the form which occurs most frequently is the two-part saying in which the reason for the accusation comes first and the announcement of judgment follows. However, at the same time it is also evident that this basic form is often varied by the prophets (cf. Wolff). Some examples should make this clear.

The basic form with the messenger formula between the two parts appears →116 e.g.in Amos 3.10f. (v.9 is an introduction and v.12 forms an independent saying); 7.16f.; Micah 2.1-3; Jer.23.13-15; here on each occasion the messenger formula is introduced by 'therefore' (*laken*). Instead of the messenger formula, in Amos 4.2 we have 'The Lord YHWH has sworn by his holiness'; in Isa.5.9 'YHWH Sabaoth (has spoken) in my ears'. In Jer.2.9 the threat is introduced with 'therefore' (*laken*), and 'saying of YHWH' (*ne'um yhwh*) is inserted immediately afterwards. Elsewhere, too, a 'therefore' (*'al-ken*, Amos 3.2) or 'Behold' (*hinne*, Amos 9.7f.) can introduce the threat.

The reason for the judgment, which comes first, can be introduced with 'Because' (*ya'an*, e.g. Amos 5.11; Isa.8.6; 29.13; Jer.7.13); occasionally the beginning of the announcement of judgment then has no special characteristics (e.g. Isa.3.16f.). However, this introduction also appears in instances in which the accusation giving the reason for judgment comes only after the announcement of judgment (e.g. Jer.5.14; 14.15; Ezek.5.5-9 [here the messenger formula is used three times: vv.5,7,8]; 11.5-8 [formula twice]; 13.18-21 [formula twice]).

Announcements of coming disaster also appear often without being introduced by a reason why. Often such sayings are introduced with particular formulas like 'On that day (it will happen)' (Amos 8.9,13; Isa.7.18,20,23; Jer.4.9, etc.), 'Behold, days will come' (Amos 8.11; Jer.7.32; 9.24), etc. These formulae usually serve as a redactional link for originally independent sayings, so that no direct context is now recognizable. The same formulas are used even more frequently for words of salvation (e.g. Amos 9.11,13; Jer.16.14; 23.5,7 etc, see below).

In addition to the announcement of imminent disaster, which can no longer be averted, we also find individual admonitions. They call for particular action, so that disaster can still be averted. Sometimes they are formulated with 'lest' (*pen*, Amos 5.6; Jer.4.3f.; 21.11f.), so that →221 they can be designated conditional announcements of disaster (cf. also Amos 5.4f.), and sometimes they make a positive announcement of the possibility of deliverance ('perhaps' [*'ulay*], Amos 5.14f.; Zeph.2.3) so that they can be designated conditional words of salvation (Isa.1.19f.; Jer.4.1f.). However, it is striking how few such admonitions there are. By and large the prophets indicate that judgment can no longer be averted. Salvation can come only after the judgment (see below).

A number of prophetic words of disaster are introduced by the cry →82 'Woe' (*hoy*). Attempts have often been made to see prophetic cries of woe as a special genre. However, more recent scholarship has worked out the derivation of this cry from the lament for the dead or lament at a downfall (in the case of political powers) and shown that this lamentation is used by the prophets after Amos as the opening of a discourse with which at the same time 'mourning metaphors' (Hardmeier) are introduced into prophetic proclamation. The judgment which cannot be averted already makes Israel seem 'dead', so that a lament can be raised (cf. Amos 5.16f.; 8.3,10; Isa.3.24; Micah 2.4). The

→82

dirge (*qina*) also belongs in this context (Amos 5.2); like Isa.3.25-4.1; Micah 1.8-16, etc., it represents an announcement of disaster in the form of a lament for the dead, whereas Isa.1.21-26 attacks the internal disintegration in Jerusalem in the form of a lament at a downfall. So this is an adoption of elements of genres from other spheres of life. However, they are not just used as a didactic means of proclamation, nor are they taken over unchanged; rather, the incorporation of these elements of lamentation over death and defeat decisively shape the prophetic preaching of judgment after the eighth century.

So in other cases too it would be wrong to regard the adoption of genres from other spheres of life as mere rhetorical means used by the

prophets. Thus, for example, the disputation sayings which appear in various prophets clearly indicate the controversies that underlie them. In Amos the question is whether YHWH is also the author of disaster (Amos 3.3-6) and whether Amos is a legitimate prophet (3.8); Deutero-Isaiah, who adopts the genre most extensively (cf. Begrich, 48ff.), stresses in his controversy with the exiles the continuity of the power of the God of Israel (e.g. Isa.40.12-17, 21-24,27-31; 46.5-11); in Haggai (1.4-6, 9-11) the question is the rebuilding of the temple and its consequences; the book of Malachi expresses its criticism of the religious behaviour of its contemporaries in the form of the disputation. In the

→90

judgment discourse Deutero-Isaiah uses a further genre which suggests a dispute (cf. Begrich, 26ff.); this is concerned above all with demonstrating that YHWH is superior to the other gods, indeed that they are not gods at all (e.g. Isa.41.1-5,21-29; 43.8-13; 44.6-8). Other prophetic texts take up forms from legal disputations for the controversy between YHWH and Israel (e.g. Isa.1.2f.,18; 5.1-7; Hos.*2.4ff.*; Micah 6.1-8; Jer.2.5ff.).

In eighth- and seventh-century prophecy the proclamation of disaster (or judgment) is dominant. However, it would be inappropriate to designate prophecy generally in Israel a prophecy of judgment. This is already inappropriate in respect of the beginnings of prophecy, which

contains words of salvation as well as sharp accusations (see below). There are also words of salvation in the prophets of the later monarchy. We have no word of salvation in connection with Amos (for Amos 9.11ff., see below III.4.3). However, proclamation of judgment and salvation are inextricably interwoven in the case of his contemporary Hosea, who like Amos emerged in the northern kingdom; indeed it can even be said that for Hosea the aim of YHWH's action in judgment is the conversion and subsequent salvation of Israel (cf. esp. *2.9,16f.*; 3.5; 11.8f.; 14). The same is true e.g. of Isa.1.21-26. (Whether Isaiah is the author of Isa.2.1-5 and the 'messianic' texts 9.*1-6*; 11 etc., is open to

dispute; the same applies to Micah 4.1-5; *5.1-3*.) In the case of Jeremiah and subsequent prophets who already experienced the onset of the great judgment on Israel, the words of salvation occupy more room. So it is impossible to distinguish between prophets of salvation and prophets of disaster, as is often attempted. Whether a prophet proclaimed disaster or salvation evidently depended on the particular situation, and not on a varied prophetic 'office'.

There are fewer common characteristics of genre in the words of salvation. In earlier prophecy the words of salvation are always introduced by the messenger formula (I Kings 11.31; 17.14; 20.13,28 etc., see below). Only rarely are they preceded by a reason for the message (e.g. I Kings 20.28; II Kings 19.20; 20.5f.). The word of salvation itself is often very short, whether as a direct word from YHWH (e.g. II Kings 9.3) or as an anonymous oracle (II Kings 4.43). (In II Kings 19.20ff. it is bound up with a taunt-song to the king of Assyria.) The frequent association of the word of salvation with particular actions is striking: it is connected with an anointing (I Sam.10.1; II Kings 9.3,6), a magical action (II Kings 2.21; 3.16f.) or a sign-action (I Kings 11.29ff.; 22.11; II Kings 13.15ff.; cf. Jer.28.10f.; 32.14f.).

The words of salvation change their character with the beginning of written prophecy (as do the words of disaster). Only in exceptional instances are they addressed to individuals (II Kings 20.5f. = Isa.38.5f. to Hezekiah; Jer.34.4f. to Zedekiah; 35.18f. to the Rechabites) or related directly to the contemporary situation (Isa.7.4ff.; 37.21ff. = II Kings 19.20ff.). They predominantly speak of a future salvation for Israel or for the whole world which lies beyond the present period of time. Before that will come YHWH's judgment over Israel, which some prophets expect in the future (Amos, Hosea, Isaiah, Micah), some experience as taking place in the present (Jeremiah, Ezekiel), and some suppose to have happened already (Deutero-Isaiah, Haggai, Zechariah, etc.).

This indicates a fundamental difference from the words of disaster, and that is also expressed in their linguistic form. The word of salvation never comes with a reason which is connected with Israel; therefore it cannot have the two-part pattern which is characteristic of the word of disaster. On the few occasions when such a pattern does appear, the first part is not a 'reason' but e.g a description of the present state of decay (Isa.1.21ff., beginning with the lament 'How', *'eka*; the word of salvation begins in v.26 with 'therefore'), instructions to perform a sign-action (Jer.32.14f.; the messenger formula occurs twice) or an admonition (Jer.33.2ff.; the messenger formula appears in vv.2,4).

Many words of salvation are introduced with stereotyped phrases which speak of 'that day' or '(those) days', which will 'come' (see below). Thus they clearly indicate that the awaited events of salvation lie in a future period of history (cf. also Isa.2.2 = Micah 4.1). At the same time these phrases mark a new beginning which does not need any justification (Hos.2.*18,20,23*; Isa.10.20,27; 11.10,11; Jer.16.14; 23.5,6 etc.).

There is a special form of the word of salvation in Deutero-Isaiah. It adopts the liturgical response of the priest to the lamentation of the

Genres

Oracle of
salvation

→103

Sayings
against foreign
nations

individual, which Begrich has designated an oracle of salvation. In Deutero-Isaiah these words of salvation are addressed to Israel, but the form of address in the singular is preserved (e.g. Isa.41.8: 'You, Israel, my servant'; 43.1: 'Thus says YHWH who has created you, Jacob, who has formed you, Israel'). Begrich saw this as an imitation by Deutero-Isaiah of the priestly oracle of salvation; von Waldow, however, assumes that in the exile there were regular popular lamentations in which Deutero-Isaiah spoke this 'prophetic cult oracle'. Finally, Westermann (1964) has drawn further distinctions. He designates the oracle of salvation in the narrower sense a 'promise of salvation' (Isa.41.8-13, 14-16; 43.1-4, 5-7; 44.1-5; 54.4-6); it contains a personal address and the promise of salvation, 'Fear not' (Isa.41.10,14; 43.1b, 5; 44.2b; 54.4), a reason for this promise and an announcement of future events, signifying salvation for Israel and disaster for the enemy. This last part can also appear independently as an 'announcement of salvation' (41.17-20; 42.14-17; 43.16-21; 45.14-17; 49.7-12) or appear within larger compositions (e.g. 49.14-26; 51.9-52.2; 54f.). Thus here Deutero-Isaiah has largely taken up cultic forms of speech for decisive themes in his proclamation, so that his language is often close to the language of the psalms. (However, that does not make him a 'cult prophet'.)

The sayings against foreign nations which appear in a number of prophetic books present a special problem. It is hard to fit them into the general picture of prophecy that we get from other texts. One basic difference is that the prophet cannot confront his audience directly. (Isaiah 18 might be seen as an exception; here perhaps we have a direct address to an Egyptian delegation.) How and in what context were these sayings uttered? Did they reach their audience (and how)? Or are they really addressed to an Israelite audience?

This latter alternative is evidently the case where a saying against a foreign nation is at the same time a word of salvation for Israel, e.g. in the context of the promise of victory to Ahab in I Kings 20.28 or the word of salvation to Ahaz in Isa.7.5-9. Here we have the two-part construction, as in the words of disaster to Israel: a reason with 'because', which contains the charge against the foreign nation (or the two nations in Isa.7) followed by an announcement of what YHWH will do to it (or them); here in Isa.7.7 the messenger formula comes only before the second part. These sayings presuppose a direct situation of war. As we also find descriptions of war elsewhere in the sayings against foreign nations, the 'war oracle' has been conjectured as their possible source (von Rad, 199). However, that would cover only a small proportion of the texts, while other important aspects and themes of the sayings against foreign nations would remain unexplained. Other attempts at explanation argue that these sayings have a cultic origin, e.g. a ritual curse on the enemy in the framework of a cultic act (thus Bentzen for Amos 1f.). It is also presupposed that the disaster announced for the foreign nations is at the same time salvation for Israel; accordingly, prophets who utter such sayings are often described as 'cult prophets' and at the same time as '(national) prophets of salvation'. Over against this is the fact that the majority of the charges against the nations do not affect Israel at all (cf. Höffken). In some cases abuse of Israel by the nations is mentioned in the reason for the saying (e.g. Zeph.2.8; Ezek.25.3,6,8; 26.2); this recalls very similar formulations in the lamentations of the people (e.g. Ps.*44.14f.*; 74.10,18,22f.). However, there the abuse of Israel is also regarded as abuse of YHWH, so these sayings cannot primarily be understood in the context of nationalistic expectations of salvation. Moreover, a cultic explanation could again cover only a small proportion of the texts.

Finally there is a further problem in the fact that the great majority of the sayings against foreign nations appear in independent collections →190, 201, 204 within the great prophetic books (Isa.13-23; Jer.46-51; Ezek.25-32). →212 The connection of these sayings with the rest of the proclamation of the prophet in question is often hard to establish. Moreover it is quite evident that these collections contain numerous sayings which could only have been composed after the time of the prophet in question, as they presuppose later historical circumstances. Often they also speak of a great future world judgment in a way which is closer to apocalyptic than the proclamation of the great prophets. But this raises the question whether and to what extent there are sayings among those addressed to foreign nations which go back to the prophets themselves. So far we do not have adequate criteria for answering this question.

In conclusion, the key term apocalyptic, mentioned above, must be taken up again. Within the prophetic books there are a variety of passages which are usually called 'apocalyptic' (e.g. Isa.24-27; 33; 34f.; →191f., 237ff. Zechariah, etc). They are thus assigned to a wider sphere of literature to which in the Old Testament only the book of Daniel belongs; otherwise it appears outside the Old Testament. This literature is dominated by an eschatological expectation which in some points is clearly distinct from that in the Old Testament. Above all it looks to the future action of God which leads to a change of fortune in Israel, not within the history of this 'aeon' but as an end to this era and the dawn of a new one. A further characteristic is the frequent attempt to calculate the onset of the events at the end of time and to outline an overall interpretation of world history which leads up to this end (cf. Dan.2; 7.9, etc.). The incorporation of apocalyptic texts into the prophetic books shows that there was a connection between the two for the final authors of the Old Testament books. More recently the connection with wisdom has also been stressed. Von Rad in particular →108ff., 125 has wanted to separate apocalyptic completely from prophecy, as its encyclopaedic quest for knowledge is typical of wisdom, and its understanding of history is incompatible with that of the prophets (315ff.); however, it is hardly possible to maintain this division. (For →273ff. Daniel see III.4.5.)

F.Baumgärtel, 'Die Formel n^eum jahwe', *ZAW* 73, 1961, 277-90; J.Begrich, *Studien zu Deuterojesaja*, 1938 (²1969); A.Bentzen, 'The Ritual Background of Amos 1.2-2.16', *OTS* 8, 1950, 85-99; H.Gunkel, 'Die Propheten als Schriftsteller und Dichter', in H.Schmidt, *Die grossen Propheten*, SAT II, 2, ²1923, XXXVI-LXXII; C.Hardmeier, *Texttheorie und biblische Exegese. Zur rhetorischen Funktion der Trauermetaphorik in der Prophetie*, 1978; G.Heinzmann, *Formgeschichtliche Untersuchung der prophetischen Visionsberichte*, Diss. Heidelberg 1978 (typescript); P.Höffken, *Untersuchungen zu den Begründungselementen der Völkerorakel des Alten Testaments*, Diss.Bonn, 1975; F.Horst, 'Die Visionsschilderungen der alttestamentlichen Propheten', *EvTh* 20, 1960, 193-205; G.von Rad, *Old Testament Theology* II, ET 1965; R.Rendtorff, '*nabi* in the Old Testament', *TDNT* 6, 796-813; id., 'Zum Gebrauch der Formel n^e'um jahwe im Jeremiahbuch', *ZAW* 66, 1954, 27-37 (= *GS*, 256-66); A.Rofé, 'The Classification of Prophetical Stories', *JBL* 89, 1970, 427-40; id., 'Classes in the Prophetical Stories', *SVT* 26, 1974, 143-64; H.-E.von Waldow, *Anlass und Hintergrund der Verkündigung des Deuterojesaja*, Diss. Bonn 1953; C.Westermann, *Basic Forms of Prophetic Speech*, ET 1967; id., 'Das Heilswort bei Deuterojesaja', *EvTh* 24, 1964, 355-73; H.W.Wolff, 'Die Begründungen der prophetischen Heils- und Unheilssprüche', *ZAW* 52, 1934, 1-22 (= *GS* 9-35).

Eissfeldt, §10; Fohrer, §52-54; Soggin, 3.I; Kaiser, §21,23,24; Smend, §22,24; Schmidt, §13; Koch, §15-18.

7 The Way to 'Literature'

In looking for the Sitz im Leben, which was our starting point in this chapter, we have not considered the Old Testament texts as 'literature' but as direct expressions of the life of Israelite society in the period when the texts came into being. This approach has produced a variety of insights into the life of this community. However, examples of the various genres have not come down to us in isolation, but as parts of texts or elements woven into wider contexts of Old Testament books and of the Old Testament as a whole. Thus for example the collections of laws are now integrated into the historical narrative of the Pentateuch; prophetic sayings proclaimed by word of mouth form parts of prophetic books, and individual psalms are parts of the book of Psalms. This leaves exegetes with the further task of pursuing the course followed by the texts up to their present final form, a course which largely corresponds to the further development of traditional material into traditional *literature*.

Putting into writing

The 'way to literature' mentioned here needs some explanation. First of all, it is not to be identified sweepingly with the process of putting material into writing (even if the existence of a written form is an obvious presupposition). For on the one hand a written form is a characteristic of some of the genres described above (e.g. annals and lists), while on the other a written form can be the result of intrinsic

→105f.

developments within the sphere in question (e.g. in the case of the **Way to Literature** codification of legal traditions). The result of the transition to literature is that in their production, reproduction and reception, texts are less bound up with particular events and situations. Thus e.g. among the psalms there are poems which evidently were not composed for a specific liturgical occasion, but are an expression of teaching and theological reflection. They can hardly still be described as cultic texts, but are rather religious 'poems' without a pre-existing cultic Sitz im Leben. Prophetic sayings spoken by word of mouth are detached from their original restricted situations by being written down and included in prophetic books, with the result that their reception is no longer limited. In addition, the prophetic books are partly shaped in a literary Literary form way by the use of texts which in each case are already 'literary' (cf. e.g. the apocalyptic sections or the redaction of the book of Jeremiah).

This development towards the shaping of the texts as 'literature' and the extension of their audience possibly began in the context of narrative genres. Longer narratives with a novellistic form (e.g. the Joseph story) and complex historical narratives (e.g. the Succession Narrative) can →86 already be seen as 'literary' genres in this sense; the large 'historical →107 works' (Pentateuch, Deuteronomistic history, perhaps the Chronicler) →157ff., 183ff., 282, 287 which integrate many traditions certainly are.

The examples of the prophetic books and historical works show that new literary genres could also develop in dealing with traditional material. However, their 'Sitz im Leben' remains very uncertain, though individual texts partly found a specific, indeed often institutionalized use (e.g. reading in the liturgy, legal findings and so on), without being limited to that.

This raises the question: who are the authors of such 'written' or 'literary' texts, which now no longer have their Sitz im Leben in one of the spheres of Israelite society? A first answer suggests itself if the examples mentioned are compared: there are marked wisdom elements Wisdom elements in many of them. The wisdom elements in the Joseph story and the →110 Succession Narrative have already long been recognized; psalms which could be understood as religious 'poems' without a fixed place in the cult are predominantly 'wisdom psalms', and the element of wisdom is →103f., 110f. similarly quite evident in apocalyptic. →123

However, this cannot mean that all these texts can be assigned to the wisdom tradition in the narrower sense. On the contrary, the emergence of elements of wisdom in so many different areas of literature shows at the same time that wisdom, too, did not remain limited to its original sphere, but that it exercised influences which transcended all earlier and limited spheres of life and looked for new forms of expression.

Appropriate 'education' is an essential presupposition for the free Levels of education use of literary forms of expression. The authors must be able to read and write, and they must know the existing literature (including that written in other languages). That presupposes an education, whether in a school or through individual instruction. At the same time the origin of new literature presupposes that there is a circle of readers, i.e. further 'educated' people capable of reading. So one can argue with a reasonable amount of certainty from the existence of 'literary' texts in the Old Testament to the presence of such an 'educated class' in Israel.

In this connection scholars have spoken of an 'intellectual tradition' in Israel which is distinct from other spheres of life above all by virtue of the fact that its representatives are in a position to participate in an intellectual and literary discussion of the problems of human life on the basis of the education that they have received. They do this by means of 'wisdom' thinking (Whybray). This tradition does not have its Sitz in Leben in a particular institution but is characterized by the fact that it transcends the traditional bounds of institutions and spheres of life.

However, the wisdom element is only one of the marks of the activity of such 'intellectual' authors or groups of authors; it points particularly to a basic education. Still, this can also be expressed in a variety of other ways. In almost all spheres of the Old Testament we can recognize literary work for which similar presuppositions hold. It can be seen above all in the way in which traditions have been collected and interpreted.

→134ff.

Thus for example it is possible to distinguish clearly several stages in the history of the tradition of the patriarchal sagas of Genesis: first of all the individual sagas; then larger or smaller compositions which still remain within the context of the narrative saga tradition; and finally one or more stages of editing which can be clearly recognized as 'literary' work. They not only collect the sagas and compositions which have been handed down but also often insert passages of text to connect them together and interpret them. This produces a new, larger context, which is governed by uniform leading thoughts. Such work can only be done at the 'desk', since it presupposes that the editor has the traditional material in writing and that he can arrange it, connect it and interpret it in accordance with his own conceptions and views. The same is true of the rest of the books of the Pentateuch and of the Pentateuch as a whole. In the historical books which follow, it is possible to distinguish very clearly between earlier traditional material of various kinds and a process (or processes) of collection and interpretation.

Theological purpose

In all cases it is evident that the editing is not only 'literary' but at the same time theological. The editors or authors of the larger works have a clearly recognizable theological purpose. They set their work in a particular theological perspective and give it a form through the entirety of which it makes particular theological statements. This is evidently the decisive purpose of these authors. (So the term 'intellectual tradition' is not to be understood in the modern sense as a critical or even negative attitude to the religious traditions.)

This is particularly interesting within the legal tradition. The 'Book

→141

of the Covenant' (Ex.20.22-23.19) contains a collection of legal statements of very different kinds which are apparently only loosely put together and hardly interpreted; we may therefore presume that the

Deuteronomy
→151ff.

statements are largely handed down in the form in which they were used in Israelite legislation. The situation in Deuteronomy is quite

different. The main part (chs.12-26) is similarly a collection of legal statements, some of which have parallels in the Book of the Covenant. But the individual statements are often extended paraenetically and interpreted theologically; above all, the collection is put in a much wider historical and theological setting which develops a quite distinctive theological conception. Here, in a unique way, for which there are no parallels in the Old Testament either before or after, an attempt is made to sum up the whole religious tradition of Israel, with its many branches and strata, in a broad new overall outline (cf. Herrmann).

**Way to
Literature**

→155

The question who the author (or authors) of this work was (or were) has so far not been answered. It has not yet proved possible to put them in the context of an institution. Without doubt they had a good education and were brilliant theologians and writers. Therefore there is much to be said for the conjecture that they should be sought among the 'scribes' who are repeatedly mentioned in the Old Testament, and who were responsible for education in the official court schools. This would also explain the striking relationship between the thought of Deuteronomy and that of wisdom – and in Jer.8.8 these are also connected with the *tora*, the central concept of Deuteronomic theology (cf. Weinfeld, 158ff.). However, if this conjecture is right, we certainly cannot regard the work of the Deuteronomistic theologians as merely the fulfilment of their professional task; it remains a quite independent intellectual and theological achievement.

Authors

Specifically in Deuteronomy, it is evident that the form-critical approach is not enough to explain the origin of the books of the Old Testament. The traditional material was collected by writers, worked over again, and interpreted theologically. These writers were not bound to fixed, pre-existing forms of expression, but made use of their own, further, theological conceptions. However, we must not just see this as the individual theological work of individual authors. It is certainly quite possible and in some cases probable that the collection and theological interpretation of a particular biblical book was carried out by just one individual. However, these writers certainly did not work in isolation from their spiritual and theological surroundings. We should understand them more as representatives of particular groups, schools, movements (or whatever one might call them) who in their work expressed and gave concrete form to what others, too, thought and reflected on.

Groups
Movements

That brings us to another important aspect: the theological work of these writers later shaped the final form of the individual books and ultimately the Old Testament. Particularly the theology which found its most comprehensive expression in Deuteronomy had far-reaching effects, The work of shaping the historical books which come after the Pentateuch has long been recognized as 'Deuteronomistic'. Deuteronomistic elements have recently been brought out increasingly clearly in the Pentateuch; here their significance is particularly evident for its final literary form.

→183ff.
→162

So far little attention has been paid to the question of a considered final form of the prophetic books; however, here too in individual books

127

Genres
→222, 213ff.
Canonization

→288ff.

we can see clear traces of Deuteronomistic redactional work (e.g. Amos, Jeremiah, etc.).

Now that means that this theological work finally attained 'canonical' character. For the books of the Bible have exercised their influence as elements of the biblical canon in their final form, i.e. in the form which they received from their final redactors. Childs above all has now put emphatic stress on this aspect. He rightly criticizes the lack of attention paid by Old Testament scholarship so far to the canonical final form of the biblical books and attempts to work out in each instance the 'canonical form' of individual books and to define their theological intention. This is a decisive further step towards understanding the whole way from the original forms of discourse, through the various stages of literary shaping, to the final form of the biblical books. These questions will be explored further in Part Three.

Bibliography

B.S.Childs, *Introduction to the Old Testament as Scripture*, 1979; S.Herrmann, 'Die konstruktive Restauration. Das Deuteronomium als Mitte biblischer Theologie', in *Probleme biblischer Theologie. Festschrift G.von Rad*, 1971, 155-70; M.Weinfeld, *Deuteronomy and the Deuteronomic School*, 1972; R.N.Whybray, *The Intellectual Tradition in the Old Testament*, 1974.

III The Books of the Old Testament

The Old Testament is the result of a long process in which material was collected, handed down, worked over and given its final form. In its final form we have it in a number of 'books'. Some of these books are clearly self-contained independent literary entities (e.g. the Psalms, Job, Proverbs). Others prove at the same time to be elements in a larger composition which on each occasion must be taken into account (e.g. the five books of the Pentateuch, the books of the 'Deuteronomistic history').

Quite different ways of dealing with the books of the Old Testament can be adopted. One can either begin with the earliest individual traditions and seek to follow their course down to their final form, or, conversely, one can start from the final form and trace a way back from it to the earlier stages of the tradition. In the first approach the development and growth of the texts is itself made the guide to the account – and here much must remain hypothetical; in the second approach the probe of the analysis backwards determines the course of the account – and here the changing methods and views of interpreters are of great importance.

The first approach was adopted by Hermann Gunkel with his programmatic demand for a 'history of the literature of Israel'. However, he himself only produced a first brief account of such a history, in which he did not get as far as the final form of the books of the Bible; that lay outside his interest. Since then, Gunkel's demand has often been recognized as justified, but nowhere has it been consistently carried through. In more recent overall accounts e.g. Kaiser opts for a middle course (12), whereas Smend explicitly chooses the second approach (11); however, he, too, is uninterested in the books of the Old Testament in their final form.

Despite various approaches, the newer general accounts work in essentially the same way. They are dominated by analysis of the texts, in which the various strata, sources, stages of the tradition, redactions and so on are worked out – but the final form of the individual books as they now are, and of the Old Testament as a whole, are hardly taken into account. Underlying this is a conception (which in the last resort goes back to Herder and the Romantics) that what is older and earlier is 'original' and therefore of greater value; what is added later is regarded as derivative and dismissed as 'secondary' or 'redactional'.

Over against this, Brevard S.Childs has now emphatically stressed that particular attention needs to be paid to the final form of the books of the Old Testament because this is not the result of a more or less fortuitous process of collection and redaction but the expression of a conscious process of the formation of binding 'canonical' writings which in their final form have become the normative basis of the religious life of the Jewish – and later also of the Christian – community. Childs combines his approach with a basic criticism of the 'decanonization' of the texts in more recent exegetical methods.

This demand is completely justified. The final form of the Old Testament books and the theological intentions expressed in them must be taken seriously in a quite different way from what has so far been the norm in Old Testament scholarship. However, in my view this must not lead to a basic contrast between this and other methodological approaches. Childs is doubtless right that the contemporary interest of scholarly work on the Old Testament is above all in investigating the earlier history of the canonical texts and interpreting the different stages of this history in its various historical contexts. One must also agree with his view that in this process, interest in the final form of the text has been lost and that at present Old Testament scholarship has no methodological approach which can make good this loss. But the question remains whether this must necessarily be and remain the case.

In my view, traditio-historical work on the Old Testament carried through consistently could and must transcend the opposition which now exists between an approach which is orientated only on the history of the tradition and one which is orientated only on the final canonical form. Once the whole course of tradition is taken seriously, then the 'canonical' final form of the individual books and of the Old Testament as a whole also has a place in it. It is then unnecessary to defend a special method of interpretation for the final canonical form which contrasts with the traditio-historical method.

However, the presupposition for such a consistent expansion of the traditio-historical method is that the literary and theological work which has led to what is now the final form of the traditions should be taken seriously. Tradition history is not just a further development of form criticism, but takes the step to the next stage, to the point where the texts have left their original setting and become the object of literary →124ff. and theological editing and interpretation (see II.7 above).

Within the framework of this book I shall attempt to take account of this change in interest in method and to give expression to it. In Part Two an attempt was made to understand the Old Testament texts as expressions of the different spheres of life in Israel; there attention was focussed above all on the history of Israel and its social and religious institutions. In Part Three we must now follow the course of the traditions as 'literature': that means above all as theological literature, which no longer remains limited to particular institutions.

Here account must be taken of the demand made by Childs, Blenkinsopp and others that the 'canonical' intention of this theological work should be noted. It is not enough to see individual theological authors or particular groups at work. The important thing is, rather, to recognize in the individual books of the Old Testament the tendencies which finally come out on top and which sum up the manifold and very varied traditions of Israel in one binding canon. If one likes to put it that way, here is a new 'Sitz im Leben': the Jewish religious community which creates out of the wealth of its literature a canon of binding religious writings that from then on will form the basis of its religious life and will finally be taken over and recognized as canonical by the Christian community which grows out of the Jewish community. (Cf. also III.5 and the literature mentioned there.)

→288ff.

However, essential preliminary work still needs to be done before this programme can be carried out. Therefore in many instances it will only be possible to indicate approaches, without at this stage being able to arrive at results. Still, I hope that it is possible to recognize the direction in which the question of the course of the Old Testament tradition up to its final stage can be taken further.

I have not given a detailed account of the history of research. It has been discussed comprehensively and in detail in the books by Kaiser and Smend. However, I have tried in each instance to sketch out the most important positions and to show how my own view relates to them.

1 The Five Books of the Pentateuch (The Torah)

The first five books of the Old Testament have been handed down as individual books with their own names; at the same time, however, they are regarded and treated as a unity. The Hebrew names of the books are formed from their opening words, whereas the titles in the Greek (and accordingly the Latin) translations denote the content:

1. *bᵉrešit*, 'In the Beginning' = Γένεσις, *Genesis* ('Origin')
2. *šᵉmot*, 'Names' = Ἔξοδος, *Exodus* ('Going out')
3. *wayyiqra* 'Then he called' = Λευιτικόν, *Leviticus* ('The Levitical [Book of the Law]')
4. *bᵉmidbar* 'In the wilderness' = Ἀριθμοι, *Numeri* ('Numbers')
5. *dᵉbarim*, 'words' = Δευτερονόμιον, *Deuteronomium* ('The Second Law' [after Deut.17.18, where the Hebrew text really means copy of the law]).

In the Jewish tradition the five books together are called 'the Torah' (or 'the Torah of Moses', 'the Books of the Torah', etc.). The division into five books is expressed in another common phrase *ḥamiša ḥumše ha-tora*, 'the five fifths of the Torah'. It is taken up in the Greek phrase ἡ πεντάτευχος [βίβλος], ' the fivefold (book)', which via the Latinized version *pentateuchus (liber)* finally led to the designation Pentateuch which is customary in academic terminology.

→162f.

The variety in the titles reflects the problem of the relationship of the individual books to the Pentateuch as a whole. Evidently the account from creation (Gen.1) to the death of Moses (Deut.34) is one large complex. But it is equally clear that each of the individual books has a more or less distinctive character of its own and that the division between them is by no means arbitrary. The independence of Deuteronomy can be seen most clearly. It is formulated as a discourse of Moses to the

Israelites before they enter the promised land and the narrative does not immediately link up with what has gone before. However, Genesis too is a self-contained entity: it contains the primal history (1-11) and the patriarchal narratives (12-50). A new beginning is explicitly marked out in Ex.1.1. The demarcation of the three middle books from one another is less clear at first sight, but on closer inspection it emerges that they too each have their own character and that thought has been taken over the demarcation.

1.1 The Book of Genesis

The book of Genesis is divided into two main sections: the primal history (chs.1-11) and the patriarchal history (chs.12-50). Each of the two parts developed in its own way, so to begin with each must be treated separately.

Primal history
→85ff.

The primal history (chs.1-11) contains a number of narratives which in terms of form may be described as sagas. The subjects of the narratives are predominantly ideal-typical figures: husband and wife (chs.2f.), the hostile brothers (ch.4), the exemplary just man (chs.6-8), 'humanity' (11.1-9); only in 9.18-27 do representatives of particular peoples from the time of the narrator appear, in the persons of Noah's sons. (Here there is a striking difference between the trio of Shem, Ham and Japheth in v.18 and Shem, Japheth and Canaan in vv.25-27; vv.18b, 22 seek to compensate for the tension.)

Creation

In this saga-tradition, the origin of the world in which human beings live is depicted from the perspective of the farmer (Crüsemann 1981); man (*'adam*) is destined by God to till the earth (*'adama*, 2.15; 3.17-19,23). The transgression of the divine prohibition in the garden leads to the more burdensome aspects of life (the toil of work, etc.)(3.14-19). The curse on Cain even separates him (and the city-dwellers, nomads, musicians and smiths who are his descendants) from the soil and thus from God himself (4.11f.,14,16). The liason of heavenly beings with human women (6.1-4) results in a reduction in the human life-span (v.3), and at the end of these narratives God responds to the hybris of humanity by scattering it and 'confusing' its language (11.1-9).

There are isolated mythological elements: most clearly in the short section 6.1-4 and in the figure of the serpent in ch.3. The narrative requires that God appears 'in person' in chs.2f., walks in the garden (3.8) and so on, since here God and man still live in undivided communion; after the expulsion from the garden, elsewhere in the primal history God converses with man only as he does in other sagas of the Old Testament.

The two great sections 1.1-2.3 (2.4a is a title to what comes next, cf. Cross, 302; Childs, 145,149) and 9.1-17 are clearly distinct from the sagas. They are not 'narrative', but contain detailed theological outlines: a systematic conception of creation within the framework of a seven-day pattern, with a strict hierarchy of the individual works of creation

– and a recapitulation of the statements about creation in the changed conditions of the time after the flood. The language and theology of these sections are closely related to ch.17 and the Priestly passages in the Jacob story (see below).

→137ff.

The genealogies in chs.5; 10; 11.10-32 form a third element in the primal history. On the one hand they draw the line from Adam (5.3) through Noah (5.29) and his son Shem (5.32; 11.10) to Abraham (11.26ff.); on the other hand, in a 'table of nations' they outline the whole world of known humanity at that time (ch.10).

The construction of the primal history can be seen quite clearly. The first section describes the beginning of human history: the creation of man and his environment (2.4-25), the transgression of the divine prohibitions and expulsion from the garden (ch.3), the first sin of man against man and the cursing of Cain (4.1-16), the further development of humanity (4.17-26). This section ends with the statement that worship of YHWH began at that time (4.26b), i.e. that in this early period he was worshipped by all men.

After a series of ten generations each of which lives to an extreme old age, the flood brings a profound break (cf. Rendtorff 1961, Clark). At the end of the very detailed narrative about the flood (6.5-8.19), God guarantees the future existence of order in creation in order to safeguard the life of humanity in the future (8.21f., again from the perspective of the farmer).

After the flood there is again sin among humanity, and this leads to a curse (9.20-27) – this time of Canaan, who is now specifically excluded from the community of YHWH worshippers. YHWH is now only the God of Shem (v.26). Finally, with the splitting up of humanity into many nations with different languages (11.1-9), the stage is set for what the author and readers or hearers of the primal history know as the reality of their own world.

The two great Priestly sections have been inserted at the key points: at the beginning (1.1-2.3), with a much more comprehensive and systematic account of creation than is offered in ch.2; and after the flood, with a renewal and modification of the blessing of fertility (animals allowed as food for humanity, 9.2-4) and a more extended and emphatic commitment on the part of God through a 'covenant', which he will remember so that another flood does not come upon the earth (9.1-17). God himself sets the 'sign of the covenant', the rainbow, in the sky (in contrast to ch.17, see below).

→137

Often another stratum within the flood narrative is assigned to the Priestly sections. There is no doubt that two different literary strata (at least) can be recognized there; however, it is impossible to reconstruct two independent narratives, so it seems more likely that we have an original narrative with additions.

A further element in the editing and shaping of the primal history can be seen in the formal titles 'these are the *tol*e*dot* of...' (2.4; 5.1; 6.9;

10.1; 11.10 [11.27]). The origin and original meaning of this formula are disputed.

tol^edot

tol^edot literally means 'begettings', i.e, series of families, generations; in the light of 5.1, some people suppose that there was once an independent 'Book of Generations', from which the formulae and the material for the genealogies would have been taken. In the present context, the formulae evidently serve to divide up the primal history and at the same time to bring out a main genealogical line: from the creation of the world, through Adam, Noah and Shem, to Terah, the father of Abraham. Here they serve as titles to very different kinds of texts: in 2.4; 6.9; 11.27 they are followed by narrative texts; in 5.1; 10.1; 11.10 by genealogies. The *tol^edot* formulae belong to a particular stage of the redaction and cannot be regarded as elements from an originally independent 'Priestly Writing'; however, they are probably connected with the Priestly texts in Gen.1.1-2.3; 9.1-17 in the history of the composition of the work. (For the role →138 of the *tol^edot* formulae in the patriarchal stories see below.)

There is no formal connection by specific references in either direction between the primal history and the patriarchal history which follows. Theological The Abraham story begins quite abruptly in 12.1-3. This marks a connection basically new beginning: from the general history of humanity there now emerges the history of the one people whose ancestor is Abraham. The promise to Abraham, and through him to all the families of the earth, which stands at the centre of these verses, points forwards to the future history of Israel and humanity. At the same time, in the present context, it also has the function of pointing backwards: the curses of primal history (3.14-19; cf.8.21) are countered and contrasted with the promise of the blessing. In this way there is a bridge from the primal history to the patriarchal history.

Von Rad has developed an interpretation of the primal history which sees it as intentionally leading up to the election of Abraham; for him, this is connected with a theological subordination of creation faith to a faith in salvation grounded in history. Westermann has stressed the independence of the primal history more strongly, and Crüsemann (1981) has shown that the primal history and the patriarchal history cannot belong together to a common 'Yahwistic' work because of the differences in the profile of their content; they were only combined at a later stage.

Patriarchal The patriarchal narratives, i.e. the tradition of the patriarchs narratives Abraham, Isaac and Jacob, and of Joseph, takes up most space in Abraham Genesis (chs.12-50). The Abraham story (12.1-25.10) contains a series →85f. of independent individual sagas, e.g. Gen.12.10-20 (connected with the context by notes of itineraries in 12.9; 13.1.3f.); 22; 23; 24. The beginnings of these are either not connected at all with what has gone before or connected only by very general phrases (e.g. 'After these things...', 22.1; 'Now Abraham was old', 24.1); each has a conclusion which does not suggest a narrative continuation.

Alongside these we can also see larger narrative complexes or combinations of individual sagas into larger compositions, (The 134 following account corresponds in essentials to the analysis given by

E.Blum, who here takes up the preliminary studies by Gunkel and
Rendtorff 1977.) Thus chapters 13; 18; 19 form an Abraham-Lot-
narrative (Gunkel called this the 'Abraham-Lot saga-cycle'); in it ch.13
is evidently already composed with an eye to chs.18f.; after the two
part, Abraham's way leads to Mamre (13.18; 18.1), where YHWH
appears to him, but Lot's way leads to Sodom (13.12f.; 19.1), where he
is almost caught up in its downfall. Whereas 18.1-16 probably takes up
an independent Abraham narrative, ch.19 is clearly composed with a
view to its context in the Abraham-Lot narrative (cf. e.g. the continuity
in the narrative with 18 in terms of characters and the time of day, and
the parallels between 18.1ff. and 19.1-3). After the destruction of
Sodom, the narrative line relating to Lot ends with the birth of the two
ancestors of Moab and Ammon in Transjordan (19.30-38); similarly,
ch.18 points above all to the miraculous birth of Isaac (word-play in
18.12-15), the ancestor of Israel (21.1-7). Thus Lot's parting from
Abraham in 13 opens a history of the origin of the peoples of Moab/ →86f.
Ammon and Israel each in its own land. (Chapter 14 also deals with
Abraham and Lot, but stands in remarkable isolation and has quite a
different picture of Abraham, who is the warrior hero.)

Chapter 20 evidently contains a variant or doublet to 12.10-20; however, what
we have here is more a theologically reflective or corrective interpretation,
which already presupposes knowledge of the narrative in 12.10-20 (Westermann,
commentary). According to Blum, along with 21.22ff. it forms a consecutive
'Abraham-Abimelech story' which – in dependence on 12.10-20; ch.26 (cf. the
sequence: danger to the ancestral mother – treaty with Abimelech) – was
originally independent and was only inserted into its literary context at a
relatively late stage (here ch.20 had to be put before 21.1-7, because in this
narrative Sarah is still childless).

In traditio-historical terms, 21.8-21 is probably a variant on the aetiology of →86f.
Ishmael in ch.16; however, in its present form it is the necessary narrative
continuation of ch.16, in which the conflict between the sons of Abraham (who
will be the heir?, cf. 21.10,12) is resolved with the expulsion of Ishmael. In this
composition the birth and expulsion of Ishmael clearly frame the episodes of
the announcement and birth of Isaac (18; 21.1-7). At the same time, however,
21.8ff. also prepares for ch.22: after Abraham has sent one son into the
wilderness by divine command, he is commanded to sacrifice the second (who
is now his only son, v.2). Both sections are connected by cross references to the
beginning of the Abraham story in 12.1-3: the Ishmael narrative by the promise
of becoming a people (cf. 21.13,18 with 12.2a) and ch.22 with 12.1, because the
command to set out, though in a different context, has a parallel structure. In
this context, opened up by 12.1-3, Abraham's career arrives at its dramatic end
and climax in ch.22 (for chs.23f. see below).

The Isaac story (26) is strikingly brief and hardly developed at all.
Evidently the narrative interest at the time when the patriarchal
narratives were collected was concentrated more on Abraham and
Jacob. So the Isaac story contains only two detailed narratives, both of
which have a parallel in the Abraham story (26.7-11 [12], 26-31, see
below). These are linked to a continuous narrative about Isaac among

and with the Philistines by brief passages, almost notes, which are concerned above all with wells in the Negeb; there are also references back (cf. e.g. v.29 with vv.11,12,16). The main theme here is the territorial division between Philistines and Israelites in the Negeb.

In the present context the Isaac story has been inserted into the beginning of the Jacob story (25.19-34; 27-35). In contrast to the Abraham story, it is almost impossible now to identify independent individual traditions in most of the main material of the Jacob story (most clearly still in 25.29-34; 28.11ff.). Everything is subordinated to one overarching theme: Jacob's conflict with his brother Esau (25.19-34; 27; 32f.) and with his uncle Laban (29-31). Here the episodes of the conflict with Esau over the right of the firstborn and the blessing (25.19-34; 27) are interwoven with the Jacob-Laban story into a self-contained 'Jacob narrative' (Blum; Gunkel calls it the 'Jacob-Esau-Laban saga-cycle') with the help of the theme of Jacob's flight (27.43ff.; 28.10,20,22) by references back from ch.31 (esp.31.13) and above all by the new

→96

'finale' in chs.32f. The two divine epiphanies at Bethel (28.1ff.) and Penuel (*32.23ff.*), at decisive turning points for Jacob, also serve to support the narrative. Without question this narrative comes from north Israel (cf. the settings for the action). According to Blum, it partly serves to legitimate the history of the beginnings of the northern kingdom of Israel, for example through its stress on the cult places of

→40

Bethel (28.11f.; 31.13) and Penuel (for a time the capital of Jeroboam I, cf. I Kings 12.25).

→86, 110

The traditions of the three 'patriarchs' are followed in Genesis by the Joseph story. Unlike the patriarchal stories, this is a large-scale narrative conceived as a unity from the start and given a novellistic form (Gunkel, cf. Donner). This is matched by the complexity of its themes; here above all the elements of wisdom theology (von Rad 1953) and the theme of 'rule' (Crüsemann 1978, 143ff.; Blum) are significant. The scene of the blessing in ch. 48, inserted at the end of the Joseph story, unites the two main figures of Jacob and Joseph and at the same time points back to the beginning of the story of Jacob in its adoption of themes from ch.27 and the beginning of the Jacob narrative. Evidently in this way it serves to bind together the Jacob narrative and the Joseph story into a comprehensive 'Jacob story' (from his birth to his death). The theme of ch. 48 is an aetiology of the pre-eminence of the Joseph tribes in Israel.

→84

By contrast, in the collection of tribal sayings in ch.49, we can see a clearly rival claim, in so far as here Judah is promised dominion over his brothers (49.8-12) – a situation made possible by the 'demotion' of the first three sons (49.3-7). Individual traditions about 'sons of Jacob' already point in this direction: the narrative about Simeon and Levi (ch.34); the note about Reuben's wickedness in 35.21f.; and the narrative about Judah in ch.38, which was evidently inserted with ch.49 into a Judaean extension to the 'Jacob story'.

The promises increasingly played a role in the formation of larger 'patriarchal narratives' as elements of composition and interpretation.

Thus the promises of land and posterity in 13.14-17 and 28.13,14a, formulated in parallel in a characteristic way, serve to link the traditions about Jacob and Abraham.

The four divine speeches in 12.1-3; 26.1-3; 31.11,13; 46.1-5a are related in another way. In the first and the third, Abraham and Jacob are commanded by God to set out from Mesopotamia to the land intended for them (Canaan); in the second Isaac is forbidden – with an allusion to Abraham's conduct in 12.10-20 (cf. 26.1!) – to leave Canaan for Egypt; finally, in the fourth, with clear references to ch.26 (46.1: Beersheba; the God of his father Isaac), Jacob is encouraged to do precisely that, though this is bound up with the promise that he will be brought back. (Further common features are the promise of becoming a people [12.2a; 46.3b; cf. also 21.13,18], the promise of God being with the patriarch [12.2a; 26.3a; 46.4], etc.) So in these divine speeches the paths of the patriarchs are continually directed towards the land of Canaan as their goal, and a deviation to the 'peripheral regions' of Mesopotamia or Egypt proves to endanger this union of the patriarchs (i.e. Israel) with their land. Thus (as with the promise of becoming a people) a concern of the narrative tradition is taken up, but is formulated more explicitly and fundamentally, and with divine authority.

Dating

Historically this is probably to be seen against the background of a situation in which the existence of the people and their possession of land was at risk, i.e. during the exile. At that point this patriarchal tradition must have acquired direct significance. The promises of blessing in 12.3 and 28.14b (each time the first promise in the Abraham and Jacob stories), which assures Israel that the nations will see it as the example of a people blessed by God, are also to be understood in this context.

Theological connection

These compositional elements bind the Abraham story, the Isaac story and the Jacob/Joseph stories together into a larger, coherent unity. The link between the patriarchal narratives and the wider Pentateuchal tradition was only achieved in the context of wider theological revisions.

Here we should mention first a group of promises (12.7; 16.10; 22.16-18; 24.7; 26.3b-5,24; 28.15; 31.3; *32.10-13*; 50.24, etc.) which are shown to belong together by virtue of their formulations, cross-references and so on. The 'main text' in this group is ch.15, in which the promises are developed into a kind of 'promise narrative': Abraham is to have as many descendants as the stars of heaven (vv.1-6), and these are to possess the land (vv.7-21). In v.18, this is expressed in a particularly solemn form. YHWH concludes a covenant (*berit*) with Abraham, the content of which is the promise of land to his descendants. Here we have the expression of a theological conception (cf. e.g. also 22.16-18; 26.3b-5) which found comprehensive expression in Deuteronomy and which is therefore usually termed 'Deuteronomistic'. Genesis 15 as a whole belongs to this Deuteronomistic stratum of revision (Rendtorff 1980, Blum). (This stratum also evidently inserted ch.24, a very late narrative.) For its significance in the growth of the Pentateuch see below.

Covenant

→151f.

→86

→143f., 161ff.

We can see a further revision in ch.17. Here the 'covenant' concept is developed in another direction. From the side of YHWH here the promise of countless descendants stands in the foreground (v.2,4), coupled with the promise that YHWH will be the God of Abraham and his descendants (v.7f.; the promise of land is also included in v.8a). Circumcision is required of Abraham and his descendants as a sign of the covenant, and this is explained in detailed cultic instructions (vv.9-14). Here we can see a 'Priestly' stratum of editing. Some sections in the Jacob story also belong here: at the beginning, in Isaac's blessing of Jacob (27.46-28.9); and at the end, in a divine speech and Jacob's reaction (35.9-15), which display a close affinity to Gen.17 (cf. also 48.3f.). Here, too, we have a thematic correction of the earlier tradition. Thus according to 27.46-28.9 – in contrast to the narrative in ch.27 – Jacob does not go to Laban in fear of Esau, but at his father's bidding, and in retrospect Esau appears in a bad light (because of his foreign wives, cf. 26.34f; 27.46; 28.1,8f.); 35.9-15 seems to be a resumption of the Bethel episode in 28.11ff., which challenges its central assertion, that God has his abode in Bethel (cf. 35.13).

→144, 162

→96

Chronology

We should also attribute to this 'Priestly revision' some chronological information which appears in the patriarchal narratives, the information about Abraham's age: on his departure from Harran (12.4: 75 years), at the birth of Ishmael (16.16: 86 years), at his circumcision (17.1,24: 99 years; Ishmael, v.25, 13 years), at the birth of Isaac (21.5: 100 years) and at his death (25.7: 175 years). There is similar information about the patriarchs. The round numbers (75, 100, 175) show that this is a well-thought-out system.

toledot
→134

The 'Priestly' editing has also substantially structured the patriarchal narratives as we now have them in a further way, by incorporating all the material into the divisions marked by the *toledot*. This first of all comprises the *toledot* formulae (11.27; 25.12; 25.19; 36.1 [,9]; 37.2). In the patriarchal narratives they serve as titles for the history of the sons of the person mentioned in the formula or for a list of his descendants (or both). A second framework (not in the case of Esau) which corresponds to this title is a note about the death and (in the main line of the Israelite patriarchs) the burial of the father by his sons (cf. 25.17; 35.29; 49.33; 50.13). (In the present text there are references back to Gen.23 in the notes about burial; however, this narrative may have had a history independent of the Priestly revision.) Only with Abraham is the *toledot* title which corresponds to the closing note (25.8ff.) 'missing' (instead we have the formula with Terah in 11.27); however, this resulted from the arrangement of the traditional material: the Abraham title would have had to introduce the Isaac story, but the bulk of this (ch.26) has been incorporated into the Jacob story.

It is clear that the different 'Priestly' passages develop the existing tradition and by no means belong together as an independent 'narrative', as is widely assumed (cf. Cross).

At the latest with the Priestly stratum of revision the primal history (see above on 1.1-2.3; ch.9) and the patriarchal narratives come to form a continuous narrative. This makes the content of the 'canonical' final form of Genesis move from creation to redemption (Childs).

Bibliography

Commentaries: Dillmann (KeH) 1875, ⁶1892; Delitzsch 1887; Holzinger (KHC) 1898; Gunkel (HK) 1902, ³1910 (⁹1977); Skinner (ICC) 1910, ²1930; Procksch (KAT) 1913, ²,³1924; Jacob 1934; Zimmerli (ZBK) I 1943, ²1967; II 1976; von Rad (ATD) 1949-1953, ET OTL ²1979; Cassuto I 1961; II 1964; Speiser (AB) 1964; Westermann (BK) I 1974, ²1976; II 1981; III 1982.
E.Blum, *Die Komposition der Vätergeschichte*, Diss. Heidelberg 1982; W.M.Clark, 'The Flood and the Structure of the Pre-patriarchal History', *ZAW* 83, 1971, 184-211; F.M.Cross, 'The Priestly Work', in *Canaanite Myth and Hebrew Epic*, 1973, 293-352; F.Crüsemann, *Der Widerstand gegen das Königtum. Die antiköniglichen Texte des Alten Testamentes und der Kampf um den frühen israelitischen Staat*, 1978; id., 'Die Eigenständigkeit der Urgeschichte. Ein Beitrag zur Diskussion um den "Jahwisten"', in *Die Botschaft und die Boten, FS H.W.Wolff*, 1981, 11-29; H.Donner, *Die literarische Gestalt der alttestamentlichen Josephsgeschichte*, 1976; G. von Rad, 'The Joseph Narrative and Ancient Wisdom' (1953), in *The Problem of the Hexateuch*, 1966, 292-300; R.Rendtorff, 'Genesis 8,21 und die Urgeschichte des Jahwisten', *KuD* 7, 1961, 69-78 (= *GS*, 188-97); id., *Das überlieferungsgeschichtliche Problem des Pentateuch*, 1977; id., 'Genesis 15 im Rahmen der theologischen Bearbeitung der Vätergeschichten', in *Werden und Wirken des Alten Testaments, FS C.Westermann*, 1980, 74-81; C.Westermann, *Genesis 1-11*, 1972; *Genesis 12-50*, 1975 (history of scholarship).
Steuernagel, §36,37; Childs, VI.
Cf. also the bibliography on I.3.1; III,1,6.

1.2 The Book of Exodus

The beginning of the book of Exodus marks a deep change in the presuppositions of the narrative. In the patriarchal narratives the protagonists were always individuals, but now the people makes an appearance. The transition is explicitly marked at the beginning. The seventy 'souls' of the families of Jacob and his sons (1.1-15) become the 'Israelites' (v.7, *bᵉne yiśra'el*, the traditional 'children of Israel') or the 'people of Israel' (v.9), who fill the whole land. Israel as a people

The nature of the narrative changes at the same time. Only occasionally is there an encounter between individuals (e.g. 2.1-10, 11-15a, 15b-22). Usually the people itself is one of the partners. Sometimes it alone is contrasted with the Egyptians or with Pharaoh (e.g. 1.8-14), or it is represented by anonymous figures (5.15-18); more often Moses represents the people, often along with Aaron (esp. chs.7ff.). But Moses does not just represent the people to outsiders; many texts speak of internal conflicts between Moses (and Aaron) and the Israelites and →12f.

of their doubt and unbelief (thus in anticipation 4.1ff.; then 5.19ff.; 6.9; 14.10ff.; 16; 17.1-7; 32). Thus these narratives also – to a greater degree than the patriarchal sagas or the heroic sagas in the book of Judges – have a largely 'theological' theme: the oppression of the Israelites (chs.1f.) is the presupposition of the promise of deliverance (chs.3f.). The sequel is therefore concerned only with how God carries out his plan to deliver Israel and how the Israelites react to the dangers on the way.

It seems questionable how far we can presuppose individual sagas here. There are only a few clearly definable individual narratives (e.g. 2.1-10,15b-22; 17.1-7, 8-16). Chapter 3 begins like an aetiological saga about a holy place (vv.1-6), but then becomes a divine discourse with a wider scope, which culminates in the calling of Moses (up to 4.31). Other narratives are so strongly influenced by the wider context that they do not display any independent narrative structure (e.g. 1.15-22; 2.11-15a). A large narrative complex about the plagues begins in 7.8, which after a provisional conclusion at 10.28f. in the narrative of the last plague (the killing of the firstborn) is continued in Pharaoh's surrender and the exodus (11.1-13.16); this is immediately followed by the narrative of the crossing of the Red Sea and deliverance from the pursuing Egyptian forces (13.17-14.31). Evidently, in contrast to the patriarchal narratives, few independent, already shaped traditional passages have been used here. That is also an important reason why the individual stages in the growth of the text can no longer be followed so clearly in the exodus tradition.

The first part of the book of Exodus (1-15) moves purposefully towards the exodus from Egypt, which is closely connected with the Passover. Therefore there has even been a concern to see this whole section as a cult legend of the feast of Passover (Pedersen). It is quite conceivable that the texts were presented and perhaps even 'performed' as a cult drama in the context of the feast of Passover/Mazzoth. However, the present version of this chapter bears witness to a very careful work of theological redaction: after the description of the oppression, the turning point is marked by YHWH hearing the lament of the Israelites and 'remembering his covenant with the patriarchs' (2.23-25); when Moses announces deliverance to the Israelites, they 'believe' (4.31). This statement about their belief is then emphatically taken up again after the deliverance from the Egyptian pursuit at the Reed Sea (14.31). With this the narrative has reached a clear conclusion. The hymn in 15.1-18 (19-21) is put at this point as a hymnic echo of the event, and also perhaps because of a corresponding liturgical usage.

Ex.15.22 describes a further departure of the Israelites. Given all that has been said so far, the destination of their journey is the land promised to them by God. However, first of all they arrive at Sinai, which in geographical terms marks a major detour. In connection with this von Rad (1938) drew attention to the striking fact that in a number of creed-like passages the exodus from Egypt is followed without a break by the entry into the promised land (Deut.26.5-9; 6.20-25; cf. I

Sam.12.8; Ex.15.12f.; Ps.135.8-12). In other texts there is more or less extended mention between these two events of the wandering in the wilderness (e.g. Josh 14.7b; Ps.78.52b; 136.16; 105.40f.; Jer.2.6; Amos 2.10), but here too there is no mention of Sinai.

Genesis

Thus in essentials the events on Sinai are evidently an independent tradition which was not initially combined in a narrative with the exodus from Egypt. In view of the marked cultic character of the passages involved, it seems obvious that we should see the reason for this in a special liturgical use of the Sinai tradition. (The term 'Sinai pericope', in a phrase derived from liturgy, is often used here.)

Sinai

The account of the stay on Sinai is an extremely complex structure and at the same time the most extensive connected passage within the Pentateuch (Ex.19.1-Num.10.10). The greater part of it is made up of collections of law and cultic regulations of very different kinds and origins, which have now been brought together within a narrative framework.

→14ff.

The first independent section is made up of Ex.19-24. This contains two legal passages: the Decalogue (20.1-17) and the Book of the Covenant (20.22-23.19; the name is taken from 24.7).

→16, 151

The Decalogue, which with slight alterations also appears in Deut.*5.6-18 (21)*, contains a series of prohibitions, the individual members of which predominantly begin with the negative *lo'*, 'not'; however, the commandments about keeping the sabbath holy (v.8) and honouring parents are given a positive formulation. It is impossible to reconstruct a uniform basic form. Ex.34.28 already presupposes that there are ten commandments (cf. Deut.4.13); however, the number already fluctuates in the tradition of the Massoretic text of the Bible, as is shown by the double system of accentuation. In particular there is a dispute as to whether the prohibition of images (vv.4ff.) should be counted as an independent (second) commandment (which would mean that v.17 contains only one commandment). In content, the Decalogue contains cultic (vv.3-11) prohibitions and commandments, and prohibitions and commandments relating to behaviour between individuals (vv.12-17); thus it embraces a wider sphere than other series of prohibitions and is to be understood as a collection of basic rules.

Decalogue

→83f., 92f.

The Book of the Covenant is a collection of legal precepts of a very different kind. 21.1ff. contains legal statements, predominantly with a casuistic formulation, about slave law (21.2-11), bodily injury (21.18-36; in vv.23f. the *lex talionis*) and crimes connected with property (*21.37-22.16*); between them is a series of apodeictic statements about crimes which bear the death penalty (21.12-17). Furthermore, the Book of the Covenant contains religious rules of various kinds, about idols and the building of altars (20.23-26); magic, bestiality, sacrificing to idols (*22.17-19*); blasphemy and cursing (*22.27*); the flesh of savaged animals which have not been cultically slaughtered (*22.30*); and instructions about cultic offerings (*22.28f.*), the sabbath year, feast days, festivals and sacrifices (*23.10-19*); there are further rules about behaviour towards aliens, the socially disadvantaged, and 'enemies' (*22.20-26*; 23.4f.,9) as well as legal proceedings (23.1-3,6-8). (For 23.20-33 see below.)

Book of the Covenant

→90ff.

→93

→144

The Decalogue and the Book of the Covenant have been inserted into a narrative framework which in turn has incorporated and worked over a variety of elements from the tradition. In Ex.19, initially the exodus from Egypt is stressed as the presupposition for the impending proclamation of the divine will (v.4, cf. also 20.2), which as a result is brought into the wider context of YHWH's historical action towards Israel. Then follow the preparations for the proclamation of the Decalogue, in which there is special stress on Moses' distinctive position as the direct recipient of the law (vv.9,20 etc.).

Moses as
mediator

After the proclamation of the Decalogue this special position of Moses is further consolidated by the fear of the people (20.18-21). This at the same time produces a distinction between the Decalogue and the laws which follow in the Book of the Covenant. Both are given by God on Sinai, but as the people was afraid at the voice of God, only Moses received the other laws in order to hand them down to the people. Thus the Decalogue is the basis and all that follows is development – and Moses is the mediator. Finally, the whole proclamation of the law in ch.24 is concluded by the solemn making of a covenant (again incorporating a variety of traditions); here the decisive key words 'covenant' and 'hearken to the voice of YHWH' from 19.5 are taken up again in 24.7f. Thus Ex.19-24 now forms a self-contained complex.

→151
→137

Cultic
decalogue

There is another 'decalogue' in Ex.34 (34.10-26, often designated a cultic decalogue), similarly within the context of a covenant ceremony (vv.10,27).

The section 34.10-26 has a number of verbal parallels in the Book of the Covenant, above all in 23.12-19 (with a different sequence of the individual commandments) and in *22.28f.* The first two commandments (34.14,17) correspond to the first (or first two) commandment(s) of the Decalogue (20.3-5; for 34.17, cf. also 20.23). It is evident from this that individual commandments and prohibitions are often handed down within several series or collections.

→16, 141

This chapter, too, has been included in a narrative framework and thus combined with the tradition of the apostasy of the Israelites from YHWH through their making of the 'Golden Calf' (ch.32). As a result of this, Ex.32-34 now forms a special narrative complex which speaks of the breaking and the renewal of the covenant. In the present 'canonical' form of the Sinai pericope we therefore see how at the beginning there was no ideal time when Israel was obedient. The covenant was broken, and the renewed covenant, valid from then on, has its basis in divine grace and forgiveness (Childs, 175f.).

Golden calf
→40

Finally, Ex.25-31; 35-40 stand out very clearly from their surroundings. They contain the instructions for the building of the sanctuary and for the institution of the cult which Moses received from God on Sinai (25-31), and an account of how the building was carried out (35-40) which is continued in the book of Leviticus (Lev.8 reports the performance of the priestly ordination ordered in Ex.29). They belong to a priestly tradition which is focussed on the cult and the exact details of its performance.

Cult traditions

→19f.

→138, 162

Their insertion at the present point is evidently well-considered. After the conclusion of the covenant Moses is again called to Sinai (24.12ff.), where he receives instructions for the sanctuary and the cult.

While he is spending forty days and nights on Sinai (v.18), the people Genesis
is committing apostasy (32.1ff.). Only after the restoration of the
covenant (34) is the building of the sanctuary undertaken (35ff.). The
institution and implementation of the cult come to a conclusion in
instructions about the Day of Atonement (Lev.16), on which the →146
sanctuary is regularly cleansed of all impurities, transgressions and sins
of the Israelites (v.16).

A further link consists in the fact that the cloud which at first covered
Sinai and at the same time concealed the 'glory' (*kabod*) of YHWH →210
(Ex.24.15-18), moved over to the sanctuary after it had been erected
(40.34f.). From now on the presence of YHWH which is expressed in
his *kabod* accompanies Israel in its journey through the wildernesss.
(In 40.36-38 the tradition of the pillars of cloud and fire has been →147f.
combined with this, cf. Ex.13.21f.; 14.19f., 24; Num.9.15-22; 10.11ff.,
etc.)

There remains the section Ex.15.22-18.27, which now stands between Wilderness
the exodus from Egypt and the arrival on Sinai. The texts brought
together here all deal with the stay in the wilderness. Some of the →17f.
narratives have local points of reference and were probably originally
transmitted as local aetiologies (Marah, 15.23; Massah and Meribah, →87
17.7; also Elim, 15.27; Rephidim, 17.1,8). What holds them together
in their present form is the 'murmuring' of the Israelites against Moses Murmuring
(and Aaron) (15.24; 16.2,7-9,12; 17.3). The reason for the murmuring →17, 148
is thirst (15.24; 17.3) or hunger (16.3), combined with a reproach to
Moses for having led the Israelites out of Egypt and brought them to
their present position (cf. also 14.11f.). So in the last resort it is directed
against YHWH himself (cf. Coats) and forms a sharp contrast with the
'faith' of the Israelites after the deliverance at the Reed Sea (14.31; →140
there too there is mention of belief in YHWH *and* Moses). At the same
time it prepares for the apostasy of the Israelites on Sinai, which
similarly contain an element directed against Moses (32.1).

Only Ex.18 does not contain the theme of murmuring. However, the narratives
connected with the figure of Jethro could hardly appear elsewhere.

The book of Exodus has been linked with Genesis in various ways Connection
in the process of redaction. Some explicit references forwards and with Genesis
backwards display marks of Deuteronomistic style: in Gen. 50.24 →137, 161ff.
Joseph announces before his death that YHWH will lead the Israelites
out of Egypt 'into the land which he swore to Abraham, Isaac and
Jacob'. In Ex.33.1 Moses receives from YHWH the command to lead
the people into the land promised to the patriarchs in the same words.

This reference to the promise of land to the fathers also appears in
Moses' intercession after the breaking of the covenant (32.13, bound
up with the promise of descendants, cf. Gen.22.17; on the promise of
land, cf. further Ex.13.5,11).

The command to set off for the land promised to the fathers is bound *mal'ak yhwh*
up in Ex.33.2 with the promise that YHWH will send an 'angel' (*mal'ak*)

before Moses. The same promise appears in 32.34 after the hearing of Moses' intercession (v.13). Evidently, then, the figure of the guiding angel belongs to this Deuteronomistic level of redaction. Therefore the paraenetic conclusion to the Book of the Covenant (23.20-33) in which the guiding angel is mentioned twice (vv.20,23) must also be included in this stratum. The leading of Israel back (cf.23.20) to the land promised to the patriarchs is one of the basic features of Deuteronomistic theology (cf. Deut.1.8; 6.10, etc.).

→162

→137f.

A further link with the patriarchal history emerges in Ex.2.23-25; 6.2-8, where there is a reference back to the 'covenant' of YHWH with the fathers. In particular the second of these texts displays a clear affinity with Gen.17 (but cf. also Ex.31.12-17) and is therefore to be attributed to the Priestly redaction. Evidently this stratum of redaction sought once again to stress the connection of the patriarchal history with the Moses tradition.

There is another attempt to divide up the book of Exodus in Weimar/Zenger (11-15; cf. Zenger 1981, 477ff.).

Bibliography

Commentaries: Holzinger (KHC) 1900; Baentsch (HK) 1903; Gressmann (SAT) 1914, ²1922; Heinisch (HS) 1934; Beer (HAT) 1939; Noth (ATD) 1959, ET OTL 1962; Cassuto 1967; Childs (OTL) 1974; Schmidt (BK) 1974ff.

G.W.Coats, *Rebellion in the Wilderness. The Murmuring Motif in the Wilderness Traditions of the Old Testament*, 1968; V.Fritz, *Israel in der Wüste*, 1970; M.Greenberg, 'The Thematic Unity of Exodus III-XI', in *Fourth World Congress of Jewish Studies* I, 1967, 151-9; H.Gressmann, *Mose und seine Zeit. Ein Kommentar zu den Mose-Sagen*, 1913; A.Jepsen, *Untersuchungen zum Bundesbuch*, 1927; J.Pedersen, 'Passahfest und Passahlegende', *ZAW* 52, 1934, 161-75; G.von Rad, 'The Form-Critical Problem of the Hexateuch', in *The Problem of the Hexateuch*, ET 1966, 1-78; id., 'Beobachtungen zur Moseerzählung Exodus 1-14', *EvTh* 31, 1971, 579-88 (= *GS* II, 189-98); A.Reichert, *Der Jahwist und die sogenannten deuteronomistischen Erweiterungen im Buch Exodus*, Diss. Tübingen 1972; P.Weimar/E.Zenger, *Exodus. Geschichten und Geschichte der Befreiung Israels*, 1975; E.Zenger, 'Tradition und Interpretation in Exodus IX 1-21', *SVT* 32, 1981, 452-83.

Steuernagel, §38-40; Childs, VII.

Cf. also the bibliography on I.3.2, 3; III.1.6.

1.3 The Book of Leviticus

The Book of Leviticus consists almost exclusively of legal material which is predominantly concerned with cultic questions. The few narrative passages also deal with cultic themes: the performance of the

priestly ordination ordered in Ex.29 (Lev.8) and the first general sacrifices on the newly built altar (9), two short narratives about problems over the right performance of sacrifice (10.1-5, 16-20) and one about dealing with a blasphemer (24.10-14,23).

The texts collected together in the book of Leviticus are of very different types and origins. Evidently they have been brought together here with the intention of depicting the whole of cultic legislation as having been given to Moses on Sinai (26.46; cf. 7.38; 25.1; 27.34). Various sub-collections can still be clearly recognized; these were not composed for their present context and initially were probably transmitted more or less independently.

Leviticus 1-7 contains a collection of rules for sacrifice which are Sacrifice →97f. further sub-divided into sacrificial rituals (1-5) and other regulations concerned with their performance (6f.). They reflect different stages in the history of Israelite sacrificial worship, as is evident above all from the fact that the sequence of the kinds of sacrifice differs in the two sections; 'sin offering' and 'guilt offering' are moved further forward (*6.17*-7.7) from last place (4f.).

The regulations for purity in Lev.11-15 stand out as a further group Purity →98 of texts. The collection consists of individual chapters on clean and unclean animals (11, cf. Deut.14.3-21), the purification of a woman after the birth of a child (12), leprosy and other eruptions on people, clothes and houses (13f.), and impurity through bodily discharges (15f.). This chapter was probably once an independent collection, as can be argued from the way in which sections keep ending with the word *tora* (11.46; 12.7; 13.59; 14.32,54,57; 15.32). →99

Leviticus 17-26 is usually designated the 'Holiness Code' and regarded as an Holiness Code independent collection of laws. At the same time, it is continually stressed that no internal order can be recognized in this collection. More recently, therefore, the existence of this 'Holiness Code' has regularly been questioned (cf. Wagner). In fact the individual chapters have very different characters. Moreover the keyword 'holy' (*qados̆*), from which this designation is derived (cf.19.2), appears only in chs.19-22 within this group of texts (19.2; 20.7f.,26; 21.6-8,15,23; 22.9, 16,32); however, it also occurs outside it (e.g. 11.44f.). So Lev.17-26 can hardly be regarded as an independent collection.

Lev.17-20 similarly deals with cultic impurity, above all that which cannot be removed. Therefore we often find here the statement that someone who transgresses against particular rules is to be 'cut off' from the worshipping community and his people (17.4,9,10,14; 18.29; 19.8; 20.3,5,6,17f.). Such 'irreparable' impurities (Wagner) could come about through offences against sacrificial regulations or through eating blood (17), illicit sexual relationships (18), crimes carrying the death penalty (20; the common factor in the various regulations collected in ch.19 is not evident). Leviticus 21f. discusses further special rules for the purity of priests (21) and sacrifical offerings (22).

The distinction between reparable and irreparable uncleanness also Day of Atonement makes clear the position of Lev.16, the regulations for the 'Day of Atonement' (*yom ha-kippurim*, cf. Lev.23.27f.), between Lev.11-15 and 17f. All removal of impurity comes to a conclusion and climax in the great annual occasion of atonement, at which at the same time the sanctuary is cleansed from the impurity caused by all the happenings for which atonement could not be made.

Primarily details of calendars are collected in Lev.23-25: the sacrificial calendar (23), supplemented by regulations for lights and showbread (24.1-9); regulations about the sabbath year (25.1-7) and the year of Jubilee (8-31). In 24.15-22 further regulations about crimes carrying the death penalty have been inserted into the narrative about dealing with the blasphemer (24.10-14,23).

These various collections now stand in a wider context which also includes parts of the book of Exodus. The final chapter, Lev.26, is probably meant as a conclusion to all the legislation on Sinai. (Cf. v.46; repeated in 27.34 after an addition.) It refers back to basic regulations:

the prohibition of images of God from the Decalogue (Lev.26.1; cf. Ex.20.4f.) and the sabbath commandment (Lev.26.2; cf. Ex.31.12ff.). It promises Israel blessing if it fulfils the laws given on Sinai (vv.3-13)

and disaster if it does not (vv.14-38), and finally expects that the 'survivors' of Israel will repent and that YHWH will 'remember his covenant' (vv.39-45).

Here we have an echo of formulations from earlier Priestly texts (e.g.

Ex.6.2-8). They show that this stratum of redaction has linked the exodus not only backwards to the patriarchal narratives and the primal history but also forwards to the legislation for the cult and its implementation at Sinai. At the same time there are also clear relationships to Deuteronomic-Deuteronomistic terminology, in the use of the phrase about observing laws and commandments, etc. (Lev.26.3,14f.,43, and also 18.4f.,26; 19.19,37). These links between the Priestly and the Deuteronomic-Deuteronomistic traditions still need further clarification (Thiel, 68ff.).

Bibliography

Commentaries: Bertholet (KHC) 1901; Baentsch (HK) 1903; Heinisch (HS) 1935; Noth (ATD) 1962, ET OTL ²1977; Elliger (HAT) 1966.

R.Kilian, *Literarkritische und formgeschichtliche Untersuchung des Heiligkeitsgesetzes*, 1963; K.Koch, *Die Priesterschrift von Exodus 25 bis Leviticus 16*, 1959; G.von Rad, *Studies in Deuteronomy*, ET 1953 , 25-36; R.Rendtorff, *Die Gesetze in der Priesterschrift*, ²1963; id., *Studien zur Geschichte des Opfers in Alten Israel*, 1967; W.Thiel, 'Erwägungen zum Alter des Heiligkeitsgesetzes', *ZAW* 81, 1969, 40-73; V.Wagner, 'Zur Existenz des sogenannten Heiligkeitsgesetzes', *ZAW* 86, 1974, 307-16.

Steuernagel §40,41; Eissfeldt, §35; Smend, §10; Childs, VIII.

Cf. also the bibliography on II.4; III.1.6.

1.4 The Book of Numbers

Of all the books in the Pentateuch, the Book of Numbers is the hardest
to survey. It contains a great deal of material of a very varied kind and
gives the impression of being very heterogeneous. It is even difficult to
decide how to divide it. A clear break comes after Num.10.10; the
Israelites set out from Sinai. So the first part of the book belongs to the
'Sinai pericope' in the wider sense, which begins with Ex.19.1. The next
part first of all deals with the stay of the Israelites in the wilderness and
in this way is connected with Ex.15.22-18.27. The narrative then goes
over to the theme of the occupation of Transjordan, so that a new
section begins with Num.20.14. (Some exegetes make the break only
within, or at the end of, Num.21.)

→141
→143

The section Num.1.1-10.10 again predominantly contains regulations
about the cult, which have a clear affinity with texts in the books of
Exodus and Leviticus.

Cultic laws

In some cases these are supplements to earlier regulations: Num.5.5-10
supplements Lev.*5.20-26* in respect of the share in the *'ašam* sacrifice which
goes to the priest (vv.8-10); Num.8.1-4 repeats Ex.25.31-40 and 37.17-24 in
abbreviated form; Num. 8.5-22 again takes up the rules about the consecration
of levites in 3.5-13 from the specific aspect of 'purification' (vv.6f.,15,21);
Num.9.1-14 supplements the passover regulations in Ex.12, above all in respect
of those taking part in the cult who are 'unclean' at the time of the feast (vv.6ff.)

→98
→97

The keyword 'purity' determines the whole section. Chapters 1-4
deal with a census of the Israelites and their organization into one great
camp; here they are divided by tribes into the four points of the compass
around the sanctuary (the 'tent of meeting'). According to 5.1-4 the
character of this camp as a holy place in which YHWH himself dwells
(v.3) is to be safeguarded by the exclusion from the camp of all those
who are 'unclean' in the cultic sense. The subsequent regulations have
then evidently been collected here from this perspective: the problem
of uncleanness is at issue in the suspicion of a wife's adultery (5.11-31),
in the case of the Nazirite (ch.6), the consecration of levites (8.5-22)
and in the Passover (9.1-14). The sanctity of the camp and the presence
of YHWH are again stressed by the priestly blessing (6.22-27), YHWH's
speaking from the 'mercy seat' of the ark (7.89; cf. Ex.25.22) and by
the cloud which covers the sanctuary (9.15ff.).

→98
→19, 142

The latter is a recapitulation of Ex.40.2,34-38. This sheds some light
on the overall conception of the Sinai pericope. The cultic legislation
of Lev.1.1-Num.9.14 is as it were a delaying factor: it gives all the
regulations which the Israelites need to be able to travel through the
wilderness with the sanctuary in their midst as the people set apart for
YHWH and made holy. Exodus 40.34-38 already speaks of the cloud
and its twofold function of concealing the divine *kabod* which fills the
sanctuary and guiding Israel on its journey. This second aspect now
comes right to the foreground in Num.9.15-23, in which the tradition
of the pillars of cloud and fire from the exodus tradition (Ex.13.21f.;

Conception

→143

14.19f., 24) is taken up and developed further. Now the cloud gives the sign to set out or to pitch camp, so that the wandering of the Israelites takes place utterly in accordance with YHWH's instructions. As well as having other functions, the signals from the silver trumpets serve to set the camp in motion in an orderly way (Num.10.1-10).

The wandering of Israel through the wilderness, which comes to a provisional end in the 'steppes of Moab' (22.1), where Moses later dies, begins in Num.10.11. Numbers 20.14 marks the beginning of the purposeful wandering towards the promised land with the sending of messengers to the king of Edom.

Numbers 10.11-20.13 again contains narrative texts which in many respects resemble the narratives about Israel in the wilderness in →143 Ex.15.22-18.27 (cf. the parallel narratives Ex.7.1-7; Num.20.1-13). In both sections the rebellion of the Israelites against Moses and thus against YHWH himself stand in the foreground. There is also mention →17, 143 of the 'murmuring' of the Israelites in the Numbers texts (14.2,27,29,36; 16.11; *17.6,20,25*); however, here this expression is not associated with complaints about hunger and thirst (cf. 11.4-6; 20.2-5; 21.5) but with protests on the one hand about the dangers of the way to the promised land (14.2f.) and on the other about the special position of Moses (16.1-11; 17.6; cf. ch.12). Thus there is a much more basic expression here of the rebellion of the Israelites against the will of YHWH (cf. Coates). Here the concept of 'holiness' plays an important role (11.18; 16.3,5,7; *17.2f.*; 20.12f.).

The passages about cultic law which occur in this section have also evidently been inserted from this perspective. Numbers 15 contains supplementary sacrificial regulations which relate to offerings in →97 addition to animal offerings (vv.1-16; cf. Lev.2; 7.11ff.) and to sin offerings (vv.22-31, cf. Lev.4f.); the chapter ends with a summons to the Israelites to observe YHWH's commandments and to be holy to him (v.40). In the present context, the stress on forgiveness for the 'whole community of the Israelites' (15.26) is perhaps related to the →20 sinning of the Israelites in the 'spy episode' in chs.13f. The reference of ch.18 to the rebellion of the Korahites, reported earlier, is easier to see: the exact observation of the rules for priestly ministry is to ensure that the wrath of YHWH does not again descend on the Israelites (18.5; cf. Childs, 198). The word 'holy' permeates the whole chapter (18.3,5,8,9,10,19,32). Finally, the water of purification prepared with the ashes of a red cow (ch.19) is in future to ward off impurities among the Israelites which endanger their worship.

→143
The narrative about the miracle with the water at Meribah in Num.20.1-13 marks a clear break: because of their 'unbelief' (which according to the narrative probably consists in the fact that they did not 'tell' the rock to produce water, as YHWH commanded them to in v.8, but used the staff for the miracle, v.11) Moses and Aaron are not to be allowed to enter the promised land (v.12, cf. v.24 and 27.14). Thus they too belong to the generation which has to die in the wilderness (cf. 14.22f., 29ff.)

Numbers 20.14-36.13 also contains narrative sections and sections dealing with cultic law. The first part is dominated by narratives which all have to do with obstacles and dangers on the way to the promised land. There are reports of clashes with five kings through whose land the Israelites want to go: with the kings of Edom (20.14-21) and Arad (21.1-3); with Sihon king of the Amorites (21.21-30) and Og king of Bashan (21.33-35), whose land the Israelites occupy; and finally with king Balak of Moab, who orders the seer Balaam against Israel (22-24). Cultic laws

→20

The Balaam narrative (Num.22-24) forms an independent literary passage which has undergone a long history of tradition (cf. Gross). The two sayings in 24.3-9, 15-19 are often understood as earlier, originally independent praises of Israel in which the 'star from Jacob' (24.17) could be a reference to David, whereas the two sayings in 23.7-10 and 18-24 probably were only formulated in the course of the further elaboration of the narrative. Balaam

Further dangers are presented by a plague of snakes, against which Moses sets up the 'brazen serpent' (21.4-9, probably an aetiology for a cultic image in the temple in Jerusalem, cf. II Kings 18.4), and the enticement of the Israelites to the cult of Baal by Moabite women (ch.25). →49f.

Here there is a clear break: in ch.26 there is a new census through which it is formally established (v.64) that the whole generation of those in the census at Sinai (ch.1) is no longer alive, as YHWH had announced (14.29). This period comes to an end with the call of Joshua to be Moses' successor (27.12-23); here, as already at the death of Aaron (20.24), there is an explicit reference back to the sinning at Meribah (27.14). Call of Joshua

→150

The narrative element now fades right into the background; only in ch.31 is there a report of a campaign against the Midianites. Rather, here ritual and ceremonial questions are in the foreground. In addition there are legal regulations: the great sacrificial calendar in Num. 28f., which here seems to be almost a legacy of Moses immediately after the announcement of his death (27.12-14); various instructions about the legal status of women (27.1-11, with the 'reformulation' in ch.36; 30.2-17; here the question of the right of inheritance in 27.3 is explicitly bound up with the context. →97

Otherwise, the concern is with the imminent settlement: the assignment of land to the tribes east of the Jordan (Num.32), which projects back into the early period a later extension of the tribal territories; instructions about the division of land west of the Jordan (33.50-34.29); the demarcation of levitical cities and cities of sanctuary (35); and in between a list of stations in the wilderness wandering (33), which in its entirety must be seen as a late attempt to reconstruct the journey, perhaps using an earlier itinerary of a 'pilgrimage' to Sinai (Noth). Assignation of land

→24

Numbers 33.50-56 and other passages of text towards the end of the book of Numbers display a marked Deuteronomistic stamp. That shows that in their present form they are connected not only backwards, with the other books of the Pentateuch, but also forwards, with the books of the Deuteronomistic history. Evidently, then, there was not only a →183ff.

comprehensive redaction of the Pentateuch but also a more overall redaction which brought together the two great literary complexes.

Bibliography

Commentaries: Holzinger (KHC) 1903; Baentsch (HK) 1903; Gray (ICC) 1903 (1956); Gressmann (SAT) 1914, ²1922; Heinisch (HS) 1936; Noth (ATD) 1966, ET OTL 1968.

G.W.Coats, *Rebellion in the Wilderness. The Murmuring Motif in the Wilderness Traditions of the Old Testament*, 1968; V.Fritz, *Israel in der Wüste*, 1970; H.Gressmann, *Mose und seine Zeit. Ein Kommentar zu den Mose-Sagen*, 1913; W.Gross, *Bileam, Literar- und formkritische Untersuchungen der Prosa in Numeri 22-24*, 1974; M.Noth, *A History of Pentateuchal Traditions* (1943), ET 1972, §23; id., 'Der Wallfahrtsweg zum Sinai (4.Mose 33)', *PJB* 36, 1940, 5-28 (= *ABLA* I, 55-74).

Steuernagel, §42; Childs, IX.

Cf. also the bibliography on I.4; III.1.6.

1.5 Deuteronomy

Deuteronomy is a self-contained, independent book, formulated as a speech of Moses to the Israelites. At the same time it is connected with the previous books of the Pentateuch: the speech of Moses is given at the place 'beyond the Jordan in the land of Moab' (Deut.1.1,5) which had already been the scene of events since Num.22.1, and the book ends with the death of Moses and the appointment of Joshua as his

→149, 154f.

successor in accordance with the announcement in Num.27.12ff. The appointment of Joshua also provides a link with the following books.

Structure

The structure of Deuteronomy is easy to recognize. It begins with a double introductory speech (1.1-4.40; 4.44-11.32), followed by the collection of laws proper (chs.12-26); the closing section (chs.27-34) is made up of a variety of elements, of which chs. 28-30 are formulated as a speech of Moses and thus form the end of the speech which begins in 1.1.

The double introductory speech is often felt to be a problem. Wellhausen saw it as an indication of two different 'editions' of Deuteronomy with different introductions, which were later combined. Others understand 1.1-4.40 as part of a 'framework', the second half of which appears in chs.31-34. Finally, Noth

→183ff.

assumed that 1.1-4.40 are meant to introduce not just Deuteronomy but the whole of the Deuteronomistic history, whereas 4.44-11.32 are the real introductory speech to Deuteronomy. However, Childs has demonstrated that the first speech too is focussed on the subsequent legislation. The two speeches probably come from different phases of the history of Deuteronomy, but now form components of a well-thought-out overall composition.

The first introductory speech (1.1-4.40) gives a retrospective survey

of the history of Israel from the departure from Horeb (1-3; the name
Horeb is used for Sinai in Deuteronomy) and ends with a long paraenetic
passage (4.1-40). It is governed by an easily recognizable leading
thought: the generation which was at Horeb did not believe the promise →14
of land and therefore was not allowed to enter the land (1.19-2.15). In
future, the new generation which has already experienced the divine
guidance and victory over the kings of Transjordan (2.16-3.21) is to →149
observe the commandments given by YHWH on Horeb when they live
in the promised land (4.1-22), otherwise they will again be led out of
the land into the dispersion (4.23-31). Finally, in 4.32-40, a central
theme of Deuteronomic theology is developed: YHWH, the creator of
the world, has chosen Israel out of love for the fathers (v.37, cf.7.6-8)
and revealed his commandments to it (cf. 10.12-17, etc.).

The second introductory speech (4.44-11.32) has a new beginning
(4.44-49; cf. 1.1-5) and then repeats the Decalogue (*5.6-21*) for the →141
present generation (5.3); the most important difference from Ex.20 is
the basis for the sabbath law in v.15 ('Remember that you were a slave
in Egypt...', cf. Ex.20.11). Moses' role as mediator (cf. Ex.20.18-21) is →142
worked out at length (*5.23-31*), so that as in the Sinai pericope all the
rest of the commandments are a development of the Decalogue. In 6.4
the central statement of Israelite religion is given in an extremely
concentrated form with a further 'Hear, Israel' (cf.5.1): 'YHWH is our
God, YHWH is one' (cf. also 4.35,39; 7.9; 10.17), coupled with the
summons to love God (v.5) and constantly keep his commandments in
their hearts and before their eyes (vv.6-9). The following paraenesis
warns above all against worshipping strange gods (6.10-19); finally, a →16
brief salvation-historical creed is quoted, to be handed on to the next →140f.
generation (6.20-25). 7.1-10.11 warns the chosen Israel of the danger
of arrogance towards the other peoples (7.6-8) in enjoying the gift of
the land (8.1-18) or even in boasting of their own righteousness (9.4-
6); the reason for this is given with a lengthy reference to the apostasy →14f.
on Horeb (9.7-10.11). The great closing paraenesis (10.12-11.32) ends
with the alternatives of blessing and curse as a consequence of hearkening, or not hearkening, to the commandments of YHWH (11.26-28).

In the second introductory speech a problem emerges which also occurs within
the collection of laws: the address to the Israelites frequently alternates between
the second person singular and the second person plural, often within a single
verse (e.g. 6.3; 7.4) or regularly within a section (e.g.6.13-19). Different
explanations have been put forward for this change in number: the combination
of several sources (e.g. Steuernagel and others); the use of a basic Deuteronomic
work by a 'Deuteronomistic' editor (e.g. Minette de Tillesse); stylistic reasons
(e.g. Lohfink). None of these solutions is completely convincing, especially as
the change in number only rarely corresponds with tensions in the text over
content. For this reason it can largely be ignored in exegesis.

The introductory speeches are stamped by characteristically
Deuteronomistic language. Their characteristic features are not only
the style, which is broad, often overloaded and seemingly prolix

(and the easy Hebrew!), but also paraenesis, i.e. constantly repeated admonitions to observe the commandments, often bound up with the promise of blessings on life in the promised land. Here stereotyped, frequently recurring phrases are used, so that scholars have even gone so far as to speak of a 'paraenetic scheme' (Lohfink, 90ff.) such as we find e.g. in Deut 4.1: 'And now, O Israel, give heed to the statutes and the ordinances which I teach you, and do them; that you may live, and go in and take possession of the land which the Lord, the God of your fathers, gives you' (cf. 4.40; 5.1,*31-33*; 6.1-3, etc.). With this also goes the admonition to love YHWH (6.5), fear him (6.2) and serve him (6.13, cf. the summary in 10.12f.), a reference to YHWH's love for the fathers which is the reason for this (4.37; 10.35), and the oath which he made to them (1.8; 6.10; 7.8,12, etc), and also a reference to the deliverance from slavery in Egypt (4.20; 5.15; 7.8). Finally there is a warning against the worship of other gods (4.19; 6.14; cf. the tables in Lohfink, 295ff.; Weinfeld, 320ff.).

→137

Laws

The collection of laws (chs.12-26) is also stamped throughout by the paraenetic Deuteronomistic language. Alongside this, even earlier legal material can be recognized, which has been included in this collection and for which there are some parallels in the Book of the Covenant.

Centralization of the cult

The collection of laws begins emphatically with the demand for the 'centralization of the cult', i.e. the regulation that sacrifice shall be performed and cultic offering made at only one place of worship (12.2-28). This demand governs the first part of the collection (chs.12-18; cf. 14.22-26; 15.19-23; 16.1-17; 17.8-13; 18.1-8 and 26.1-11). Beyond question it is not one of the earlier traditions taken up by Deuteronomy but is a distinctive postulate which is new in this form. It has two aspects: cultic purity (i.e. delimitation from the outside world, cf.12.2-7) and cultic unity (i.e. concentration within the community, cf. 12.8-12). Here the place of worship is not mentioned by name, but is paraphrased as 'the place which YHWH will choose', frequently with the addition 'to make his name dwell there', etc. (12.5,11,14,18,21; 14.23-25, etc.). It has therefore been conjectured that the original reference was not to Jerusalem but to another place of worshiip (e.g. Shechem, see below); however, there is no firm reference in the Old Testament to any other place of worship which would ever have been accorded such central significance.

Division

It is difficult to divide up the collection of laws successfully, as a systematic arrangement by content is only partly recognizable. Perhaps it is based on earlier sub-collections, the arrangement of material within which was retained (cf. Merendino and Seitz); perhaps we no longer understand the associations by which texts were related to one another; perhaps, too, connections have been changed by later additions. However, we may follow Horst in calling the first part of the collection (chs.12-18) 'YHWH's law of privilege', because it is predominantly concerned with cultic questions or with ministers who are in a special relationshp to YHWH. It could be further subdivided: 12.1-28 centralization of the cult; 12.29-14.21 prohibition of alien worship; 14.22-15.18 offerings, sabbath year and social duties; 15.19-17.1 (without 16.18-20) firstborn

and festivals; 16.18-20 and 17.2-18.22 ministers and legal proceedings.
However, this division still remains very crude.

In the second part of the collection (chs.19-26), it is even more difficult to recognize an overall division. However, we can frequently mark off groups of texts which have points of content and/or form in common. Thus first of all, chs.19f. consist predominantly of regulations which above all relate to the community as a whole, whereas from ch.22 on individual conduct stands in the foreground: ch.19: legal regulations, above all those about murder (vv.1-13) and the law of witnesses (vv.15-21), separated by a rule against moving a landmark (v.14); ch.20: laws of war, leading into 21.1-9: victims of unknown killer; 21.10-14: women taken captive (the beginning synonymous with 20.1), in turn leading into 21.15-17: the rights to inherit of the children of two wives; 21.18-21: dealing with a refractory son; 21.22f.: procedure for hanging (the beginnings of vv.15,18, 22 have identical wording); 22.1-4: responsibility for a neighbour's property; 22.5,9-11: prohibition of various kinds of mixing, separated by 22.6f.: the mother bird and its nestlings; 22.8: parapets on the roof of a house, and leading into: 22.12: tassels on a garment; 22.13-*23.1*: laws on sex and marriage, leading into *23.2-9*: rules for purity for the cultic community (a →98, 145 series of prohibitions in *23.1,2,3,4,8a,8b*); *23.10-15*: prohibitions for the war →83 camp; *23.16-21*: a series of prohibitions about runaway slaves (vv.*16f.*), sacral prostitution (v.*18*); fines for immorality (v.*19*) and the taking of tithes (vv.*20f.*); *23.22-26*: a series beginning with 'if' (*ki*) about vows (vv.*22,23f.*) and theft of food (vv.*25,26*); 24.1-4,5 marriage laws; 24.6-25.18: a collection of prohibitions →91 and casuistic legal statements about human society ('laws of humanity'): prohibitions (some extended by paraenesis) about taking pledges (24.6), paying wages (24.14f.), kinship (24.16), the socially disadvantaged (24.17f.), threshing oxen (25.4), two kinds of weights and measures (25.13-16); interspersed are causistic statements about kidnapping (24.7), taking pledges (24.10-13), gleaning (24.19-22), restricting flogging (25.1-3), marriage between kindred (25.5-10), indecency in fighting (25.11f.); in 25.17-19 there is a saying against the Amalekites. Chapter 26 stands out clearly from what has gone before: this contains confessions on offering the firstfruits (vv.1-11, 'short creed', vv.5b-9) and the tithe (vv.12-15), and a final paraenesis about the binding nature of the covenant (vv.16-19).

A comparison of the collection of laws with the Book of the Covenant is particularly interesting. There are countless points of contact between the two, but the differences are more striking than the points in common. Only occasionally are sentences competely identical in both (e.g. Ex.23.19b = Deut 14.21b); in the latter, however, Ex.23.19b is →141 combined with Ex.*22.30* in a different formulation); occasionally the formulation in Deuteronomy is shorter and seems like an extract from sentences in the Book of the Covenant (thus the rules for the judge in Deut.16.19 as opposed to Ex.23.2f.,6-8), or a section from the Book of the covenant appears in Deuteronomy divided into individual statements and put in other contexts (cf. Ex.*22.20-26* with Deut 24.17f.; 23.20; 24.10-13).

In most cases, however, the version in Deuteronomy is more detailed. Thus a statement about the offering of the firstborn of domestic animals (Ex.*22.29*) is developed from various aspects, so that one could now call the passage a set of rules of procedure. The same is true of the rules

153

about the three regular festivals (23.14-17; Deut.16.1-17), the rules about sanctuary (Ex.21.12-14; Deut.19.1-13), dealing with false witnesses (Ex.23.1b and Deut 19.16-21), help for other people's domestic animals (Ex.23.4f. and Deut. 22.1-4) and the offering of the firstfruits (Ex.23.19a and Deut. 26.1-20).

There are also important changes in content. According to Ex.23.10f., the sabbath year is a fallow year on religious grounds (cf. also Lev.25.2-7) with social connnotations: the poor can take what grows spontaneously. However, in Deut.15.1-11 the concern has developed in the direction of money-lending, and the social perspective dominates the foreground. In slave law the social demands of Deuteronomy are even in conflict with the Book of the Covenant. There the slave is to be freed after six years without compensation, and even without his wife and his children if he has married in slavery (Ex.21.2-4); according to Dan.15.12-15, however, his master must not let him go away 'empty handed' but is to 'furnish him liberally' from his cattle, threshing floor and barn. Finally, the legal position of a seduced girl is improved in Deut.22.28f. in comparison to Ex.*22.15f.*: the father cannot forbid the marriage and the man may not dismiss her in accordance with the law of divorce which was otherwise in force. Here we have changes in social and economic structure, and above all in ethics.

Is Deuteronomy meant to replace the Book of the Covenant or even to suppress it (Eissfeldt)? The very fact that only half of the regulations contained in the Book of the Covenant are taken up into Deuteronomy itself suggests otherwise. Are the others tacitly regarded as obsolete? It is more probable that they are presupposed as being known and still valid (Fohrer). Deuteronomy probably incorporated only those regulations which had a new and different contribution to make: extensions, corrections and rules for detailed implementation.

In the closing section (chs.27-34), chs.28-30 stand out by virtue of the fact that they continue the speech of Moses begun in 1.1 and bring it to

a conclusion. (Chapter 27 speaks of Moses in the third person and gives an instruction for a cursing ritual which is later to be performed on Mount Ebal and Mount Gerizim, cf. Josh.8.30-35.) Chapter 28 develops the theme of blessing (vv.1-14) and cursing (vv.15-68) and thus takes up again the end of the introductory speech in 11.26-28. Chapter 29 is a new beginning; it once again stresses the 'today' of the covenant making (vv.*11f.*) and its validity for future generations (vv.*13f.*), and then announces the destruction of the land and the exiling of its inhabitants (vv.*21-27*) as a consequence of worshipping other gods (vv.*15-20*); 30.1-10, however, explicitly opens up the possibility of return to YHWH and the restoration of the exiles. At the end it is stressed that the commandment given here can be fulfilled (30.11-14), and once again there is a presentation of the alternatives of blessing and curse, indeed of life and death (30.15-20).

After the end of the Moses speech, chs. 31-34 describe the last actions

and instructions of Moses. He appoints Joshua his successor (31.1-8) and gives instructions for further presentations of the Torah (31.9-13,

24-29). In addition we have a song which Moses is to write down and **Deuteronomy**
teach the Israelites (31.16-22). The 'song of Moses' (32.1-43) certainly Song of Moses
had an independent existence before it was inserted into the present
context. Here it now has a clearly recognizable function; Moses is to
write it down like the Torah (31.19, cf. v.9) and it is to be a 'witness'
against the Israelites (31.19,21), again like the Torah (31.26), i. e. it is
to depict again and in another form the consequencs of apostasy from
YHWH, but at the same time to confirm that in the end YHWH will
again turn to his people and that he alone is God (vv.36-43).

After the announcement of the death of Moses (32.48-52) there follows a further
poetic text, the 'Blessing of Moses' (33.2-29), a collection of tribal sayings which Blessing of
doubtless also initially had an independent existence. Its function in the present Moses
context can no longer clearly be recognized: v.4, 'Moses commanded us a →84
Torah', provides a link.

Deuteronomy ends with the death of Moses and Joshua's entry into
office (34.1-9). This opens up a perspective on the next stage in Israel's
history, but the real interest is ultimately again focussed on Moses: the
unique and incomparable 'prophet', who knew YHWH 'face to face'
(34.10-12; cf. Ex.33.11).

Deuteronomy is a theological book. There is probably no other book
in the Old Testament of which this could be said so clearly. It outlines Theological
an overall view of Israel's faith in the one God and in the unique conception
relationship of this God to the people whom he has chosen; such a view →150
did not exist either before or after. This outline is intrinsically very
consistent. At the same time, however, in many places the book seems
not to be a literary unity, and this has led to many attempts to
demonstrate different strata within Deuteronomy or different stages in
its composition (see above). None of these attempts has found universal
acceptance. Above all, it has transpired that hardly any tensions or →127
differences in content can be recognized. The different editors or
redactors who may have been at work here all evidently belonged to
the same school, and despite its literary unevennesses, the final form
seems very much to be a unity.

Where does this book come from? Once it was seen to be independent, Josiah's reform
it was also recognized to have a connection with the report about of the cult
Josiah's reform of the cult in II Kings 22f. (first by de Wette, cf. Kaiser, →50f.
118; Smend, 77). It is said there that 'the book of the Torah' was found →163
in the temple (22.8); this expression otherwise appears only in the
closing chapters of Deuteronomy (e.g. Deut. 30.10; 31.26) or in texts
which relate to Deuteronomy (e.g. Josh.1.8; 8.31-35; Neh.8.1-3).
Above all, the measures taken in Josiah's reform as reported in II Kings
23 show striking affinity to the demands of Deuteronomy. So the ⌐
connection is indisputable.

However, there is a dispute as to whether Deuteronomy in its present form
could have been the basis for the reform or whether there was an earlier →180
'Ur-Deuteronomy'; this again raises the question of the form of this 'Ur-
Deuteronomy' and its relationship to what are supposed to be the literary strata
in Deuteronomy. The discussion is incomplete, especially as in more recent times

it has been argued that II Kings 23 originally did not describe a comprehensive reform of the cult and that the centralization of the cult in particular was only introduced by a later Deuteronomistic redaction (Würthwein, Kaiser). In that case II Kings 22f. could not be regarded as an argument for the age of Deuteronomy.

If one does maintain the connection between Deuteronomy and Josiah's reform, the question remains whether it was composed for the reform or had already been in existence for some time and only now became effective. However, we can hardly answer this question, since we have no evidence. There is also no agreement as to the circles from which the author(s) came. Levitical →127 groups, either in Judah (von Rad 1947), or in the north (Wolff), have often been suggested. Alt above all argued that Deuteronomy came from the north. →218 The affinity between Hosea and Deuteronomy is also relevant here. Finally, Weinfeld looked for the author in the groups of 'scribes' in the Jerusalem court.

The character of Deuteronomy as systematic theology is decisive for the question of its origin. Over against this the possibility that the authors belonged to an institution fades into the background, since the distinctive feature of this outline is its novelty; it is not stamped by any tradition. So first of all we must content ourselves with the assertion Deuteronomic that presumably towards the end of the monarchy in Israel (or Judah) movement a theological movement came into being which made the successful →127 (and momentous) attempt to bring together the 'complex experiences of Israel in decisive formulae which were appropriate for understanding and interpreting the past and giving a constructive shape to the future' (Herrmann, 161).

Mention must also be made of von Rad's (1938) theory that the structure of Covenant Deuteronomy reflects the liturgy of a festival, a covenant festival or covenant festival renewal festival originally celebrated in Shechem, the centre of which he hypothesis supposed – with a reference to Deut. 31.10f. – to be a solemn proclamation of →166f. the law. He also found the same liturgical structure in the Sinai pericope (Ex.19-Covenant 24) and in Josh. 24. In the wake of this hypothesis, the covenant formulary formulary which was supposed to underlie the festival was compared with treaty texts from outside Israel (Baltzer, etc.). However, this comparison can hardly be confirmation of such a festival and its great age; it is more probable that here Deuteronomy has taken up and made literary use of earlier traditions (Weinfeld).

Bibliography

Commentaries: Bertholet (KHC) 1899; Driver (ICC) ³1902; König (KAT) 1917; Steuernagel (HK) ²1923; Junker (HS) 1933, ²1952/54; von Rad (ATD) 1964, ET OTL 1966.

A.Alt, 'Die Heimat des Deuteronomiums', *KS* II, 250-75; J.Baltzer, *The Covenant Formulary*, ET 1971; S.Herrmann, 'Die konstruktive Restauration. Das Deuteronomium als Mitte biblischer Theologie', *Probleme biblischer Theologie. FS G. von Rad*, 1971, 155-70; F.Horst, *Das Privilegrecht Jahwes. Rechtgeschichtliche Untersuchungen zum Deuteronomium*, 1930 (= *Gottes*

Recht, 1961, 17-154); N.Lohfink, *Das Hauptgebot. Eine Untersuchung literar-* **Deuteronomy** *ischer Einleitungsfragen zu Dtn 5-11*, 1963; R.P.Merendino, *Das deuteronomisti- sche Gesetz. Eine literarkritische, gattungs- und überlieferungsgeschichtliche Untersuchung zu Dtn 12-16*, 1969; G.Minette de Tillesse, 'Sections "tu" et sections "vous" dans le Deuteronome', *VT* 12, 1962, 29-87; M.Noth, *Überlieferungsgeschichtliche Studien*, 1943, partial (1-110) ET *The Deutero- nomistic History*, 1981; J.G.Plöger, *Literarkritische, formgeschichtliche und stilkritische Untersuchungen zum Deuteronomium*, 1967; H.D.Preuss, *Deutero- nomium*, 1982 (account of research); G.von Rad, 'Das Gottesvolk im Deutero- nomium, 1929 (= *GS* II, 9-108); id., 'The Form-Critical Problem of the Hexateuch', in *The Problem of the Hexateuch*, 1966, 1-78; id., *Studies in Deuteronomy* (1947), ET 1953; G.Seitz, *Redaktionsgeschichtliche Studien zum Deuteronomium*, 1971; M.Weinfeld, *Deuteronomy and the Deuteronomic School*, 1972; J.Wellhausen, *Die Composition des Hexateuchs und der histor- ischen Bücher des Alten Testaments*, ³1899 (⁴1963); H.W.Wolff, 'Hoseas geistige Heimat', *TLZ* 81, 1956, 83-94 (= *GS*, 232-50); E.Würthwein, 'Die josuanische Reform und das Deuteronomium', *ZTK* 73, 1976, 395-423.

Steuernagel, §43, Eissfeldt, §34; Fohrer, §25; Soggin, 2.III; Kaiser, §11; Smend, §12; Schmidt, §10; Childs, X.

1.6 The Pentateuch as a Whole

Since the end of the nineteenth century, the 'newer documentary Source theory hypothesis' has become established, above all under the influence of Julius Wellhausen. It assumes that the books of the Pentaeuch (or Hexateuch, see below) are composed of several 'sources' or 'docu- ments', which at first existed by themselves as independent writings and were only combined as a result of one or more redactions. Each of them (with the exception of Deuteronomy) had its own narrative account from the creation (or at any rate from Abraham) to the settlement (or at any rate to the death of Moses). However, when the sources were brought together in the redaction, parts of them were lost, so that they can no longer be reconstructed in their entirety; still, that does not alter the basic assumption that they were originally independent and complete.

Since Wellhausen, in general at least three sources have been posited Three sources (outside Deuteronomy). Two earlier narrative sources are distinguished, among other things, by the use of different divine names: the Yahwist (J), who uses the divine name YHWH, the Elohist (E), →17 who uses the divine designation *'elohim*, and the latest source, the Priestly writing (P, for Wellhausen Q, as an abbreviation for 'Book of four [*quatuor*] covenants'). There have been all kinds of shifts within this hypothetical construction over the course of the last hundred years, but on the whole, down to most recent times it has only be questioned by some outsiders (e.g. Cassuto and Engnell).

The internal changes relate above all to the splitting up of J into two Fourth source sources. Smend Sr distinguished an earlier and a later Jahwist (J^1 and J^2); Eissfeldt called the earlier source the lay source (L) – in explicit contrast to the Priestly Writing; while Fohrer designated the latter the nomad source (N), because of its 'marked nomadic character'.

Elohist

The Elohist presented a problem, since most exegetes did not feel themselves in a position to reconstruct this source with any degree of completeness. Once Volz and Rudolph had disputed that there was an Elohist at all, scholars often contented themselves with talking of the 'Elohistic fragments' (Wolff, Smend Jr). Here Noth attempted to explain the preservation of E only in fragments by the argument that J was the basis of the redaction and E had been used only to supplement it. So scholars were often content to call the earlier narrative stratum 'Jehovistic' and to refrain from more detailed analysis.

Jehovist

The designation 'Jehovist' (JE) was already used by Wellhausen, who was mainly concerned with the contrast between this earlier stratum and the later Priestly codex. He also explicitly challenged the assumption 'that all the three sources continued to exist separately until some one at a later date brought them together simultaneously into a single whole' – as the Elohist has come down to us only as an element in the Jehovistic writing (*Prolegomena*, 7).

Priestly Writing
→142f., 144ff.
147ff.

There was no unanimity over the extent and content of the Priestly Writing. Wellhausen summed up all the priestly material including the texts of cultic legislation as the 'Priestly Codex', but distinguished from it 'Q' as the 'original nucleus' (*Composition*, 135). Other strata had crystallized around this, and in particular independent collections of laws like Lev.1-7. Later a distinction was often drawn between a basic stratum or basic narrative (P^g) and secondary extensions (P^s, often further differentiated), which were also attributed to P's final work. By contrast, Noth wanted to protect the character of P as a narrative work and therefore rejected the addition of legalistic passages to P. Others, too, stressed the narrative character of P, because P was understood as a consecutive 'source' parallel to the earlier narrative works.

→145

Extent of
sources
→132f.

A further point of controversy was the question of the beginning and the end of the individual sources. While the beginning of the Priestly Writing was generally accepted to be Gen.1.1 and the beginning of the Yahwist Gen.2.4b, there was always a dispute over the beginning of the Elohist. Some scholars wanted to find traces of E in the primal history; the majority for a long time saw its beginning in Gen.15, which then proved to be Deuteronomistic, so that finally Gen.20 was accepted as the beginning. The main questionn in connection with the end of the sources was whether they led up to a fulfilment of the promise of land to the fathers and therefore had an account of the settlement. On this presupposition the book of Joshua was often brought in, leading to talk of the Hexateuch (six-part book). (Some played the game with Greek numbers even further and spoke, after adding further books, of the Heptateuch, Octateuch or Enneateuch; alternatively they took Deuteronomy away and spoke of the Tetrateuch.) Other interpreters saw the death of Moses as the end of one or more sources which accordingly they tried to find in the last chapters of Deuteronomy. Wolff even made the Yahwistic narrative end with the Balaam story in Num.22-24. This question is closely associated with the understanding

→137
→135

→136f.

Hexateuch

→155

→149
158

of Deuteronomy and its association both with the other books of the Pentaeuch and with the later books.

Pentateuch as Whole
→162f., 185f.
Literary dependence

There was also always a dispute about the relationship between the individual sources. What was at issue here was whether the later sources were independent of the earlier ones in literary terms, i.e. whether they were to be understood as new editions or new versions meant to replace the earlier versions, or whether they had been composed and transmitted independently of these. Noth assumed that J and E drew the nucleus of their content from a common basis (Grundlage, G), and a number of scholars followed him here. On the other hand, there was a dispute over the question how the combination of the individual sources was to be understood, i.e. whether a redactor had brought them all together at one time or whether the combination had taken place step by step, so that it was necessary to presuppose several redactors.

Since Wellhausen there has been widespread agreement over the relative age of the sources. The Yahwist was regarded as the earliest source (where an even earlier one, L or N, was not assumed), the Elohist came somewhat later, Deuteronomy third and the Priestly Writing fourth. It was thought that there were relatively certain points of reference for dating the two latter sources: for Deuteronomy in the late pre-exilic period and for the Priestly Writing in the exilic or post-exilic period. However, the points of reference for the dating of P were only indirect. Wellhausen's most important argument derived from his observation that the pre-exilic prophets do not seem to know the 'Mosaic law' as presented in P. For J and E, similarly there were no direct points of reference, but J was usually dated in the early monarchy and E in the later monarchy (with great variations); E was often thought to come from the northern kingdom, in contrast to J, which came from Judah.

Age of the sources

→155f.

The history of the 'newer documentary hypothesis' shows that the questions and problems could always be formulated much more clearly than the answers and solutions. There was agreement over accepting this hypothetical model in principle rather than over specific details, so that reports have always had to note the existence of different opinions, from the first – and most detailed – account by Holzinger onwards.

In the course of time the uncertainty over the demarcation of sources became greater, so that even in the case of the main source, the Yahwist, it was necessary to be content with a 'critically assured minimum' (Wolff 1964, 147) or even to attempt to define it negatively by a 'process of subtraction' (Smend Sr, 86). The existence of the two other sources has been emphatically challenged quite recently. Cross (like Volz and others before him) declared that the 'Priestly Writing' never existed as an independent source, but represented a stage in the revision of the earlier traditions (JE) (similarly Van Seters); in his commentary on Genesis Westermann came to the conclusion that the Elohist cannot be demonstrated even in the form of related fragments, but that the passages assigned to him are to be understood as interpretative supplements which do not belong to a common 'source'.

Uncertainties

159

Finally, the prevalent tendency to date the Yahwist in the early period of the monarchy is also disputed, and its close connection with the Deuteronomic-Deuteronomistic tradition has been stressed (Van Seters; H.H.Schmid). As a result the whole previous picture of the history of the origin of the Pentateuch within Israelite history has been shaken, because now the overall outline of the Pentateuchal narrative can only be envisaged for the late pre-exilic period (or even later). Schmid does not see the 'Yahwist' as a writer, but more as a 'process of redaction and interpretation'.

These critical approaches meet up with others which start from a consistent application of form criticism and tradition criticism. Gunkel's approach through the 'smallest literary units', i.e. for the Pentateuchal narrative above all the individual sagas (thus also Gressmann), was basically incompatible with the documentary hypothesis. In the course of time this became increasingly clear when source criticism was virtually ignored in the development of Gunkel's approach by von Rad, Westermann and others. The reason why source criticism was not explicitly challenged was simply that it was taken as a presupposition. Here von Rad declared that the combination of various sources was not a 'clear process which allowed of any satisfactory explanation' (*Hexateuch*, 74). He himself developed another model by assigning the

traditions in the Pentateuch to individual complexes of tradition (primal history, patriarchal history, exodus tradition, Sinai tradition, settlement traditions) which originally were separate and independent of one another before they were combined together. In attributing this overall composition to the Yahwist, von Rad was deliberately not thinking of a number of sources; rather, he was making use of this designation which had been introduced to express something quite different: that here a great theologian had been at work, alongside whom there was room for no other. This no longer has any connection with the classical documentary hypothesis.

I have attempted to take this approach of von Rad's further in discussing the individual books of the Pentaeuch above. Here some of my own observations and considerations (cf. my book mentioned in the bibliography) have been combined with those of Childs and others. To sum up my present view of the history of the origin of the Pentateuch once again:

Larger units
→132f.
→134ff.
→149

→140
→141ff.

The narrative traditions were first combined in the individual complexes of tradition. The formation of independent 'larger units' can still be recognized in the present text, at least in the case of the primal history and the patriarchal narratives (but cf. also the Balaam story in Num.22-24). Each has a distinct profile of its own and each is self-contained. This is not true to the same degree of the exodus traditions and the Sinai pericope, though Ex.1-15 now forms a 'rounded' composition and the Sinai tradition doubtless had an earlier history of its own.

The independent profile of the individual units is already given by the character of the texts. The sagas of the primal history deal with ideal-typical figures from the beginning of human history; they are depicted as having led an agricultural life. The patriarchal narratives tell of the ancestors of Israel and thus of the beginnings of the history of the people: they presuppose that the figures they depict are leading a nomadic or semi-nomadic way of life. In the stories of the stay in Egypt and the exodus the individual figures fall back in favour of the people as a whole and its representatives or its opponents. This is also →139f. largely true of the books Exodus-Numbers (and of Deuteronomy), where now the internal contrast between Moses (and Aaron) and the →143, 148 people is the governing factor.

The individual units have been collected and shaped from very Leading ideas different perspectives and leading ideas. The primal history runs from the beginnings of human history, through the deep break marked by the flood, after which God gives a guarantee that the order of creation will stand, to a further differentiation of humanity which accords with reality as the readers or hearers now know it; it does not suggest a narrative continuation. Each of the patriarchal stories (Abraham, Isaac, Jacob and Joseph) has a different form; they have then been combined into a larger unit above all by the insertion of divine promises and thus →136ff. given a distinctive stamp. The exodus narrative is deliberately focussed on the exodus and moreover is broken up and given a theological interpretation by the theme of 'faith'. The first basic feature of the →140 Sinai pericope is the reciprocal relationship between narrative and →141f. communication of the law; this brings out on the one hand the special position of Moses and on the other the breaking of the covenant and its restoration. In addition, different collections of cult laws have been added which have been similarly combined under the overall leading ideas. In the further course of the books of Exodus and Numbers the normative leading ideas are sometimes less recognizable (or we have not yet fully recognized them).

In these complexes of tradition, the narrative content of the primal Connections narrative (pre-Priestly) and the patriarchal narratives has not been combined (neither the two together, nor one or other with the sequel). The situation is rather different in the traditions of the books Exodus to Numbers. Continuity is provided here by elements like the figure of Moses (and Aaron), guidance by the pillars of cloud and fire, the 'murmuring' of the Israelites during and after the exodus, and so on. →143, 148 The Sinai pericope also introduces the features of the tent and the ark, which are important in the subsequent wandering through the wilderness. So here, too, the narrative material in the traditions which →19f., 142f. we have is also shaped by overarching patterns of tradition (partly Deuteronomic-Deuteronomistic and Priestly). (This needs to be worked out in more detail in a compositional analysis.)

By contrast, it is clear that the integration of the larger units in Genesis into a comprehensive whole took place at a level that can be described as theological redaction. This connection is particularly Theological redaction obvious between the patriarchal narratives and the exodus story. In →143f. Gen.50.24, on the death of Joseph there is an emphatic reference 161 forward to the return of the Israelites to the land which YHWH promised to the fathers by an oath. This reference is taken up again immediately before the exodus of the Israelites from Egypt in Ex.13.5,11; again at the moment when this return is endangered by the apostasy of the people from YHWH (32.13); and again after this danger has been averted (Ex.33.1). Even after that, these references continue, always in situations of crisis (Num.11.12; 14.23; 32.11; cf. Rendtorff, 77ff., 163). Here we have an overall view of the history of Israel from the patriarchs to the settlement, in which the promise of YHWH and his keeping of it form the decisive ongoing factor.

Deuteronomis-
tic language The texts mentioned have all been formulated in language with a Deuteronomic stamp. In particular, the mention of the 'oath' by which YHWH has promised the land to the fathers appears often in Deuteronomy (Deut.1.8,35; 6.10,18,23; 7.13 etc.). The theological collectors and editors who were at work here therefore stand more or less close to Deuteronomy. The work of these groups can also be recognized elsewhere within the individual books of the Pentateuch. It may therefore be taken as certain that a collection of Pentateuchal traditions (probably the first) came from this theological school.

Priestly
language
→144

→137f.
→97 Another group of texts which similarly provide an overall connection has been formulated in the language of the Priestly tradition. Thus at the beginning of the exodus narrative in Ex.2.23-25 and 6.2-8 there is mention of the 'covenant' of YHWH with clear reference to the Abraham covenant in Gen.17. Echoes of Gen.17 are also recognizable in the institution of the Passover (Ex.12) and the sabbath (Ex.31.12ff.): circumcision, passover and sabbath are called 'signs' ('ot, Gen.17.11; Ex.12.13; 31.13,17); circumcision and sabbath are also called 'eternal covenant' (berit 'olam, Gen.17.13; Ex.31.16; cf. Gen.9.16) and there is stress on its validity for all generations (Gen.17.9,23; Ex.12,14,16,52; 31.13,16). The relationships between this Priestly stratum of revision and the cultic traditions in the books Exodus to Numbers call for even closer investigation (here the question of the relationship between Pg and Ps comes up again on a different basis). Similarly, its relationship with the Deuteronomistic revision is still largely unexplained.

Relationship to
the sequel Finally, the Deuteronomistic character of the comprehensive revision of the Pentateuch again raises the question of its relationship to the books which follow. So far it has been answered by means of two different models, by positing a Hexateuch or a Deuteronomistic history. The nucleus of the problem lies in the fact that there is no longer any account in the Pentateuch of a final fulfilment to the wanderings of the →149 patriarchs and the exodus generation (or only the beginnings of one, in Transjordan). The Hexateuch hypothesis solves the problem by including the account of the conquest in the book of Joshua with the Pentateuchal sources. By contrast, in his hypothesis of the Deutero-nomistic history, Noth assumes that the original conclusions of the Pentateuchal sources were 'simply omitted' in favour of this newly composed work (ET 1972,16).

However, if we no longer begin by assuming continuous 'sources' in the Pentateuch, the picture looks different. The Deuteronomic-

Deuteronomistic circles who had played a crucial part in shaping the subsequent books were also key figures in giving the outline of the Pentateuch its shape. In both places they have worked over earlier traditions of different kinds and given them a theological interpretation. Initially, the transition from the Pentateuch to the following books was made without any fundamental break. Later, however, the first five books were regarded and treated as an independent entity. This separation obviously took place deliberately because of the special significance which the Torah, received and handed on by Moses, had gained in the meantime. Therefore the independence of the Pentateuch and the fact that it shares with the following books a common Deuteronomistic revision is by no means a contradiction, but reflects different stages of the history of the Old Testament canon.

Pentateuch as Whole

Overall conception

As there is already mention in the Old Testament of the '*tora* of Moses' (I Kings 2.3; Mal.3.22 etc.) and even of the 'book of the *tora* of Moses' (Josh.8.31; II Kings 14.6; Neh.8.1, etc.), it was natural, after the extension of the concept of *tora* to the whole Pentateuch, to see Moses as its author. This is presupposed by the Jewish authors Philo and Josephus, writing in Greek at the end of the first century AD, by the Babylonian Talmud (Baba Bathra 14b), and by the New Testament (Matt.19.7f.; Mark 12.26; Acts 15.2, etc.). It was first put in question by modern biblical scholarship.

→131, 155

Bibliography

E.Blum, *Die Komposition der Vätergeschichte*, Diss. Heidelberg 1982; U.Cassuto, *The Documentarty Hypothesis and the Composition of the Pentateuch*, 1961; D.J.A.Clines, *The Theme of the Pentateuch*, 1978; F.M.Cross, 'The Priestly Work', in *Canaanite Myth and Hebrew Epic*, 1973, 293-325; I. Engnell, 'The Pentateuch. A Rigid Scrutiny', in *Critical Essays on the Old Testament*, 1970, 50-67; H.Gressmann, *Mose und seine Zeit. Ein Kommentar zu den Mose-Sagen*, 1913; H.Gunkel, *Die israelitische Literatur*, 1925 (1963); id., *Die Sagen der Genesis. Einleitung zum Genesis-Kommentar* (HK), ³1910 (⁹1977); G.Hölscher, *Geschichtsschreibung in Israel. Untersuchungen zum Jahvisten und Elohisten*, 1952; H.Holzinger, *Einleitung in den Hexateuch*, 1893; S.Mowinckel, *Tetrateuch, Pentateuch, Hexateuch. Die Berichte über die Landnahme in den drei altisraelitischen Geschichtswerken*, 1964; id., *Erwägungen zur Pentateuch-Quellenfrage*, 1964; M.Noth, *A History of Pentateuchal Traditions* (1948), ET 1972; G.von Rad, 'The Form-Critical Problem of the Hexateuch' (1938), in *The Problem of the Hexateuch*, ET 1966, 1-78; R.Rendtorff, *Das überlieferungsgeschichtliche Problem des Pentateuch*, 1977; W.Rudolph, *Der 'Elohist' von Exodus bis Josua*, 1938; H.H.Schmid, *Der sogenannte Jahwist, Beobachtungen und Fragen zur Pentateuchforschung*, 1976; R.Smend Sr, *Die Erzählung des Hexateuch auf ihre Quellen untersucht*, 1912; J. van Seters, *Abraham in History and Tradition*, 1975; P.Volz/W.Rudolph, *Der Elohist als Erzähler – ein Irrweg der Pentateuchkritik?*, 1933; J.Wellhausen, *Die Composition des Hexateuchs und der historischen Bücher des Alten Testaments*, ³1899 (⁴1963); id., *Prolegomena to the History of Israel*, ET 1885, reissued 1957; C.Westermann, 'Arten der Erzählung in der Genesis', in *Forschung am Alten Testament* I, 1963, 9-91 (= *Die Verheissungen an die Väter*, 1976, 9-91); H.W.Wolff, 'Das Kerygma des

Jahwisten', *EvTh* 24, 1964, 73-98 (= *GS*, 345-73); id., 'Zur Thematik der elohistischen Fragmente im Pentateuch', *EvTh* 29, 1969, 59-72 (= *GS²*, 402-17).

Steuernagel, §32-60; Eissfeldt, §23-32, 36; Fohrer, §17-28; Soggin 2.I; Kaiser §4,7-10; Smend, §6-14; Schmidt, §4.6-8; Childs, V.

2 The Former Prophets

In Jewish tradition the prophets (*nᵉbi'im*) follow the 'Torah' as the second part of the canon. In addition to the prophetic books in the narrower sense, this part also comprises the books of Joshua to Kings, the authors of which were regarded as prophets: Joshua, Samuel, who was regarded as the author of Judges and the books which bear his name (and also of the Book of Ruth), and Jeremiah, to whom the books of Kings were attributed (Babylonian Talmud, Baba Bathra 14b/15a). Since the Middle Ages a distinction has been drawn between the 'former prophets' (*nᵉbi'im rišonim*) and the 'latter prophets' (*nᵉbi'im 'aharonim*); given their content, the 'former prophets' are often termed 'historical books'.

In the Hebrew canon, the Book of Ruth appears among the 'Writings', while in the Greek canon it follows the book of Judges. The latter is the position which it occupies in most English Bibles.

→131f.   The problem arises with the historical books, as with the Pentateuch, that the individual books are more or less independent entities but at the same time are part of a larger complex. Here the independence of the first two books, Joshua and Judges, is more marked than that of Samuel and Kings. This is evident, for example, from the fact that the Greek Bible and, following that, the Latin Bible count Samuel and Kings as four books of Kingdoms (Βασιλειων or *Regum*; this should be noted in looking up references in the Septuagint and the Vulgate).

Theological   That the books from Joshua to Kings belong together is evident above
conception   all from a common basic understanding of a theology of history which in language and theology is clearly akin to Deuteronomy and which is therefore usually termed Deuteronomistic. There is no agreement as to whether this is merely a Deuteronomistic redaction or whether these
→183ff.   books were brought together into a 'Deuteronomistic history', and further whether the latter is a unity or shows signs of various redactions. Here we shall not begin from a particular hypothesis, but first treat the individual books independently, taking account of their connections with other books. Only to end with will we take up again the question
→183ff.   of their overall conception and their relationship to the Pentateuch.

2.1 The Book of Joshua

The Book of Joshua deals with the time between the death of Moses (1.1) and the death of Joshua (24.29). A clear division may be observed: occupation of Transjordan (chs.1-12); division of the land (chs.13-21, 22); farewell speeches and last actions of Joshua (chs.23-24). It is evident that in its present form the book is meant to be independent. It owes its formation to the Deuteronomistic redaction; the introductory speech (1.1-9) and the rest of ch.1 are formulated in Deuteronomistic language, as are the closing notes of the first part (11.15,23) and the closing section 21.43-22.6 with the subsequent farewell speech of Joshua in ch.23.

Division

The material from which this Deuteronomistic book of Joshua has been constructed differs widely in character. In the first part, chs.2-11 contain a series of narratives about events in the settlement. Noth (Commentary) has pointed out that the narratives in chs.2-9 are predominantly aetiological in character and relate to places more or less close to Gilgal: the ruins of the walls of Jericho (ch.6) and the house of Rahab's family (ch.2; 6.22-25); the sanctuary stones of Gilgal (4.3,8,20-24) and twelve other stones in the bed of the Jordan (4.9); the name Gilgal (5.9) and the 'hill of foreskins' (5.2-8); the heap of ruins at Ai (8.28), a pile of stones in the valley of Achor (7.26) and another at Ai (8.29); the obligation of the inhabitants of Gibeon to minister at the Israelite sanctuary (ch.9). (Here we almost always find the aetiological formula 'to this day'.) Chapters 10 and 11 also contain narratives from the time of the conquest, which Noth designated 'war narratives'. A list of conquered kings (ch.12) ends this section. The individual narratives have undergone differing degrees of Deuteronomistic revision.

Settlement
Aetiologies
→20f., 87

→87

The texts in the second part are of a very different kind. In some passages in chs.13-19 the boundaries of the individual tribal regions are described within a narrative framework about the division of Transjordan by Joshua (e.g. 15.2-12; 16.1-3, 5-8; 17.7-11, etc.); in others there are lists of place names (e.g. 15.21-62; 18.21-28; 19.41-46). Alt conjectured that two quite different documents underlie this part: a system of tribal boundaries which comes from the time of the judges, and a list of places in the twelve districts into which Josiah divided the state of Judah after it had been extended northwards. However, this hypothesis has been challenged, especially as the relationship of these texts to Num. 32-36 has not yet been explained adequately. Chapters 20 and 21 contain further information about sanctuary cities and levitical cities. 22.10-34 reflect a conflict about the cultic associations between the inhabitants of Transjordan and those of the land east of the Jordan.

Distribution of
land

→105f.

→51f.

This traditional material, which is varied and sometimes disparate, has been incorporated into the book of Joshua within an overall perspective the main factor in which is the influence of its relationship with Deuteronomy. Joshua is Moses' successor – but he is not a second Moses! He is often portrayed like Moses. He makes the people 'consecrate' themselves before an important event (3.5; 7.13; cf.

Overall
conception
→150f.

Ex.19.10); he is honoured by the people like Moses (4.7; 4.14); he makes intercession for Israel (7.6ff.; cf. Deut.9.25); shortly before his death he makes known his last will (23.1ff.; cf. Deut.31.1ff.). At the same time, however, it is important for him to follow the commands of Moses exactly (1.7,13; 4.10; 8.30ff.; 11.15 etc.). Above all, the Torah has been completed; he has it as a 'book' which he must use as a guide (21.8; 8.31,34).

Here we can see clearly not only the continuity between Deuteronomy and the book of Joshua but also the qualitative difference. If we reflect on the close connection between Deuteronomy and the previous books and especially on its function as a concluding summary interpretation of the Torah, we will already find in the Deuteronomistic conception of the book of Joshua a hint of the later distinction between the 'Torah' (i.e. the Pentateuch) and the following books.

There remains the question of the relationship between the book of Joshua and those which follow. Here we must stress a marked tension within the Deuteronomistic conception of the book. Joshua 1.5 says that no one will withstand Joshua; consequently, in 11.16,23; 21.43f. (cf.24.18) it is asserted that Joshua and the Israelites had occupied the whole land. Things sound rather different in ch.23. Here too there is mention of the fulfilment of YHWH's promise (vv.3,9), but at the same time we are also told of the peoples who are still 'left behind' (vv.4,7,12)

and whose expulsion still lies in the future. It is even suggested that YHWH will not continue to drive out these peoples (v.13) if Israel deviates from the Torah of Moses; in particular, that means, if they mix with the people who are left behind and thus turn to other gods (vv.6f.13). That might result in the expulsion of Israel from the land (vv.13b); and just as formerly all the 'good words' of YHWH were fulfilled, so too his 'bad words' will also be fulfilled (vv.15b,16).

Thus here full possession of the promised land is made dependent on observance of the Torah. Evidently this is a different stratum of interpretation (though similarly Deuteronomistic) from that in 1.5; 21.43-45 etc. (Smend, Childs). However, in view of the book of Judges, which follows immediately afterwards, it must be said that here we have no more than the announcement of such a possibility, and that (with the exception of ch.7, which is quickly dismissed) in Joshua the predominant picture is of an obedient Israel to whom the fulfilment of the promises is granted – as long as Joshua lived and the generation which still knew what YHWH had done for Israel (24.31). Here there is already an echo of the negative resumption of this statement in

Judg.2.10.

Chapter 23 is followed directly, in 24.1ff., by a further concluding scene involving Joshua. After a retrospect on salvation history (vv.1-13), this deals with the obligation of the Israelites to YHWH and the renunciation of strange gods (vv.14ff.). Often this chapter has been regarded as an independent tradition, and scholars (e.g. Noth) have attempted to make a historical evaluation of it in terms of the early period. However, the text probably already has essentially a

Deuteronomic-Deuteronomistic stamp (cf. Perlitt, 239ff.). It has parallels and references in the Deuteronomistic history and in the Pentateuch (e.g. Gen.35.1ff.) and is to be seen within the framework of the formation of a Deuteronomistic historical tradition which goes beyond this collection of texts (cf. Blum).

Bibliography

Commentaries: Holzinger (KHC) 1901; Gressmann (SAT I,2) ²1922; Steuernagel (HK) ²1923; Schulz (HS) 1924; Noth (HAT) ²1953 (³1971); Hertzberg, ATD 1953 (⁵1974); Soggin (OTL) 1972.
    A.Alt. *Das System der Stammesgrenzen im Buche Josua* (1927), *KS* I, 193-202; id., *Judas Gaue unter Josia* (1925), *KS* II, 276-88; E.Blum, *Die Komposition der Vätergeschichte*, Diss.Heidelberg 1982; M.Noth, *Überlieferungeschichtliche Studien*, 1943 (⁴1973), partial (1-110) ET *The Deuteronomistic History*, 1981; L.Perlitt, *Bundestheologie im Alten Testament*, 1969; R.Smend, 'Das Gesetz und die Völker. Ein Beitrag zur deuteronomistischen Redaktionsgeschichte', in *Probleme biblischer Theologie. FS G. von Rad*, 1971, 494-509.
    Steuernagel, §61-64; Eissfeldt, §38; Fohrer, §30; Soggin, 2.VI; Kaiser, §12; Smend, §18-20; Schmidt, §11; Childs, XII.

2.2 The Book of Judges

Even at first glance there is evidently a basic difference between the book of Joshua and the book of Judges. In the former a single figure dominates both the individual narratives and the composition of the whole book, while in the latter the picture is governed by a variety of extremely varied figures between whom there is hardly any continuity; moreover the book as a whole does not suggest any single overall shape comparable to that of the book of Joshua. Evidently other viewpoints were determinative here in the collection and composition of the traditions.

To begin with, a quite formal division of the book of Judges can be Division →25f., 27f. made. 1.1-2.5 serve as an introduction. The main section, 2.6-16.31, deals with the 'judges'; the material collected here is very varied and suggests all kinds of subdivisions, but these have not been taken up in the overall approach. Chapters 17-21 look like an appendix which introduces other traditions from the same period of the history of Israel.

The absence of a coherent concept behind the book of Judges can hardly be explained in terms of a lack of skill on the part of the authors or redactors; rather, it reflects their view of this period. Between the time of the strict leadership by Joshua and the beginning of the monarchy (which I Samuel records) this was a time in which everyone did what he wanted (Judg.17.6; 21.25). This remark, formulated in the 'appendix', Time without a applies to the whole book, and indeed to its main part, in an even more king emphatic, markedly theological sense: not only did everyone do 'what was right in his eyes' (17.6; 21.25), but the Israelites did 'what was evil in the eyes of YHWH' (2.11; 3.7,12; 4.1; 6.1; 10.6;13.1). That determined their fate in this period (cf. Veijola).

This can already be seen in the introduction. Chapter 1 collects together individual traditions from the time of the settlement. Towards the end, the almost stereotyped statement, 'they did not drive out the

→21, 106

Canaanites' (vv.19,21,27,28,29,30,31,32,33), is dominant, and finally we even hear how the tribe of Dan is itself driven out by the Amorites (vv.34f.). This is interpreted in 2.1-5, in Deuteronomistic language, by

→144

the 'angel of YHWH' (cf. Ex.23.20-33; 33.2!) as follows: because the Israelites have come to terms with the inhabitants of the land, YHWH will not drive them out but allow them to dwell in the land as a 'snare'

→166

for the Israelites. Here we have a fulfilment of the threat in Josh. 23.13, but with an essential difference. In Judg.2 (as throughout the whole of the book of Judges) there is no announcement of the Israelites being driven out of the land. Here different strata can be recognized within the Deuteronomistic redaction (Childs).

In 2.6ff., similarly in Deuteronomistic language, the conclusion of

→166f.

the book of Joshua (Josh.24.31) is taken up again, but made a negative one: the new generation was no longer aware of the mighty acts of YHWH (v.10); therefore they did 'what was evil in the sight of YHWH'

Programme

(v.11). In 2.11-19 a kind of programme for the time of the judges is worked out, which is regularly repeated: the Israelites leave YHWH and worship other gods (vv.11-13); YHWH is angry and 'sells' them into the hands of enemies (vv.14f.); the Israelites cry out to YHWH (this is absent here, but occurs regularly in 3.9,13; 4.3; 6.6; 10.10); he raises up judges who free them from the hands of the enemy (vv.16-18).

2.20-3.6 take up the announcement of 2.1-5 that YHWH will not drive out the peoples, and enumerates these peoples. The theme is clearly different from the one previously developed, which is concerned with warlike conflicts with 'enemies'. Here again we can see the many strata in the Deuteronomistic redaction (Smend).

Now this pattern has been used as a framework in the subsequent narratives. First of all in 3.7-11 there is a purely Deuteronomistic 'model passage' (Richter 1964), in which the pattern is presented as it were in

**Forty years'
rest**

a pure form with the closing formula: 'the land had rest forty years' (v.11). Here we see clearly that the presentation of the period of the judges is essentially not a chronological sequence of events but the regular recurrence of a cycle of apostasy, distress, conversion and salvation. The disobedient Israel of the time of the judges is compared with the obedient Israel of the time of Joshua; however, even disobedient Israel is not abandoned by YHWH, but continually experiences, at least temporarily, the establishment of the promised state of

→166

'rest' in the land (cf.Deut.12.10; 25.19; Josh.21.44; 23.1).

Otherwise the Deuteronomistic framework is only put loosely around the

individual narratives or narrative complexes, as with Ehud (3.12-15a, 30; the

eighty years of rest probably apply at the same time to Shamgar, cf. v.31);
Deborah and Barak (4.1-3,23f.; 5.31b); Gideon (6.1-6 [7-10]; 8.28 [33-35]);
Jephthah (10.6f.,10 [11-16]; 11.33b; here the forty years' rest is absent because
of the other chronology in 12.7); Samson (13.1: here forty years are mentioned
as the period of alien rule; information about 'rest' is missing, but cf. 15.20;
16.31).

The narratives themselves are of a very varied kind. First of all the Minor judges
list of 'minor judges' clearly stands out (10.1-5; 12.7-15). This is →27, 106
interrupted by the complex of narratives about Jephthah (10.6-12.6),
evidently because he was reported in both forms of the tradition; thus
he could be included among both the major and the minor judges, and
the narratives were inserted where his name appeared in the list. (This
possibly led to the transference of the designation 'judge' to the
charismatic deliverer figures, Noth 1950.) A whole collection of narra- →25ff.
tives about Gideon has also been preserved (chs.6-8); here apparently
two different people, Gideon and Jerubbaal, have been identified
(cf.6.32; 7.1; 8.29f., 35). In chs.4; 5 there is an interesting parallel
tradition, in the form of a narrative and in the Song of Deborah, a
victory song in which numerous tribal sayings have been incorporated.
(Richter conjectures that chs.3-9 formed a pre-Deuteronomistic 'Book
of Deliverers'.)

The narrative of Abimelech (ch.9) falls outside the framework because he does Kingship of
not belong to either of the two groups of judges. However, it is not only a Abimelech
valuable historical source but shows above all an acute anti-monarchical →106
tendency which comes to a climax in the Jotham fable about the uselessness and
harmfulness of the monarchy (vv.8-15). An anti-monarchical text has also been →83
handed down within the Gideon narratives (8.22f.). Both are strikingly opposed
to the narratives in chs.17-21, which are particularly concerned to bring out the
need for the monarchy in the face of the anarchic circumstances of the
pre-monarchical period. They reflect from two different perspectives the
controversies over the monarchy which were carried on in the time of David →29, 171
and Solomon (Crüsemann).
The Samson narratives (chs.13-16) are 'almost in a world of their own' Samson
(Smend), because nowhere is it even hinted that Samson's activity in the frontier →87
territory between Israelites and Philistines had anything at all to do with the
fate of Israel. The notes about the 'judging' of Samson (15.20; 16.31) are quite
isolated. In the context of the book, however, the Samson stories are a further
example of everyone doing what they wanted.

This tension also demonstrates the pluralistic character which the
Deuteronomistic redaction of the traditions of the book of Judges has
allowed itself. This redaction has given the reader only very isolated
aids to interpretation. However, by placing chs.17-21 at the end of the
book it has made its tendency quite clear. Everything is moving towards
the establishment of the monarchy.

Bibliography

Commentaries: Budde (KHC) 1897; Moore (ICC) [2]1898 ([8]1966); Nowack 1902; Gressmann (SAT I,2) [2]1922; Schulz (HS) 1926; Hertzberg (ATD) 1953 ([5]1974); cf. Soggin (OTL) 1981.

W.Beyerlin, 'Gattung und Herkunft des Rahmens im Richterbuch', in *Tradition und Situation. FS A. Weiser*, 1963, 1-29; F.Crüsemann, *Der Widerstand gegen das Königtum. Die antikönigliche Texte des Alten Testaments und der Kampf um den frühen israelitischen Staat*, 1978; M.Noth, *Überlieferungsgeschichtliche Studien*, 1943 ([4]1973), partial ET (1-110) in *The Deuteronomistic History*, 1981; id., 'Das Amt des Richters Israels', in *FS A.Bertholet*, 1950, 404-17 (= *GS* II, 71-85); id., 'Literarische Analyse von Ri.19-21', in *Das System der zwölf Stämme Israels*, 1930 (1978), 162-70; W.Richter, *Traditionsgeschichtliche Untersuchungen zum Richterbuch*, 1963; id., *Die Bearbeitungen des Retterbuches in der deuteronomistischen Epoche*, 1963; R.Smend, 'Das Gesetz und die Völker. Ein Beitrag zur deuteronomistichen Redaktionsgeschichte', in *Probleme biblischer Theologie, FS G. von Rad*, 1971, 494-509; T.Veijola, *Das Königtum in der Beurteilung der deuteronomistischen Historiographie*, 1977.

Steuernagel, §65-67; Eissfeldt, §39; Fohrer, §31; Soggin, 2.VII; Kaiser, §13; Smend, §18-20; Schmidt, § 11; Childs, XIII.

2.3 The Books of Samuel

The books of Samuel are dominated by three great individual figures: Samuel, Saul and David. The tense relationships between them are governed by one all-embracing theme: the rise of the monarchy. Here in the account of the books of Samuel (as also in the books of Kings) the various judgments on the monarchy in the course of the history of Israel have found expression.

Samuel
→29, 112

Chapters 1-7 cover the story of Samuel. Here the story of his birth and youth (chs.1-3) can be seen as an independent unit in which Samuel is designated a 'prophet' (3.19f.); in 7.15-17 there is a final summary of the activity of Samuel as 'judge'.

Ark narrative
→33, 97, 172

4.1-7.1 has incorporated the first part of the ark narrative, which ends in II Sam.6 with the bringing of the ark to Jerusalem (Rost). Samuel does not appear in it other than in 4.1a; the central figure is the priest Eli of the temple of the ark in Shiloh, with whom according to 1.24ff. Samuel grew up and was trained in the service of the sanctuary (2.18ff.).

Saul

Saul enters the scene in ch.8. Chapters 8-15 are dominated by the shifting relationship between Samuel and Saul. Here the farewell discourse of Samuel in ch.12 marks a clear division.

→176f.

170

This section is also marked by the introductory formula for Saul's monarchy in 13.1. Similar formulae appear from here on as introductions or conclusions in connection with all the kings, cf. II Sam.5.4f. (= I Kings 2.11); I Kings 11.42, etc.).

In chs.8-12, very different traditions have been combined, so that **Samuel** there is a very contradictory picture of the beginning of the monarchy, On the one hand are two narratives in which Samuel secretly anoints →29f. Saul as the future ruler at YHWH's behest (9.1-10.16) and the people publicly makes king the man who has successfully delivered them from the enemy (ch.11). Here the monarchy is portrayed positively, without Positive picture qualification, and as being willed by YHWH.

The two narratives did not originally belong together, but represented two different traditions about the appointment of Saul as king. The tension is compensated for by the fact that 11.13 talks of the 'renewal' of Saul's kingship. A third tradition perhaps underlies 10.17-27, according to which an oracle foretells that the one who towers head and shoulders everyone else is to be king (Eissfeldt, cf. vv.22f.).

On the other hand we have chs. 8 and 12 (and the present version of 10.17-27), in which the desire for a king is sharply condemned as apostasy from YHWH. This negative judgment does not derive from Negative the Deuteronomists who have given these chapters their present form, picture but reflects an opposition to the monarchy from the early period of the →29 kingdom. It appears particularly clearly in the 'law of the king' (8.11-17), which describes the *de facto* power relationships polemically from the viewpoint of the well-to-do Israelite farmers for whom the rise of the monarchy had a negative effect particularly in economic terms (Crüsemann). This anti-monarchical tradition has been adopted by the Deuteronomistic revision and supplemented and reinforced by the inclusion of theological arguments.

In the present composition, the sections favourable to the monarchy Composition (9.1-10.16; ch.11) are framed by negative ones (ch.8; 10.17-27; ch.12), so that the latter clearly dominate. Moreover, in his farewell discourse Samuel is presented as a positive counterpart to the king: the king wants to take everything (8.11ff.) – Samuel took nothing (12.3ff.). Nevertheless the people is given the chance to live with the king if he keeps the commandments of YHWH (12.14,20-24); if not, they will be destroyed along with the king (v.25, cf.v.15).

The continuation of Saul's monarchy is overshadowed by this threat and is presented as a history of apostasy from YHWH and of failure. The narratives about Saul's battles against the Philistines (ch.13) Saul's failure and the Amalekites (ch.15) are now completely coloured by Saul's disobedience and his rejection by YHWH (13.11-14; 15.10ff.). Here there are already references to the other man who will become king in Saul's place.

With I Sam.16 there begins the history of David, which ends in I →31ff. Kings 2.11. The first part overlaps with the history of Saul. The present division of the books has produced a break with the death of Saul in I Sam.31, which interrupts the History of the Rise of David (I Sam.16-II David's rise Sam.5), an independent piece of tradition. →107

The beginning of the history of David, like that of Saul, is reported in different versions. In 16.1-13 we are told of a secret anointing of David by Samuel; the narrative was probably composed to match Saul's anointing by Samuel (9.1-10.16) in order to stress the legitimacy of the monarchy of David. In 16.14-23 David is invited to the court for Saul's personal service and entertainment, while in the narrative about the combat with Goliath (ch.17), he sets out from his father's house (vv.17ff.) and Saul does not know him at all (vv.55ff.).

Conflict
between Saul
and David
→31f.

The dominant theme of the History of the Rise of David is the conflict between Saul and David. Saul's jealousy over David's success and popularity (18.5-9,12,14-16,28f.) leads him to attempts on David's life (18.10f.; 19.9-17); David finally flees (19.18ff.). This provides the framework into which the other narratives have been inserted: David's flight and his persecution by Saul. In a skilful literary composition narratives about David the fugitive (*21.2-10,11-16*; 22.1-5,20-23; 23.1-5; 25.2-42; 27.8-28.2; 29.30) alternate with others about Saul his persecutor (*22.6-19*; 28.4-25; 31), often being directly interwoven (23.6-15, 19-28). There are even personal encounters, though these are not noticed by Saul (chs.24; 26). At the beginning, to heighten the tension

Jonathan

we have the story of the friendship between David and Jonathan (18.1,36; 19.1-7; 20.1-21.1).

Finally, the whole History of the Rise of David is permeated by interpretative notes to the effect that in this battle David will emerge victor and gain the kingdom; these comments are often emphatically attributed to Saul, still reigning as king (18.8; 20.31; 24.21; 26.25), or to the 'crown prince' Jonathan (20.13-16; 23.16-18; cf. also 25.28,30; II Sam.3.9f.,18; 5.2,12). Here it becomes particularly clear that the History owes its present form to a deliberate plan of composition (cf. Weiser, Rendtorff).

Abner and
Eshbaal
→32

In the closing part of the History of the Rise of David, after the death of Saul (II Sam. 1-5) two large narrative complexes (2.12-32; 3.6-4.12) depict the struggles for the succession. Here the rivalry of the two generals Abner and Joab stands in the foreground. After the death of Saul's son Eshbaal, the way is free for David to add rule over 'all the tribes of Israel' (5.1-3) to his kingly rule over Judah (2.4). The capture of Jerusalem and the proclamation that it is the 'city of David' (5.6-9), along with the summary interpretative notes (vv.10,12), mark the end of the History. As an appendix there is a report of David's victory over the Philistines (5.17-25), which forms the basic presupposition for the success of his kingly rule.

There is a dispute as to where the History of the Rise of David ends. This is bound up with the question of the beginning of the Succession Narrative. There is much to suggest that these narrative works were combined by the Deuteronomistic redactors through the insertion of various interludes in 5.17 (or 5.11) – 8.18 (Veijola). Here some pieces of independent tradition stand out

→170

clearly: the conclusion of the ark narrative (ch.6), which Rost regarded as the beginning of the Succession Narrative (especially because of the Michal episode in vv.16,20-23, which gives the reason for the barrenness of Saul's daughter

Nathan's
prophecy
172

Michal); the Nathan prophecy (ch.7) with the rejection of the plan to build the temple (vv.1-7); and the promise of a dynasty to David (vv.8ff.), the

Deuteronomistic character of which has long been recognized; the summary of the foreign successes of David which derive from 'official' documents (8.1-14, cf. Noth) and the list of David's officials (8.16-18, cf. 20.23-25).

Samuel

→33, 106

The second part of the history of David is formed by the history of the succession to the throne, the Succession Narrative (II Sam.9-I Kings 2). Like the History of the Rise of David, it has been interrupted by the present division into books, evidently with the intention of making a new book begin with the accession of Solomon. Thus David is the only king to have a whole book devoted to him (II Sam.).

Succession to the throne
→107, 110

Unlike the History of the Rise of David, the Succession Narrative is not composed of independent pieces of narrative and tradition, but forms a major literary entity. Only in 10.6-11.1; 12.26-31 has the author incorporated an 'official' document, the 'account of the Ammonite war' (Rost), which he integrated into his work by linking it with the Bathsheba episode (11.2-12.25). Otherwise he gives a continuous narrative of the dangers to which the kingly rule of David was exposed: first of all by the existence of a direct descendant of Saul, Merib-baal (ch.9), then through the two rebellions of Absalom (ch.13 [prehistory]; 15-19) and Sheba (ch.20). Only a few hints indicate his theological interpretation of this history (II Sam.11.27b; 12.24b; 17.14; cf. von Rad).

→107
→117

The 'appendices' (chs.21-24) presuppose the present division of the books and form the conclusion to the history of David. They are skilfully composed; at the beginning and the end there are stories about David, in each of which a 'plague' plays a decisive role (21.1-14; 24); towards the middle there are lists of 'David's heroes' and their acts (21.15-22; 23.8-39); finally, at the centre, there are two songs or poems (ch.22 [= Ps.18] and 23.1-7).

Appendices

→106

In both narratives David is confronted with a sin (in 21.1f. with a sin of Saul, and in 24.10 with one of his own), but he is able to turn away the wrath of God from Israel by virtue of his own exemplary conduct (21.14; 24.25). The second event also determines the place where the temple is to be built. In the first section, about the 'heroes', David is expressly released from fighting by his soldiers (21.17), so that he can devote himself wholly to the praise of YHWH (22; in 22.29 the expression 'lamp of Israel' is taken up again from 21.17, cf. also I Kings 11.36; 15.4; II Kings 8.19). Here David's righteousness is emphatically stressed (22.12-15; cf.23.3).

In the present composition of the books of Samuel accents have been placed which extend beyond the original narrative complexes. Thus we can recognize a clear distinction between 'David under the blessing' (II Sam.2-5) and 'David under the curse' (II Sam.9-24) (Carlson). In 5.12 the period in which David was 'the shepherd of Israel' (5.2) is emphatically concluded by the statement that YHWH raised up the kingly rule of David 'for the sake of his people Israel'; after the Bathsheba affair this is contrasted with Nathan's saying that YHWH will raise up 'evil out of your own house' against David (12.11); this then comes about in the rebellions.

Composition

The two books of Samuel are put in an even wider context by the

poetic texts, which are related to each other. In the 'Psalm of Hannah'
(I Sam.2.1-10), themes are touched on which are taken up again in II
Sam.22; 23: God is described as a 'rock' (I Sam.2.2; II Sam.22.3,32,47;
23.3); his epiphany is depicted in the same way (I Sam.2.10; II
Sam.22.8ff.); the theme of raising up and bringing down, killing and
making alive, appears in both places (I Sam.2.6-8; II Sam.22.17-20,28);
and at the conclusion of each there is mention of YHWH's blessing for
the king and 'anointed' (*mašiah*, I Sam.2.10b; II Sam.22.51); in II
Sam.22 the name of David is mentioned, but it is not yet known in I
Sam.2.

The Nathan prophecy in II Sam.7 forms a bridge between these texts
at the beginning and the end of the books of Samuel. The 'messianic'
expectation of I Sam.2.10 is taken up and directed beyond the person
of David into the future: the promise to the house of David is to hold
'for all time' ('*ad 'olam*, II Sam.7.13,16,25,29), and it continues in force
despite the sin of David (II Sam.23.5) (Childs).

Bibliography

Commentaries: Budde (RHC) 1902; Nowack (HK) 1902; Gressmann (SAT 2,1)
²1921; Caspari (KAT) 1926; Hertzberg (ATD) 1956 = ET OTL 1964; Stoebe
(KAT²) 1 Sam. 1973.
    R.A.Carlson, *David, the Chosen King. A Traditio-Historical Approach to the
Second Book of Samuel*, 1964; R.Crüsemann, *Der Widerstand gegen das
Königtum. Die antiköniglichen Texte des Alten Testamentes und der Kampf
um den frühen israelitischen Staat*, 1978; O.Eissfeldt, *Die Komposition der
Samuelisbücher*, 1931; M.Noth, *Überlieferungsgeschichtliche Studien*, 1943
(⁴1973), partial (1-110) ET *The Deuteronomistic History*, 1981; G.von Rad,
'The Beginnings of Historical Writing in Ancient Israel', in *The Problem of the
Hexateuch*, ET 1966, 166-204; R.Rendtorff, 'Beobachtungen zur altisraelit-
ischen Geschichtsschreibung anhand der Geschichte vom Aufstieg Davids', in
Probleme biblischer Theologie, FS G. von Rad, 1971, 428-39; L.Rost, *Die
Überlieferung von der Thronnachfolge Davids*, 1926 (= *Das kleine Credo und
andere Studien zum Alten Testament*, 1965, 119-253); T.Veijola, *Die ewige
Dynastie. David und die Enstehung seiner Dynastie nach der deuteronomistischen
Darstellung*, 1973; A.Weiser, 'Die Legitimation des Königs David. Zur Eigenart
und Entstehung der sogen. Geschichte von Davids Aufstieg', *VT* 16, 1966, 325-
54.
    Steuernagel, §68-74; Eissfeldt, §40; Fohrer, §32; Soggin, 2. VIII; Kaiser, §14;
Smend, §18-19,21; Schmidt, §11; Childs, XIV.

2.4 The Books of Kings

The books of Kings present quite a different picture from the books of
Samuel. They contain only a few larger narrative units, and their division
is not immediately obvious.

There could have been practical reasons for the division into two books, which is only demonstrable after the fifteenth century (division into two parts of approximately the same size). The death of king Ahab was chosen as the break. (The note in II Kings 1.1 'after the death of Ahab' is parallel to II Sam.1.1 'after the death of Saul' and Josh.1.1 'after the death of Moses'.) In this way the clashes between Elijah and Ahab form the end of the first book, while Elijah's activity is reported at the beginning of the second book; this finally leads to the overthrow of the dynasty of Ahab by Jehu (II Kings 9f.).

The history of Solomon forms the first major section (I Kings 1-11). The conclusion of the Succession Narrative has been incorporated at the beginning; this deals with the appointment of Solomon as king (ch.1) and the removal of those rivals who are still alive (ch.2); in 2.10-12 we have the concluding formula for the rule of David and the transition to Solomon. The rest of the account of Solomon's reign is divided up by accounts of two epiphanies which are granted him. In the first (3.4-15), Solomon is presented as the model, pious king, who asks God for an "understanding mind' (v.9) in order to be able to fulfil his duties as king; in the second (9.1-9), which follows immediately after the consecration of the temple, the possibility of the apostasy of the kings from YHWH appears (vv.6ff.); soon afterwards the same thing is reported of Solomon himself (11.1ff.). This heralds the end of Solomon's rule and thus also of the Davidic empire.

Solomon →34ff.

Two epiphanies

A variety of material has been collected within this framework; some of it consists of official documents (e.g. the two lists in 4.2-6, 7-19) and historical notices (e.g. 3.1; 5.6-8; 9.15-28; one in 10.28f.) and some of traditions with a narrative form which seek to paint a particular picture of Solomon. These are concerned above all with three themes.

→105f.

The dominant theme is Solomon's wisdom. In the introductory dream vision (3.4-15) wisdom is given him (v.12), and in the subsequent story of the judgment of Solomon (3.16-28) there is proof of it; in 5.9-14 and the narrative of the visit of the Queen of Sheba (10.1-13) there is an indication of its worldwide superiority; in the closing note about Solomon's reign (11.41-43) wisdom is stressed once again as Solomon's decisive characteristic (v.4). Here we see quite different aspects of wisdom: in 5.9-14 it is concerned with nature (v.13); in 3.16-28, on the other hand, it is concerned with giving judgment, which is also specially praised by the Queen of Sheba (10.9); whereas in 10.1-3 there is more general mention of the wisdom of Solomon.

Wisdom

→108

The second theme is Solomon's royal power and the development of his splendour. Three lengthy sections are devoted to this: 4.1-5.8; 9.10-28; 10.14-29; however, it also plays a major role in the narrative of the visit of the Queen of Sheba (10.4f. and the insertion vv.11f.); in the summary section 10.23-25 it is explicitly connected with the wisdom of Solomon.

Splendour

The accounts of Solomon's building activities, the third theme, take up a good deal of room (5.15-8.66). In them the development of Solomon's splendour is taken further, and in addition we have the picture of Solomon as the founder and patron of the temple cult. Here

Building activity

his piety (cf.3.4-15) finds its lasting expression, in particular in the speeches and prayers in 8.14-21, 22-53 ('Prayer at the dedication of the temple'), 54-61 and in the great sacrificial ceremony in 8.62-66 (cf. 3.4,15; 9.25; 10.5). Here too there is initial stress on the wisdom of Solomon which finds its expression in his pious plans to build the temple and in the peace which prevails abroad (*5.21* with reference to vv.*18f.*; *5.26*).

Piety

The picture of Solomon as the wise, just, pious king of peace is disturbed towards the end of his rule because he allows himself to be enticed by his foreign wives into worshipping strange gods and establishing alien cults in Jerusalem (11.1-8). This brings down on him the threat made in the second epiphany (9.1-9); only 'for David's sake' will it not come into force in the lifetime of Solomon (v.12), and even thereafter not completely (v.13).

Strange gods

→181ff.

This provides the transition to the reports about the decline of Solomon's kingdom. An Edomite (11.14-22) and an Aramaean (11.23-25) 'adversary' (*śatan*) threaten his power abroad, and in Jeroboam he has a dangerous opponent at home (11.26-40) who is, moreover, appointed by the prophet Ahijah of Shiloh to fulfil the announcement that the kingdom of Solomon will be rent asunder (11.29-39; cf. 11.9-13). The accomplishment of this is postponed until the death of Solomon because of Jeroboam's flight (v.40), so that the final note about Solomon's reign (vv.41-43) at the same time marks the end of the Davidic empire.

Decline
→36

In the closing note, reference is made to the 'Book of the Acts of Solomon' as an additional source of information (11.41). This reference indicates that the author of I Kings 1-11 has not used all the information available to him but has selected from it according to a particular perspective. Otherwise the reference presupposes that the source cited is accessible to the readers. The same is true of the similar references to the 'Chronicle of the Kings of Israel' (I Kings 14.19, etc.) or 'of Judah' (I Kings 14.29, etc.).

→106

In its present form the history of Solomon has marked Deuteronomistic features, above all in the sections dealing with Solomon's piety, as in 'the prayer for the consecration of the temple' (8.22-53).

The historical account which follows is orientated on the person of the king reigning at a particular time, so it can be summarily described as the history of the kings of Israel and Judah. Its main characteristic is a framework with introductory and concluding notes about the individual kings, which is arranged in accordance with a fixed scheme and is only interrupted when the course of events makes that necessary. The scheme contains:

History of the
kings

Framework

1. Chronological information about the date of the accession and the duration of the reign of each individual king. As long as Israel and Judah stand side by side as two separate kingdoms, a 'synchronistic' form of dating is used; i.e. the accession of a king is dated in accordance with the regnal year of the king ruling in the neighbouring kingdom (I Kings 15.1,9,25,33,etc.). In the case of the kings of Judah the king's

Synchronisms

age on accession (e.g. I Kings 14.21; 22.42) and the name of his mother (e.g. I Kings 14.[21]31; 15.2) is also given.

Jepsen has conjectured that the chronological information comes from a 'synchronistic chronicle' which was available as a source to the authors of Kings; according to Noth it is taken from the 'Chronicles of the Kings of Israel or Judah', while Bin-Nun posits separate king lists from the northern and southern kingdom as sources. →106

2. A religious assessment of the king in question. The kings of Israel always receive a negative evaluation because they have continued the 'sin of Jeroboam' (I Kings 15.26,34; 16.26, etc.). In the case of the kings of Judah there are also positive verdicts, but except in the cases of Hezekiah (II Kings 18.3-6) and Josiah (22.2; 23.25) these are qualified, because the 'high places' (*bamot*) continue to exist (I Kings 15.11-15; 22.43f.; II Kings 12.3f.; 14.3f.; 15.3f.,34f.). Otherwise there is often a reference back to David: as a model by which the king in question is measured (e.g. I Kings 15.3,11; II Kings 14.3; 16.2; 18.3; 22.2) or as a reason why YHWH allows Judah to continue to exist (cf. already I Kings 11.12f.; also 15.4f.; II Kings 8.19, etc.). Religious verdict →40f.

These verdicts and the reasons for them are stamped with Deuteronomistic language and theology. They display numerous stereotyped phrases, and at the same time also a great many variations. H.Weippert has argued from this for a number of strata of Deuteronomistic revisions, the earliest of which is to be put a long way before the reform of the cult by Josiah. However, Hoffmann sees here references to a comprehensive Deuteronomistic history of the cult.

3. In the closing note there is a reference to the 'Chronicles of the Kings of Israel or Judah', often with schematic indications of the further information to be found there (I Kings 14.19,29f.; 15.7,23,31f., etc.). →106

4. A concluding comment on the death (in the case of the kings of Judah also the burial) of the king and the name of his successor (I Kings 14.20 [here, by way of exception, the information about the duration of his reign is given at the end because the note at the beginning is missing],31; 15.8-24; 16.6, etc.).

Within this scheme the history of the individual kings is handled very differently. In the majority of cases there is little information other than what is given in the scheme itself: e.g. in the case of Joash of Israel (II Kings 13.10-13), only the comment within the closing note that he 'fought against Amaziah king of Judah' (v.12); in the case of Abijah of Judah (I Kings 15.1-8) there is a similar report in an independent sentence (v.6). Elsewhere, too, there are often only one or two sentences, though these make statements of very different importance: e.g. about sickness (II Kings 15.54), about a conspiracy to which the king concerned fell victim (II Kings 15.10,14,25,30; 21.23f.), and also about important political events abroad (e.g. II Kings 15.19f., 29,37) or about the foundation of a new capital (I Kings 16.24).

For the insertion of the political notes into the framework cf. Hoffmann (33f.);

177

also for the striking use of the scheme for judges in II Kings 13.3-5 (113ff.) and 14.26f.

Only at a few points does the account become more detailed, evidently because here the authors had extensive material at their disposal which seemed important to them for their overall account. These are almost all turning points in the history of Israel and Judah and, almost always, prophets are involved. This stress on the prophetic element doubtless lies within the purpose of the authors of Kings. However, it is now impossible to discover whether they had other material at their disposal which they did not include (e.g. from the sphere of court historiography).

Division of the
kingdom
→38ff.

A first major narrative complex discusses the division of the kingdoms of Israel and Judah (I Kings 12.1-14). The section begins immediately after the closing note about Solomon (11.41-43) and ends with the closing notes about Jeroboam (14.19f.) and Rehoboam (14.29-31).

→38f., 107

Various traditions have been combined in this framework: a historical narrative about the separation of the northern tribes from the Davidic dynasty (12.1-19, cf.Plein); an account of Jeroboam's cultic measures (12.26-32; v.33 is an introduction to ch.13); three very different

→40
→113f.

prophetic narratives: about the prevention of a war between Rehoboam and the northern tribes by Shemaiah (12.21-24); about the fate of an anonymous 'man of God' at the altar of Bethel (13.1-32); and about a forecast of judgment to Jeroboam by Ahijah of Shiloh (14.1-18, a continuation of 11.29-39). There are also various individual notes about Jeroboam, some serving as links (12.20 [taking up 11.40, cf. 12.2f.], 25; 13.33f. [resumption of 12.32f.]), and about Rehoboam within the overall framework (14.21-31).

This section has several functions within the overall account of the

→175f.

monarchy. The forecast made to Solomon (11.9-13, cf. 11.29-39) is fulfilled (12.15; cf.14.8) by the division of the kingdoms of Israel and Judah. At the same time, however, Jeroboam is also told of the coming end of his dynasty (14.9-16; cf.15.29f.). Finally, a cultic development begins in both kingdoms which is to determine future events: in the

→38

northern kingdom the 'sin of Jeroboam' (12.30; 13.34), and in the southern kingdom the continuation of the cult on the high places and other 'abominations of the nations' (14.22-24, cf. Hoffmann).

Prophets v.
kings

The next major narrative complex deals with the controversy between the prophets and the kings of Israel (I Kings 17-II Kings 10). Various prophetic narratives have been collected here, combined with reports about the kings reigning at the time: the two great complexes centred on Elijah (I Kings 17-19; 21; II Kings 1) and Elisha (II Kings 2.1-9.10 [interrupted by information about the kings reigning at the time in 3.1-3; 8.16-24, 25-29], the conclusion comes in 13.14-21), the narrative

Micaiah ben
Imlah
→44, 112
→45, 107

about Micaiah ben Imlah (I Kings 22.1-28, connected with the end of the history of Ahab in 22.29-40 and the information about further kings in 22.41-51, 52-54) and the collection of prophetic narratives in I Kings 20. At the same time, the end of the Elisha narrative marks the beginning of the narrative of Jehu's revolution (II Kings 9.11-10.36), in which the fulfilment of prophetic announcments is stressed several times (9.25f.,36; 10.10,17).

Kings

In its present form, the Elijah narrative is dominated by the opposition between Elijah and Ahab. This opposition also closely determines the details of the story of Naboth's vineyard (I Kings 21) and the framework of the narrative complex in chs.17f., which deals with a drought and a famine (17.1-6; 18.1-20,41-46). Two miracle stories have been inserted into it (17.8-16, 17-24) and above all the scene on Carmel (18.21-40). Here the question 'YHWH or Baal?' comes to a dramatic climax; and there is no mention of Ahab anywhere. In the narrative about the epiphany on Horeb (19.1-18; the call of Elisha follows in vv.19-21), Ahab's wife Jezebel is the real opponent (vv.1f.); in II Kings 1 it is her son Ahaziah. However, although the protagonists change, the religious conflict is always the dominant feature and gives the Elijah narrative its distinctive stamp.

Elijah →43

In the Elisha narrative, the dominant picture is that of the miracle worker (II Kings 4.1-7, 8-37 show striking parallels to I Kings 17.8-16, 17-24!). The miracles sometimes take place within a closed circle, but sometimes they also have military and political consequences (II Kings 3; 6.8-7.20). Elsewhere, too, Elisha is shown as exercising a political function (8.7-15; 13.14-19); here his involvement in Jehu's revolution had far-reaching consequences for the history of the northern kingdom. However, his image remains contradictory and strikingly different from that of Elijah (cf. Schmitt).

Elisha →112f., 114

→45

For more than a hundred years (and therefore for the rest of the history of the northern kingdom) we have no further detailed accounts. The only historical narrative is connected with the episode of the reign of Athaliah in II Kings 11; in 12.5-17 there is an account of an alteration to the financing of the temple by Joash of Judah, and in 14.5-14 the account of Amaziah's political activities at home and abroad is rather more extended than usual; the same is true in 16.5-18 of the Syro-Ephraimite war and the measures taken by King Ahaz in connection with the cult. Otherwise, the reports about individual kings are always limited to a few sentences.

→45, 106f.

The account of the destruction of the northern kingdom by the Assyrians is extremely brief (17.3-6). However, a detailed theological reason is attached to it (17.7-23): the downfall of the northern kingdom is the result of the sin of the Israelites (v.7) who practised many forms of illegitimate cults (vv.8-12,16f.). Despite the warning given by the prophets (v.13) they thus rejected the covenant with YHWH (v.14f.). All this is rooted in the 'sin of Jeroboam' (vv.21f.) which finally inevitably led to the rejection and exile of Israel (vv.18,23; in vv.19f. this reason is later also extended to Judah). With this the aberrant history of the cult in the northern kingdom, which had begun with Jeroboam (I Kings 12.16-32), comes to an end (cf. Hoffmann).

Destruction of the northern kingdom →47f.

An appendix follows in 17.24-41 which is divided into a number of sections: vv.24-28 deal with the settlement of alien population groups in the northern kingdom and its consequences; vv.29-33 depict the religious conditions in this area; vv.34-41 criticize these conditions by the standards of Deuteronomy. Here, in contrast to the earlier sections, the inhabitants of this northern province

→47f.

are not called foreigners but 'sons of Jacob (= Israel)' with whom YHWH made a covenant and whom he brought out of Egypt (vv.34-36).

This last section is probably an addition related to the later controversies with the Samaritans (Hoffmann, for the whole question cf. Talmon).

Another major narrative complex begins with the Isaiah narratives (II Kings 18.13-20.19). It is embedded in the history of Hezekiah (18.1-20.21) and is primarily connected with the siege of Jerusalem by Sennacherib in 701.

18.13-19.37, about the siege of Jerusalem by Sennacherib, is composed of different sections. 18.13-16 contains a brief account of the subjection of Hezekiah and his payment of tribute, which is probably based on official annals. In the following section the theme of the siege and deliverance of Jerusalem is developed with some legendary elements; here two parallel versions have been combined (18.17-19.9a, 36f. and 19.9b-35). Both are clearly stamped by Deuteronomistic theology; the second is more firmly concentrated on the person of the pious king, as is evident especially from the prayer in 19.15-19 (Childs 1967). The taunt song about the king of Assyria (19.21-28) stands out clearly as an independent piece.

The legendary narrative of Hezekiah's sickness (20.1-11) also stresses this aspect of the king's piety, while the narrative about the delegation from Babylon (20.12-19) presents Hezekiah's wrong behaviour as the reason for the subsequent exile.

The whole section II Kings 18.13-20.19 has been incorporated, with minor differences, into the book of Isaiah (Isa.36-39), along with a major addition, the Psalm of Hezekiah (38.9-20).

After the extended, essentially Deuteronomistic, passage about Manasseh (II Kings 21.1-18) and the brief information about Amon (21.19-26), the last detailed narrative complex is the history of Josiah (22.1-23.30), at the centre of which is the account of the discovery of the book of the law and the reform of the cult (22.3-23.25). In the overall context of the description of the monarchy this is presented as being of decisive importance. The cultic reform set in motion by the discovery of Deuteronomy takes up all the previous cultic reforms of the monarchy, both positive and negative, and brings them to completion. Explicit mention is made of the removal of high places and altars which had been erected by Solomon (23.13; cf. I Kings 11.5,7), Jeroboam (23.15; cf. I Kings 12.32), and Manasseh (23.12; cf. 21.5); in connection with other reform measures summary mention is made of the kings of Judah (23.5,11,12) and the kings of Israel (23.19). Here there is always criticism in religious assessments of the continued existence of the high places or the 'sin of Jeroboam'. In some cases reforms are also mentioned, which were already reported in connection with earlier kings, like the removal of cultic prostitutes (23.7) by Asa (I Kings 15.12) and Jehoshaphat (I Kings 22.47) and of the cult of Baal (23.4) by Joram (II Kings 3.2), Jehu (9.18-28) and Jehoiada (11.18); here Josiah's reform marks the final conclusion. (For details see Hoffmann, 251ff.)

Josiah's reform
of the cult
→51

→176
→40f., 50f.

→177

180

The accounts in II Kings 22f. are largely regarded as a historical source for Josiah's reform. Thus e.g. Noth assumes the basis of 22.3-23.3 to be an official memorandum and regards 23.4-20a as extracts from the 'Chronicles of the Kings of Judah'. More recently, Würthwein in particular has questioned the character of the sources. Finally, Hoffmann has pointed out the interweaving of the accounts, sketched out above, with the overall presentation of the books of Kings. arguing from this that it is to be regarded *in toto* as the work of the Deuteronomist.

Kings
→54, 155f.

→106

The reports about the last kings of Judah again move within the usual framework. The accounts of the two captures of Jerusalem and the deportation of Judaeans at the time of Jehoiachin (24.8-17) and Zedekiah (24.18-25.21) are also very brief and have neither been developed into narratives nor been provided with detailed theological motivations or interpretations (cf. 24.20). The closing section, concerned with the pardon for Jehoiachin (25.27-30), has also been left without an interpretation.

Occupation of Jerusalem
→52f.

→187

The books of Kings as a whole have been systematically planned. This is evident first of all from the framework, which is applied thoroughly and consistently. In it the religious assessment of the individual kings forms the element of continuity. Here the behaviour of the kings is measured by the criterion whether it corresponds to or conflicts with the demands of Deuteronomy for purity and unity in the cult. All these statements culminate in Josiah's reform of the cult in II Kings 23 and find their conclusion there. The report of the discovery of the book of the law in II Kings 22 indicates explicitly that Deuteronomy is the basis of this reform of the cult.

Composition of the books of Kings

Assessment of the cult

Another element of continuity lies in the pattern of promise and fulilment which runs through the books of Kings. Here it is always prophets who announce usually to the king a particular action by YHWH or a particular fate; we are then informed when this comes about (cf. von Rad, Dietrich). Thus at the consecration of the temple Solomon already refers back to the prophecy of Nathan to David (I Kings 8.20; cf. II Sam.7.12f.). Then prophecies are made by the prophet Ahijah to Jeroboam (I Kings 11.29-39, fulfilment → 12.15; 14.7-11 → 15.29), by a prophet named Jehu to Baasha (16.1-4 → v.12), by Elijah to Ahab (21.21-24, 27-29, cf. II Kings 9.7-10 → 10.17), by Micaiah ben Imlah to Ahab (I Kings 22.17 → vv.35f.), by Elijah to Ahaziah (II Kings 1.6 → v.17), by Isaiah to Hezekiah (20.17 → 24.13), by anonymous prophets to Manasseh (21.10-15 → 24.2) and by Huldah the prophetess to Josiah (22.15-17 → 24.20; 22.18-20 → 23.30). The prophecy about the altar of Bethel also belongs in this context (I Kings 13 → II Kings 23.15-18).

Prophecy and fulfilment

→173f.
→39
→43f., 179
→178f.

→179f.

→113f., 178

In some cases the agreement between prophecy and fulfilment appears within an independent story which has been adopted by the author of the books of Kings (e.g. I Kings 22; II Kings 1). In other cases prophetic narratives are incorporated by such references into the wider context (e.g. the Elijah narrative in I Kings 21, the Elisha narrative in II Kings 9 and the Isaiah narrative in II Kings 20) or are shaped in accordance with it (e.g. I Kings 11.29-39; 13; 14.1-

18; II Kings 22.14-20). Finally, the Deuteronomistic author of the books of Kings has also introduced prophets for whom he evidently had no model (e.g. I Kings 16.1-4; II Kings 21.10-15). Here it is possible for us to gain some insight into the way in which the author worked.

Orientation on
David

→163

Finally, the orientation on David forms another continuous thread (cf. von Rad, Cross). It begins with the repeated emphasis that Solomon sat on the throne of David (I Kings 2.12,14; 3.6f.). We are then told that Solomon loved YHWH in that he walked according to the statutes of his father David (3.3), i.e. in accordance with all that was written in the 'law of Moses' (2.3). On several occasions the future fate of Solomon (3.14), the kingdom (9.4f.), and all Israel (6.12) is explicitly bound up with the succession to the throne of David, and it is finally affirmed that in his old age Solomon ceased to correspond to the the model established by David (11.4,6). The threat of the loss of the kingdom is not, however, to come about in Solomon's lifetime 'for David's sake' (11.12); moreover his son will retain rule over the tribe of Judah 'for David's (and Jerusalem's) sake' (11.13, cf. vv.32,34); therefore a 'lamp' is to be kept before YHWH in Jerusalem for David (11.36).

This provides the keywords for what follows. Jeroboam, too, is measured by the standards of David (11.38) and fails (14.8); the destiny of the monarchy in the northern kingdom is thus sealed. In the southern kingdom, after the death of Rehoboam, Abijah appears as a king who does not correspond to the Davidic model (15.3); however, again the

Lamp in
Jerusalem

→45

→45

→47, 49

→49ff.

→50f.

→51

182

'lamp' is preserved in Jerusalem 'for David's sake' (vv.4f.). The next king of Judah, Asa, lives up to the Davidic model (15.11), and his son Jehoshaphat also follows the example of his father (22.43). It is only his son Joram who departs from this way and walks in the 'ways of the kings of Israel' (II Kings 8.18), to which he was allied through his marriage with Ahab's daughter Athaliah. However, again Judah is spared destruction 'for the sake of David', to whom YHWH had promised an everlasting 'lamp' (v.19). Joram's son Ahaziah is killed in Jehu's revolution in the northern kingdom; but after the interlude of the illegal rule of Athaliah, his son Joash again proves to be a king on the throne in Jerusalem who 'did what was pleasing to YHWH' (12.3); the same is true of his son Amaziah, albeit with the qualification that he did not completely correspond to the Davidic model (14.3). Azariah and Jotham follow the same line, and only with Ahaz does a king again ascend the throne who does not correspond to the Davidic model (16.2). The report about him clearly shows the danger to Judah and its decline, above all in the cultic sphere, but his son Hezekiah again takes up the Davidic line and makes good the cultic transgressions of his father (18.3-6). He is given the promise of YHWH that 'for my sake and for the sake of my servant David' he will protect and deliver the city of Jerusalem (19.34; 20.5f.). Manasseh's cultic sins are particularly bad because YHWH had promised to David and Solomon that he would 'make his name dwell' in the temple in Jerusalem (21.7); but Josiah again follows the ways of David without deviation (22.2), and with his cultic reform sets everything back in order.

Thus here an unbroken line is drawn from David to Josiah, and at the points of greatest danger – at the collapse of Solomon's kingdom and in the rule of kings who do not continue the way of David – YHWH's promise comes into force: he will keep a lamp for David in Jerusalem (I Kings 11.36; 15.4; II Kings 8.19). Along with the notes about the cult, this orientation on David maintains a firm structure within the framework of the book of Kings which is supplemented by the references to the fulfilment of promises.

The question of the end of the Books of Kings is discussed in connection with the Deuteronomistic history. →186f.

Bibliography

Commentaries: Benzinger (KHC) 1899; Kittel (HK) 1902; Gressmann (SAT 2,1) ²1921; Montgomery-Gehman (ICC) 1951; Gray OTL ²1970 (³1977); Noth (BK) *I Könige* 1-16, 1968; Würthwein (ATD) *I Könige* 1-16, 1977; *I Könige* 17-II Könige 25*, 1984.

S.Bin-Nun, 'Formulas from Royal Records of Israel and of Judah', *VT* 18, 1968, 414-32; B.S.Childs, *Isaiah and the Assyrian Crisis*, 1967; F.M.Cross, 'The Themes of the Book of Kings and the Structure of the Deuteronomistic History', in *Canaanite Myth and Hebrew Epic*, 1973, 274-89; W.Dietrich, *Prophetie und Geschichte. Eine redaktionsgeschichtliche Untersuchung zum deuteronomistichen Geschichtswerk*, 1972; H.-D.Hoffmann, *Reform und Reformen. Untersuchungen zu einem Grundthema der deuteronomistischen Geschichtsschreibung*, 1980; A.Jepsen, *Die Quellen des Königsbuches*, 1953 (²1956); M.Noth, *Überlieferungsgeschichtliche Studien*, 1943 (³1973), partial (1-110) ET *The Deuteronomistic History*, 1981; I. Plein, 'Erwägungen zur Überlieferung von I Reg 11,26-14,20', *ZAW* 78, 1966, 8-24; G.von Rad, *Studies in Deuteronomy*, ET 1953, 74-92; H.C.Schmitt, *Elisa. Traditionsgeschichtliche Untersuchungen zur vorklassischen nordisraelitischen Prophetie*, 1972; S.Talmon, 'Polemics and Apology in Biblical Historiography – 2 Kings 17:24-41', in R.E.Friedman (ed.), *The Creation of Sacred Literature. Composition and Redaction of the Biblical Text*, 1981, 57-61; H.Weippert, 'Die deuteronomistischen Beurteilungen der Könige von Israel und Juda und das Problem der Redaktion der Königsbücher', *Bib* 53, 1972, 301-39.

Steuernagel, §75-81; Eissfeldt, §41; Fohrer,§53; Soggin, 2.IX; Kaiser, §15; Smend, §18-10, 21-23; Schmidt, §11; Childs, XV.

2.5 The Deuteronomistic History

In their present form, the books from Joshua to Kings have a largely Deuteronomistic stamp. In 1943 Noth argued that what we have here is not a Deuteronomistic redaction but rather a systematically planned Planned history history.

According to Noth, Dtr (in Noth this abbreviation denotes the work and its author) put Deuteronomy at the beginning of his work and for this purpose gave it a new introduction (Deut.1-3 or 4). In so doing at the same time he had created a basis on which he could shape and interpret the subsequent history: 'Here Dtr usually just allowed the sources at his disposal to speak for themselves and simply combined the individual passages by a connecting text'. However, Dtr 'made a deliberate selection from the material at his disposal' (10), as is

→106

evident, e.g., in his references to the 'Chronicles'. Otherwise Dtr made his own arrangement of all the material and gave his theological interpretation 'at all the important points in the course of the history', either in speeches by the leading characters (Josh.1; 23; I Sam.12; I Kings 8.14ff.) or in his own summaries (Josh 12; Judg. 2.11ff.; II Kings 17.7ff.) (5f.). So his 'central theological ideas' (89ff.) can best be brought out here.

In essentials, Noth's impressive and coherent view has largely been accepted, and has governed discussions since then. The term 'Deuteronomistic History' has found a firm place in Old Testament scholarship as a designation for the books of Joshua to Kings. However, it was established very soon, and from a wide variety of perspectives, that Noth's hypothesis excessively simplified the problems of this history and did not take enough account of the many levels and the complexity of the traditions or the way in which they were revised.

Independently of Noth, Jepsen had already developed the theory that several redactions could be recognized in the books of Kings: one priestly, one nebiisitic (i.e. prophetic) and one levitical (though he did not regard this as having been very important). He identified his second, prophetic redactor explicitly with Noth's Dtr. Cross, too, posits two 'editions' of the Deuteronomistic history but identifies the first editor with Noth's Dtr. This leads to a basic difference in the matter of dating: Noth and Jepsen put Dtr chronologically after the last event

→55

mentioned in II Kings, the pardoning of Jehoiachin (II Kings 25.27-30), and thus arrive at a time after 562/1 for the whole work (Noth) or for the decisive redaction (Jepsen). By contrast, Cross dates the basic first redaction in the time of Josiah and only the second editor in the exile. This difference in dating has a substantial influence on the overall understanding of the work.

Smend and his pupils Dietrich and Veijola now also posit a multiple redaction of Dtr: the Deuteronomistic 'historian' proper (DtrG or DtrH), a 'prophetic' (DtrP) and a 'nomistic' (DtrN) redactor, the latter so called because of his interest in the law (Smend 1978, 115). They date DtrG (or DtrH) after the destruction of Jerusalem (Dietrich) or after the pardoning of Jehoiachin (Smend); the two revisions are to be dated accordingly. This approach works with the literary-critical separation of individual sections, verses and parts of verses. The method is often termed redaction-critical, because it not only attempts to bring out the later revisions in order to extract the original text but also investigates the intention of the different strata of the revision. However, the text as it is now is not made the object of the interpretation.

Hoffmann adopts a quite different approach. He himself claims that his work is consistently traditio-historical, i.e. he does not attempt to

establish the pre-history of the material but rather derives the present final form 'more strongly than before from the deliberate and planned work of the author or authors of Deuteronomy' (20). By means of the

central theme of the writing of a history of the cult he succeeds in **Deuterono-
bringing out the unity and coherence of the Deuteronomistic history **mistic**
and at the same time showing that Dtr was much more of an active **History**
'writer' than had been assumed since Noth; i.e. he had not just taken
over source material which he had provided with a linking text.

It is difficult to reconcile these two methodological approaches. We shall have
to see how the Deuteronomistic history can be explained in a better and more
convincing way.

The problem of the Deuteronomistic history lies in a wider context.
Recently it has become increasingly clear that 'Deuteronomistic' Deuteronomis-
revisions can also be recognized in many other areas of Old Testament tic movement
literature. This holds not only for the Pentateuch but also for the
prophetic books, psalms and so on. Evidently this 'school' (or 'movement') worked widely in collecting, editing and reshaping the religious →126ff., 156,
traditions of Israel. Therefore the Deuteronomistic history cannot be 161ff., 290
treated in isolation.

Above all, the question of the derivation and origin of Deuteronomy
itself must be seen in this connection. Without doubt it represents the →156
final stage of a lengthy theological work. Work could also have been
carried on during this period on other passages with the same theological
intentions. That means that not all 'Deuteronomistic' formulations (i.e.
formulations outside Deuteronomy which are related to it in language
and theology) need be later than Deuteronomy and in the literary sense
dependent on it. We can entertain the possibility of 'pre-Deuteronomistic' elements outside Deuteronomy (which can also be designated
'early Deuteronomistic' or 'proto-Deuteronomistic', cf. Brekelmans;
Lohfink, 17f.; Weippert, 337).

These considerations influence the question of date. The starting Dating
point here is often that Deuteronomy was unknown before Josiah's
reform and that therefore all the 'Deuteronomistic' texts could only
have come into being after this point in time. Moreover, as the origin
of the Deuteronomistic History is often only put after the end of the
state of Judah and as the rest of the 'Deuteronomistic' texts are usually
regarded as being later than Deuteronomy, the almost inevitable
consequence was that 'Deuteronomistic' texts naturally derived from
the time of the exile. Over against this it was pointed out that
Deuteronomy has clear connections with theological tendencies existing
towards the end of the northern kingdom, as is evident, for example,
from Hosea. If we keep to the usual dating of the 'Deuteronomistic' →218
texts, the result is a vacuum of almost a century and a half in which the
basic ideas of Deuteronomy were already present but not influential.
So in my view it seems better to assume that at this point they were
influential at various points and in different ways.

If the report of the discovery of the book of the law and Josiah's reform (II
Kings 22f.) in its present form is the work of the Deuteronomist, there is no
objection to the assumption that Deuteronomy was known and was influential

earlier. In my view, this question must be connected with a closer investigation of religious circumstances in the time before Joshua, above all with the opposed cultic activities of Hezekiah and Manasseh which are also stressed by Dtr. We can hardly imagine that such events could have failed to influence the theological work of the circles of reformers whose presence can be recognized at the latest after the last decades of the northern kingdom.

In my view there is much to be said for the view that both the origin of Deuteronomy and the beginnings of 'Deuteronomistic' work are to be put in the time of Hezekiah and Manasseh.

→150f.

There still remains the question of the beginning and end of the Deuteronomistic history. Noth took the first introductory speech in Deuteronomy (Deut.1-3 or 4) as the beginning. However, this view leads to a series of difficulties. First of all, Deuteronomy has to be torn apart, and there are no other convincing reasons for that. This also mortgages research into Deuteronomy, because it means that the first chapters are often ignored; similarly, in the question of the relationship of the Deuteronomistic texts to Deuteronomy this separation is often left unquestioned, so that Deuteronomy is no longer considered in its

→158

present form. Moreover, this hypothesis suggests that we have to presuppose the existence of a Tetrateuch, for which otherwise there is no evidence. Finally, this Tetrateuch has no conclusion; in the last chapters of the book of Numbers everything points towards a continuation. Here numerous 'Deuteronomistic' formulations are striking

→149f.

(especially from Num.33.50-56 on); these show clearly that here the same redaction was at work as in the Deuteronomistic history.

Deuteronomy forms the connecting link without which neither the preceding four books of the Pentateuch nor the subsequent Deuteronomistic history can be understood. Therefore we should probably not suppose that there were two self-contained literary 'works' which existed independently of each other as independent 'books'. Rather, the Deuteronomistic writers are to be thought of as having worked in such a way as to shape the individual major complexes of tradition and connect them together. This is supported by the fact that the individual books of the Deuteronomistic history were clearly separate and were given very different forms.

→166

To a certain extent the beginning of the book of Joshua marks the begining of the historical account. A completely new period of the history of Israel begins with the conclusion of the Torah and the death of Moses. To this degree there are good reasons for the separation of the Pentateuch from the following books, which is what happened later.

The conclusion of the Deuteronomistic history poses several problems. First of all, it is striking that the Deuteronomistic author, who elsewhere at important places gives his theological interpretation of events very clearly, has left this out at the end. Therefore there is much to be said for the conjecture that the real conclusion is to be sought in

→180f.

the account of Josiah's reform (II Kings 22f.: Cross); this is all the more likely if II Kings 22f. was formulated by the Deuteronomist himself and represents the concluding summary of the history of the cult in Israel and Judah.

Deuterono-mistic History

The final chapters would then have been added in accordance with the same basic scheme, though in a rather different form (Weippert). In this approach, the final remark about the pardoning of Jehoiachin (II Kings 25.27-30) does not bear the full weight of the conclusion of the Deuteronomistic history. It leaves open the question whether and in what form the Davidic kingdom still has a future.

→55

Noth has argued that this closing note does not have any openness to the future. Dtr simply 'passed on his information as a simple fact' (98), because 'it too belongs in the account of the fate of the Judaean kings' (74). Moreover, Dtr evidently regarded the divine judgment on Israel as 'final and definitive' (97). This view has been rejected by many interpreters ('At all events, the passage must be interpreted by every reader as an indication that the line of David has not yet come to an irrevocable end', von Rad ET 1953, 90f.,cf. Dietrich, 142; Wolff, 185 [323], differs. Baltzer even sees this text as a contribution to the rise of messianic expectation.) It is in fact improbable that Israelite readers would not have thought here of a possible future for the Davidic monarchy.

If II Kings 22f. represents the original conclusion of the Deuteronomistic history, then the question of dating arises again. It seems likely in that case that the composition of the main part of the work should be put in the time of Josiah (Cross). However, further investigation must be made to see whether this dating holds and what detailed exegetical conclusions are to be drawn from it.

Time of Josiah

Bibliography

K.Baltzer, 'Das Ende des Staates Juda und die Messias-Frage', in *Studien zur Theologie der alttestamentlichen Überlieferungen, FS G.von Rad*, 1961, 33-43; C.Brekelmans, 'Die sogenannten deuteronomistischen Elemente in Gen.-Num. Ein Beitrag zur Vorgeschichte des Deuteronomiums', *SVT* 15, 1966, 90-6; F.M.Cross, 'The Themes of the Book of Kings and the Structure of the Deuteronomistic History', in *Canaanite Myth and Hebrew Epic*, 1973, 274-89; W.Dietrich, *Prophetie und Geschichte. Eine redaktionsgeschichtliche Untersuchung zum deuteronomistischen Geschichtswerk*, 1972; H.-D.Hoffmann, *Reform und Reformen. Untersuchungen zu einem Grundthema der deuteronomistischen Geschichtsschreibung*, 1980; A.Jepsen, *Die Quellen der Königsbuches*, 1953 (²1956); N.Lohfink, *Die Landverheissung als Eid*, 1967; M.Noth, *Überlieferungsgeschichtliche Studien*, 1943 (³1973), partial ET *The Deuteronomistic History*, 1981; G.von Rad, *Studies in Deuteronomy*, ET 1953, 74-91; R.Smend, 'Das Gesetz und die Völker. Ein Beitrag zur deuteronomistischen Redaktionsgeschichte', in *Probleme biblischer Theologie, FS G. von Rad*, 1971, 494-509; T.Veijola, *Die ewige Dynastie. David und die Entstehung seiner Dynastie nach der deuteronomistischen Darstellung*, 1975; id., *Das Königtum in der Beurteilung der deuteronomistischen Historiographie. Eine redaktionsgeschichtliche Untersuchung*, 1977; H.Weippert, 'Die deuteronomistischen Beurteilungen der Könige von Israel und Juda und das Problem der Redaktion der Königsbucher', *Bib* 53, 1972, 301-39; H.W.Wolff, 'Das Kerygma des

deuteronomistischen Geschichtswerk', *ZAW* 73, 1961, 171-86 (= *GS*, 308-24).
Cf. also A.D.H.Mayes, *The Story of Israel between Settlement and Exile*, 1983.
Eissfeldt, §37; Fohrer, §29; Soggin, 2.VI §1; Kaiser, § 16; Smend, §19;
Schmidt, §11; Childs, XI.

3 The Latter Prophets

The prophetic books are collected together in the Hebrew canon as the latter prophets (*nᵉbi'im 'aharonim*). At the beginning stand the books of the three 'major prophets' (in terms of their length), Isaiah, Jeremiah and Ezekiel. The order of these books varies in the tradition, but this particular sequence has become established in the mainstream, Hebrew and Greek. There is evidence for the combination of the shorter prophetic books into one, the Book of the Twelve Prophets (Dodeka-propheton), as early as 190 BC; this is mentioned in the book of Jesus Sirach (49.10).

However, in the Greek canon of the Septuagint the 'minor prophets' come before the 'major' prophets. Moreover, the apocryphal books Baruch and the 'Letter of Jeremiah' (combined in the Vulgate into one book) have been inserted after the book of Jeremiah, with Lamentations (Threni), also attributed to Jeremiah, between them. In the Greek and Latin tradition the book of Daniel comes last in the series of major prophets, but in the Hebrew canon it comes in the third part, among the Writings.

Prophetic books as collections

The prophetic books are not unitary, self-contained books, but collections. That is quite evident in the case of the Book of the Twelve Prophets. More recent Old Testament scholarship has also demonstrated this in the case of Isaiah: in this book only chs.1-39 are connected with the prophet Isaiah from the last third of the eighth century BC; chapters 40-66 derive from the time of the Babylonian exile or the post-exilic period. Finally, the books of Jeremiah and Ezekiel also consist of such varied material that they too must be regarded as collections.

→198ff.

Some of the prophetic sayings collected here go back to the time of the prophets whose names the various books bear, and some derive from later times and different situations. That is true not only of larger sections within the books but also of numerous individual texts and shorter sections; these have often been worked over and enlarged, so that the text as we now have it is often the result of a lengthy process of interpretation and supplementary development of the sayings of the prophet concerned.

Literary criticism

Scholarly exegesis has attempted above all to use the resources of literary criticism to free the original, 'authentic' sayings of the prophets from later revisions. Hardly any special attention has been paid to the latter; they have been 'cut out'. In more recent times, increasing attention is being paid to the intentions and main interests of the collectors and editors, so that there is now consideration of the texts and also the whole books in their present form. (The beginnings of this approach can already be found in Birkeland and Mowinckel.) This method is often described as redaction criticism. However, the questions asked and the ways in which exegetes work vary immensely. Some attempt to bring out the various strata of redaction and interpret them separately, so that – as in the literary-critical method – the present text as a whole is not taken into account (cf. e.g. H.Barth on Isaiah); others, however, are particularly concerned to understand the present text as a whole (cf. e.g. Ackroyd on Isaiah; also Clements, Tucker). The discussion of the prophetic books which follows will also be governed by this composition-critical approach.

Composition criticism

So exegesis can do more than simply investigate the original, personal words (the *ipsissima verba*) of the prophets. Evidently it was not the aim of those who handed down the biblical material to give us the most faithful 'historical' picture possible of a particular prophet and his preaching. If we look for that, as modern readers, then we do so against the intention of the texts. That does not mean that such questions are unjustified; however, we must remember that they are governed by our modern interests and that they fall short of grasping the purpose of the biblical text. Rather, we must pursue our questioning further, in order also to understand the text as it now is, a text which has formulated the prophetic sayings anew in a changed situation so that they speak to the editors' own day and to the future.

A concern to discover the 'authentic' words of the prophets is often motivated not only (perhaps even not primarily) by historical interests but also by religious or theological ones. Particularly great importance is attached to the prophetic words because they claim to be the word of God in a direct sense. When this evaluation is detached from the present text and attached to what modern historians can discover of the person of the prophet and his prophetic understanding of himself, the result is often a combination of modern historical critical questions with religious value judgments antedating criticism or lying outside it. The result is a canon within the canon, in that certain words of scripture are given a greater status than others, the criteria being derived from a historical judgment on the authenticity of a prophetic saying.

'Authentic' prophetic sayings

Here the question of 'authenticity' introduces an inappropriate value category into exegesis, because it must necessarily go with a similar concept of 'inauthenticity' which denies legitimacy to the texts in the form in which we now have them. But this cannot be the function of exegesis. So the misleading concept of 'authenticity' should be avoided.

Bibliography

H.Birkeland, *Zum hebräischen Traditionswesen. Die Komposition der prophetischen Bücher des Alten Testaments*, 1938; R.E.Clements, 'Patterns in the Prophetic Canon', in G.W.Coats and B.O.Long (eds.), *Canon and Authority; Essays on Old Testament Religion and Theology*, 1977, 42-55; S.Mowinckel, *Prophecy and Religion*, 1946; G.M.Tucker, 'Prophetic Superscriptions and the

**Latter
Prophets**

Growth of a Canon', in G.W.Coats (see Clements), 56-70.
Steuernagel, §97; Eissfeldt, §42; Fohrer, §54; Soggin, 3.1; Kaiser, §24; Smend, §24; Schmidt, §13; Childs, XVI.
See also the bibliography on III.5.

3.1 The Book of Isaiah

Three parts

From as early as the end of the eighteenth century, many interpreters saw two independent parts in the book of Isaiah: in chs.1-39 the book of Isaiah proper, from the eighth century BC, and in chs.40-66 a prophetic book from the Babylonian exile. Finally, the view put forward by Duhm (1892) became established: a further distinction had to be made in chs.40ff. between two different parts, the unknown authors of which are usually called 'Deutero-Isaiah' (the Second Isaiah, chs.40-55), and 'Trito-Isaiah' (the Third Isaiah, chs.56-66).

Since then, most exegetes have treated the individual parts of the book of Isaiah quite separately, hardly discussing the reasons which led to the addition of chs. 40ff. and whether there are connections between the two parts. Only in more recent times has a discussion of the composition of the book of Isaiah got under way. As this is also related to the question of the composition of the individual parts, especially 'Proto-Isaiah' (1-39), we shall first consider the parts separately, but take into account their reciprocal relationships; in conclusion we shall again take up the question of the composition of the book of Isaiah.

3.1.1 Isaiah 1-39

Division

→180

→122

Not only the book of Isaiah as a whole, but also chs.1-39, forms a collection of texts of different kinds. That this part is a collection already becomes clear from the fact that the Isaiah narratives from II Kings 18.13-20.19 have been incorporated in chs.36-39. The sayings against foreign nations (chs.13-23) stand out as an independent complex; here the word *massa'*, which can mean 'saying' but also 'burden' (cf. Jer.23.33ff.), often appears (13.1; 14.28; 15.1 etc.). (Chapter 22 is not directed against foreign nations; vv.1-14 are directed against Jerusalem and vv.15-19, 20-25 against two court officials, Shebnah and Eliakim.)

Chs.1–12

→215

190

Chapters 1-12 form a subsidiary collection, with many strata but clearly self-contained. The introductory formula 'Vision (*hason*) of Isaiah' (1.1), a summary designation of the message of the prophet (cf. II Chron.32.32), relates to this collection. Chapter 12 brings it to an end with a psalm, which was probably composed specially for this position; it thanks YHWH for deliverance and in so doing takes up the keyword 'Zion' (v.6), which runs through this collection from the first chapter on (1.8,27; 2.3; 3.16f.; 4.3-5; 8.18; 10.12,24,32), and the designation of YHWH as the 'holy one of Israel' (*qᵉdoš yiśra'el*, v.6; cf. 1.4,5,19,24; 10.20), which is characteristic of Isaiah (Ackroyd).

Isaiah 1–39
→199

This collection evidently had a lengthy prehistory. *6.1-9.6* (or up to 8.18) are usually regarded as an originally independent passage and are often described as a memorial (taking up 8.16): the promise of the birth of a king (of salvation?) in (*8.23*) *9.1-6* is often regarded as an eschatological-messianic addition. Whereas hitherto most exegetes have regarded this passage with its historical references (6.1; 7.1-9; 8.1-4,5) as an important and historically reliable source for the activity of Isaiah at the time of the Syro-Ephraimite war, a number of scholars now understand it as a retrospective interpretation from the exilic period (Ackroyd, Kaiser 1981).

Memorial

›47

The section *6.1-9.6* interrupts the sequence of another composition, which consists of a group of seven 'woes' (5.8-24; 10.1-4) and an associated poem with a refrain (5.25-30; *9.7-20*; the refrain occurs in 5.25b; *9.11,16,20*; in 10.4b it is added as a link with the 'woes'); the Song of the Vineyard (5.1-7) has been put at the beginning of this composition. In 10.5 a further composition with 'Woe' has been attached: sayings about Assyria (10.5-15, 16-19, 24-27, 28-34) coupled with sayings of comfort and salvation for Israel (10.20-23 [link in v.24]; 11.1-10,11-16 [mention of Assyria in vv.11,16 alongside Egypt, cf. 7.18f.]).

'Woes'
→119

→90, 120

At the beginning we have the composition consisting of 1.2-2.5, which speaks of Israel's sin (1.2-3,10-17 [criticism of the cult]), YHWH's judgment (1.4-9, 18-20) and the future purification of Jerusalem (1.21-26,27f. [29-31]) and is concluded with the eschatological saying about the pilgrimage of the nations to Zion (2.1-4.5). (The introductory formula in 2.1 states explicitly that this saying, which has been handed down twice [cf. Micah 4.1-5], is a 'word of Isaiah' [Ackroyd].) We can also recognize a separate composition in 2.6-4.6, in which sayings about the day of YHWH (2.6-22) and against the upper class in Jerusalem (3.1-15; 3.16-4.1) are concluded with a word of promise for the remnant of Zion' (4.2-6)(Fohrer).

→228

The collection in chs. 1-12 is evidently meant to outline a particular picture of the prophet Isaiah. On the one hand he is the prophet of judgment on Israel, on Jerusalem, on the leading classes and on the royal house itself; here the focal point is his meeting with king Ahaz and his vain attempt to move the king to hold fast to the divine promises about Jerusalem and the royal house (7.1-9). On the other hand he is the prophet of future salvation for Israel, for Jerusalem and for the dynasty of David. Here it becomes quite evident that these promises will only come into force after the fulfilment of the announcements of judgment; this is also demonstrated by the position of the words of promise (2.1-5; 4.2-6; *9.1-6*; 11.1-16) within the individual subsidiary collections (see also 6.11). However, the psalm in ch.12 already strikes up in eschatological anticipation the thanksgiving song of those who have been delivered; here there is repeated stress on the word *yᵉšuʿa*, 'help, salvation' (three times in vv.2f.) which clearly echoes the name of the prophet Isaiah *yᵉšaʿyahu*, YHWH has helped).

Judgment
→47

Salvation

So far the structure and division of the remaining chapters 24-35 have proved less clearly recognizable. Isaiah 24-27 is often called the Isaiah apocalypse. However, these chapters do not form a literary unit and can only be termed 'apocalyptic' with considerable qualifications.

Apocalypse

191

Alongside the expectation of YHWH's judgment on the world (24.1-13,16b-20,21-23; 26.20-27.1) and the annihilation of an unnamed city (24.10-12; 25.1-5; 26.1-6; 27.10f.) we find eschatological thanksgiving songs from those who have been delivered (24.14-16a) in which the 'mountain' (Zion) has a central place (25.6-8, 9-12 [27.7-9?] 12f.), a popular lament with a wisdom stamp (26.7-19) and a resumption of the 'Song of the Vineyard' (5.1-7) with a different preface (27.2-6). The relationship between the individual sections is often difficult to see; the whole section has been called a 'cantata' (Lindblom) or a collection of 'prophetic liturgies' (Fohrer), terms which above all are meant to express its composite character.

→123

Assyrian cycle

The frequent designation of chs.28-32 as an Assyrian cycle is meant to express the origin of the majority of the texts in the time of Assyrian rule. We can see historical references in the threat to Samaria (28.1-4), the warning against a coalition with Egypt (30.1-5; 31.1-3), the mention of Assyria (30.31; 31.8) and the threat to Jerusalem (29.1-8; 31.4f.). Moreover the texts reflect controversies with various groups in Jerusalem (28.7-13,14-22 [23-29]; 29.9-12,13f.,15f.; 30.8-17; 32.9-14). In between there are eschatological words of salvation (28.5f.; 29.17-24; 30.18-26; 32.1-8, 15-20). It is uncertain which texts go back to Isaiah himself and whether a coherent conception underlies this collection (cf. Barth).

→47ff.

→122f.

Gunkel called the obscure ch.33 a 'prophetic liturgy'. Some scholars have termed chs.34f. a 'little apocalypse', with the same limited justification as in the case of 24-27. Chapter 34 deals with YHWH's eschatological judgment, especially on Edom (vv.9-15). Chapter 35 contains a prophecy of salvation which has clear echoes of Deutero-Isaiah.

→199

In this many-layered collection which is associated with the name of Isaiah, the figure of the prophet himself appears only in the first (chs.1-12) and the last subsidiary collections (chs.36-39) – that is, if we leave aside the sign in ch.20. In both cases his portrait has been deliberately shaped in retrospect, so we must be careful in using it to establish his historical profile.

Period of
activity

The period of Isaiah's activity falls in the reigns of Ahaz and Hezekiah (according to 1.1; according to 6.1 also in those of their predecessors Uzziah and Jotham). Confrontations with the kings reigning at the time are reported from the crisis periods of the Syro-Ephraimite war (734/33) and the siege of Jerusalem (701). It has been inferred from this that Isaiah had special relations with the royal court and that he was a man from the upper classes of Jerusalem society, a patrician, indeed a man of royal blood. The texts say nothing about this. Nor does a comparison with other prophets lend any support to the view which is often expressed that his language is particularly 'educated'.

Isaiah's appearance before kings, as depicted in the texts, may be compared with that of Nathan and Elijah. They too are said to have appeared directly before the kings of their time and announced to them salvation and disaster (whereas in the case of other prophets, like Elijah and Amos, the proclamation of disaster stands in the foreground). A

→112f.

discrepancy is often noted in Isaiah between chs.1-12 and 36-39, but Isaiah 1–39 →179f. here it must be remembered that both portraits have been shaped to a literary pattern, so that it remains questionable whether one is more authentic than the other.

Bibliography

Commentaries: Duhm (HK) 1892, ⁴1922 (⁵1968); Marti (KHC) 1900; Procksch (KAT) 1930; Fohrer (ZBK) I ²1967; II ²1967; III 1964; Kaiser (ATD) I, 1960, ET OTL 1972;⁵1981, ET OTL 1983; II 1973, OTL 1974; Wildberger (BK) I 1972; II 1978; III 1982.

P.R.Ackroyd, 'Isaiah I-XII, Presentation of a Prophet', *SVT* 29, 1978, 16-48; H.Barth, *Die Jesaja-Worte in der Josiazeit. Israel und Assur als Thema einer produktiven Neuinterpretation der Jesajaüberlieferung*, 1977; R.E.Clements, 'The Prophecies of Isaiah and the Fall of Jerusalem in 587 BC', *VT* 30, 1980, 421-36; G.Fohrer, 'Entstehung, Komposition und Überlieferung von Jesaja 1-39', in *Studien zur alttestamentlichen Prophetie*, 1967, 113-47; id., 'Der Aufbau der Apokalypse des Jesajabuches (Jesaja 24-27)', ibid., 170-82; H.Gunkel, 'Jesaja 33, eine prophetische Liturgie', *ZAW* 42, 1924, 177-208; J.Lindblom, *Die Jesaja Apokalypse. Jes.24-27*, 1938.

Steuernagel, §98-106; Eissfeldt, §43; Fohrer, §56; Soggin, 3.IV; Kaiser, §22c; Smend, §25; Schmidt, §16; Childs, XVII.

3.1.2 Isaiah 40-55 (Deutero-Isaiah)

It is now almost universally recognized that Isaiah 40ff. cannot come from the prophet with whom chs.1-39 are concerned. The situation Exilic situation which is initially the setting of chs.40-55 is fundamentally different: Israel is in captivity, far from its homeland, and is promised comfort and speedy deliverance. There can be hardly any doubt this is a reference to the Babylonian exile: that is suggested above all by the mention of →55ff. the name of Cyrus the Persian king (44.28; 45.1). →59

But who is the author of these chapters? No name is given anywhere, Authorship nor is there any reference to a particular person. Moreover, in contrast to all the independent prophetic books, there is no title which mentions the name of the prophet and the period of his activity. So the designation 'Deutero-Isaiah' is hardly more than a cipher for the author of chs.40-55, who remains completely in the dark. There is even a dispute as to whether he can be called a prophet, as the characteristic basic forms of prophetic speech do not occur with him. Rather (according to Begrich), the most important genres used here are the oracle of salvation (sub- Genres →121f. divided by Westermann into promise of salvation and announcement →90 of salvation), the invective, and the disputation saying. The two →120 latter also appear in other prophets and reflect controversies with contemporaries. There is some dispute as to whether the words of salvation came into being in direct association with worship among the exiled Judaeans. Were this the case, the profile of the figure standing behind Isa.40-55 would be somewhat clearer.

Despite their intractable anonymity, Isa.40-55 display a marked independence and coherence in form and theological expression. The texts of the various genres all serve the one main purpose which is

Prologue

already formulated in the prologue (40.1-11): to proclaim to the Judaeans living in exile that their 'forced labour' is at an end (vv.1f.), that YHWH will bring them on a way through the wilderness (vv.3-5) to Jerusalem and lead those who are freed from exile like a shepherd

Epilogue

(vv.9-11). This is confirmed in the epilogue (55.8-13): YHWH's word will come about (vv.10ff.) and those who are freed will return home in joy to the jubilation of creation (vv.12f.).

→115f.

40.1-8 are often understood as the account of a call (changing the Massoretic text in v.6 from 'he said' to 'I said'). Scholars point to echoes of other prophetic call narratives, especially Isa. 6; Jer.1. However, here too there is uncertainty, and the prophetic 'I' in the emended text would be the only one in chs.40-55.

The promise and announcement of deliverance is repeated with many variations in the words of salvation. The other genres are concerned above all to counter objections and to overcome doubts (this is already true of 40.6-8; 55.8f.). The disputation sayings and some of the invective are addressed to Israel; the majority of the invective is addressed to other nations and their gods, the power and even the existence of which is challenged.

Composition

Only in most recent times has more attention been paid to the structure and composition of Isa.40-55.

Earlier exegetes tried to arrange the individual texts by keywords (Mowinckel) or in smaller collections shaped by content (Elliger), while Muilenberg posited a number of longer poems divided into strophes. Westermann then observed that in a number of cases brief hymnic passages (Westermann called them 'songs of praise') have the function of concluding larger units. This was taken further by Melugin and Mettinger.

Division

This produces the following division of Isa.40-55.

40.1-11	Prologue
40.12-42.13	(concluding hymn, 42.10-13)
42.14-44.23	(Hymn 44.23)
44.24-45.8	(Hymn 45.8)
45.9-48.22	(Hymn 48.20f.)
49.1-13	(Hymn 49.13)
49.14-51.3	(Hymn 51.3)
51.4-52.12	(Hymn 52.9f.)
52.13-54.3	(Hymn 54.1-3)
54.4-55.7	
55.8-13	(Epilogue vv.12f. theme of hymns)

Here the song about Israel as the 'servant of God' who is made the 'light of the Gentiles' (49.1-12) serves as a bridge between the two main parts of Isa.40-55 (Nielsen, Mettinger). In the first part (40-48), which can be described in terms of its theme as the 'Jacob-Israel part' (Hessler, Melugin), the saying about Cyrus stands out as a short passage framed by hymns (44.24-45.7; only here is the name of Cyrus mentioned: 44.28; 45.1); this is matched in the 'Zion-Jerusalem part' (49-55) by the saying about the suffering servant of God (52.13-53.12). Each time contrasting sayings follow: the saying about the victorious Cyrus is followed by the overthrow of Babylon (chs.46f.), and that about the suffering 'anti-hero' is followed by the exaltation of Jerusalem (ch.54)(Mettinger).

Elsewhere, too, the formation of contrasts is recognizable as an overall principle of composition (Melugin). In the first major unit (40.12-42.9) an introductory composition of four disputation sayings (40.12-31) is followed by two sections each of which consists of invective against the nations with subsequent words of salvation (41.1-7 and 8-20; 41.21-29 and 42.1-9); the latter are addressed to the servant ('ebed) who in the first instance is explicitly identified with Israel (41.8). The second major unit (42.14-44.22) has a similar structure. After an introduction (42.14-17) come three (or four?) invectives against Israel with a subsequent word of salvation (42.18-25 and 43.1-7; 43.8-13 and 14-21; 43.22-28 and 44.1-5; 44.6-7 and 8[?]). There are similar contrasts in 45.9-13 and 14-17; 45.18-21 and 22-25; 46.1-7 and 8-13; 50.1-3 and 4-11; 51.9-11 and 12-16; 51.17-20 and 21-23; 52.3-6 and 7f.; 54.7f. and 9f.; 54.11-14a and 14b-17 (and perhaps also in some other passages which there are difficulties in understanding).

The so-called servant songs pose a special problem. Duhm had singled out the sections 42.1-4; 49.1-6; 50.4-9; 52.13-53.12 as 'Ebed-YHWH' songs and attributed them to a later author. Since then this hypothesis has held almost undisputed sway (though some exegetes extend the first song to 42.1-9, the second to 49.1-12 and the third to 50.4-11) and this has become one of the most discussed themes of Old Testament scholarship, though without leading to any tangible or even generally recognized results.

Most open to dispute is the question whether the servant of God is meant to be an individual figure or whether the texts refer to Israel (collective interpretation). The latter view is supported by the fact that elsewhere too in Isa.40-55 Israel is often designated the servant of YHWH (41.8,9; 42.19 [twice]; 43.10 [?]; 44.1,2,21 [twice]; 45.4; 48.20) and that this identification is also made in the second 'servant song' in 49.3 (which the proponents of the individual interpretation have to explain as a later addition). In the case of the individual interpretation the question remains open whether the texts refer to a specific historical figure (here interpretation in terms of the prophet Deutero-Isaiah himself has recently come to dominate the field), or whether they have a future, perhaps 'messianic' mediator figure in view.

Such questioning has fundamentally shifted ground in the light of the new insights into the composition of Isa.40-55. The first song (42.1-9) is closely parallel to 41.8-13; in both texts Israel is the 'servant' (Melugin), and both stand in the composition as contrasts to the preceding references to Cyrus (Mettinger). This corresponds on a small scale to the contrast that has already been mentioned between Cyrus (44.24-45.7) and the suffering servant of God (52.13-53.12) in the overall structure of Isa.40-55. The second song (49.1-12) also has its fixed, central place in the composition. So it is not possible to detach the 'servant songs' as a separate group of texts. (The significance of the designation of Israel as servant for the whole composition is also evident from the statements in 44.21 and 48.20 which stand emphatically at the end of larger units, and in 45.4.) The ambivalence of the picture of the servant of YHWH who in part is clearly identified with Israel and partly has more or less evident individual features, must be explained from its context in the proclamation of Deutero-Isaiah; here it should be remembered that in many other passages in the Old Testament Israel is spoken of as a person.

Bibliography

Commentaries on Isa.40-66: Volz (KAT) 1932; Muilenburg (IB) 1956; Westermann (ATD) 1966, ET OTL 1966; Elliger (BK) 1978 (to 45.7).

J.Begrich, *Studien zu Deuterojesaja*, 1938 (1963); K.Elliger, *Deuterojesaja in seinem Verhältnis zu Tritojesaja*, 1933; E.Hessler, *Gott der Schöpfer. Ein Beitrag zur Komposition und Theologie Deuterojesajas*, Diss.Greifswald 1961; R.F.Melugin, 'Deutero-Isaiah and Form Criticism', *VT* 21, 1971, 326-37; id., *The Formation of Isaiah 40-55*, 1976; T.N.D.Mettinger, 'Die Ebed-Jahwe-Lieder. Ein fragwürdiges Axiom', *ASTI* 11, 1978, 68-76; S.Mowinckel, 'Die Komposition des deuterojesajanischen Buches', *ZAW* 49, 1931, 87-112, 242-60; E.Nielsen, 'Deuterojesaja. Erwägungen zur Formkritik, Traditions- und Redaktionsgeschichte', *VT* 20, 1970, 190-205; C.Westermann, 'Sprache und Struktur der Prophetie Deuterojesajas', in *Forschung am Alten Testament*, 1964, 92-170 (separate new impression with a survey of research by A.Richter, 1981).

Steuernagel, §107-109; Eissfeldt, §44; Fohrer, §57; Soggin 4.II; Kaiser, §22k; Smend, §25; Schmidt,§ 21; Childs, XVII.

3.1.3 Isaiah 56-66 (Trito-Isaiah)

The last major section of the book of Isaiah is similarly anonymous. It seems much less of a unity and less coherent than the previous section. At all events, a specific individual can be recognized in 61.1, where there is mention of a commissioning and sending in the first person; however, this text is less reminiscent of the accounts of prophetic calls than of the remarks about the 'servant of YHWH' in 42.1-9; 49.1-12, so it remains questionable whether there is an underlying prophetic figure. The term 'Trito-Isaiah' thus essentially denotes the collection of texts in Isa.56-66.

→195

That these chapters come from a single author has been stressed particularly emphatically by Elliger, but in recent times he has found hardly any supporters. An alternative hypothesis occasionally put forward is that at least the basic material in Isa.56-66 goes back to Deutero-Isaiah, who after 538 returned home to Jerusalem from exile and continued to work there (Haran, Maass). However, despite the manifest relationships between the two collections of texts the coherent character of the composition of Isa.40-55 makes this assumption very improbable.

One special problem in the collection Isa.56-66 lies in the fact that quite different themes appear in it side by side: on the one hand there is lamentation and accusation because of severe infringements of justice (chs.56-59) and correct worship (chs.65f.); on the other hand there is the promise of imminent salvation (chs.60-62; 64f.). The themes are associated and related in the composition of the collection. This is already clear in the introductory verse 56.1: the motivation behind the invitation to do 'right and justice' is that YHWH's salvation and righteousness will come soon. The word z^edaqa in its twofold meaning also dominates both groups of texts: as an accusation and as a lament over the decline of human righteousness (57.1,12; 58.2,8; 59.4,9,14; *64.4f.*), and as an expectation and promise of the 'righteousness' of the divine salvation to come (59.16f.; 60.17; 62.1; 63.1), which at the same time means the restoration of human justice (60.21; 61.10f.; 62.2).

Infringements
of the law
Imminent
salvation

z^edaqa

The words of salvation in chs.60-62 mark the centre of the book; they have numerous echoes of Deutero-Isaiah. In 59.1-14; 63.7-*64.11* they are framed by popular lamentations, and between them stands a description of the intervention of YHWH (59.15-21; 63.1-6). In the introductory complex chs.56-58 the invective (56.9-57.13) is followed by an announcement of the coming of YHWH, which echoes Deutero-Isaiah (57.14-21). Chapter 58 again begins with an accusation and admonition about fasting which leads to a popular lament in ch.59. The closing complex, chs.65f., shows a similar construction: between two passages of accusation and admonition (65.1-16a; 66.1-24, the latter interspersed with words of salvation) there is an announcement of imminent salvation (65.16b-25), which is depicted as new creation (*bara'* v.17, cf. 41.20; 48.7). The beginning (56.2-8) and end (66.18-24) are connected by the keywords sabbath (56.2,4,6; cf. 66.23), house of God and holy mountain (56.5,7; cf. 66.20), name (56.5; cf. 66.22), and by the announcement of the addition of foreigners to the Israelites who are brought home (56.6-8; cf. 66.18-21) (Lack, 142; for the composition cf. also Westermann and Pauritsch, and for the relationships with Deutero-Isaiah Zimmerli, Michel and Kraus).

Division
→101
→90
→119

The texts collected here all reflect the post-exilic period. Deutero-Isaiah's promise of return has been fulfilled, but the dawn of the time of salvation is still to come. It is delayed and put in question by circumstances in the community which are described in terms of numerous infringements of the law and the cult. Here controversies between different groups seem to have played a part; these are sometimes clearly (e.g. 56.3-7) and sometimes less clearly (e.g. 66.14,24) recognizable in the texts.

Dating

It is hardly possible to date the individual texts or the collection more closely. Some exegetes put the lamentation over the destruction of the temple in 63.15-*64.11* in the exilic period. The nucleus of the texts is often put in the time between the return from exile in 538 and the rebuilding of the temple in 515, although the texts do not contain any specific references. Moreover there are also said to be additions of apocalyptic (Westermann) or Deuteronomistic (Semsdorf) origin, which further complicates the picture. The question of the origin of the collection can only be answered in the context of the book of Isaiah as a whole.

Bibliography

For commentaries see on 3.1.2.

K.Elliger, *Die Einheit des Tritojesaja*, 1928; id., 'Der Prophet Tritojesaja', *ZAW* 49, 1931, 112-41; M.Haran, 'The Literary Structure and Chronological Framework of the Prophecies in Is.XL-XLVIII', *SVT* 9, 1963, 127-55; H.-J.Kraus, 'Die ausgebliebene Endtheophanie. Eine Studie zu Jes.56-66', *ZAW* 78, 1966, 317-32 (= *Biblisch-theologische Aufsätze*, 1972, 134-50); R.Lack, *La Symbolique du Livre d'Isaie. Essai sur l'image littéraire comme élément de structuration*, 1973; F.Maass, ' "Tritojesaja"?', in *Das ferne und nahe Wort, FS L.Rost*, 1967, 153-63; D.Michel, 'Zur Eigenart Tritojesajas', *ThViat* 10, 1965/66, 213-30; K.Pauritsch, *Die neue Gemeinde: Gott sammelt Ausgestossene und Arme (Jesaja 56-66). Die Botschaft des Tritojesaja-Buches literar-, form-, gattungskritisch und redaktionsgeschichtlich untersucht*, 1971; E. Sehmsdorf, 'Studien zur Redaktionsgeschichte von Jesaja 56-66', *ZAW* 84, 1972, 517-61, 562-76; W.Zimmerli, 'Zur Sprache Tritojesajas', *STU* 20, 1950, 110-22 (= *Gottes Offenbarung*, 1963, ²1969, 217-33).

Steuernagel, §110-11; Eissfeldt, §45; Fohrer, §58; Soggin, 4.V; Kaiser, §22k; Smend, §25; Schmidt, §21; Childs, XVII.

3.1.4 The Composition of the Book of Isaiah

There are many connections between the three parts of the book of Isaiah (in this section designated I-III). The relationship between II and III has often been explained in terms of Trito-Isaiah being a pupil of Deutero-Isaiah (Elliger, etc.). Mowinckel extended the idea of an Isaiah school to all three parts (see also Eaton, Schreiner). Most recently, too, the question of the composition of the book of Isaiah has come more clearly into focus (Lack referring to Liebreich, Melugin, Childs, cf. also Becker). Here it is evident that on the one hand the three parts have their very clear independence and distinctiveness and that on the other there are many connections and relationships between them which are evidently the result of a conscious process of composition.

The best way of recognizing the relationships is to start from II, which comes in the middle. The first words, 'Comfort, comfort my people, speak tenderly to Jerusalem' (40.1f.), take up the opening words of the

psalm which in I brings the collection 1-12 to an end (12.1). These words
of comfort (*nihham*) are then echoed in some of the hymns which in II
conclude the larger units; here the people are comforted in 49.13, Zion
(i.e. Jerusalem) in 51.3 and both in 52.9 (as in 40.1f.); in 51.12 YHWH
says that he himself is the one who comforts. In III to comfort those
who mourn is the task of YHWH's messenger (61.2) and finally at the
end YHWH himself reappears as the one who comforts his people and
Jerusalem (66.13).

The next keyword in 40.1 goes back to the beginning of the book. The guilt
(*'awon*) of Israel, which was first mentioned emphatically in 1.4, is forgiven.
Towards the end of I, 33.24 anticipates the announcement of the forgiveness of
sins. In that case the representative bearing of guilt has a decisive function in
the sayings about the suffering servant (53.5,6,11); finally, in *64.4-8* there is
another detailed confession of guilt. Here the line which leads from I (1.4) to
II (40.1) seems to be broken.

The keyword Zion/Jerusalem plays a dominant role in all three parts. In I it
again appears in the first chapter (1.8) and permeates this part right to the end
of the psalm (12.6). The mention of the forsaken 'daughters of Zion' in
1.8 indicates the theme of II (especially from 49.14 on) and III (especially
chs.60ff.).The saying about the purification of Jerusalem to become the 'city of
righteousness' (1.21-26,27) is taken up in 54.14 and in 60.14,21; 62. That the
glory (*kabod*) of YHWH will be revealed (40.5) is a clear echo of 6.3. There
the statement that YHWH's glory fills the earth appears in Isaiah's vision; in
35.2, as in II, it is proclaimed as a reality which will be manifest in the future
(42.12); in III it forms an essential element in the proclamation of salvation for
Zion (60.1-3; 62.2; 66.18).

One characteristic element is the designation of YHWH as the Holy
One of Israel (*q*e*doš yiśra'el*), which appears in all three parts of the
book of Isaiah, but elsewhere in the Old Testament only in isolated
passages (II Kings 19.22 = Isa.37.23; Jer.50.29; 51.5; Ps.71.22; 78.41;
89.19). However, at the same time there is a striking difference here:
in I this designation of YHWH is predominantly used in accusations
(1.4; 5.19,24; 30.11f.,15; 31.1), whereas in II it appears exclusively in
words of salvation (41.14,16,20; 43.3,14f.; 45.11; 47.4; 48.17; 49.7;
54.5; 55.5; cf.40.25). This usage also occurs in a series of eschatological
sayings in I, which are clearly akin to II (10.20; 12.6; 17.7; 29.19,23;
37.23) and similarly in III (60.9,14; cf. 57.15).

A similar difference in terminology is also evident with the word
righteousness (*zedeq/z*e*daqa*). In I it primarily denotes human conduct,
frequently in connection with the word 'right' (*mišpat*)(1.21,27; 5.7;
9.6; 16.5; also 1.6; 5.23; 11.4f.; 26.10), but this combination of right
and righteousness also occurs in connection with the action of YHWH
(5.16; 26.9; 28.17). In II, by contrast, this connection is completely
absent. Instead, the combination of righteousness and salvation (*yeša*ʿ/
*y*e*šu*ʿ*a/tešu*ʿ*a*) is used for the actions of YHWH (45.8; 46.13; 51.5,6,7;
with *šalom* 48.18; 54.13f.; cf. also 41.2,10; 42.6,21; 45.13,19,21,23f.;
54.14; of man, 46.12; 48.1; 51.1,7). The two pairs of concepts are linked
in the first statement in III (56.1); here at the same time the double

theme of this part is indicated. So this verse has a key function in the composition of the book as a whole.

Thus the third part binds the themes and the terminology of the first and second parts together. This is an indication that III did not exist as an independent collection which was attached to I and II, but that the origin of III must be taken in connection with the composition of the whole book of Isaiah. The numerous passages in I which echo II clearly indicate that the composition of the first part in its present form cannot be understood apart from the composition of the book of Isaiah as a

**Chs.40-55
as nucleus**

whole. At most the second part, with its well-planned and integrated composition, could have existed independently before being inserted into the present composition.

This fits in with our observations on the first part. There it was possible to see that in the subsidiary collection chs.1-12, words of salvation sometimes stand at the end of smaller collections (2.1-5; 4.2-6; *9.1-6*; 11.1-16). That recalls the construction of contrasts between invective and words of salvation which was recognizable in II as a constant principle of composition. Evidently this model was also used for the shaping of the first part. (In chs.28-35 we can similarly recognize an alternation of invective and words of salvation', which needs to be investigated further.)

**The
compostion
as a whole**

Accordingly, the book of Isaiah has not been composed by the combination of three independent 'books', but is a work with many strata and a lengthy history behind it. It has two specific focal points: the activity of the prophet Isaiah in the second half of the eighth century and the collection of the sayings of a prophet or preacher, who remains anonymous, towards the end of the Babylonian exile. The latter's proclamation of salvation became the starting point for a wider collection in which Isaiah's message of judgment was continued and met a response in the message of salvation at the time of the exile, and was

**Judgment and
salvation**

taken up and developed in the post-exilic period. Now judgment and salvation belong indissolubly together and are related to each other. The post-exilic community does not hear one without the other: the message of judgment does not remain the last word, but salvation has not yet made a final appearance. Israel is still required to bring right and righteousness to fulfilment, because YHWH's salvation and righteousness call for realization (56.1).

Bibliography

J.Becker, *Isaias – der Prophet und sein Buch*, 1968; J.H.Eaton, 'The Origins of the Book of Isaiah', *VT* 9, 1959, 138-57; J.Elliger, *Deuterojesaja in seinem Verhältnis zu Tritojesaja*, 1933; R.Lack, *La Symbolique du Livre d'Isaïe*, 1973; L.J.Liebreich, 'The Compilation of the Book of Isaiah', *JQR* 46, 1955/56. 259-77; 47, 1956-57, 114-38; R.E.Melugin, *The Formation of Isaiah 40-55*, 1976; S.Mowinckel, *Prophecy and Tradition*, 1946; J.Schreiner, 'Das Buch jesajanischer Schule', in J.Schreiner (ed.), *Wort und Botschaft*, 1967, 143-62. Childs, XVII.

3.2 The Book of Jeremiah

Several complexes of texts have been combined in the book of Jeremiah, but in contrast to the book of Isaiah, they have all been explicitly connected with the person of the prophet Jeremiah. One exception is the appendix taken over from II Kings 24.18-25.30, in ch.52, but the adoption of a section from II Kings has a parallel in Isaiah, as does the incorporation of a self-contained block of sayings against foreign nations (chs.46-51).

→180f.

The main sections of the book of Jeremiah produce the following division:

→122
Division

1-25 Predominantly sayings of Jeremiah (closing note 25.13)
26-45 Predominantly reports about Jeremiah
46-51 Sayings against foreign nations (closing note 51.64)
52 Appendix

In chs.1-25, there are not only numerous texts in the 'poetic' language characteristic of prophetic sayings but others written in a broad prose style which shows a clear affinity to the language of Deuteronomy. Mowinckel (1914) saw an 'independent' source here (as also did Rudolph and others). Other interpreters explain these texts as 'sermons' which Jeremiah gave on particular occasions (Eissfeldt, Weiser, Miller). Most recently the view is increasingly gaining ground that this should be seen as the work of a Deuteronomistic redaction which worked over both the sayings of Jeremiah in chs.1-25 and the reports about him in chs.26-45 and gave the whole passage its present form (Thiel following Hyatt, cf. also Nicholson; Weippert differs, cf. McKane). The sayings against foreign nations (chs.46-51) are regarded by most exegetes as an independent complex of tradition which was only connected with the first two parts in the final redaction.

Deuteronomistic prose style
→151f.

For a long time a particular topic of discussion was the question of the original scroll, i.e. the earliest collection of sayings of Jeremiah which stood on the scroll that Baruch wrote at Jeremiah's dictation and then read aloud to King Jehoiakim (ch.36). Here quite contradictory answers are given: the content of the original scroll is sometimes seen in the short sayings formulated in the 'classical' prophetic style, and sometimes in the prose sayings with a Deuteronomistic formulation (Robinson, Eissfeldt, Miller). The more recent redaction-critical approach makes the attempt at reconstructing such an 'original' collection seem no longer to make sense (though cf. Holladay, 1980), as it has shown that we have the texts largely in an edited form.

Original scroll

The collection of the sayings of Jeremiah (chs.1-25) is a composition with many strata which was presumably based on shorter subsidiary collections. There is much to suggest that the redactional shaping took place in several phases, but here many questions remain open. In what follows I shall attempt to cover the origin and intention of the present text as far as possible (cf. Thiel, especially 1973, 273ff., and Holladay).

Sayings of Jeremiah

Some divisions can be seen within chs.1-25. First of all chs.1-10 clearly stand out from what follows by virtue of the fact that here prophetic

Chs.1-10

words with a poetic formulation are dominant (with the exception of 7.1-8.3), whereas later the prose language emerges more strongly. Moreover, in ch.10, in the hymn (vv.12-16) and the prayer (vv.23-25), there are passages which serve as conclusions. A further section can be recognized at the end of ch.6, where 6.27-30 are evidently the conclusion of chs.2-6. Finally, further sub-sections are marked by 4.4. and *9.24f.* This produces a division into the following sections: 1; 2.1-4.4; 4.5-6.30; 7.1-8.3; 8.4-*9.25*; 10 (Holladay 1976 and to some degree others).

Division

The introduction (1.1-3), which is probably that to the collection in chs.1-25, is followed in 1.4-19 by a self-contained composition. The call account (4.1-10) is developed in two visions (vv.11f.,13f.) and a saying of YHWH (vv.15-19): YHWH's word (vv.7,9) will be fulfilled (v.12) as YHWH summons the nations (vv.5,10) from the north to judge Israel (vv.14f.); he will protect Jeremiah despite all attacks (vv.8,17-19).

→114f.

In 2.1-4.4, first of all in ch.2 Israel, who in the wilderness period was intimately associated with YHWH (vv.1-3), is accused in a piece of invective of apostasy from YHWH after the settlement (vv.4-13); Israel's refractory behaviour against YHWH is then developed further from different aspects in a composition stamped by elements from the genres of the disputation saying and the invective (vv.14-37). In ch.3 the question emerges whether repentance is possible (3.1-5). This is affirmed first of all in respect of the northern kingdom of Israel (3.6-10,11-13) and then opened up in several stages as a future possibility for all Israel and Judah (3.14-18,19-25; 4.1-14). The section 2.1-4.4 thus forms a composition which links judgment and salvation; here the call to conversion has central significance (3.12,13,22; 4.1; cf. v.4).

Repentance

In 4.5-6.30 on the one hand the approach of an enemy from the north is depicted in constantly changing dramatic imagery (4.5-31; 6.1-5,22-26); and on the other hand the guilt of Israel is given as the cause of this judgment (4.13b,14,18,22,26b; 5.1-31; 6.6-21). The closing section (6.27-30), which is perhaps meant to bring the whole collection chs.2-6 to an end, compares the prophet's task of disclosing the guilt of his contemporaries with that of a metal assayer. It thus reflects a prophetic self-understanding which does not limit itself merely to handing on sayings of YHWH which have been received, but promises the prophet an indepedent critical function over against his environment. Thus at the same time it leads into the 'temple speech' which follows.

Enemy from the north

→117

Whereas prophetic sayings in 'poetic' form dominate in chs. 2-6, the picture alters in 7.1-8.3. Here we find an expansive prose speech which bears all the marks of Deuteronomistic style. The temple speech (7.1-15, cf.ch.26) with its polemic against a wrong understanding of the temple cult is followed by further sections which criticize behaviour in the cult: the cult of the 'queen of heaven' (7.16-20), sacrifices (7.21-29) and child sacrifices (7.30f.), and finally the announcement of a fearful judgment (7.32-8.3). As a whole the section was probably formulated by the Deuteronomistic redaction and puts the proclamation of Jeremiah completely in this context.

Temple speech

In 8.4-*9.25* there are again the same elements as in 4.5-6.30: a description of the disaster which is imminent (8.16-23) and lamentation about it (8.14f.; *9.9f.,16-21*), along with accusations against those whose guilt is the cause of judgment (8.4-13; *9.1-8*). Here the composition is arranged under the keyword 'be wise': in 8.8f. inculcated wisdom is criticized as being worthless, but wisdom is necessary in order to understand the judgment of YHWH (*9.11-15*); however, anyone

Be wise

who has gained this insight should not boast of his wisdom but of insight into
YWHH's actions (*9.22f.*). The call to lamentation (*9.16-21*) is also attached to
this keyword by the summons of the 'wise women' (*v.16*). The obscure conclusion
of the section (*9.24f.*) again takes up the invitation to circumcise the heart which
in 4.4. similarly marks the end of a section.

Chapter 10 contains a number of quite different elements. In vv.1-16 polemic
against the self-made idols which has many echoes of Deutero-Isiaiah (and in
which the keyword 'wise' is taken up again on many occasions, vv.7,9) is bound
up with a hymn (vv.12f.,16) ending with the phrase 'YHWH Sabaoth is his →100
name'. 10.12-16 is repeated in 51.15-19; furthermore, similar hymns are to be
found in 31.35; 32.18; 33.2 (and often in the book of Amos). In some cases they →222
evidently have a special function in the composition. Here a lament on the
destruction of Jerusalem (vv.17-22) also follows, and finally a prayer (vv.23-
25), the last verse of which corresponds to Ps.79.6f. This prayer again makes it
quite clear that here we have the end of a division in the composition of the
sayings of Jeremiah.

From ch.11 on, the prose language with a Deuteronomistic stamp Chs.11-20
comes more strongly into the foreground. At the same time larger
compositions in this language can be recognized. These can be described
as stylized scenes of the proclamation of Jeremiah (Thiel): 11.1-12.6; Stylization
14f.; 18; 19f. They all display a similar structure: the occasion for the
proclamation – message of judgment (- word of judgment) – persecution
of the prophet – lamentation. In details these compositions differ
because of the different traditional material which is incorporated into
them. The lamentation which always stands at the end is particularly
characteristic; here texts are incorporated which in very personal
formulations express the suffering of the prophet in his office; these are
usually called the confessions of Jeremiah (11.18-23; 12.1-6; 15.10f.,15- Confessions
21; 17.12-18; 18.18-23; 20.7-12,14-18; only 17.12-18 are not incorporated into such a composition).

In terms of genre the confessions are individual lamentations (Baumgartner). →108f.
There is dispute as to whether they are to be understood as a quite individual
expression of the suffering of Jeremiah in his ministry (von Rad). There is little
to be said for understanding them as liturgical formularies (Reventlow); it is
also improbable that they are later interpretation of the proclamation and
person of Jeremiah (Gunneweg). Rather, the very fact that they are incorporated
into larger compositions shows that they were already available to the authors
as Jeremianic traditions (Thiel). This also helps us to understand the apparently
scattered distribution in chs.11-20.

Within chs.11-20 there are other texts between these larger scenes,
sometimes in 'poetic' style, sometimes in prose. The perspectives from
which they have been collected and inserted are often difficult to
recognize. Sometimes associations by keywords and sometimes
thematic arrangements could have determined the pattern (cf. Thiel
1973, 288f.). Sayings

Finally, chs. 21-24 stand out as an independent composition. They against the
contain sayings against the leaders. Two sub-headings indicate that leaders
earlier collections have been incorporated here: 21.11, 'On the royal

house of Judah', now introduces 21.11-23.8; it contains sayings against various kings and ends with a composition consisting of messianic sayings (23.1-8); 23.9, 'On the prophets', opens the collection of sayings against prophets in 23.9-40. The framework is provided by 21.1-10, where the fate of the last king, Zedekiah, is connected with the imminent conquest of Jerusalem, and ch.24, where this fate is contrasted with the promising future of those deported to Babylon in 597.

Conclusion

25.1-13 form the conclusion of the collection of the sayings of Jeremiah. The section is divided according to the basic form of prophetic speech into accusation (vv.1-7) and announcement of judgment (vv.8-13). It takes up themes in sayings from the preceding collection (above all from ch.7) and at the same time points forward (e.g. to ch.29). It displays clear connections with the summary Deuteronomistic interpret-

→179f.

ation of the history of Israel in II Kings 17.

Judgment on
the nations

The section 25.15-38 poses a particular problem. It deals with the judgment of YHWH on the nations. It stands in striking isolation between the sayings of Jeremiah about Judah and Jerusalem in chs.1-25 and the reports about Jeremiah in chs.26-45. However, it is bracketted with what has gone before by the last words of v.13, 'what Jeremiah prophesied about all the nations', and by vv.12 (and 14?), where judgment on Babylon is announced. In the Septuagint, the sayings against the foreign nations follow this saying; they appear in the Massoretic text in chs.46-51, but in a different order. Some exegetes regard the Septuagint version as the earlier, because in Isaiah too the sayings about foreign nations stand immediately after the first complex of prophetic sayings. However, the reverse conclusion can also be derived from this comparison, namely that the Septuagint has made a transposition to assimilate the content to the book of Isaiah. Moreover, the question remains open why 25.15-38 was allowed to stand in its present position if there was a subsequent transposition of the sayings about foreign nations. At present it is impossible to give an illuminating answer. (Elsewhere, too, the Septuagint text often differs from the Massoretic text in Jeremiah; overall it is about an eighth shorter.)

Reports

→53
Conflicts
→90

→202

→114

Letter of
Jeremiah
204

The collection of reports about Jeremiah (chs.26-45) is clearly divided into two parts. Chapters 26 and 36 correspond to each other. Both begin with a saying of YHWH to Jeremiah at the time of Jehoiakim (whereas chs.27ff. already take place in the time of Zedekiah); the public appearance of Jeremiah in ch.26 first of all leads to conflict with the priests and prophets (only in 34.1-7 is there a brief mention of king Zedekiah), while the confrontation with the king and the court officials, in which Jeremiah is in danger of his life, begins in ch.36. (For the composition cf. also Thiel 1981, 100ff.).

As an opening to the first part (chs.26-35), the programmatic temple speech from 17.1-8.3 is repeated in ch.26 and expanded by the addition of a narrative (vv.7ff.). Chapters 27-29 are held together by the theme of false prophets: Jeremiah's sign with the 'yoke of the king of Babylon' (ch.27) sparks off the controversy with the prophet Hananiah (ch.28), and the false prophets also have a role in the letter of Jeremiah to the exiles (29.8f. 15,21-23, cf.24ff.) .

The theme of future hope which is struck up in ch.29 is developed in chs.30-33; here only ch.32 has the character of a report. Chapters 30f. are often called the Book of Consolation (there is mention of a book in 30.2); they contain a collection of very different words of salvation which are introduced by an announcement of the return from exile (30.3) and brought to an end with the saying about the new covenant (31.31-34) and with hymnic statements about YHWH as the creator (31.35-37). (31.38-40 contain a supplementary announcement of the rebuilding of Jerusalem.) The account of the sign given by Jeremiah's purchase of a field in ch.32 also indicates a promising future (vv.15,42-44). Finally, in ch.33 there follows a further collection of words of salvation in which keywords from chs.30f. are taken up: the turning (*šebut*) which YHWH will bring about (33.7,11,26; cf.30.3,18; 31.23; 32.44) and the covenant (33.20f., 25f.; cf. 31.31-34); here the latter is now related to David (and the Levites) and the promise of its permanence is bound up with hymnic statements about YHWH as creator which recall 31.35-37.

Jeremiah

Book of Consolation

New covenant →100

Purchase of field

Chapters 34f. form a contrast with the words of salvation which have gone before: these do not hold for Zedekiah (34.1-7) and the upper classes of Judah who break the covenant (34.8-22), whereas the Rechabites stand under the divine promise because of their exemplary obedience (ch.35).

Rechabites

The second part (chs.36-45) contains no further words of salvation to Judah or Israel; there are only two individual promises of salvation which are clearly parallel: to a Cushite court official whom Jeremiah had helped (39.15-18; cf. 38.7-13) and to Baruch (ch.45). The latter at the same time serves as a framework for this part: Baruch is first mentioned in ch.36, where he writes down words at Jeremiah's dictation and then reads them publicly in the temple. Both texts bear the same date, the fourth year of Jehoiakim; so the composition goes back to the beginning.

Individual promises of salvation

Chapter 36 is a clear parallel to ch.26 and at the same time an intensification of it: in ch.26 Jeremiah himself appears in the temple; there is conflict with the 'priests and prophets' (vv.8,11,16), but this is resolved by the royal justices in favour of Jeremiah (vv.10,16). In ch.36, by contrast, Jeremiah does not dare to make a public appearance in person but commissions Baruch to read out his words (vv.4-8); the royal officals react in agitation (vv.11-20), but the king himself demonstrates his contempt for the words of Jeremiah by burning the inscribed scroll piece by piece (vv.21-23); moreover, he gives orders for the arrest of Baruch and Jeremiah (v.26). This opens the conflict. It is also important to note that Jer.36 is explicitly stylized as a contrasting parallel to the account of the discovery and reading of the 'book of the law' before Josiah in II Kings 22 (Nicholson, Wanke): Josiah 'rends his garments' (II Kings 22.11, cf.v.19), while it is explicitly stressed that Jehoiakim does not do this, nor does he heed the warnings of his court officials (v.25). Cf. also the contrast between Jehoiakim and Josiah in Jer.22.13-19. (For the relationship between Jer.26; 36 and II Kings 22 cf. also Lohfink.)

→204

→180

Chapters 37-44 contain a consecutive account of the fate of Jeremiah from his arrest (37.11ff.), through his liberation by the Babylonians

Fate of Jeremiah

205

(39.11f.) to his forced journey to Egypt (43.5ff.); it is embedded in reports about the capture of Jerusalem by the Babylonians and its consequences. This account has been called a 'passion narrative' of Jeremiah (Kremers). Its literary unity has often been stressed (e.g. Wanke, Lohfink; Pohlmann differs), but this does not exclude the discovery of Deuteronomistic redaction work in the larger sermon-like passages, 42.10-22 and 44 (Thiel).

Baruch's
writing

Since Duhm the reports in Jeremiah 26 (often also including 19.1-20.6) have often been regarded as the work of Baruch. Mowinckel regarded them as an independent 'source', but kept the question of authorship open. Following others, Wanke above all has stressed the difference between chs.37-44 and the preceding narrative sections, so that they can hardly continue to be regarded as an original unit. The question of authorship cannot be decided, as the texts themselves give no indication, nor do we have any exact information about the relationship between Jeremiah and Baruch.

Person of
Jeremiah

→54

→203

As to personal details, we learn from 1.1 that Jeremiah came from a priestly family in Anathoth, a Benjaminite city a few miles north-east of Jerusalem. According to 1.2 (cf. 25.3) his prophetic activity began in the thirteenth year of Josiah, i.e. in 627/6. (The exact date can hardly be a subsequent invention, so a later dating of the beginning of his activity is improbable.) We learn details of his personal fate in the last years from chs.37-44, but many other texts, too, clearly indicate that he was involved in many conflicts as the result of his prophetic activity and therefore suffered personally (cf. e.g. 1.8; 20.1ff; chs.26; 28 and above all the 'Confessions'). Finally, he himself was caught up in the judgment which he had proclaimed and thus became the type of the suffering prophet.

Proclamation

As in the case of Isaiah, it is no longer possible to reconstruct Jeremiah's proclamation in its original form, because the book of Jeremiah as it has come down to us outlines a specific picture of the prophet which is already stamped by the realization of his proclamation of disaster. Therefore more space has been given to the proclamation of salvation, as the book is addressed to those who were affected by the catastrophe. However, there can be hardly any doubt that Jeremiah himself, too, was not just a prophet of disaster, but that some of the announcements of salvation actually go back to him, in intention if not in actual wording. Here individual sayings which originally applied to the northern kingdom were later extended to all Israel including Judah (e.g. 3.6ff., cf. Herrmann).

Relationships to
Deuteronomy
→51,180f.

The relationship between Jeremiah and Deuteronomy is a particularly disputed question. Many exegetes note the lack of an explicit reaction to the 'book of the law' and Josiah's cultic reform which, according to II Kings 23.2f., was introduced in the time of the prophetic activity of Jeremiah. But should we expect such a reaction? Would Jeremiah, whose prophetic proclamation concentrated entirely on criticism of the conduct of his contemporaries, have had to declare publicly, in prophetic speech (which is the only way in which it would have been handed

down), his assent to the measures of a king whom he never criticized?
Moreover, the introduction of Deuteronomy probably took place in a less spectacular way than that depicted in the account in II Kings 22f. There can hardly be any doubt that Jeremiah agreed with the intentions of Deuteronomy and Josiah's reform, since the central place given to criticism of the Canaanite cult (which had already appeared in Hosea) is a common factor between the two (cf. e.g. Jer.2.5-8, 20 with Deut.6.12-14; 12.2, etc.; cf. also the tables in Weinfeld, 359ff.). The Deuteronomistic redaction has intensified this tendency; in so doing it brought the prophetic words up to date so that the intentions of the proclamation of Jeremiah were taken up and developed in a changed situation.

Bibliography

Commentaries: Duhm (KHC), 1901; Giesebrecht (HK) ²1907; Volz (KAT) 1922, ²1928; Rudolph (HAT) 1947, ³1968; Weiser (ATD) 1952, ⁹1979; Hyatt (IB) 1956; Bright (AB) 1965; cf. also Carroll (OTL) 1986.

W.Baumgartner, *Die Klagegedichte des Jeremia*, 1917; A.H.J.Gunneweg, 'Konfession oder Interpretation im Jeremiabuch', *ZTK* 67, 1977, 395-416; S.Herrmann, *Die prophetischen Heilserwartungen im Alten Testament*, 1965; W.L.Holladay, *The Architecture of Jeremiah 1-20*, 1976; id., 'The Identification of the Two Scrolls of Jeremiah', *VT* 30, 1980, 452-67; J.P.Hyatt, 'The Deuteronomic Edition of Jeremiah', in *Vanderbilt Studies in the Humanities* I, 1951, 71-95; H.Kremers, 'Leidensgemeinschaft mit Gott im Alten Testament. Eine Untersuchung der biographischen Berichte im Jeremiahbuch', *EvTh* 13, 1953, 122-40; N.Lohfink, 'Die Gattung der "Historischen Kurzgeschichte" in den letzten Jahren von Judah und in der Zeit des Babylonischen Exils', *ZAW* 90, 1978, 319-47; W.McKane, 'Relations between Poetry and Prose in the Book of Jeremiah with Special Reference to Jeremiah III 6-11 and XII 4-17', *SVT* 32, 1981, 220-37; J.W.Miller, *Das Verhältnis Jeremias und Hesekiels sprachlich und theologisch untersucht mit besonderer Berücksichtigung der Prosareden Jeremias*, 1955; S.Mowinckel, *Zur Komposition des Buches Jeremia*, 1914; E.W.Nicholson, *Preaching to the Exiles. A Study of the Prose Traditions in the Book of Jeremiah*, 1970; K.-F.Pohlmann, *Studien zum Jeremiabuch. Ein Beitrag zur Frage nach der Entstehung des Jeremiabuches*, 1978; G. von Rad, 'Die Konfessionen Jeremias', *EvTh* 3, 1936, 265-76 (= *GS* II, 224-35); H.Graf Reventlow, *Liturgie und prophetisches Ich bei Jeremia*, 1963; T.H.Robinson, 'Baruch's Roll', *ZAW* 42, 1924, 209-21; W.Thiel, *Die deuteronomistische Redaktion von Jeremia 1-25*, 1973; id., *Die deuteronomistische Redaktion von Jeremiah 26-45*, 1981; G.Wanke, *Untersuchungen zur sogenannten Baruchschrift*, 1971; M.Weinfeld, *Deuteronomy and the Deuteronomic School*, 1972; H.Weippert, *Die Prosareden des Jeremiabuches*, 1973.

Steuernagel, §112-120; Eissfeldt, §46; Fohrer, §59; Soggin, 3.VII; Kaiser, §22h; Smend, §26; Schmidt, §19; Childs, XVIII.

3.3 The Book of Ezekiel

The Hebrew name y^{e}heskel is given the Greek form Ἰεζεκίηλ in the Septuagint, from which the Latin form *Ezechiel* developed in the Vulgate; our Ezekiel is a variant spelling.

Compared with the other major prophetic books, the book of Ezekiel give the impression of being much more uniform and coherent. The main reason for this is its clear division. In fourteen cases a unit is introduced by a date or an indication of time (1.1f.; 3.16; 8.1; 20.1; 24.1; 26.1; 29.1,17; 30.20; 31.3; 32.1,17; 33.21; 40.1). However, these dates are not distributed evenly throughout the book. They initially cover the period from the fifth year after the deportation (1.2; the figure thirty in 1.1 remains obscure) to the eleventh year (33.21), the time of the arrival of the news of the fall of Jerusalem in 586; the concluding great temple vision is dated fourteen years later (40.1). In numerous

other instances units are introduced by the word-event formula, 'Then the word of YHWH came to me (or, to Ezekiel)' (1.3; 3.16; 6.1; 7.1; 11.14; 12.1 etc.). On the basis of these two criteria, Zimmerli, for example, has discovered fifty (or fifty-two) independent units (Commentary, 25f.).

A further characteristic of the book is the distinctive language, which puts its stamp on it almost throughout: this is an expansive, idiosyncratic prose which shows clear affinities with the 'Priestly' parts of the Pentateuch, and in some respects also with Deuteronomistic language. Another striking peculiarity is the way in which YHWH addresses the prophet as 'Son of man' (*ben-'adam* in the sense of individual man, as distinct from the collective meaning of *'adam* as mankind, 2.1,3,6,8; 3.1,3,4,10,17,25, etc.).

However, most distinctive of all is that fact that the prophetic saying gives way completely to other methods of expressing the prophetic message. The book is stamped by four great visions (1.1-3.15 [22-24]; 8-11; 37.1-14; 40-48). The prophet is personally involved very deeply here. There is often mention of the 'hand of YHWH' which comes upon him (1.3; 3.14,22; 8.1; 37.1; 40.1); he falls down (1.28; 3.23; 9.8; 43.3; 44.4) and is raised up again (2.2; 3.24) or transported elsewhere (3.12,14; 8.3; 11.1,24; 40.11; 43.5) 'by the spirit' (*ru^{a}h*); he has to eat a scroll of scripture (3.1f.), wade through water (47.3f.), speak to dead bones (37.4ff.), etc.

Even more numerous are the sign-actions which the prophet is asked to perform (4.1-3, 4-8, 9-17; 5.1-17; 12.1-16, 17-20; *21.11f., 23-29*; 24.15-24; 37.15-28). It is striking here that almost always we just have reports of YHWH's command to perform the sign-action, often with a detailed interpretation, but not of its actual performance. However, it is evident from the reactions of the Judaeans in 12.8ff.; 24.19 that the

performance of the sign-action is taken for granted (cf. also 4.14ff.). A further characteristic element is provided by the metaphorical speeches (15;16; 17; 19 [in the form of the dirge, the *qina*]; 23; 27 [similarly as a *qina*]; 31). Some of them contain a large-scale retrospective survey of the history of Israel (16; 28), which we also find in ch.20 without the imagery.

In addition to the 'word-event formula' (see above), the regular, almost stereotyped, recurrent elements in the language of the book of Ezekiel include the phrase 'I YHWH have spoken', with which speech-units are often concluded (5.13,15,17; 17.21,24; *21.22,37*; 22.14; 24.14; 26.14; 30.12; 34.24; 36.36; 37.14). Of the various extensions which the formula can undergo, its connection with the recognition formula 'you will (they will) know that I (am) YHWH' (5.13; 17.21; 37.14) is significant. This statement is one of the most frequent and characteristic elements, and permeates the whole book (outside 40-48). It usually has an emphatic position at the end of a speech unit (6.7,10,13,14; 7.2,9,27; 11.10,12 etc.); often it can be taken as the real culmination of the divine discourse, so that it is possible to talk of a genre of proof saying, which is concerned with the divine 'proof of identity' (Zimmerli 1957, cf. 1954).

Thus the book of Ezekiel has a quite distinctive stamp. Nevertheless, there are many indications that, like the other prophetic books, in its literary form it does not come from one hand. The images of the prophet Ezekiel, his activity and his message, which are given us in this book are without doubt the result of a history of tradition and composition.

There is a wide difference of opinion over the details of this earlier history of the book. Hölscher assigned only a small proportion of the texts of the book to the 'poet' Ezekiel and attributed the most distinctive elements to a redactor; Torrey even wanted to understand the whole book as a pseudepigraphical writing from the third century BC. Then Zimmerli (following Mowinckel) sought to understand the manifest complexity of many texts, which indicates a kind of constant interpretative rewriting, as the work of a school (Commentary and 1980). This view is particularly illuminating because it provides an explanation why despite work which presumably went on over a long period and in many phases, the book has kept its special stamp and its relative coherence. Most recently there has again been a tendency to divide up the book into numerous redactional levels (e.g. Schulz, Garscha, Hossfeld); here the results at present differ widely. In this process the misleading term 'Deutero-Ezekiel' has cropped up (used with different meanings by Schulz and Garscha); in view of the terminology introduced into scholarship which uses Deutero-Isaiah and Deutero-Zechariah to denote individual parts of the books in question, the use of such a term for a redactional stratum should be avoided.

As we now have it, the book of Ezekiel is clearly divided into three parts:

1-24	Announcements of judgment on Judah and Jerusalem
25-32	Announcements of judgment on foreign nations
33-48	Announcements of salvation for Israel.

The individual parts are linked together in many ways (cf. Zimmerli, Commentary, 2; Garscha). The link between the first and the third parts is very close. At the beginning of the announcements of judgment we find, 'They will again know that a prophet was in their midst' (2.5); this saying is repeated at the beginning of the announcements of salvation (33.33): it was the task of the prophet whom YHWH had sent to Israel to proclaim judgment and salvation. At the beginning of the first and third parts we find quite emphatically the statement that the

Prophet as
watchman

prophet has the office of watchman (3.16-21; 33.1-9). Finally, the dumbness which had been inflicted on the prophet according to the call vision (3.25-27) is removed again with the report of the fall of Jerusalem (33.21f.; cf.24.25-27).

The visions, too, form a span between the first and the third parts.

kabod of
YHWH

At the beginning the prophet sees the 'glory' (*kabod*) of YHWH, while he is among the exiles in Babylonia (1.1ff.); then he is carried off to Jerusalem and there sees the *kabod* of YHWH a second time (chs.8-11), first of all within the temple, and then going out of the city, on the 'hill which lies east of the city' (11.22f.); finally, he is witness to the return of the *kabod* to the temple 'from the east' (43.1ff.). In the last passage reference is explicitly made to the two previous appearances of the *kabod* (43.3). The vision of the revival of the dead bones in 37.1-14 also has a clear parallel in the first part, in the remarkable song in 24.1-14, in which there is constant stress on the bones (vv.4,5 [twice], 10) with the very word ('*ezem*) used in ch.37 to denote the dead bones.

Exiles

There is a further important parallel in the contrast between the exiles and those who are left behind in the land. In 11.14-21 there is a contrast between the claim of those who have been left behind, that they have sole possession of the land (v.15), and a promise of salvation to the exiles; in 33.23-29 the claim of those left behind is again rejected and their annihilation is forecast because of their idolatry. This opens the way for the renewal of life in Jerusalem and in the land of Israel through those who returned from exile. The word of disaster on the 'mountains of Israel' (ch.6) is also matched by a word of salvation (36.1-15).

Finally, the great word of salvation in 36.16-38 takes up in a broad sweep the earlier words of disaster; it has particularly close connections with ch.20, since 36.16-38 form the continuation of the historical retrospect.

Even in Egypt and in the wilderness YHWH had wanted to 'pour out his wrath' over Israel (20.8,13,21), but he did not do so 'for my name's sake' (20.9,14,22); however, even in the wilderness he had announced the dispersion of Israel 'among the nations' (20.23f.). This has now taken place: YHWH has poured out his anger and scattered them among the nations (36.18f.). However, again 'for my name's sake' (vv.22f.) YHWH will bring them from the nations and restore them to their land (v.24). There he will cleanse them from all uncleanness (v.25), give them a new heart and a new spirit, so that they observe his commandments and laws (vv.26f.), and finally they will live as YHWH's people in the land which was already promised to the fathers (v.28). Nature, too, will be drawn into this future state of salvation (vv.29f.); the land will be rebuilt (vv.33-35) and inhabited (vv.37f.), so that finally the nations too will recognize that YHWH has done all this (v.36).

The perspectives of the composition are also often clearly visible within the individual parts (cf. Cassuto; Zimmerli, Commentary, 68; Garscha). The theme of the first part (ch.1-24) is determined by the siege of Jerusalem. The great opening vision (ch.1) which is connected with the call of the prophet and the description of his office as watchman (chs.2f.) is first followed by a sign-action in which the siege of Jerusalem is depicted (4.1-3); then the actual beginning of the siege is reported in 24.1. This provides the framework for this part.

Ezekiel

Siege of
Jerusalem

Call

A group of four sign-actions has been collected in 4.1-5.4 (4.1-3, 4-8, 9-17; 5.1-4), all to do with the siege of Jerusalem; they are followed in 35.5-17 by an extensive interpretation which begins with the words 'That is Jerusalem' (5.5). Two great invectives follow in chs. 6; 7: against 'the mountains of Israel' (6) and the imminent 'end' (7, as the development of a quotation from Amos 8.2). Here the recognition formula appears particularly frequently (6.7,10,13,14; 7.4,9,27).

→114f.

→209

The great vision of the judgment on Jerusalem (ch.8-11, cf. Greenberg), which begins with a date (8.1), ends with a word of salvation to the exiles (11.14-21), which marks the first clear break. The following complex again begins with a group of sign-actions (12.1-16, 17-20) in which the theme of siege or exile is again taken up; they spark off a discussion about the reliability of visions (12.21-25, 26-28), to which are attached various sayings under the keyword 'prophets' (13.1-16, 17-23; 14.1-11, cf. Talmon-Fishbane), and about the impossibility of deliverance through pious individuals like Noah, Daniel and Job (14.12-23).

Judgment on
Jerusalem

There is a group of similitudes in chs.15-19. The first two, dealing with the useless wood of the vine (15) and the faithless foundling (16) are about Jerusalem; the second again ends with a word of salvation (16.53-56) in which the term 'covenant' (bᵉrit) appears (vv.59-62, cf.also 34.25; 37.26). Chapters 17; 19 are about the king. The first is a complex poem about the eagle, the cedar and the vine which culminates in the metaphorical announcement of a new king (of salvation, 17.22-24); the second is a dirge (19). In between, in ch.18, is a text of quite a different kind: a sacral-law discussion about the problem of individual responsibility. In the form of the apodeictic law of death (Schulz), there is a defence of the theory that a son does not have to bear the guilt of his father nor a father the guilt of his son; each bears only his own. The chapter could have been put between the two similitudes on the fate of the king to stress that the sons of Josiah, Jehoiakim and Zedekiah, were responsible for their own sins.

Similitudes

The historical retrospect in ch.20 (see below) again begins with a date (v.1) and ends with a word of salvation (vv.39-44), the last in the first part of the book (cf.11.14-21; 16.53-63; 17.22-24). This divides the first main section into three (chs.1-24); only in the middle part between the vision of judgment on Jerusalem (chs.8-11) and the historical retrospect (ch.20) are there words of salvation.

Historical
retrospect

The following chapters contain several sign-actions, all of which indicate the end which is about to come upon Jerusalem (*21.11f., 23-29*; 24.15-25). The first two are incorporated into a larger composition under the keyword 'sword' (ch.21, cf. Zimmerli, Commentary), which is framed by sayings about fire (*21.1-4, 36f.*). Various sayings about judgment have been combined in chs.22f.; here in 22.1-16 we can again recognize traditions from sacral law (Schulz), while the imagery in ch.23 extends the saying about the unfaithful wife Jerusalem (ch.16) to the two 'sisters' Jerusalem and Samaria (cf. also already 16.44ff.). In 24.1-14 the inevitability of the fate of Jerusalem is depicted in the form of a song about the cauldron and the fire (see below on 37.1-14). In the last sign-action the prophet himself once again becomes the 'sign' (*mopet*, 24.24, cf. v.27; 12.6,11).

Judgment on foreign nations
→122f.

The second part (chs.25-32), which contains announcements of judgment on foreign nations, is more clearly integrated into the overall composition of the book than is the case with other prophetic books. This is achieved above all by the inclusion of dates, which run through all three parts. Here, however, they are not equally distributed: in ch.25 there is no date in the judgment sayings – each with the same construction – against Israel's immediate neighbours, the Ammonites (vv.2-5, 6f.), Moab (vv.8-11), Edom (vv.12-14) and the Philistines (vv.15-17). In 26.1, a date then introduces the cycle of sayings against Tyre (26.1-28.19), which are followed by a saying against Sidon (18.20-23), the construction of which resembles the sayings in ch.25. There follows a word of salvation to Israel (28.24,25f.) which marks a clear division. Then follows a collection of sayings against Egypt (29-32), in which there is now a series of dates (29.1,17; 30.20; 31.1; 32.1,17), with the exception of 29.17 all in the tenth to the twelfth year after the deportation. Thus the sayings about Egypt are related chronologically to the events of the siege and destruction of Jerusalem.

Salvation for Israel

Despite being thus bracketted off, the first and the third parts (chs.33-48), which predominantly contain announcements of salvation for Israel, are very much more closely connected. Chapter 33 is wholly governed by relationships with the first part (cf. 33.1-9 with 3.16-21; 33.10-20 with ch.18; 33.21f. with 3.25-27; 24.25-27, 33.23-29 with 11.14-21; 33.30-33 with 2.3-5 and 24.24). Here the central significance of the prophet and his office is brought out once again by the shift from proclamation of disaster to proclamation of salvation.

David as shepherd

→210

In ch.34 the image of the shepherd and the flock is varied and developed from different aspects. The former leaders of the people were bad shepherds, and YHWH relieved them of their office (vv.1-10); he himself will pasture his flock and bring it together again from dispersion (vv.11-16); he will also see to justice within the flock (vv.17-22). Finally, he will appoint a new David sole shepherd (vv.23f., cf. 17.2-24) and conclude the covenant of peace with the flock, so that it can live without danger and hunger (vv.25-31). Chapters 35 and 36 are related: an announcement of disaster upon the 'hill country of Seir' (ch.35; the name Edom associated with it is mentioned only in v.15, but cf. 25.12-14) is followed by the announcement of salvation for the mountains of Israel (36.1-15, cf. ch.6) which are again to be fertile and populated. This is followed by the continuation of the historical retrospect from the first part (36.16-38, cf. ch.20), the focal point of which is the land in which Israel is to live in the future, purified and freed from all former uncleanness. The vision in 37.1-14 finally announces as

Revival of Israel the decisive basis for future salvation the revival of Israel; moreover, a sign-action (37.15-28) forecasts the reunion of Judah and Israel under the Davidic

Gog of Magog monarchy.

212

In the strange section 38.1-39.22, Gog, the great prince of Meshech and Tubal

(= Magog 38.2; 39.6), is introduced as the 'last enemy' (38.14-16) by whose overthrow YHWH will once again show himself to be 'holy' (39.1-7; cf.38.16). This text contains marked apocalyptic elements (especially in 38.17-23). In 39.23-29 this part of the announcement of salvation is concluded with a word of salvation for Israel which takes up much from the previous chapters and is comparable with 28.24-26 in its function of providing a conclusion.

The final great vision (chs.40-48) is again explicitly connected with Temple vision the first part of the book. It corresponds to the two visions in chs.1-3 and above all in chs.8-11. There the prophet saw the *kabod* of YHWH departing from the desecrated temple (11.22ff.) which was thus given →210 over to destruction; now he sees it return to the new pure temple (45.1ff., cf. Greenberg). Much material from cultic legislation has been used in the description of this new temple, its organization and its cult, together with the account of the division of the land and the city of Jerusalem (for the division cf. also Gese).

In 40.1-43.12, a plan of the temple, which is measured exactly in the presence of the prophet, is framed by the vision of the *kabod* (cf. Talmon-Fishbane); there follow details of the size of the altar (43.13-17) and instructions for its consecration (43.18-27). The east door through which the *kabod* had entered (cf.43.4) is in future to remain shut (44.1-3). One last time the prophet sees the *kabod* which fills the temple, and prostrates himself (44.4; cf. 1.28; 3.23; 43.3). Now he is given instructions for entering the temple (44.5ff.), especially instructions for the service of Levites (44.10-14) and priests (44.15-27), their income (44.28-31) and possessions within the bounds of the city (45.1-8, the name Jerusalem is not used, cf. 48.35). The keyword 'prince' (*naśi'*) (which is used in chs.40-48 instead of the word king [*melek*], cf. also already 34.24; 37.25) attracts further sayings about the prince(s) (45.9ff.), above all about the offerings to be made to them (vv.13-17, also in vv.10-12 the fixing of measures) and their duties in sacrifices (v.17). This is followed by further regulations about sacrifice, in which particular stress is laid on the cultic duties of the prince (45.18-46.15); finally there are regulations about the prince's inheritance (46.16-18). In 46.19-24 the 'circuit' is taken up again ('he brought me', cf. 40.2f., 17, 24, 28, etc.; 44.1,4) in order to show a supplementary detail of the sacrificial cult: the cooking of sacrifices.

The last stage of the 'circuit' (47.1-12) introduces a surprising new element: water flows from under the temple threshold, down into the land, and then to the Dead Sea, making its water sweet. Once again the measuring procedure of 40.5ff. is taken up, this time involving the prophet, who has to measure (or demonstrate) the depth of the water with his body (v.3f.). He has now left the →115 temple precinct, and the visionary description is also at its end. In 47.13-48.29 there is an outline of a reordering of the land and with it a reordering of the people by a new assignation of plots of land as *naḥala* ('hereditary inheritance', 47.13f.; 48.29); this takes up the old order of the twelve tribes (cf. Machholz). The conclusion is formed by 'the city' with its twelve gates (48.30-35) and its new name 'YHWH is there' (v.35). Thus the return of YHWH into the new, purified Jerusalem is sealed.

The book of Ezekiel is such a complex and artistic composition that Person it is virtually impossible to discover much from it about the person of →52f. the prophet. It emerges from 1.1-3 that he was a priest and was among those deported to Babylon from Judah in 597. 24.15ff. mentions a sign-action he performed on the death of his wife. It is as uncertain whether this is to be understood in biographical terms as whether the abnormal physical states like temporary dumbness (3.25-27; 33.21f.) and immobility (4.4-8) which are depicted as sign-actions can be interpreted as manifestations of illness and whether the sometimes eccentric sign-actions and expressions, like clapping hands, stamping feet, etc. (6.11; *21.19*) are symptoms of an abnormal personality. At the latest by the transportation scenes, in which the prophet is carried to and fro between Babylon and Jerusaelm (8.3; 11.24; 40.1f), psychological and biographical explanations are automatically ruled out. The ingredients of the portrait of the prophet as presented in the book of Ezekiel can no longer be analysed.

586 as a break

→58

The conquest and destruction of Jerusalem in 586 marks a very striking break in the proclamation of Ezekiel described in the book (33.21f.). Before this the proclamation of disaster dominates; afterwards the proclamation of salvation. Both parts are related to each other in many ways. Therefore it is highly improbable that we should suppose that none of the proclamation of salvation goes back to the exilic prophet himself, because without it the whole book would fall apart and nothing comprehensible would remain. However, in view of the composition of the book we cannot attempt a reconstruction of an 'original' proclamation by the prophet.

Bibliography

Commentaries, Bertholet (KHC) 1897; Kretzschmar (HK) 1900; Herrmann (KAT) 1924; Fohrer/Galling (HAT) 1955; Eichrodt (ATD) I 1959, II 1966, ET OTL 1970; Zimmerli, BK I/II, 1969, ET Hermeneia I 1979, II 1983.

U.Cassuto, 'The Arrangement of the Book of Ezekiel', in *Biblical and Oriental Studies* I, 1973, 227-40; J.Garscha, *Studien zum Ezekielbuch. Eine redaktionsgeschichtliche Untersuchung von Ez 1-39*, 1974; H.Gese, *Der Verfassungsentwurf des Ezechiel (Kap.40-48) traditionsgeschichtlich untersucht*, 1957; M.Greenberg, 'The Vision of Jerusalem in Ezekiel 8-11. A Holistic Interpretation', in *The Divine Helmsman, FS L.H.Silberman* (ed. J.L.Crenshaw and S.Sandmel), 1980, 143-64; S.Herrmann, *Die prophetischen Heilserwartungen im Alten Testament*, 1965; G.Hölscher, *Hesekiel. Der Dichter und das Buch*, 1924; F.Hossfeld, *Untersuchungen zu Komposition und Theologie des Ezechielbuches*, 1977; G.S.Macholz, 'Noch einmal: Planungen für den Wiederaufbau nach der Katastrophe von 587', *VT* 19, 1969, 322-52; S.Mowinckel, *Prophecy and Tradition*, 1946; H.Schulz, *Das Todesrecht im Alten Testament*, 1969; S.Talmon/M.Fishbane, 'The Structuring of Biblical Books. Studies in the Book of Ezekiel', *ASTI* 10, 1976, 129-53; C.C.Torrey, *Pseudo-Ezekiel and the Original Prophecy*, 1930; W.Zimmerli, 'Knowledge of God according to the Book of Ezekiel' (1954), and 'The Word of Divine Self-Manifestation (Proof-Saying): A Prophetic Genre' (1957), in *I Am Yahweh*, ET 1982; id., 'Das Phänomen der Fortschreibung im Buche Ezechiel', in *Prophecy. FS G.Fohrer*, 1980, 174-91.

Steuernagel, §121-7; Eissfeldt, §47; Fohrer, §60; Soggin, 4.I; Kaiser, §22i; Smend, §27; Schmidt, §20; Childs, XIX.

3.4 The Book of the Twelve Prophets

From as early as the first quotation that has come down to us, the prophets from Hosea to Malachi are summed up as 'The Twelve Prophets' (Jesus Sirach 49.10). This Hebrew designation also appears in the Babylonian Talmud (Baba Bathra 14b/15a); it is matched by the expression Δωδεκαπρόφητον in the Greek Septuagint, while the Vulgate designates them *Prophetae Minores*, which has given rise to the common designation 'Minor Prophets'. Here the twelve prophets are always counted as one book.

In the Talmud, the arrangement of the individual books within this collection is explicitly said to be chronological, in that Hos.1.2 is understood to mean that God spoke *first* to Hosea. The sequence is orientated on the dates at the beginning of the books of Hosea, Amos, Micah, Zephaniah, Haggai and Zechariah, and in the case of Jonah on the mention of him in II Kings 14.25. The order of the other books shows how they were understood at the time when the Book of the Twelve Prophets was formed. This gives a chronological grouping: the first six prophets are assigned to the eighth century, the next three to the seventh century and the last three to the post-exilic period. (In the Septuagint the sequence of the first six books is rather different: Hosea, Amos, Micah, Joel, Obadiah, Jonah.)

The titles over the individual books indicate different stages of the collection. The title in Hos.1.1, 'The word of YHWH which came to Hosea', is matched precisely in Joel.1.1; Micah 1.1 and Zeph.1.1; in Jonah 1.1 it is altered by having the verb in a narrative form, 'Then the word came...'; in Hag.1.1; Zech 1.1 it is in each case preceded by a date (moreover in Hag.1.1 we also have 'through' [*b*ᵉ*yad*] Haggai), in Mal.1.1 it is: 'The word of YHWH *to* Israel *through* Malachi'. So these eight books form one group in which the title speaks of the 'word of YHWH'. Another group uses the term 'vision' (*hason*) in the sense of 'prophesying' (Obad.) or 'saying' (*massa'*) in connection with that (Nah.1.1) or with the verbal expressn 'which he saw' (Hab.1.1); this latter is also added in Micah 1.1, as in Amos 1.1, to the independent heading 'The words of Amos'. Through this the books from Amos to Habakkuk (but without Jonah) are again brought together as a special group. (For *hason* cf. also Isa.1.1; for the prefixed date with the following 'The word of YHWH', Ezek.1.1-3; in Jer. 1.1 'The words of Jeremiah', which is reminiscent of Amos 1.1, is bound up with the 'word of YHWH' formula.)

Finally, it is worth noting that at the end of the collection there are three sections with the title 'Saying' (Zech.9-11; 12.14; Malachi), the first two of which have been incorporated into the book of Zechariah. The last has been given its own title, perhaps in order to make the number of the books up to twelve. (For the whole question see Tucker.)

Bibliography

Commentaries: Nowack (HK) 1897, ³1922; Marti (KHC) 1904; Sellin (KAT) 1922, 1929, ²,³1930; Robinson/Horst (HAT) 1936, ²1954 (³1964); Weiser/Elliger (ATD) 1949/50, ³,⁴1959 (1979/⁴75); Rudolph (KAT 2) 1966-76.

G.M.Tucker, 'Prophetic Superscriptions and the Growth of a Canon', in G.W.Coats and B.O.Long (ed.), *Canon and Authority. Essays in Old Testament Religion and Theology*, 1977, 56-70.

Eissfeldt, §48.

3.4.1 Hosea

Division

The book of Hosea provides only a few clear pointers towards division. Chapters 1-3 are a thematic unity in which the relationship between YHWH and Israel is described with the image of marriage and symbolically by Hosea's marriage. Chapters 4-11 are marked off as a further unit by the introductory formula, 'Hear the word of YHWH, you Israelites' (4.1) and the concluding formula 'Saying of YHWH' (11.11). Along with the closing section, chs.12-14, this produces three major units. Common to them is that each of them begins with an accusation

Judgment and salvation

and an announcement of judgment against Israel and ends with an announcement of salvation (3.5; 11.8-11; *14.2-9*); here an important role is played on the one hand by the keyword 'legal dispute' (*rib, 2.4*; 4.1; *12.3*) and on the other by the word 'return' or 'lead back' (*šub* 3.5; 11.11; 14.2,3,8).

→116

Moreover it is striking that the introductory and concluding formulae which characterize most of the prophetic books are almost completely absent. The messenger formula does not appear; apart from 11.11, the formula 'saying of YHWH' appears only in ch.2 (v.*15* as a concluding formula, also vv.*18,23*). This indicates that the collection and redaction of the sayings of Hosea was not made with the intention of preserving the original speech units. Rather, thematic perspectives and associations by keywords seem to have been largely the determining factor. Therefore the characteristic forms of prophetic speech in Hosea can hardly be recognized either.

Hosea's marriage →114f.

In chs.1-3, two narrative texts (chs.1 and 3) have been brought together with a series of prophetic sayings to make a composition. Both the narratives deal with Hosea's marriage. This happens in ch.1 in the form of a third-person report and in ch.3 in the form of a first-person report. It is hard to define the relationship between the two texts. Do they deal with the same marriage? Or with a second marriage of Hosea to the same woman? Or with two different women? The name is given only in ch.1. The question of the biographical background to the texts

→114

cannot be resolved, but it is decisive for understanding the texts to see that they are accounts of a sign-action (Wolff). The function of the sign is different in each case: in ch.1 it is the name of the children (vv.4,6,9) and in ch.3 it is the segregation of the woman from (other) men (vv.4f.). Both have a parallel passage, within the composition chs.1-3, in the announcement of salvation (*2.1-3,25* or 3.5).

The fact that the names of the children are included twice in an announcement of salvation (*2.1-3.25*) probably indicates that the composition was developed gradually. In the present context the first sign-action with the ominous names of the children (1.1-9) is followed by a full-blooded announcement of salvation for Judah and Israel (*2.1-3*); the accusation then begins afresh in the form of a legal dispute (*rib*) which YHWH has with Israel, the mother of the children (*2.4ff.*). This again ends in an announcement of salvation (vv.*16f.*); a further group of words of salvation has been added.

There are no clear dividing lines in the two other major units. Wolff is guided by 'beginnings of speeches' which are sometimes marked by a new address and sometimes by a clear change of theme (4.1,4; 5.1,8; 8.1; 9.1,10; 10.1,19; 11.1). Other sayings are added to the opening one to produce 'kerygmatic units' which Wolff understands as 'sketches of scenes' in which each appearance of the prophet has been recorded; here he addresses a variety of audiences (Commentary XXX). Other exegetes construct larger groups of sayings (e.g. Frey, Willi-Plein, Buss).

Thus in chs.4-11 Buss distinguishes four cycles: I (4.1-9 [10], 11-14, 15-19; 5.1-7) with the theme 'cult' and the keyword 'whoredom'; II (5.8-10; 5.11-7.7; 7.8-16; 8.1-7, 8-10) with the theme 'social and political abuses' and frequent mention of the 'king' (5.13; 7.3,5,7; 8.4,10) and 'prince' (5.10; 7.3,5,16; 8.4,10); III (8.11-13; 9.1-9), again with the theme 'cult' and the motive of a return to Egypt; IV (9.10-17; 10.1-8,9-15; 11.1-11) with a series of historical retrospective surveys.

In chs.12-14 the sections *12.3-15*; 13.1-*14.1* can be marked off (Buss also makes a division at 13.11); here there are 'quotations' from the cultic tradition about Jacob (*12.4-7,13*), the exodus (*12.10f.,* 14; 13.4f.) and creation (13.14, Buss). The concluding announcement of salvation (14.2-9) is followed by a postlude in the style of wisdom (14.10).

As to personal details: the title (1.1) gives us the time of Hosea's activity. As in the case of Isaiah, mention is made of kings Uzziah, Jotham, Ahaz and Hezekiah of Judah, and also of Jeroboam II of Israel, though his reign overlaps only with that of Uzziah. But most exegetes assume that Hosea's activity extended beyond the time of Jeroboam. Alt saw a reference in 5.8-6.6 to the Syro-Ephraimite war, but the fall of Samaria is not yet presupposed. So the period of Hosea's activity is usually put between 750 and 725.

Hosea's proclamation is entirely addressed to the northern kingdom. As early as 1.4 the dynasty of Jehu is addressed with a recollection of the 'blood-guilt of Jezreel' (cf. II Kings 9); the capital of Samaria is mentioned (7.1; 8.5f.; 10.5,6; *14.1*) and also the cult-places Bethel (10.5; 12.5; cf. 4.15; 5.8) and Gilgal (4.15; 9.15; *12.12*); Judah appears as the enemy of 'Ephraim', i.e. of the northern kingdom (5.10; in 1.7; 5.5; 6.11 etc. there is evidence of a Judaean revision).

Latter
Prophets

Marriage
between
YHWH and
Israel

It remains uncertain how far we are to take the accounts of Hosea's marriage(s) biographically. However, with them a central theme appears in the proclamation of Hosea which in this form is new. The relationship between YHWH and Israel is described by a picture of love and marriage. Here we may certainly see an adoption of Canaanite ideas, in which the sexual element played an important role in the cult. However, to begin with this adoption is polemical, with the imagery of whoredom and adultery (Wolff), so that only a departure from the cultic practice now dominant makes possible the (re-)establishment of a loving relationship between YHWH and Israel.

Wolff has put forward the theory that the 'wife of harlotry' whom Hosea has to marry (1.2) is a normal 'average Israelite woman' who has taken to the 'modern' practice of cultic prostitution to ensure fertility. However, this view is disputed (cf.Rudolph).

Another special feature of Hosea lies in the explicit reference to the traditions of the early period of Israel. He mentions Jacob (*12.4f.,13*), the exodus from Egypt (2.17; 11.1; *12.10,14*; 13.4) and the guidance in the wilderness (2.16f.; 9.10; 13.5). It remains uncertain whether this suggests a tradition from Israel, i.e. the north. However, it is clear that Hosea stands in the context of tradition from which Deuteronomy emerged (Wolff 1956).

Bibliography

Commentaries, see on 3.4; also Wolff (BK) 1961, ³1976, ET Hermeneia 1974 ; Jacob (CAT) 1965; Mays (OTL) 1969; Andersen/Freedman (AB) 1980.

A.Alt, *Hosea 5.8-6.6. Ein Krieg und seine Folgen in prophetischer Beleuchtung* (1919), in *KS* II. 163-87; J.Buss, *The Prophetic Word of Hosea. A Morphological Study*, 1969; H.Frey, 'Der Aufbau der Gedichte Hoseas', *WuD* NF 5, 1957, 9-103; I.Willi-Plein, *Vorformen der Schriftexegese innerhalb des Alten Testaments. Untersuchungen zum literarischen Werden der auf Amos, Hosea und Micha zuruckgehenden Bücher im hebräischen Zwölfprophetenbuch*, 1971; H.W.Wolff, 'Hoseas geistige Heimat', *TLZ* 81, 1956, 83-94 (= *GS*, 232-50).

Steuernagel, §128; Eissfeldt, §49; Fohrer, §61; Soggin, 3.III; Kaiser, §22b; Smend, §28; Schmidt, §15; Childs, XX.

3.4.2 Joel

The character of the book of Joel is not easy to define. Two particular elements stand out; on the one hand marked liturgical forms of speech (especially in 1.5-20; 2.12-17) and on the other hand large-scale eschatological descriptions (especially in 2.1-11; 3f.) (English versions count chapter 3 as 2.28-32 and ch.4 as ch.3). Both have been combined into an artistic composition (Wolff). Here two parts clearly stand out from each other: chs.1f. and *3f.*

After the opening 'call to receive instruction', which has a wisdom stamp (1.20), the first part indicates the occasion of the work in a narrative statement: a catastrophic plague of locusts has devoured everything (v.4). This is the reason for the ensuing extended invitation to proclaim a ceremony of lamentation, centred on a fast (v.5-14); this invitation is followed by a lament (vv.15-18), in which the day of YHWH is mentioned for the first time (v.15), and a short prayer (vv.19f.). 2.1-11 then extends talk of the day of YHWH far beyond the specific occasion of the plague of locusts which has already taken place, to an eschatological attack by a hostile army which is still to come. Here we have the beginning of a call to penitence (vv.12-14) which in turn goes back to the summons to fast (vv.15-17).

Joel
→110

Ceremony of popular lamentation
Day of YHWH

2.18 marks the turning point and with 1.4 forms the brief narrative framework: YHWH becomes 'jealous' and has pity on his people. His response takes the form of a promise that he will hear them (2.19-27); this has a characteristic repeated 'Fear not!' (in the singular and in the plural,vv.21f.) which culminates in a recognition formula (v.27). The themes of the acute distress caused by the plague of locusts and the great eschatological threat are brought together in this word of salvation (Childs): YHWH sends food and fertility and at the same time deliverance from his 'army' (v.25b, cf.11), and he is not only in the midst of Israel now but will remain so for the future (v.27).

→208f.

Both chapters in the second part are a development of 2.27 within the composition: YHWH will pour out his spirit on Israel (*3.1f.*) and send cosmic signs of the day of YHWH (vv.*3f.*), but whoever confesses YHWH will find deliverance on Mount Zion and in Jerusalem (v.5). And when YHWH judges the nations in the great eschatological final battle (*4.1-17* [vv.4-8 are probably a later addition]) the Israelites who were scattered in the Diaspora (vv.1-3) will also find refuge on Zion (v.16). Here the recognition formula from 2.27 is taken up again: YHWH himself dwells on Zion and hallows it and Jerusalem by his presence. Further eschatological promises have been added in vv.18-21.

Spirit of YHWH

Zion

In more recent interpretation two particular approaches to understanding the book of Joel have emerged. In contrast to early questioning, both maintain that the book is a unity. Rudolph (following Kapelrud and others) sees Joel as a cult prophet who in chs.1f. reports a ceremony of lamentation among the people in which he himself played a decisive part; in chs.3f. the prophet develops further the consequences of the announcements of YHWH's salvation. He assumes that the book was written before the destruction of Jerusalem, but after 597, because of the 'foreigners' who have entered the city (*4.17b*); this puts it in the decade between 597 and 587/6.

Author

→122f.

Wolff, by contrast, puts more stress on the literary character of the whole book. This is evident not least in the frequent echoes of the sayings of earlier prophets (cf.1.15 with Isa.13.6; 2.1f. with Zeph. 1.14f.; 2.10a,b with Isa.13.13,10; 2.13b with Jonah 4.2b; *4.16* with Amos 1.2, etc., see Wolff, 10f.). Moreover the eschatological language and thought shows that the author is already 'on the way to apocalyptic', but has not yet crossed the threshold (Wolff, ET 14). With Plöger, Wolff puts him in the eschatological circles of the fourth century BC, which also include the author of the Isaiah apocalypse in Isa.24·27 and the author of Zech. 12-14.

→191f.
→240f.

The position of the book of Joel within the Book of the Twelve
Prophets between Hosea and Amos could be based on a similar dating.
However, it is remarkable that Amos 1.2 begins with a 'quotation' from
Joel *4.16*, so that here there may be an association by keywords;
moreover the theme of the Day of YHWH which dominates the book
of Joel also occurs in Amos 5.18-20, with echoes of Joel 2.2.

Bibliography

Commentaries see on 3.4; also Keller (CAT) 1965; Wolff (BK) 1969, ²1975, ET
Hermeneia (*Joel and Amos*) 1977; A.S.Kapelrud, *Joel Studies*, 1948; O.Plöger,
Theocracy and Eschatology, ET 1968.
   Steuernagel, §129; Eissfeldt, §50; Fohrer, §62; Soggin, 4.IX; Kaiser, §22o;
Smend, §29; Schmidt, §23; Childs, XXI.

3.4.3 Amos

The book of Amos gives us a very clear profile of this prophet. The
reason for this is not least that the individual units are almost always
clearly separated and are more obviously defined by numerous opening
and closing formulae. This often gives the impression of proximity to
the spoken words of the prophet himself. However, further analysis
shows that the present collection has undergone a lengthy history in
which a number of stages can be distinguished, though here (in contrast,
say, to the book of Hosea) the original units have largely been preserved.

First of all, two cycles of speech units with uniform constructions
Sayings clearly stand out: the proclamations of disaster against the nations (1.3-
against the 2.16: against Damascus 1.3-5; Gaza 1.6-8; Tyre 1.9f.; Edom 1.11f.; the
nations Ammonites 1.13-15; Moab 2.1-3; Judah 2.4f. and Israel 2.6-16. Here
→122f. the strophes against Tyre, Edom and Judah are to be assigned to a later
redaction) culminate in catastrophe over Israel; in them Amos makes
his characteristic accusations of oppressing the poor and despising the
Cycle of visions law (2.6f.), and forecasts disaster (vv.13-16). The cycle of visions in 7.1-
→114ff. 8; 8.1-3 contains no kind of reason for the disaster which is to come.
Intercession However, it does show a clear drift; in the first two visions (7.1-3, 4-6)
the prophet's intercession is successful, but in the two others (7.7f.; 8.1-
3) the possibility that the announcement of disaster will be withdrawn
is explicitly ruled out. It can now no longer be avoided: 'The end has
come upon my people Israel' (8.2). In 8.4-8 the reason is given for this
in accusations which are taken up verbatim from 2.6f. (vv.4,6; in v.5
extended by the accusation of dishonest dealings) and developed into
YHWH's oath that he will not forget this action (v.7). Here the
irrevocable nature of the judgment is again confirmed. In v.8 there
Composition follows a rhetorical question which takes up the keyword 'mourn' from
220 1.2. The earth must tremble and mourn. Here the composition of the

book completes a span: what was announced in chs.1f. has now become irrevocable. The imminent disaster is developed further in 8.9-9.6: here we have three sayings with the introductory formula 'On that day' (8.9f.,13f.) or 'Days will come' (8.11f.), a saying introduced as the account of a vision (9.1-4) and a hymnic passage (9.5f., see below). Here the keyword 'mourn' is repeated again several times (8.10 twice, 9.5). Thus chs.1f.; 7-9 (for 7.10-17; 9.7-15 see below) encircle the rest of the book like a ring (Wolff).

Amos

→119

Further structured compositions can also be recognized within this framework. In 3.1-4.3 there is a two-membered invective which begins programmatically with a more extended summons to hear (3.1f.): YHWH will also pay special attention to the guilt of Israel, with whom he has dealt in such an exceptional way. This is followed by a disputation saying (vv.3-8, v.7 is a redactional expansion, v.8 perhaps an originally independent saying) which in the present context has the function of legitimating this message of the prophet. Three (or four) further words of judgment against the upper classes in the capital of Samaria are attached (3.9-11 [12] 13-15; 4.1-3).

Invective

Disputation
saying
→120
→46

Three admonitions with similar constructions appear in the following section 4.4-5.17, all of which are to do with the cult (4.4f.; 5.4; 6.14f.); they clearly come to a climax which has a specific function within the composition. In 4.4f. (often designated a parody of a priestly *tora*) the Israelites are ironically invited to offer their cult in the way they like. As a contrast, there is attached to this in 4.6-11 a retrospect on YHWH's action, which should have made the Israelites repent, with the refrain 'but you did not return to me' (vv.6,8,9,10,11). The announcement that YHWH will 'do' something to Israel and the invitation to prepare to meet YHWH (v.12, taken up in the hymnic passsage v.13, which is concluded with the emphatic, 'YHWH, God Sabaoth is his name') is followed by the parody of a dirge (*qina*, 5.1f.) on the 'virgin of Israel'; this is made more vivid by an oracular threat of the imminent decimation of Israel (v.3). However, the second admonition (vv.4-6) makes a new beginning, calling on the Israelites to seek YHWH and not the cult places (in contrast to 4.4f.) so that he does not (*pen*) burn the house of Joseph (= Israel) like fire. A further accusation of failure to observe justice (vv.7,10; interrupted by a hymnic passage in vv.8f.) and an invective (vv.11f.; v.13 is a later note) is followed by the third admonition (vv.14f.). This invites the people to seek the good and preserve justice, so that YHWH may then perhaps (*'ulay*) be gracious to the remnant of the house of Joseph. But all in vain – the dirge is struck up (vv.16f.), 'for I go in the midst of you': the encounter with YHWH has taken place (cf. 4.12f.; also 5.16, 'YHWH, God Sabaoth').

Admonitions
→119

qina
→82,119f.

A collection of further sayings is attached with the cry *hoy*, 'woe' (5.18; 6.1), which derives from the lament for the dead: these are about the day of YHWH (5.18-20); against the way in which the cult is currently performed (vv.21-27; in v.22 the Israelite account is presented as overdrawn); an extended attack on luxurious life in Samaria followed by an announcement of judgment (6.1-7), and two further invectives (vv.8-10 [11] 12-14, ending again with 'YHWH, God Sabaoth').

→119f.
Day of YHWH
→98

The section 7.10-17 on the controversy at the sanctuary of Bethel stands out as an independent passage. It is probably not to be understood as a prophetic narrative or as part of a longer narrative about Amos,

→114

now lost, but as a prophetic word with an extended introduction to describe the situation (Wolff, Bach 1981). Amos' remark in v.14, 'I am not a prophet', is to be understood in terms of the argument in the accusation: Amos, who is not a prophet (v.14), has been given a prophetic commission by YHWH (v.15); because Amaziah seeks to prevent him from carrying it out (v.16), disaster is proclaimed for him (v.17). The much-discussed question whether Amos is now a prophet lies outside the scope of this text, which is focussed completely on the invective against Amaziah (Bach). The insertion of this section in the cycle of visions has probably been occasioned above all by the mention of the name of Jeroboam in 7.9, which is taken up in 7.10f. At the same time, however, the invective against Amaziah leads to the announcement of the end in the fourth vision (8.1-3).

Hymnic
passages
→100

The hymnic passages, which should be taken to include 1.2 and 8.8 as well as 4.13; 5.8f.; 9.5f., pose a special problem. Taking up Josh.7.19a, etc., Horst has attempted to understand the first three, with their identical conclusion 'YHWH is his name' (extended in 4.31), as judgment doxologies. The approach by Koch is more illuminating (1974); he regards them as elements of the composition. 1.2; 9.5f. (together with 8.8, see below) form the framework of the composition of the book and 4.13 is a turning point within the composition 4.4-5.17 (see above, Koch differs; 5.8f. are explained by de Waard in the context of a chiastic composition consisting of 5.1-17). Elsewhere, too, Koch (1976) makes many observations on the composition of the book which need further evaluation.

Concluding
word of
salvation

The section 9.7-15 stands outside the composition marked out by the hymnic passages. However, the conclusion (apart from the collection of sayings in vv.7-10, which seems like a later addition) once again gives the book quite another stamp. It contains announcements of salvation of a kind which do not appear elsewhere in the book: the restoration of the rule of David over 'the remnant of Edom and all the nations' (vv.11f., probably an allusion to 1.3-2.3), paradisal fertility (v.13) and the homecoming of the exiles to dwell safely in the land (vv.14f.). In this way, in Amos too, as in all the other prophetic books, the proclamation of disaster is incorporated into the eschatological proclamation of salvation.

Time of
composition

The book certainly underwent this last transformation only in the post-exilic period. Before that, too, we can suppose that there were several stages in the composition. Koch (1976) assumes that the whole book was composed in Judah in the pre-exilic period. Schmidt has indicated a Deuteronomistic revision to which he assigns e.g. the reshaping of the title in 1.1 and the address in 3.1, the expansion of the sayings against the nations, the references to salvation history in 2.10-12 and the saying about the prophets in 3.7. Wolff, moreover, posits a Bethel interpretation from the time of Josiah to which he also assigns the hymnic passages. However, these approaches fall short of raising the question of the composition of the book as a whole, so that they need to be examined again from that perspective. Above all, the texts assigned to the individual strata of redaction must not be interpreted apart from their context, since their precise purpose is to provide a new understanding of the whole work (Childs).

The title tells us that Amos came from Tekoa (in the hill country south of Jerusalem), i.e. from Judah, where he lived as a herdsman until his prophetic call (cf. 7.14ff.). However, his prophetic activity probably took place exclusively in the northern kingdom of Israel, as is evident from his accusations against King Jeroboam (7.9,11), against the upper classes of Samaria (3.9; 4.1; 6.1; 8.14) and against the northern Israelite sanctuaries of Bethel and Gilgal (4.5; 5.5f., cf. further 7.13; 3.14). Only Bethel is expressly mentioned as a place where he appeared (7.13). His period is indicated by a mention of Jeroboam II (787-747) but cannot be defined any more closely than that.

→40,165

→46

The question of the prophetic self-understanding has been discussed more intensively and controversially in the case of Amos than in that of any other prophet. This has often at the same time raised basic questions about the understanding of prophecy. Thus Amos was sometimes regarded as the embodiment of the cultic prophet (Wurthwein, Reventlow), a theory which has again been almost universally abandoned. As it were on the rebound his 'spiritual home' has been sought in country tribal wisdom (Wolff 1964); early Israelite legal traditions have also been seen as the basis of his speech (Bach 1957). A great many apt comments have been made in this connection, but no clearly defined area has emerged within the traditions of Israel and Judah from which Amos could and must be understood.

Bibliography

Commentaries, see on 3.4; also Amsler (CAT) 1965; Wolff (BK) 1969, ²1975, ET Hermeneia (*Joel and Amos*) 1977; Mays (OTL) 1969.

R.Bach, 'Gottesrecht und weltliches Recht in der Verkündigung des Propheten Amos', in *FS G.Dehn*, 1957, 23-24; id., 'Erwägungen zu Amos 7.14', in *Die Botschaft und die Boten, FS H.W.Wolff*, 1981, 203-16; H.Gese, 'Komposition bei Amos', in *SVT* 32, 1981, 74-95; F.Horst, 'Die Doxologien im Amosbuch', *ZAW* 47, 1929, 45-54 (= *Gottes Recht*, 1961, 155-66); K.Koch, 'Die Rolle der hymnischen Abschnitte in der Komposition des Amos-Buches', *ZAW* 86, 1974, 504-37; id. (and colleagues), *Amos. Untersucht mit den Methoden einer strukturellen Formgeschichte*, three vols, 1976; H.Graf Reventlow, *Das Amt des Propheten bei Amos*, 1962; W.H.Schmidt, 'Die deuteronomistische Redaktion des Amosbuches', *ZAW* 77, 1965, 168-93; J.de Waard, 'The Chiastic Structure of Amos V.1-17', *VT* 27, 1977, 170-1; H.W.Wolff, *Amos geistige Heimat*, 1964; E.Würthwein, 'Amos Studien', *ZAW* 62, 1950, 10-52 (= *Wort und Existenz*, 1970, 68-110).

Steuernagel, §130; Eissfeldt, §51; Fohrer, §63; Soggin, 3.II; Kaiser, §22a; Smend, §30; Schmidt, §14; Childs, XXII.

3.4.4 Obadiah

Theme
→215

The theme of this brief work handed down under the title 'Vision (*ḥason*) of Obadiah' seems at first sight to be simply judgment on Edom. However, if one considers the twenty-one verses as a whole, another dominant theme emerges: the day of YHWH. These two themes are linked in v.15. Most exegetes divide the work into two parts; to do that, however, they have to reverse the two halves of v.15 and thus destroy what was evidently a deliberate composition (Childs).

Division

Obadiah is composed of a variety of passages. If we follow the indications of divisions provided by formulae and the manifest stylistic characteristics, we have the following sub-divisions: vv.1-4, 5-7, 8-11, 12-15,16,17f., 19-21. These are in part clearly related, so it is not to be assumed that they all had an independent existence.

Edom

→53

Verses 10f., 12-14, which speak of the shameful behaviour of Edom to his 'brother' Jacob, form a starting point for understanding the first part, which speaks exclusively of Edom (vv.1-15, apart from v.15a, which is a link). The reference is evidently to the cooperation of the Edomites with the Babylonians at the time of the annihilation of the kingdom of Judah in the year 586. The preceding verses (vv.1-4,5-7, 8f.) depict with varying imagery the judgment on Edom which its behaviour has brought upon it. Here it is striking that vv.1-4, 5 largely correspond to the saying against Edom in Jer. 49 (vv.14-16,9). However, the discrepancies between the two are better explained as the use of a common (perhaps oral) model than in terms of literary dependence (Wolff).

Day of YHWH

In v.15 punishment is proclaimed for Edom because of its behaviour, but this is preceded by the announcement 'for the day of YHWH is at hand for all nations'. So now the judgment on Edom becomes an element in the eschatological judgment on the nations; all nations must drink from the 'cup of reeling' (v.16, cf. Jer.35.15ff., etc.) – but 'on Mount Zion there is deliverance' (v.17). Now circumstances are reversed. The house of Jacob will again take possession of what was taken from it and will become an annihilating fire over Edom (vv.17b, 18). Getting back what has been taken is again depicted in concrete terms (vv.19f.). However, the judgment on Edom is not an end in itself but serves an eschatological purpose: 'The kingly rule will belong to YHWH' (v.12b).

→122

Many exegetes regard Obadiah as a 'nationalist prophet of salvation' (often also as a 'cultic prophet') and find the inclusion of the work in the canon problematical. This verdict has to be changed if the second part is not just regarded as an 'addition' or 'appendix' and it is seriously noted that the first part has not been handed down on its own, but as an element of this composition. Moreover, there are numerous texts of the same kind in the sayings against foreign nations in the great prophetic books, but they too are only handed down within the wider contexts in which they now stand.

We may perhaps conclude from the fact that this small work was handed down separately that the name Obadiah in fact relates to an individual prophet whose words formed the focal point for this collection. The best explanation for their insertion at this point in the

Book of the Twelve Prophets is the use of the keywords 'day of YHWH' and 'Edom', which provide a link with the previous books of Amos (cf. 5.18-20; 9.12) and Joel (cf.1.15; 2.1, etc.).

Obadiah
→221f.
→219

Bibliography

Commentaries see on 3.4; also Keller (CAT) 1965; Wolff (BK) 1977.
Steuernagel, §131; Eissfeldt, §52; Fohrer, §64; Soggin, 4.VI; Kaiser, §22j; Smend, §31; Schmidt, §18; Childs, XXIII.

3.4.5 Jonah

The book of Jonah occupies a special position within the prophetic books. It contains a prophetic narrative in which there is only one brief prophetic saying (3.4b). In all probability its incorporation into the prophetic canon arises from the fact that not only was the name of the prophet Jonah rooted in the tradition (II Kings 14.25) but he was also assigned a particular place in the prophetic tradition.

Prophetic narrative
→114

The narrative is very clear and vivid. It is divided into two main parts with parallel constructions (cf.Cohn), both of which begin with the almost synonymous commissioning of the prophet to preach judgment on the city of Nineveh (1.1f.; 3.1f.). This is followed in the first part by Jonah's flight on a ship which gets into difficulties; this situation finally leads the seamen to recognize YHWH as God (1.3-16). In parallel to this, the second part reports how Jonah carries out his task and how the inhabitants of Nineveh repent (3.3-10). In both main parts there then follows a prayer by Jonah (with a similar introductory formula in *2.2* and *4.2*): in *2.3-10* (with a narrative framework in vv.1,11) there is a 'psalm' (see below); in 4.2f. a prayer which leads to a discussion between YHWH and Jonah, in which YHWH justifies his action (vv.4-11). The feature of the narrative that has particularly influenced the tradition, how Jonah is thrown into the sea, swallowed by a whale and spewed up again after three days (1.15; *2.1,11*), is not given any particular emphasis.

Two main parts

The narrative makes very skilful use of a variety of stylistic means in its construction (repetitions, contrasts, chiasmus and so on) and terminology (formations of leading words, repetitions, the use of ambiguous words and so on). This indicates a deliberate process of shaping (cf. Wolff 1965, Cohn, Magonet). Despite this the unity of the narrative has been repeatedly questioned (thus recently by L.Schmidt); however, none of the literary-critical analyses has become established. The psalm (*2.3-10*; its genre is that of the individual thanksgiving) is widely regarded as a later addition. However, it has clear references to the context of the narrative. Moreover, Magonet has shown that the 'quotations' from other psalms have often been changed to fit the special situation of the Jonah narrative (e.g. the stress on Jonah in the first person in

Stylistic means

the comparison of Ps.120.1 with Jonah *2.3* [transposition in the Hebrew text] or of *Ps.31.23b* with Jonah *2.5b*; the omission of 'I hate' from *Ps.31.7* in Jonah *2.9*, etc.) and that the parallels from other psalms are absent in the central part of the account, about the drowning (vv.*6b,7a*). Thus the prayer was probably formulated for its present context using themes from the language of the psalms and put in parallel to the prayer in 4.1f. (Landes).

Genre

The narrative has been called a midrash (Loretz following Wellhausen), a Novella (Wolff) or a parable (Rofé), while Keller expressly wants to keep the concept of the prophetic narrative. This question is as much connected with the overall understanding of the book of Jonah as the other, whether and to what extent we can find elements of irony or even satire in it (Burrows).

Theme

The book of Jonah is concerned with a central problem: are the announcements of YHWH's judgment valid? Jonah knew that YHWH is a gracious God, who repents of his announcements of judgment (4.2); therefore he escaped so as not to be a false prophet (cf. Deut.18.21f.).

→211

There are discussions of the same problem in the books of Jeremiah and Ezekiel (cf. Jer.18, esp. 7f.; Ezek.18, esp. vv.25-29); in Jer.18 there is explicit mention of the judgment on other nations. The problem is discussed in the Deuteronomistic History with reference to Israel, precisely at the point where the prophet Jonah is mentioned (II Kings 14.25-27). Here the view that the judgment of YHWH proclaimed over Israel is final is rejected (v.27; if there is criticism of Amos here, Jonah could be an exact contemporary and be meant as a corrective to him, cf. Clements). In Jonah 4 we have the reason for this: human life (and even animal life) is more important to YHWH than consistently keeping to a word of judgment once spoken (cf. also Heinrich). Thus it is also

YHWH wants
repentance

said in Ezek.18.23,32: YHWH does not will the death of a sinner but that he should repent and live.

This is also the message of the book of Jonah (Clements, Rofé). The book therefore stands in the context of a broad discussion of the kind that is carried on in the Deuteronomistic History and has found expression in the editing of most of the prophetic books: particularly clearly in Jeremiah and Ezekiel, but also in the others, in which judgment and salvation have been combined. Here the call to repentance has an important role, so that another aspect of the book of Jonah can be seen to be a concern to demonstrate that the possibility of repentance

Parallel to
Jeremiah

is always open. The figure of Jonah is portrayed as a clear counterpart to Jeremiah (Keller); the initial refusal to carry out the proclamation (cf. Jer.1.6) and the compulsion under which it is then done (1.7; 20.9), the angry solitude (15.17), the death wish (20.14ff.; 15.10; here too we can see a parallel to Elijah, cf. I Kings 19.4), the protest against YHWH's long-suffering nature (Jer.15.15b), YHWH's corrective answer (12.5; 15.19). For all the differences the common feature is obvious: here is a disobedient, rebellious prophet who remains YHWH's prophet even

→203

against his will.

The book of Jonah has often been interpreted from quite different aspects. The

central theme is often taken to be the relationship between Israel and the
Gentiles, and the figure of Jonah is understood as a deliberately negative model
of a selfish Israel concerned only for its own salvation, which like Jonah would
rather go under than see the conversion of the Gentiles (Kaiser 1973, cf. also
Wolff, Rudolph, etc.). Thus indications of irony, satire and the grotesque are
often found in the text, and Jonah's comments from the religious tradition (e.g.
1.9; 4.23) are seen as dishonest, cynical and indeed blasphemous (cf. Wolff,
Commentary). However, the contrast between Jews and Gentiles does not
become a theme anywhere in the book of Jonah (otherwise than, say, in Gen.20,
where Abraham is portrayed in sharp contrast to the godfearing Gentiles), and
there is no indication that Jonah is to be understood as the representative of a
contemporary Judaism (which is criticized by the author of the book) – quite
apart from the question whether the picture of post-exilic Judaism presupposed
here, for which there is nowhere any exegetical support, is an apt one. The main
thing against this exegesis is that contrary to the biblical tradition it removes
Jonah from the historical context of prophecy instead of trying to understand
him in this context.

→135

The dating of the book of Jonah is in essentials dependent on an
understanding of it as a whole. It is only rarely dated in the time of
Jeroboam II (following II Kings 14.25); this has been attempted most
recently by Porten following Kaufmann. The widespread conception
which sees Jonah as a negative reflection of post-exilic Judaism usually
dates the book rather vaguely in the Persian or early Hellenistic period.
Clements proposes the end of the sixth century, but thinks it impossible
to make a more accurate dating.

Dating

Bibliography

Commentaries, see on 3.4; also Keller (CAT) 1965; Wolff (BK) 1977.
    M.Burrows, 'The Literary Category of the Book of Jonah', in *Translating and
Understanding the Old Testament, FS H.G.May*, 1970, 80-107; R.E.Clements,
'The Purpose of the Book of Jonah', *SVT* 28, 1975, 16-28; G.H.Cohn, *Das Buch
Jonah im Lichte der biblischen Erzählkunst*, 1969; K.Heinrich, *Parmenides und
Jona*, 1966; O.Kaiser, 'Wirklichkeit, Möglichkeit und Vorurteil. Ein Beitrag
zum Verständnis des Buches Jona', *EvTh* 33, 1973, 91-103; C.A.Keller, 'Jonas.
Le portrait d'un prophète', *TZ* 21, 1965, 329-40; G.M.Landes, 'The Kerygma
of the Book of Jonah. The Contextual Interpretation of the Jonah Psalm',
Interpretation 21, 1967, 3-31; O.Loretz, 'Herkunft und Sinn der Jona-Erzäh-
lung', *BZ* NF 5, 1961, 18-29; J.Magonet, *Form and Meaning. Studies in Literary
Techniques in the Book of Jonah*, 1976; B.Porten, 'Baalshamem and the Date
of the Book of Jonah', in *De la Tôra au Méssie. FS H.Cazelles*, 1981, 237-44;
A.Rofé, 'Classes in the Prophetical Stories: Didactic Legenda and Parable',
SVT 26, 1974, 143-64; L.Schmidt, *'De Deo'. Studien zur Literarkritik und
Theologie des Buches Jona, des Gesprächs zwischen Abraham und Jahwe in
Gen.18.22ff. und von Hi 1*, 1976; H.W.Wolff, *Studien zum Jonabuch*, 1965,
²1975.
    Steuernagel, §94; Eissfeldt, §53; Fohrer, §65; Soggin, 4.X; Kaiser, §19;
Smend, §32; Schmidt, §23; Childs, XXIV.

3.4.6 Micah

The book of Micah is a complex collection of prophetic texts which has a long history behind it. It is stamped in particular by the combination of judgment and salvation which also appears in other prophetic books. That is true first of all of the book as a whole. It begins with a large-scale composition in which, after a summons to open a trial (1.2), YHWH's coming to judge the guilt of Israel (vv.5-7) is announced in a theophany (vv.3f.). This is followed by a long lamentation (vv.8-16). At the end of the book there is a long prayer (7.14-20) with a petition to YHWH to show his faithfulness to Israel as in the time of the exodus (v.15) and the fathers (v.20).

Further subdivisions can be seen: in chs.1f. the announcement of judgment against Israel and Judah in ch.1 (see above) is followed by an accusation (2.1ff.) with a subsequent announcement of judgment (vv.3-5) on the economically powerful who exploit others. The accusation is developed further within the framework of a discussion with the audience (vv.6-11). This section ends with an announcement of salvation (vv.12f.) which clearly presupposes that judgment has already taken place and that the people are scattered in the Diaspora.

→191

A new series of invectives begins with ch.3: against those responsible for justice (vv.1-3 accusation, v.4 announcement of judgment) and against the prophets who mislead the people by corrupt prophecies (v.5 accusation, vv.6f. announcement of judgment); in v.8 Micah contrasts himself with them as a prophet of disaster whose credentials come from YHWH. In vv.9-12 the accusations against the leadnng groups are continued (the priests are added to the two groups already mentioned, v.11), and there is an announcement of the complete destruction of Jerusalem (v.12). There again follows a word of salvation about Jerusalem (4.1-8; vv.1-3 correspond almost word for word with Isa.2.2-4). Here, as in 2.12f., there is a promise that those scattered in the Diaspora will be gathered together (vv.6f.) and the kingdom restored (v.8b – in contrast to the kingship of YHWH, v.7b).

The following section 4.9-5.14 also proves to be a carefully planned composition: in 4.9-5.5 there is a series of sayings each of which is introduced by 'Now' ('atta, 4.9 [10] 11, 14), while the following sayings in 5.6-14 are each introduced with 'Then' (wehaya, literally, 'it will be or happen', vv.6,7,9). The first group speaks above all of the distress of Zion. Here, however, there are already clear hints of future salvation in YHWH's 'thought' of Zion (4.12f.) and above all in the announcement of a new ruler from Bethlehem (5.1,3). The second group is dominated by the announcements of salvation for the remnant of Jacob (5.6,7), who will no longer have to suffer under his enemies (vv.7f.) and will ultimately no longer need to use weapons and fortifications because YHWH himself will remove them (vv.9f.), along with all alien cult objects (vv.11-13).

A clear break in the composition can be recognized in 5.14. A word of YHWH against the 'people who do not hearken' obviously resumes the introductory cry, 'Hear all nations' from 1.2 (Wolff). This brings us full circle: the nations were to be witnesses of YHWH's judgment upon Israel but they have not lived up to this task. However, that does not bring the whole composition to an end. The mountains and hills are called upon with another 'Hear' (6.1: as witnesses or as accused?). This opens the fourth sub-section which again contains an alternation of judgment and salvation (chs.6f.).

6.2-8 deals with a legal dispute between YHWH and Israel in which YHWH's speech in his own defence (vv.3-5) brings up the question of Israel's guilt towards him in connection with possible cultic offerings (vv.6f.). This question is answered by a summary of YHWH's religious and ethical demands (v.8). The whole passage forms a skilful didactic sermon (Wolff and others). 6.9-16 contain a renewed accusation against the leading classes for their transgression of the law and oppression of the poor (v.10-12), followed by an announcement of judgment (vv.13-16 with YHWH's emphatic 'I' in v.13 and the thrice-repeated 'you' in vv.14,15a, 15b). In 7.1-6 there follows a lamentation on the overthrow of law and the destruction of trust between human beings, to which is attached in v.7 a psalm-like expression of hope for YHWH's help. The theme of Zion is also taken up again (7.7-13), but now (in comparison to 4.9-5.5) with an even more confident expectation of the saving future. Then YHWH will bring justice to Jerusalem and lead it to the light (v.9b), build up its walls again (v.11) and reunite its people scattered throughout the world (v.12). Attached to this is the great prayer for YHWH to demonstrate his faithfulness (7.14-20); at the same time this forms the conclusion to the whole book (see above).

Legal dispute with YHWH
→89f.,120

→110f.

This collection evidently contains elements from quite different periods. Its basic material consists of words of the prophet Micah from the eighth century (see below). Opinions over the extent of this basic material differ; most scholars attribute to it the greater part of the sayings in chs.1-3 (but without the announcement of salvation in 2.12f.), and often also some material in the following sections. There, however, the later strata of redaction clearly predominate. There is especial dispute over the saying about the future ruler from Bethlehem (5.1ff.) and over 6.1-8, a passage particularly well known because of its last verse; here a minority of exegetes continue to maintain that Micah himself is the author. Furthermore, there are very different assessments of the course of the history of redaction and composition of the book. Often a revision in the exile (early on) is assumed, which seeks to interpret the events of 586 as fulfilment of the forecasts of judgment made by the prophet Micah (Jeremias and others), and one or more post-exilic revisions (Willi-Plein, Renaud, etc, cf. Wolff 1982, XXXVI). In the dating of the latter some exegetes go down to the Hellenistic period, among other reasons because they see a polemic against the Samaritans in the announcement of the destruction of Samaria (Lescow). (Here the uncertainty of such datings becomes evident, as other exegetes see these verses as evidence for the activity of Micah before the destruction of the northern kingdom in 722!) Finally, the clearly recognizable connections with the book of Isaiah play a role, as is evident in the themes they share (Childs mentions Messiah, remnant, plan of YHWH, etc.) and not least in the striking (and perhaps deliberate) parallelism between Isa.2.2-4 and Micah 4.1-3. At all events they are an indication that the interpretative revisions of the individual prophetic books did not take place independently of one another.

The title (1.1) first of all tells us that Micah was a rather later

Basic material

Revisions

→191

Person
229

contemporary of Isaiah and also came from Judah (from Moresheth-gath, cf.1.14). This tradition is confirmed by the mention of Micah in Jer.26.18, where Micah 3.12 is also cited literally. He also comes close to Isaiah (and Amos) in his criticism of the social conduct of the upper classes. Wolff (1978) wants to conclude from Micah's emphatic assertion in 3.8 (deleting the words 'spirit of YHWH') that Micah was one of the local elders of Moresheth, but this interpretation is disputed.

Bibliography

Commentaries, see on 3.4; also Wolff ((BK) 1982; Mays (OTL) 1976; van der Woude (POuT) 1976.

J.Jeremias, 'Die Deutung der Gerichtsworte Michas in der Exilszeit', *ZAW* 83, 1971, 330-54; T.Lescow, 'Redaktionsgeschichtliche Analyse von Micha 1-5 (or 6-7)', *ZAW* 84, 1972, 46-85 (or 182-212); J.L.Mays, 'The Theological Purpose of the Book of Micah', in *Beiträge zur alttestamentlichen Theologie. FS W.Zimmerli*, 1977, 276-87; B.Renaud, *La formation du livre de Michée*, 1977; I.Willi-Plein, *Vorformen der Schriftexegese. Untersuchungen zum literarischen Werden der auf Amos, Hosea und Micha zuruckgehenden Bücher im hebräischen Zwölfprophetenbuch*, 1971; H.W.Wolff, 'Wie verstand Micha von Moreschet sein prophetisches Amt?', *SVT* 29, 1978, 408-17.

Steuernagel, §132; Eissfeldt, §54; Fohrer, §66; Soggin, 3.V; Kaiser, §22d; Smend, §33; Schmidt, §17; Childs, XXV.

3.4.7 Nahum

At first sight, two passages clearly stand out in the book of Nahum: an introductory psalm (1.2-8) and an announcement of disaster for Nineveh (2.4-3.19) consisting of several strophes. There is a dispute about the relationship of these and about how the intervening verses 1.9-2.3 are to be understood.

Psalm   Without doubt the psalm offers an interpretation of the book as a whole: YHWH is the penal and gracious God (1.2-3a); because he is Creator and Lord of the world (vv.3b-5) no one can resist him (v.6), and whereas he is a refuge for those who trust in him (v.7), he is making an end for his adversaries (v.8).

→268   The psalm is evidently constructed in alphabetical order; however, in a number of passages this is no longer clearly evident; moreover, it covers only half the alphabet, though this was perhaps deliberate (Humbert). It is impossible, given this form, to determine whether the psalm was an original element of the proclamation of Nahum, as we know nothing about Nahum himself (see below). At all events, in its present form the book is a planned composition consisting of a variety of texts which are meant to be understood in the light of the introductory psalm (Keller, Childs, etc.).

230   The section 1.9-2.3 is also governed by the contrast between danger

from enemies and preservation by YHWH (as long as the verses are not transposed or emended, see below): those addressed (according to *2.1*, Judah) are not to make their own plans (1.9a) because YHWH will annihilate (1.9b, 10,12a, 13f.; *2.1b*) the enemies who rise up against Jerusalem (2.2), especially those who make ungodly plans (*yo'ez b^eli-ya^cal*, 1.11, cf.2.1b), and whose yoke Judah must now bear (1.13). YHWH will no longer humiliate Judah (1.12b), so that jubilation prevails in it (*2.1a*), because YHWH is restoring all Israel (*2.3*).

These verses are often understood in quite a different way. Jeremias sees 1.11,14 and *2.2f.* as original invective against Israel; he sees *2.1* as being dependent on Isa.52.7 and reckons the verse, with 1.12f., as an exilic or post-exilic interpretation which has completely changed the original meaning. He sees 3.1-5, 8-11 as invective against Jerusalem and understands Nahum generally as a prophet of judgment against Israel who – like other pre-exilic prophets – only made some utterances against a foreign nation (Assyria). Schulz regards 1.11,14; *2.2* as part of a battle song which he reconstructs by numerous transpositions of the text; however, he sees the present association of these verses with an original word of salvation to Judah (1.12f.; *2.1*) as a planned composition. Rudolph interprets the whole section 1.11-*2.3* as 'consolation for Judah' on the basis of textual emendations.

The next section, *2.4*-3.19, is directed as a whole against Nineveh, Nineveh which is explicitly mentioned in *2.9*; 3.7 (cf. 'Assyria' in 3.18). It is clearly divided into three sub-sections; in *2.4-14* there is the dramatic portrayal of the conquest of Nineveh by an uncanny enemy who is not mentioned by name; after a taunt song (vv.*12f.*) the conclusion is made →82 up of YHWH's threat 'Behold I will..' (*2.14*). 3.1-7 begins with a 'Woe' on the 'bloody city' and continues the description of the annihilation, again with the threatening 'Behold, I will. . .' (vv.5f.) and a taunt song (v.7). In 3.8-19 Nineveh is compared with the city No-Amon (= Thebes) which also had to fall; again there is a taunt-song at the end (vv.18f.).

This conclusion to the book seems very abrupt. Evidently the Powers hostile to God interpretative work of the composition was concentrated right at the beginning – in contrast, say, to the book of Obadiah, where a saying against another people (Edom) has been set in a wider theological context by an interpretative second part. In the book of Nahum it is made clear from the begining that Nineveh is simply the representative and example of the powers opposed to YHWH and that none of these powers can withstand him since he is creator of the world (1.3b-6). Here we also have escahtological overtones: they are clearest in the discourse about the 'day of distress' (1.7) which recalls the 'day of YHWH', but also in the portrayal of the theophany and its connection with the theme of judgment which shapes the whole psalm (Schulz). This also contains a promise of salvation for 'those who trust in him' (1.7).

The title of the book (1.1f.) similarly indicates that it has been made up of Title →215 different elements. It contains two elements, the word *maśśa'* (saying) and the word *ḥason* (vision). The former occurs frequently as the title of independent, often anonymous prophetic sayings, above all against other nations (e.g. Isa.13.1; 15.1; 17.1, etc.; Zech 9.1; 12.1); the latter is a title only at the beginning of prophetic books in conjunction with the name of the prophet (Isa.1.1; Obadiah 1; Nahum 1.1), so that it must be regarded as an element in the composition; the addition of the word *šeper* (book) also indicates this.

Person

We know nothing about the person of the prophet other than his name and that he came from the (unknown) place Elkosh. The book does not introduce us at any point to a prophetic figure. The date of the sayings against Nineveh can be determined from the mention of Thebes

Time

(3.8), which was destroyed in 667 (by another reckoning 662); the destruction of Nineveh in 612 is evidently still to come. Some exegetes date the books as a whole in the period between these two events (e.g. Keller, Rudolph), but in my view it is more likely that the whole composition, like that of the other prophetic books does not antedate the exile.

Bibliography

Commentaries, see on 3.4; also Keller (CAT) 1971.

P.Humbert, 'Essai d'analyse de Nahoum 1,2-2,3', *ZAW* 44, 1926, 266-80; J.Jeremias, *Kultprophetie und Gerichtsverkündigung in der späten Königszeit Israels*, 1970; C.A.Keller, 'Die theologische Bewältigung der geschichtlichen Wirklichkeit in der Prophetie Nahums', *VT* 22, 1972, 399-419; H.Schultz, *Das Buch Nahum. Eine redaktionskritische Untersuchung*, 1973.

Steuernagel, §133; Eissfeldt, §55; Fohrer, §67; Soggin, 3.VI; Kaiser, §22f.; Smend, §34; Schmidt, §18; Childs, XXVI.

3.4.8 Habakkuk

The prophetic speech spoken at the behest and in the name of YHWH is completely absent from the book of Habakkuk (cf. Keller 1973). However, the book contains other forms of speech which also occur elsewhere in the prophetic books, so that it remains within the spectrum offered by the prophetic traditions of the Old Testament.

Division

The division of the book is clear: a lament by the prophet is twice (1.2-4, 12-17) followed by a divine answer (1.5-11; 2.1-5); the second

→119f.

answer is followed by a series of woes (2.6-20) concluded by a psalm

→247

(ch.3), which is provided with an introduction of its own (v.1) and a closing note about the musical way in which it is to be performed (v.19b).

As with other prophetic books, the psalm indicates how the book as a whole is to be understood. However, in contrast to the book of Nahum

→230

it does not come at the end so that everything culminates in it. Similar

Lamentation

stresses are placed throughout the book. The opening of the first lament,

232

'How long, Lord...?' (1.2), already points forward. In the way in which

it addresses YHWH as the holy God from primal times (1.12), the
second lament anticipates themes of the psalm (cf.3.2f.). The prophet
then watches for an answer from YHWH (2.1); here there is mention
of a vision which points to the future (2.2ff.). Finally, within the woes
and at the end there are also references to YHWH's future (2.13a,
14,20). The psalm itself depicts a theophany of YHWH (cf. Jeremias
1965) in which themes of creation and the end-time are interwoven.

The sayings in 1.2-2.5 seem to move on two different levels. The prophet
complains about violence (*ḥamaś*) and injustice (*'amal*) and the decline of justice
(*mišpat*) among his own people (1.2-4). However, instead of announcing the
hoped-for help the divine answer (vv.5-11) forecasts the attack of a hostile
people (according to v.6 the Babylonians) which will exercise its own right
(*mišpat*, v.7) and practise violence (*ḥamaś*, v.9). In the renewed lamentation
(vv.12-17) the speech about the people destined by YHWH for judgment
(*mišpat*, v.12b) is combined with a lamentation over injustice (*'amal*, v.13a) and
the oppression of the righteous (*ṣaddiq*) by the unrighteous (*raša'*, v.13b, cf.
v.4b). Otto sees here an original lament by the prophet criticizing the society
in which he lives, which has later been reinterpreted by the insertion of the
Babylonians in vv.5-11,12b; Rudolph (like others before him), however, refers
the speech about the unrighteous who swallow up the righteous (v.13b) to the
Babylonians; they are summoned by YHWH to punish the unrighteous and
now themselves prove to be unrighteous. So the second lament is an 'accusation'
(cf. 2.1b), and the criticism of the conduct of the Babylonians who have
arrogantly exceeded the task set them (vv.15-17) is understandable in this
context. (If the texts are based on such a critical lament, it has not only been
altered by secondary additions but consistently reinterpreted.) YHWH's second
answer (2.1-5) must similarly be understood in that light: against present
appearances the prophet is told in a future-orientated 'vision' that in the end
the righteous person who has so far kept faith (*'emuna*) will live (v.4), while the
violent ruler who exceeds himself will perish (v.5).

In the subsequent five woes (2.6b-8, 9-11, 12f., 15-17, 18f.), statements
about social abuses (exorbitant interest, vv.6f.; struggle for illicit profit, v.9;
unscrupulous building, v.12; drunkenness, v.15; idolatry, vv.18f., cf. Jeremias
1980, Otto) are also reinterpreted in terms of oppression by 'nations'
(vv.8.10,13b, cf. v.17) so that they are now addressed to the conquerors
mentioned in ch.1, i.e. the Babylonians. The connection with what has gone
before is provided by the introduction in v.6a. The assembled peoples (v.5b)
begin a taunt song (*mašal*) about the fallen conqueror with the cry 'woe' (*hoy*),
which derives from the lament for the dead.

The internal tensions which dominate the book of Habakkuk are
essentially a result of the history of its tradition; here social criticism
has been turned into invective against the Babylonians. However, this
new interpretation goes far beyond the present historical occasion and
points to an eschatological theophany of YHWH (ch.3). The 'vision'
which the prophet has (2.1-3) is a last pointer to this, and it is the basis
of his confidence (3.18f.), into which the promise that the righteous will
live (2.4) has also been incorporated (cf. Childs).

We learn nothing about the person of Habakkuk but his name. He is
often designated a 'cultic prophet' because the whole book is understood

as a cultic-prophetic 'liturgy' (Humbert); alternatively, at least the nucleus of the prophetic sayings are assumed to have a 'liturgical' character (Jeremias 1970). By contrast, other exegetes stress the social-critical aspect (Otto) or at any rate that of the suffering in the unrighteousness of the world (Keller). Because of the mention of the 'Chaldaeans' (= Babylonians) in 1.6, the date of the prophet's activity is usually put in the last third of the seventh century. (Some exegetes arrived at later datings, e.g. in the time of Alexander the Great, by reinterpreting the Chaldaeans, Duhm et al.) If we see the book as the result of redaction or composition, then its completion, like that of the other prophetic books, can hardly be put before the time of the exile.

Bibliography

Commentaries see on 3.4: also Duhm 1906; Keller (CAT) 1971.

P.Humbert, *Problèmes du livre d'Habacuc*, 1944; J.Jeremias, *Theophanie. Die Geschichte einer alttestamentlicher Gattung*, 1965; id., *Kultprophetie und Gerichtsverkündingung in der späten Königszeit Israels*, 1970; P.Jöcken, *Das Buch Habakuk*, 1977 (history of research); C.A.Keller, 'Die Eigenart der Prophetie Habakuks', *ZAW* 85, 1973, 156-67; E.Otto, 'Die Stellung der Wehe-Worte in der Verkündigung des Propheten Habakuk', *ZAW* 89, 1977, 73-107.

Steuernagel, §134; Eissfeldt, §56; Fohrer, §68; Soggin, 3.VI; Kaiser, §22g; Smend, §35; Schmidt, §18; Childs, XXVII.

3.4.9 Zephaniah

The book of Zephaniah seems more coherent and more of a unity than the prophetic books which immediately precede it. The picture of prophecy which appears in it is in continuity with the great eighth-century Judaean prophets (Amos, Isaiah, Micah). At the same time we can also see that in its present form the book is the result of a planned composition which can hardly go back to the prophet.

Themes

Three thematic focal points emerge in the course of the book. First of all, invective against Judah and Jerusalem predominates (1.2-2.3). This section is stamped by mention of the day of YHWH (1.7,14 etc.). Judgments on other nations begin in 2.4. However, they are not separated in a self-contained group of texts, since in 3.1-7 there follows another saying against Jerusalem, in turn followed by a concluding saying against the nations (3.8). Next follow words of salvation (3.9-20), first for the nations (vv.9f.), then for Jerusalem and Israel. However, the division into three that is often proposed, which takes its guidelines from the book of Ezekiel, does not do justice to the construction of the book. It would be better to think in terms of a catena-like composition in which each section is linked to the preceding one, taking the theme further and developing it in a particular direction.

Composition

234

After the title (1.1), the book begins with the announcement of YHWH's **Zephaniah**
judgment on the whole creation (v.2f.). It is then focussed on a judgment on
Judah and the inhabitants of Jerusalem (vv.4-6), who worship other deities and
'do not seek (*biqqeš*) YHWH (v.6b). The phrase 'for the day of YHWH is at Day of YHWH
hand' (v.7) introduces the theme of this whole section (cf. Isa.13.6; Joel.1.15; →219, 224
Obadiah 15). It is developed in the alternation of words in the first person by
YHWH (vv.8f.,12f.,17 [18.3 third person]) and descriptions of the day of
YHWH formulated in an impersonal way (vv.10f., 14-16). The conclusion is
formed by an admonition (2.1-3) with the invitation to seek (*biqqeš*, v.3, cf.
1.6) YHWH before the day of YHWH's wrath (vv.2f.; cf.1.15,18) comes.

The sayings against other nations are composed of sayings against the →122f.
Philistine cities (2.4-7), against Moab and the Ammonites (vv.8-11), against the
Cushites (= Ethiopians, v.12) and against Assyria and its capital Nineveh
(vv.13-15). YHWH will 'stretch out his hand' (v.13) against these as earlier
against Judah and Jerusalem (1.4). Announcements of salvation for the
'remnant' of Judah who will receive back their possession have been inserted
at two points into these sayings against the nations (2.7, 9b). This makes the
juxtaposition between the announcement of judgment on the city of Nineveh Judgment on
(*'ir*, 2.15) and on the city of Jerusalem (3.1-7, *'ir*, v.1) all the more harsh. The Jerusalem
woe is directed against the city and especially against its officials, judges,
prophets and priests (v.3f.), who do their mischief 'in its midst' (v.3), while
YHWH alone is righteous 'in their midst' (v.5). Even the example of the
destruction of other cities has not led to Jerusalem 'accepting instruction' (vv.6f.,
cf.v.2).

The transition to the last section is made by invective against the nations Salvation for
(3.8), on whom YHWH will 'pour out his wrath'; this is followed by a word of Zion
salvation (vv.9f.). According to this, pure lips wil be given to them so that they
worship YHWH and sacrifice to him (cf. also 2.11). 'On that day' salvation will
also begin for Jerusalem. 'In their midst' (vv.11f., cf. vv.3,5) YHWH will remove
all the arrogant and 'leave behind' (*hiš'ir*) a humble people who will seek refuge
in YHWH and like the remnant (*še'ar*) of Israel will do nothing evil and live in
peace (v.13). There follow a brief imperative hymn (vv.14f.) which summons
Zion to rejoice becuse YHWH will be king 'in its midst', a promise of salvation
(vv.16-18) that YHWH will be its god and helper 'in its midst' and a two-part
promise of help against the enemy, the reunion of the Diaspora and the turning
of captivity (vv.19f.; cf.2.7b).

The composition has been worked out in many ways by means of Stylistic means
keywords and word repetition, through which connections within the
book have been brought out: the often and varied mention of the day
of YHWH (1.7,14); day of wrath (of YHWH) (1.15,18; 2.23); day of
distress, of oppression, of darkness, and so on (1.14-16); day of sacrifice
(1.8); day on which YHWH raises himself up (3.8); or simply 'that day'
(1.9,15; in the introductory formulae 1.8,10; 3.11,16; cf. 'at that time',
1.12; 3.19,20). Then there is what happens 'in the midst' of Jerusalem
(3.3,5,11,12,15,17); 'seeking YHWH' (1.6; 2.3); 'accepting instruction'
(3.2,7); 'worshipping' (1.5; 2.11; cf. 3.9f.); 'fearing' (3.7,15,16);
'visiting' (1.8,9,12; 2.7; 3.7); 'raising the hand' (1.4; 2.13); 'gathering'
(*'asap, kibbez*) in different contexts (1.2; 3.8,19,20); '(leaving a)
remnant' (2.7,9; 3.12,13; cf. 1.4b); 'turning the captivity' (2.7; 3.20),
the city (2.15; 3.1); the 'arrogant' (2.15; 3.11); *mišpat* ('right', etc.) with

various meanings (2.3; 3.5,8,15), etc. This shows that we have more than a combination of various units; on many occasions the choice of word has determined the composition. The consequences of these observations need to be investigated more closely (as also in other books).

The title (1.1) matches that in Hos.1.1. The long genealogy when the prophet's name is given is striking; it has been argued that the offensive name of his father (Cushi = the Ethiopian, the 'Negro', cf.Amos 9.7) is compensated for by the demonstration of his descent from King

Hezekiah; however, this remains sheer conjecture. The date is given as the reign of Josiah; the book does not contain any specific indication of particular events, but the nature of Zephaniah's prophecy suggests a date before the exile (see above). As a composition, however, the book presupposes the exile (cf. e.g. the 'gather' and the 'turning of captivity', 3.19f.).

Bibliography

Commentaries on 3.4; also Keller (CAT) 1971.

A.S.Kapelrud, *The Message of the Prophet Zephaniah*, 1975; G.Krinetzki, *Zefanjastudien. Motiv und Traditionskritik und Kompositions- und Redaktionskritik*, 1977; L.Sabottka, *Zephania. Versuch einer Neuübersetzung mit philologischem Kommentar*, 1972.

Steuernagel, §135; Eissfeldt, §57; Fohrer, §69; Soggin, 3.VI; Kaiser, §22e; Smend, §36; Schmidt, §18; Childs, XXVIII.

3.4.10 Haggai

The book of Haggai marks the beginning of the group of three post-exilic prophets in the Book of Twelve Prophets. The first two, Haggai and Zechariah, are associated by exact dating with the rebuilding of the temple in the years after 520.

The book of Haggai is divided into four sections by the dates it contains. Chapter 1 (the last half probably belongs to what comes next), 2.1-9, 10-19, 20-29. The introductory datings in 1.1; 2.1, 10, 20 (in 1.15

there is also a closing date) are all associated with the word-event formula 'The word of YHWH came through/to (the prophet) Haggai'. The narrative sections 1.2f., 12-15; 2.2 also belong to this well planned framework. It contains a number of prophetic sayings which are also sub-divided through further introductory and concluding formulae (for

the whole question see Beuken).

The dominant theme is the rebuilding of the temple. The arrangement of the book first of all brings out the role of the prophet Haggai in the

resumption of work on the temple: the first section (ch.1) reports how

his admonitory sermon (vv.4-8, 9-11 are expansions of the same theme) makes his audience 'hearken to the voice of YHWH' and fear him (v.12). He 'arouses' their 'spirit' by YHWH's promise that he will be with them (v.13), and so they begin work.

Here the exact designation of the audience is significant. Zerubbabel is addressed as the son of Shealtiel and therefore as a member of the house of David (1.12,14; 2.2; cf. I Chron. 3.17). Not only is Joshua given his title, high priest, but we are also told the name of his father, Jehozadak, the son of the last high priest from the tribe of Levi in Jerusalem (cf.I Chron.5.40f.; II Kings 25.18), who had consequently been taken into exile. Thus the two figures represent the continuity of the Davidic monarchy and the levitical priesthood. The population addressed is termed the 'whole remnant (*še'erit*) of the people' (1.12,14; 2.2); this doubtless takes up the frequent mention of the 'remnant' in the prophetic books (e.g. →223, 235 Amos 5.15; Jer.31.7; Zeph.3.12). That YHWH 'rouses the spirit' for work on the temple is reminiscent of Ex.35.29; 36.2, so here there is probably meant to be an explicit parallel to the building of the first temple (Mason). →142f.,175f.

In the second section (2.1-9), Zerubbabel, Joshua and the people are summoned, in view of the sorry state of the new building (v.3), to be strong and set to work (v.4, cf. I Chron.22.11-16; 28.10,20; also Josh.1.6f.), because YHWH will be with them (v.5; cf.1.13). This is followed by an eschatological proclamation of salvation about the glory Eschatological of the new temple (vv.6-9) in which YHWH will give salvation (*šalom*).   salvation Thus the last resistance to the building of the temple is overcome in the structure of the book.

A new theme emerges in the third section (2.10-19). The prophet is charged to give a priestly *tora* on the question whether cultic impurity Priestly *torah* is contagious (vv.11-3). Verse 14 gives the interpretation: 'this people' →98f. is unclean. This is often related to the Samaritans, but Koch and (independently of him) May have shown that the passage should more probably be interpreted in terms of the people themselves (cf.1.2). In →62 that case the continuation in vv.15-19 unconditionally belongs to it (for the new beginning with 'But now' [*we'atta*] cf.1.5; 2.4): from the day of the laying of the foundation stone of the new temple onwards YHWH will not only give the fertility which he has so far withheld (cf.1.6,9-11), but with his 'good pleasure' in the temple (1.8), with salvation (2.9) and blessing (2.19b), the impurity will also cease (Koch). However, this is hardly meant in a purely cultic sense: the beginning of the building of the temple was indeed already the sign of a new spirit (Childs, cf. Townsend).

In the fourth section (2.20-23), the eschatological trend of the book reaches its climax. The eschatological phenomena which have been foretold (2.6ff.) will begin (vv.21f.), and Zerubbabel will be YHWH's chosen king of salvation (v.23). This is the expression of a clear messianic →62 expectation which is connected with the person of Zerubbabel.

The framework of the book has given the words of Haggai a particular Dating shape and trend, but hardly altered their original intention. Therefore there is no occasion to put the composition of the book too far after Haggai's activity, i.e. beyond the year 520. Granted, there are manifest connections between the framework and the Chronistic tradition (Beuken), but similarly there are Deuteronomistic elements and echoes of the Priestly traditions in the Pentateuch (Mason). We should probably not seek to separate the post-exilic traditions too strictly, especially as they still need further investigation. One last reason for the dating of the book soon after 520 lies in the easy juxtaposition of Zerubbabel and Joshua and in the unbroken messianic expectation, focussed on Zerubbabel. In the book of Zechariah, slightly later, both these things have become questionable. (However, it is improbable that the book is an 'apologia for Haggai' which seeks to demonstrate his priority over Zechariah in taking offence at the building of the temple [Rudolph].)

Bibliography

Commentaries, see on 3.4. Cf. also Petersen (OTL) 1984.

P.R.Ackroyd, *Exile and Restoration*, 1968, 153-70; W.A.M.Beuken, *Haggai-Sacharja 1-8. Studien zur Überlieferungsgeschichte der frühnachexilischen Prophetie*, 1967; K.Koch, 'Haggais unreines Volk', *ZAW* 79, 1967, 52-66; R.A.Mason, 'The Purpose of the Editorial Framework of the Book of Haggai', *VT* 27, 1977, 413-21; H.G.May, ' "This People" and "This Nation" in Haggai', *VT* 18, 1968, 190-7; T.N.Townsend, 'Additional Comments on Haggai II.10-19', *VT* 18, 1968, 559f.

Steuernagel, §136; Eissfeldt, §58; Fohrer, §70; Soggin, 4.III; Kaiser, §22m; Smend, §37; Schmidt, §22; Childs, XXIX.

3.4.11 Zechariah

The book of Zechariah is the only one within the Book of the Twelve Prophets to contain a collection with clearly divergent parts. The datings in 1.1,7; 7.1 closely connect the first part (chs.1-8) with the book of Haggai and the rebuilding of the temple. The second part (ch.9-14) is not included in the datings. It is clearly divided from the first part by the title *maśśa'*, 'saying', in 9.1 and 12.1 and at the same time is further subdivided. These chapters are often called 'Deutero-Zechariah', although they do not have so clear a profile as Deutero-Isaiah. Occasionally this designation is limited to chs.9-11, and 12-14 are known as 'Trito-Isaiah'.

The first part (chs.1-8) is divided into three equal sections by the datings. 1.1-6 is prefaced to the whole section as an introduction, a call to conversion (v.3) which refers to the example of the 'fathers'. This example is initially negative, because they did not listen to the words of the 'former prophets' (v.4f.), and then positive, because they repented after the accomplishment of what the prophets had foretold. The post-exilic community is to learn its lesson from these experiences of the fathers.

The second, most extensive, section (1.7-6.15) contains a series of visions which are usually called 'Night visions' (cf.1.8; 4.1). The eight successive accounts of visions reveal a very marked basic pattern; they have partly been expanded by further sayings of YHWH.

1.7-15: Horsemen, 16f. word of salvation for Jerusalem taking up v.12; *2.1-4* horns and smiths; *2.5-9* measuring line for Jerusalem; vv.*10-17* expansion of the first three visions; summons to set out from exile (vv.*10-13*); hymn to the return of YHWH to Zion (vv.*14-16*), both with clear echoes of Deutero-Isaiah (cf. Isa.52. 1-12, also 48.20f.; 40.9) and the twofold formula, 'You (first/second person) will know that YHWH Sabaoth has sent me' (vv.*13,15*). Closing notice, 'Keep silent before YHWH' (v.*17*; cf. Hab.2.20; Zeph.1.7); 3.1-7 rehabilitation of Joshua; vv.8-10 supplementary words of salvation for Joshua; 4.1-5, 10b-14 lampstand and oil trees, inserted words of salvation for Zerubbabel (vv.6-10a); 5.1-4 flying scroll with curses; 5.5-11 evil in the bushel; 6.1-8 chariot; vv.9-15, appendix: a crown for Joshua (see below).

The visions are evidently composed as a consecutive cycle. This becomes particularly clear if we take the section about the high priest Joshua in ch.3 as an independent tradition (Jepsen), as here the characteristic elements of the vision account are missing. The remaining seven visions are a self-contained composition with a symmetrical construction (Gese, cf. Galling, Seybold). At the centre is the fourth (in the present collection the fifth) vision (4.1-14) of the lampstand and the two olive trees, i.e. the anointed, framed by a pair of visions which depict the outward, political liberation of Jerusalem (*2.1-5, 5-9*) and inward liberation from sins (5.1-4, 5-11); at the beginning and end there are two more visions which announce the intervention of YHWH in the history of the world (1.8-15) and finally set it in motion. Everything happens for the sake of Jerusalem (1.12,14; cf. 16f.). (Cf. the table in Gese, 36 or 218.)

The relationship between Zerubbabel and Joshua poses a particular problem. In 4.14 the two figures are juxtaposed as the two anointed ('sons of oil', thus without the word *mašiᵃḥ*). In 4.6-10a Zerubbabel is addressed separately and emphasized as the builder of the temple (v.9), whereas in ch.3 Joshua alone stands in the centre and is rehabilitated for his ministry in the temple (v.7) by 'YHWH who has chosen Israel'. According to 6.9-15, finally, Joshua is to be crowned (v.11), but a man by the name of 'Branch'(*zemaḥ*) will build the temple (v.13a with verbatim allusions to II Sam.7.13; I Kings 5.19, cf. Beuken) and reign; however, for the moment his crown remains hidden in the temple (v.14). This could be a veiled expression of messianic expectation with an eye to the Persian occupying forces. (Other exegetes think in terms of a disappointment in messianic expectations and the transfer of the functions of the ruler to the high priest; however, v.13 clearly tells against this.)

The third section (chs.7f.) contains a collection of prophetic sayings which is again dominated by the reciprocal relationship of judgment and salvation. The starting point is a question about the fast day in commemoration of the destruction of the temple (7.1-3; cf. II Kings 25.8). The question is first of all answered with criticism of the practice of fasting (7.4-7); its gist is continued only in 8.16f.: the enquirers are to do what the former prophets said, bring truth and right to fruition in their midst; then the fast days will become days of joy (8.18f.). Two groups of texts have been inserted into this framework: 7.8-14 contain a survey of history which depicts judgment as a consequence of disobedience to the words of the 'former prophets' (v.12; cf. v.7)

Salvation for
Jerusalem
→237

described in terms of Deuteronomistic theology. Words of salvation for Jerusalem and Judah have been collected in 8.1-15. Verses 1-5 are words of salvation for Jerusalem; vv.6-8 words of salvation for the Diaspora; vv.9-13 words of salvation in connection with the building of the temple, with clear echoes of Haggai (cf. Hag.2.15-19); vv.14f. words of salvation for Jerusalem and Judah taking up 1.1-6: YHWH's wrath at the fathers is turned to salvation. Finally, further words of salvation are added in 8.20-23; according to these, Jerusalem and Judah will be the eschatological centre of the world of nations.

Composition
Dating

The recapitulation of the introduction (1.1-6) in the word of salvation 8.14f. clearly shows that Zech. 1-8 in their present form are a well-considered composition. The basic material of the collection is formed by the visions of Zechariah, which by their dating in 1.7 are put soon after the appearance of Haggai (February 519). According to the introductory dating in 1.1 the activity of Zechariah already began some months earlier, so that he could still have been a contemporary of Haggai; the dating in 7.1 puts the sayings of chs.7f. a bare two years after the visions (December 518). The chapters do not contain anything that could not be explained in terms of these years. We cannot discover whether Zechariah himself was also responsible for the composition as

Person

a whole. The only personal details we have are the names of his ancestors (1.1,7; cf. Ezra 5.1; 6.14), who according to Neh.12.16 could have been a priestly family.

Chs.9-14

The second part of the book of Zechariah (chs.9-14) contains quite a variety of passages, the relationship between which is not easy to recognize. First of all there is a clear sub-division into two parts, each

maśśa'
→215

of which is introduced by the title *maśśa'*, 'saying' (chs.9-11; 12-14). There is also a sub-division into the sections chs.9f.; 11; 12f.; 14 (Otzen, Saebø; Lamarche differs).

Chapters 9f. begin and end with sayings against foreign nations (9.1-8; 10.11b-12). According to Otzen this is a chiastic circular composition: the victorious entrance of the king (9.9f.) - YHWH's victorious epiphany (10.11a); home-coming of the northern kingdom from exile (9.11f.; 10.6-10); battle against the enemy (9.13-15; 10.3b-5); 'positive' and 'negative' pictures of the shepherds (9.16; 10.2b-3a); 'positive' and 'negative' themes of fertility (9.17-10.1; 10.2a). The keyword 'shepherd' (10.2b, 3a) also provides a connection with ch.11; the

Shepherd
allegory

shepherd allegory here (11.4-7, with vv.1-3 as an introduction) contains a prophetic sign (vv.7,10-14) and historical allusions which are difficult to interpret (esp. v.8). (For the composition of chs.9-11 cf. also Willi-Plein.)

Final battle over
Jerusalem

In chs.12f., 12.2-13.16 first of all form a consecutive section which is shaped by the frequently recurring phrase, 'On that day (it will come about)' (12.3,4,6,8,9,11; 13.1,2,4). Here Jerusalem is in the centre, withstanding the assaults of the enemy (12.2-8; in vv.5-7 there is a strange contrast between Judah and Jerusalem), after which it is purified (vv.9-14; the identity of the 'pierced one' of v.10, the subject of the lamentation, remains obscure) by the outpouring of a 'spirit of compassion and supplication' (v.10). One aspect of the purification from sin and impurity (13.1) is the removal of 'the prophets and the unclean spirit' (v.2); according to vv.3-6 this evidently refers to an ecstatic form of prophecy which is regarded as being incompatible with the new spirit. Finally, the removal of the unfaithful shepherds (13.7-9; cf. ch.11) is part of the purification and cleansing of the people; two thirds of the people have to succumb, and only the last third will be YHWH's people (v.9b).

Chapter 14 contains a great eschatological description of the struggle for Jerusalem. In contrast to 12.2-8, here Jerusalem is initially drawn right into the suffering (vv.2f., cf. Lutz); it then becomes the eschatological centre of the world (vv.8-11), to which the peoples make pilgrimage (v.16), and in which even the most everyday things will be cultically pure (vv.20f.).

Thus ch.14 takes up the theme of the pilgrimage of the nations to Zion, with which the first part of the book of Zechariah ends (8.20-23). Here we can see a deliberate combination of the two parts of the book. Further cross-references can be seen, like the undisturbed security of Jerusalem (2.8; 9.8; 14.11), the 'covenant formula' (8.8; 13.9), the return of the Diaspora (8.7; 10.9f.), the outpouring of the spirit (4.6; 12.10), the removal of those who bear impurity (5.4; 13.2) and the figure of the powerless Messiah (4.6; 9.9f.). The addition of chs.9-14 has given the book of Zechariah a new eschatological dimension which goes far beyond the framework of chs.1-8 (Childs).

The time of the origin and collection of chs.9-14 and the combination of the whole book is difficult to establish, as the allusions to contemporary history which it obviously contains largely remain incomprehensible and our insight into the post-exilic situation as a whole is still too incomplete.

Bibliography

Commentaries, see on 3.4. See also Petersen (OTL) 1984.

On Zechariah 1-8: P.R.Ackroyd, *Exile and Restoration*, 1968, 171-217; W.A.M. Beuken, *Haggai – Sacharja 1-8. Studien zur Überlieferungsgeschichte der frühnachexilischen Prophetie*, 1967; K.Galling, 'Die Exilswende in der Sicht des Propheten Sacharja', in *Studien zur Geschichte Israels im persischen Zeitalter*, 1964, 109-126; H.Gese, 'Anfang und Ende der Apokalyptik, dargestellt am Sacharjabuch', *ZTK* 70, 1973, 20-49 (= *Vom Sinai zum Zion*, 1974, 202-30); A.Jepsen, 'Kleine Beiträge zum Zwölfprophetenbuch III', *ZAW* 61, 1945/48, 95-14; C.Jeremias, *Die Nachtgesichte des Sacharja*, 1977; A.Petitjean, *Les oracles du Proto-Zacharie*, 1969; K.Seybold, *Bilder zum Tempelbau. Die Visionen des Propheten Sacharja*, 1974.

On Zechariah 9-14: A.Jepsen, 'Kleine Beiträge zum Zwölfprophetenbuch II', *ZAW* 57, 1939, 242-55; P.Lamarche, *Zacharie IX-XIV. Structure littéraire et messianisme*, 1961; H.-M.Lutz, *Jahwe, Jerusalem und die Völker. Zur Vorgeschichte von Sach.12-18 and 14.1-5*, 1968; R.A.Mason, 'The Relation of Zechariah 9-14 to Proto-Zechariah', *ZAW* 88, 1976, 227-39; B.Otzen, *Studien über Deuterosacharja*, 1964; O.Plöger, *Theocracy and Eschatology*, ET 1968; M.Saebø, *Sacharja 9-14; Untersuchungen von Text und Form*, 1969; I. Willi-Plein, *Prophetie am Ende. Untersuchungen zu Sacharja 9-14*, 1974.

Steuernagel, §137; Eissfeldt, §59, 60; Fohrer, §71, 72; Soggin, 4.IV and VIII; Kaiser §22 n and q; Smend, §38; Schmidt, §22; Childs, XXX.

3.4.12 Malachi

The transition from the book of Zechariah to Malachi is surprising. After the eschatological battle over Jerusalem (Zech.14), there is now again a discussion of the problems of everyday life. Both aspects are

→74f. evidently concerns of the post-exilic community, so that prophetic sayings have been handed on to us about both.

Disputation
sayings
→120

The book of Malachi has a quite distinctive literary structure. It consists of six units clearly divided off from one another, all of which have the basic form of the disputation saying: 1.2-5; 1.6-2.9; 2.10-16; 2.7-3.5; 3.6-12; 3.13-*21*. Each begins with a saying of YHWH or of the prophet which is disputed by the conversation partners, thus sparking off the discussion (cf. Pfeiffer). In some cases the audience is obviously made up of priests (1.6; 2.1,8; cf. 3.3); however, it is hardly possible to use this to divide the book into a speech to laity and one to priests (thus Wallis; for the literary problems of the book see also Renker, 63ff.).

Sacrifice

The individual themes are: 1.2-5: YHWH's love for Israel shows itself in the contrast with his treatment of Edom; 1.6-29: the worship of YHWH called for is incompatible with faulty sacrifices. Here the critical questions to the priest are at the same time an accusation (1.8-10), which is contrasted with the behaviour of the nations towards YHWH (1.11-14); it is then followed in 2.1-9 by an announcement of judgment; 2.10-16: faithlessness towards YHWH is evident, as it was right at the beginning of the history of Israel, (vv.11f.) in the form of adultery. Here the discussion becomes an admonition (vv.15b, 16); 2.17-3.5: YHWH's judgment comes upon those who doubt this (2.17) and therefore offend against his will (3.5). Again we have the forms of the accusation (2.17) and the invective (3.1-5); 3.6-12; return to YHWH consists in the

Tithe correct provision of the tithe. Here the admonition (v.10a) is followed by an annoucement of salvation (vv.10b-12); 3.13-*21*: the doubters are told that the

Righteous and coming judgment will make a distinction between the righteous and the
unrighteous unrighteous.

3.22-24 are often regarded as additions. Doubtless these closing sections are meant to give a final overall interpretation to the book of Malachi. (According to Rudolph they serve as a conclusion to the whole of the prophetic canon, but that is improbable.) In v.*22* the cultic and

Tora of MOses ethical demands of the prophet are expressly based on the *tora* of Moses,
→155f.,163 i.e. on Deuteronomy. Verses *23f.* announce that the prophet Elijah will
Prophet Elijah come before the day of YHWH in order to provide a last possibility of repentance and thus of deliverance from judgment. This is directly bound up with the last disputation in 3.13-*21*. At the same time the

announcement of a messenger (*mal'ak*) whom YHWH will send before
the coming of judgment is taken up again (3.1); the messenger will be
Elijah!

We are told nothing about the person of the prophet. Even his name
is disputed. It is often assumed that this was an anonymous writing and
that the term 'my messenger' from 3.1 was later interpreted as a name
and put at the beginning; however, the form *mal'aki* can certainly be
understood as a proper name (perhaps as a short form of *mal'akiyahu*,
cf. Rudolph); moreover, the 'messenger' of 3.1 is interpreted in v.23 in
terms of Elijah.

The date of Malachi cannot be defined more closely. The existence
of the temple cult is presupposed. In 1.8 there is mention of the
governor, and this indicates the post-exilic (Persian) period. This is also
matched by the place in which the book has been handed down, after
Haggai and Zechariah. Finally, mention of the Torah of Moses in *3.22*
is a clear pointer to the tradition which is expressed in Ezra.

Bibliography

Commentaries, see on 3.4: also see Bulmerincq, 1926-1932.

J.A.Fischer, 'Notes on the Literary Form and Message of Malachi', *CBQ* 34,
1972, 315-20; E.Pfeiffer, 'Die Disputationsworte im Buche Maleachi', *EvTh*
19, 1959, 546-68; A.Renker, *Die Tora bei Maleachi*, 1979; G.Wallis, 'Wesen
und Struktur der Botschaft Maleachis', in *Das ferne und nahe Wort, FS L.Rost*,
1967, 229-37.

Steuernagel, §128; Eissfeldt, §61; Fohrer, §73; Soggin, 4.VII; Kaiser, §22p;
Smend, §39; Schmidt, §22; Childs, XXXI.

3.5 The History of the Composition of the Prophetic Books

This account of the prophetic books has shown that their present form
is the result of a shorter or longer history of revision and composition.
Here in most cases we can see more or less clearly the intention of
the final formation of the individual books. If we compare these
compositions in retrospect, we can see both basic common features and
also characteristic differences.

The most striking common feature is that all the prophetic books
contain announcements of salvation for Israel. In some cases (e.g.
Amos) evidently no announcements of salvation were handed down as
words of the prophet in question. Often the addition of these words is
regarded as a falsification of the original harsh announcement of
judgment. However, this is to misunderstand the purpose with which the
prophetic books were handed down. Their composition and collection
doubtless took place for the most part only after the catastrophe of 586.

The judgment announced by the prophets had therefore evidently come about. The preservation and handing down of pure prophecies of judgment would therefore no longer have had any point for the generations of the exilic and post-exilic period. (A purely 'historical' interest in prophecy is certainly unthinkable for the people of that time.) The prophetic books could only become significant again in a form which matched the changed situation.

→74f.

However, it is equally striking that no single prophetic book contains only announcements of salvation for Israel. The onset of judgment certainly did not mean that everything proclaimed by the pre-exilic prophets was out of date and finished. On the contrary, the post-exilic prophets specifically take up the 'former prophets' (Zech.1.4; 7.7,12), and the demands, admonitions and accusations of the pre-exilic prophets are resumed, repeated and developed. That means that in the tradition of the words of the former prophets the invective – in fact, above all the invective – continued to be seen as valid and therefore to have a message for the contemporary generation. However, it could no longer be understood as the announcement of an inevitable and final judgment. For not only had the judgment announced by the prophets come about, but it had also emerged that YHWH did not want to annihilate his people utterly. It was his intention to give them 'future and hope' (Jer.29.11). However, this hope for a saving future was now always within the perspective of the experience of judgment.

→239f.

→204f.

Words of
judgment
remain valid

Tension
between
judgment and
salvation

This tension between judgment and salvation stamps the prophetic books individually and the collection as a whole. This is clearly evident, for example, from the book of Isaiah. Here not only are the announcements of judgment by the pre-exilic Isaiah and the announcements of salvation made by Deutero-Isaiah in the exile combined, but in 'Trito-Isaiah', in a new approach, there is a further development of the tension between the demands and accusations directed at the present generation and the salvation which has already dawned with the return from exile, and which is moving towards its complete realization. Each of the prophetic books deals with this tension in a distinctive way. Right from the beginning, words of judgment and salvation were handed down from a series of prophets (e.g. Hosea, Jeremiah, Ezekiel), so that these beginnings could be developed further. In the case of the book of Amos, the announcements of salvation were evidently added only in the last phase of the history of its origin, whereas the actual composition of Micah is wholly stamped by the relationship between judgment and salvation. With the post-exilic prophets, announcements of judgment and salvation were combined from the start.

Eschatology

A further feature common to the prophetic books is that in their present form (apart from the book of Jonah) they all contain an eschatological element, i.e. they expect a future which is still to come when present circumstances will be changed or fundamentally transcended through the action of YHWH. In this respect the differences between the individual prophetic books are particularly great, because this element was present in different ways in the proclamation of the individual prophets. For example, in the book of Amos the **Composition History** expectation of the 'end' (8.2) has been interpreted by hymnic passages in an eschatological sense and has finally been given yet another →220f. interpretation by the closing words of salvation in 9.7-15. In Hosea, on →222 the other hand, the announcements of a new beginning are part of →216ff. the basic element of the prophet's proclamation, so that a basic reinterpretation was not felt to be necessary. The books of Isaiah and →198ff., 228ff. Micah in their present form contain very marked eschatological features, bound up with messianic expectations. In the case of Jeremiah and Ezekiel, the prophets' activity in the time after 586 has already produced →201ff., 208ff. an expectation of a basic change which has been further intensified in later work on the books. In some prophetic books (e.g. Joel, Zephaniah, Haggai, Zechariah, Malachi) the eschatological expectation is a basic element of the proclamation; in others (e.g. Obadiah, Nahum, Habakkuk) it stamps the present composition and thus governs the overall understanding of the book.

These common features show an understanding of prophecy in post-exilic Israel which is unanimous in its basic concerns. The prophets retain their fundamental significance by virtue of the fact that even Significance of prophecy for the present generation they proclaim the demand that both the community and the individual should live in accordance with the will of YHWH. The seriousness of the demand is intensified by the fact that the experience of judgment constantly remains present. At the same time the prophets are understood as heralds of a future salvation for Israel, indeed for the whole world and humanity. The way to this final salvation can once again lead through judgment and serious catastrophe, but the final goal is clearly indicated.

4 The Writings

The third part of the Hebrew canon contains the 'writings' (k*etubim*). The contours of this part are more blurred than those of the two preceding parts. It contains writings of very different character, the common feature of which is essentially that they have not been incorporated in one of the two other parts of the canon. It too was open for a long time, as is clear from the divergent order in the Septuagint.

There the book of Ruth follows Judges; Chronicles, the books of Ezra and Position in canon Nehemiah (as one book with the title II Ezra, which is preceded by the apocryphal book I Ezra) and the book of Esther come after Kings; Lamentations (Threni) is attached to the book of Jeremiah (or Baruch), and Daniel brings the series of major prophets to a close.

The sequence of the individual books also fluctuates in the Jewish Sequence tradition. Thus according to the Babylonian Talmud (Baba bathra 14b), the book of Ruth comes at the beginning of the Writings, probably because it is dated in the time of the judges. In some mediaeval Jewish manuscripts Chronicles comes at the beginning. However, the present sequence became established in the printed editions: at the beginning the group of the 'three great writings' (thus the Babylonian Talmud, Berakoth 57b), Psalms, Job and Proverbs; then the group of the five m^egillot ('scrolls', see 4.4) and finally Daniel, Ezra, Nehemiah and Chronicles.

English translations of the Bible usually follow the Vulgate, which puts Job before Psalms and Proverbs, and otherwise also contains the deviations in the Septuagint mentioned above.

Bibliography

Eissfeldt, §62; Childs, XXXII.

4.1 The Psalms

The book of Psalms (t^ehillim, 'songs of praise', LXX ψαλμοί) consists of a collection of psalms of very different genres from very different periods of the history of Israel. Many of them originally had particular functions in public worship in the temple in Jerusalem (e.g. hymns of different kinds, popular lamentations, royal psalms); others accompanied the cultic acts of individual Israelites (individual lamentations and thanksgivings); yet others are to be regarded more as religious poems without a particular place in the cult (e.g. individual hymns, wisdom psalms).

→99ff.

The book as it now stands represents the final stage of a lengthy history of collecting psalms. The main motives here have certainly been cultic and liturgical. A popular modern title for Psalms is the 'hymnbook of the post-exilic temple'. The parallel with modern hymnbooks is justified insofar as these too only contain the congregational part, and not the liturgical features of in the service which are performed by the priest or pastor, and that they too juxtapose hymns from very different periods. However, we can clearly see that the present final form of the collection is not only governed by liturgical considerations but also seeks to give a more far-reaching theological interpretation of the psalms (see below).

→78

Five books

The book of Psalms is usually sub-divided into five books: Pss. 1-41; 42-72; 73-89; 90-106; 107-50. This division is also orientated on the fact that at the end of the last psalm of each book there is a doxology which ends 'amen 'amen (41.14; 72.18f.; 89.53; 106.48), while Ps. 150 is regarded as the concluding doxology for the fifth book. However, this subdivision is not marked in the Massoretic text; it is probably a later tradition of interpretation in which the five books of the Psalms were considered in analogy to the five books of the Pentateuch (cf. Gese). But the sub-division is very formal and partly goes against other groupings of the psalms.

Following Gese, we can posit the following individual collections, though they are not all equally clear:

3-41	Psalms of David
42-49	Psalms of Korah (50 a concluding Psalm of Asaph)
51-71	Psalms of David (72 a concluding Psalm of Solomon)
73-83	Psalms of Asaph
84-89	Psalms of different guilds of singers (except 86)
90-107	Psalms of related content (105 [including 104.35 to the end] to 107 have the same introduction)
108-110	Psalms of David, with additional psalms introduced with *hallᵉlu yah* (111-118)
119	Acrostic (alphabetical) Torah psalm
120-134	*ma'alot* ('pilgrimage') psalms, followed by *hallᵉlu yah* psalms 135, 136 and Ps.137 with a similar theme
138-145	Psalms of David, ending with the *hallᵉlu yah* psalms 146-150

The individual groups are characterized in very different ways. Usually the groupings are indicated by common titles, but these are of very different kinds. The majority of titles are formed of names prefixed with the preposition *lᵉ*. The prevailing view (though it is often challenged) is that this denotes the author. (That this is the view of the final editor of the book of Psalms is clearly evident from the references to particular situations in the life of David in the title to Pss.3; 18, etc., see below.)

Seventy-three psalms are attributed to David (also to Solomon [Ps.72; 127] and Moses [90]); apart from this most of them bear the names of guilds of levitical singers who are mentioned in the books of Chronicles and who probably functioned in the cult of the post-exilic temple: Korah (Pss.42/43; 44-49; 84f.; 87f., cf. II Chron.20.19); Asaph (Ps.50; 73-83; cf. I Chron.6.35; 25.1f.); Heman (Ps.88; cf. I Chron.6.18; 25.1,4); Jeduthun (Pss.39; 62; 77, cf. I Chron.25.1,3); Ethan (Ps.89; cf. I Chron.6.29). In the latter cases it is uncertain whether these are the names of the actual authors; in the case of David (as in that of Solomon and Moses) this is very improbable.

Psalms 120-134 have another kind of title; they all begin with *šir ha-ma'alot*, which is usually rendered 'pilgrimage psalms'. This is a thematic group or one that is held together by a connection with a specific occasion. On the other hand, it is questionable whether we can regard the psalms introduced with *hallᵉlu yah* as an individual group.

There are also numerous enigmatic expressions in the titles which are probably instructions for the musical performance of the psalms (cf. Kraus, 'Einleitung', §4; Delekat). *šir* and *mismor* both denote a song, but presumably of different kinds, *tᵉhilla* a song of praise, *tᵉpilla* a prayer, *toda* a thanksgiving (connected with the thank-offering), *maśkil* perhaps an art song. The term *la-mᵉnazeᵃḥ* which is often used is obscure; it is usually rendered as 'leader of the chorus', etc., but that is quite uncertain. The numerous other expressions, which often occur only a few times, could contain references to musical instruments, melodies or other musical details; they are largely incomprehensible to us, as is the word *śela*, which often occurs at the end of a strophe or elsewhere.

The division into five books is based on existing subsidiary collections, since Pss.41; 72; 89 each stand at the end of a larger or smaller group. Moreover, in 72.20, after a detailed doxology there is the note: 'The end of the prayers of David, the son of Jesse', which will once have ended a collection of psalms of David. Another collection spills over this division: Pss.42-83 have undergone an 'elohistic' revision; in other

→16f.

words, the divine name YHWH has been replaced throughout (though not completely consistently) with the divine designation *elohim*. That is particularly clear from the comparison of versions of a psalm which has been handed on twice, 14 = 53; it can often also be seen elsewhere in the text. So this revision has covered the collections Pss.42-50; 51-72; 73-83 (with 84-89 probably as an appendix).

Some of the subsidiary collections predominantly contain psalms of a particular genre. Thus the psalms of the individual are predominant in Pss.3-41, 51-72, most of them lamentations; outside these two collections there are individual lamentations only in 77; 94; 102; 109, with a small group in 140-143. This can be a starting point for

Composition

observations about the composition of the book (cf. Westermann): at its beginning(42-50) and end (73-83) the 'elohistic psalter' predominantly contains community psalms, with psalms of the individual in the centre

→108

(51-72). However, this central section ends with the royal psalm 72, which evidently changes the 'private' character of the collection into a public one. (This is also suggested by the concluding doxology in vv.18f., with the 'amen' as the community's answer, cf. Gese.) As a result of the 'appendix' in 84-89 a further royal psalm comes to stand at the end of the section; here again it must be left open whether this is meant to conclude only the 'elohistic' collection (42ff.) or the whole collection including 3-41. Any answer given here must also take account of the position of two further royal psalms. Psalm 2 now stands before the larger composition which begins with Ps.3. Westermann assumes that

Framework

it corresponds with Ps.89, so that these two royal psalms serve as the framework for the composition made up of 3-88. However, in my view the next step of the history of the composition must also be included: in Ps.110 we again have a royal psalm which has particularly clear parallels to Ps.2: both speak of the king as the ruler of the world who has been appointed by YHWH himself. Psalm 110 is followed by the group of *hallᵉlu yah* psalms, 111-118, which here evidently serves to provide a solemn conclusion. Finally, the whole work ends with the great Torah psalm, 119, which again corresponds with the Torah psalm

Composition
Pss.1-119

1. Thus the two Torah psalms 1 and 119 frame the whole composition. At the same time there is a connection between the two royal psalms 2 and 110.

The major composition made up of Pss.1-119 is first followed by the collection of 'pilgrimage psalms' (120-134), which are clearly independent (cf. Seybold); they end with the *hallᵉlu yah* psalms (135f.) and the 'appendix' (137). The last group of Davidic psalms (138-145) again ends with *hallᵉlu yah* psalms (146-150). The principle of composition is

evident. One large (2-118) and two smaller compositions (120-136; 138-

150) each end with a group of *hallᵉlu yah* psalms; moreover the larger one is still framed by the two Torah psalms 1 and 119.

We can draw some conclusions from this for our understanding of the collection of psalms as a whole. First of all it is clear that the way in which it develops towards the praise of God in the *hallᵉlu yah* psalms determines the character of the whole collection; this is also expressed by the use of the word *tᵉhillim*, songs of praise (derived from the same root *hll*) in their title. Secondly, the emphatic position of the royal psalms is of great significance. They conclude subsidiary collections (72; 89) and provide a framework for the first collection (2; 110). There can be no doubt that at this stage they were understood in messianic terms: the praise of God is not only directed to the past and the present, but also includes the messianic future. In addition to this the surrounding Torah psalms 1; 119 introduce a further basic element: the psalms have become the word of God, which is to be read and meditated on again and again; like the Torah, they manifest God's will and show the right way to those who observe it (cf. Childs). Moreover Reindl stresses the wisdom character of the collection.

Overall
understanding

Messianic

Word of God

Wisdom

The titles which relate to particular events in the life of David (Pss. 3; 18; 34; 51; 52; 54; 56; 57; 59; 60; 63; 142) afford us an interesting glimpse of the beginnings of the history of the exegesis of the psalms (cf. Childs 1971). These are all events or contexts which are described in the books of Samuel. Here is evidence of a midrashic exegesis which relates particular texts to situations in the life of well-known people and thus enables the reader of the Bible to relive them. Here the concern is not with the royal side of the image of David but with the difficulties and dangers which he personally had to withstand. 'David the psalmist' here gives evidence of his weak human side.

→171ff.

It is hard to define the time of origin of the individual psalms and the various collections. We should reckon with the presence of very old elements in individual psalms, thus e.g. in Ps.*19.2-7*, which taken together looks like a Canaanite psalm, or in Ps.29, which is probably a rewriting of a psalm to the Canaanite storm god Baal-hadad. The royal psalms doubtless presuppose the existence of the monarchy, as is particularly clear in quite unmessianic psalms like the wedding song, 45, or the obligation to maintain a just order (101; cf. also 20; 21; 144); this also emerges from a liturgical text like Ps.132. So we must certainly presuppose the existence of pre-exilic texts. It is equally certain that some psalms presuppose the Babylonian exile (e.g. 126; 137), i.e. that they come from the post-exilic period. As we know little about the details of worship in the Jerusalem temple and as cultic procedures may well have remained unchanged for centuries, an exact dating is impossible in the case of most psalms. This is true to an even greater degree of the psalms of the individual, which are usually quite devoid of any feature by which they might be dated. The psalm quotations in the books of Chronicles could serve as a *terminus ad quem*; these presuppose the existence of a collection, as e.g. in I Chron.16.8ff., where passages from Pss.105; 96; 106 have been combined (including

Dating

→43

→108

→57f.

→285

Writings

→5

the closing doxology Ps.106.48, with the communal 'amen', cf. I Chron. 16.36). Therefore dating some of the psalms in the time of the Maccabees, an approach which was often argued for earlier, has now generally been abandoned.

Bibliography

Commentaries: Delitzsch (BC) 1859, ⁵1894; Duhm (KHC) 1899, ²1922; Kittel (KAT) 1914, ⁵·⁶1929; Gunkel (HK) 1926, ⁵1968; Schmidt (HAT) 1934; Weiser (ATD) 1950, ET (OTL) 1962 ; Kissane I 1953; II 1954; I/II ²1964; Kraus (BK) I/II 1960, ²1978; Dahood (AB) I 1966; II 1968; III 1970.
   B.S.Childs, 'Psalm Titles and Midrashic Exegesis', JSS 16, 1971, 137-50; L.Delekat, 'Probleme der Psalmenüberschriften', ZAW 76, 1964, 280-97; H.Gese, 'Die Entstehung der Büchereinteilung des Psalters in Wort, Lied und Gottesspruch', FS J.Ziegler, 1972; II 57-664 (= Vom Sinai zum Zion, 1974, 159-67); J.Trinfl, 'Weisheitliche Bearbeitung von Psalmen. Ein Beitrag zum Verständnis der Sammlung des Psalters', SVT 32, 1981, 33-56; K.Seybold, 'Die Redaktion der Wallfahrtspsalmen', ZAW 91, 1979, 247-68; C.Westermann, 'Zur Sammlung de Psalters', ThViat 8, 1961/62, 278-84 (= Forschung zum Alten Testament, 1964, 336-43).
   Steuernagel, §152-157; Eissfeldt, §63; Fohrer, §43; Soggin, 5.I; Kaiser, §28, 29.
   Cf. also the bibliography on II.4.

4.2 The Book of Job

At first sight, two different elements can be recognized in the book of Job: a narrative framework written in prose (chs.1f; 42.7-17) and a main poetic section, containing a dialogue between Job and his friend (3-37) and speeches by God with Job's answers (38.1-42.6). The relationship between these parts is one of the main problems of the book of Job.

Narrative framework

The narrative framework deals with the pious and righteous Job who, despite severe suffering as a result of the loss of his possessions and his family, and a severe illness, keeps his devout piety and is finally rehabilitated. Apart from a few short sentences (1.2; 2.10) he suffers silently. By contrast, the speeches of Job in the dialogue part are marked by lamentations and invective against God which are unique in the Old Testament for their profundity, acuteness and their often challenging statements. Both parts can hardly have been written together and at the same time. Rather, there is much to be said for assuming that the narrative framework first had an independent existence (some scholars, e.g. Hoffmann, doubt this).

→110f.

250

The narrative framework often used to be called a 'folk book'. In the meantime, however, its 'cultured and developed narrative art' (Fohrer) has been recognized and it has been termed a didactic wisdom narrative (Müller 1977). There is argument as to whether the narrative had its present form and present extent from the very beginning. Some exegetes assume that the two scenes in heaven were only added later (cf. Horst) or that the figure of Satan was inserted at a secondary stage (Fohrer) so that originally YHWH himself caused Job's suffering. The role of the friends also raises questions: in the last part of the narrative framework there is mention of a visit by Job's kinsfolk and acquaintances (42.11) which the preceding scene (42.7-9) does not seem to presuppose. It has been argued from this that there was originally no mention of the friends in the narrative (Alt) or that the visitors in 2.11-13 were primarily Job's kinsfolk and acquaintances who were changed into friends only subsequently, because of the following dialogue. By contrast, Müller (1970) sees the friends as having originally had the role of Job's tempters, a role which is now taken by his wife (2.9). However, the narrative can no longer be detached from its function as a framework, so that all such attempts at reconstruction remain hypothetical.

The main part begins with the dialogues between Job and his friends (3-37). Here there is a further sub-division. First of all there is the dialogue between Job and the three friends who were introduced in 2.11: Eliphaz, Bildad and Zophar (3-27). It is divided into three sets of speeches, each of which begins with a speech by Job to which the friends reply; the order of the replies changes each time. The first two series are carried through completely: I: Job (3), Eliphaz (4f.), Job (6f.), Bildad (8), Job (9f.), Zophar (11), II: Job (12-14), Eliphaz (15), Job (16f.), Bildad (18), Job (19), Zophar (20). The third ends in a fragmentary way: III: Job (21), Eliphaz (22), Job (23f.), Bildad (25), Job (26f.); Bildad's last speech is very short (6 verses). Zophar does not speak again. Whether parts of the text have been lost here or whether this is a deliberate move on the part of the author or editor (namely to demonstrate the failure of the friends' arguments) is disputed. Job again issues a great challenge (29-31, for 28 see below) in which he demands an answer from God (31.35ff.). However, instead of an answer a new section of speeches begins in which Elihu, who has not previously been mentioned, takes up and continues the arguments of Job's three friends (32-27). These speeches probably did not belong originally in this context but have a clearly recognizable function within the composition (see below). Finally Job receives his answer in two speeches by God (38.1-40.2; 40.6-*41.26*), each of which is followed by a short retort from Job (40.3-5; 42.1-6).

Dialogue

Three sets of speeches

Elihu speeches

Speeches of God

Other passages than the speeches of Elihu (32-37) are often regarded as additions: the song of wisdom (28), as an extension of the last speech of Job in the dialogue section (often parts of chs.26f. are also regarded as later additions: 26.5-14; 27.7-10, 13-23, and ch.24, cf. Fohrer), and the sections about the two great animals *bᵉhemot* (40.15-24, hippopotamus? or a mythical creature?) and *liwyatan* (40.25-41.26: crocodile?, but cf. 74.14) as additions to the second divine speech, parts of which are then often combined with the first (Keel and Kubina now argue against this separation).

Despite the literary tensions, the general pattern of the book of Job can be recognized clearly. The introduction (chs.1f.) tells how the

General pattern

→135
Job's lament

Accusation

Experiential
wisdom
→109ff.
→101ff.

→89ff.
Theophany

Crisis of
wisdom

exemplary pious man Job was made to suffer with divine consent but that nevertheless he did not depart from his piety nor did he 'sin with his lips' (2.10). (Here the reader is given more information than Job: he knows that Job's piety is being tested, whereas Job himself does not. Cf. Gen.22!) When Job's friends visit him (2.11-13), Job bursts out in a violent lament in which he curses the day he was born (3). Neither here nor in the narrative framework does Job ask for an end to his suffering, quite unlike the psalms of lamentation, to which otherwise there are close relationships in form (Crüsemann, against Westermann). So here the lament has another function: it is a protest which later intensifies to become an accusation. Job keeps stressing to his friends that he is innocent (6.24 etc.), above all before God himself (7.20; 9.20; 23.10-12; 27.2-6 and above all ch.31). Behind this lies the view that all suffering has its cause in sin ('the connection of action and outcome'). Because Job is conscious of no sin he sees his suffering as unjustified: God deprives him of his rights (27.2).

The starting point of the friends is the same, but they argue the other way round: if someone suffers, he must have sinned. They try to make this clear to Job with constantly new approaches and impress on him that his suffering is an indication of his sin (4.7; 8.5-7; 11.4-6 etc., above all ch.22). Here they do not simply argue from a dogmatic position, as is often claimed, but continually base their statements on the experience of many generations (8.8; 15.9f.,17f.; 20.4 etc.). Job's problem, however, lies in the fact that he cannot see the rule of this 'experiential wisdom' confirmed in his own suffering. He suffers without reason. Therefore he feels not only abandoned by God, as do those whose voices are heard in the psalms (Ps.22.2f; 31.23; 88.6 etc.), but also attacked and persecuted. God has become his enemy (6.4; 7.12; 9.17f.; 16.9-14; 19.6-12, etc.), so that Job can reverse the supplication in the psalms for God's care (Pss.6.5; 13.4; 25.16, etc.) and even say, 'Look away from me' (10.20; cf. 7.16; 13.21; 14.6,13). The decisive reason for this is that God himself no longer observes the right: he destroys innocent and guilty (9.22f.; 10.14-17 etc.). Therefore Job challenges him to stand trial (23.3-5; 31.35-37).

God's answer emerges in a theophany speech (38.1-42.6). However, it is no answer to Job's challenge – on the contrary: Job's limitations are shown up. In a long series of rhetorical questions he is made to see the infinite distance between God the creator of the world and himself (chs.38f.), so that his challenge can even seem absurd (40.1f.). The parallel second divine speech (40.6-*41.26*) endorses this yet again. Job recognizes that his whole speech was out of place (40.3-5; 42.1-6).

How one interprets the book of Job as a whole essentially depends on how one understands God's speech(es). Many exegetes see them above all as an answer to Job himself, whom God inwardly convinces by them, 'so that he finds the way to authentic and radical repentance before God' (Fohrer); or, he now 'knows that his fate has been transcended in the mystery of this God' (von Rad). However, we must also see them as an answer to Job's friends. According to the structure of the book they do not succeed in convincing Job (cf.32.3-5; 42.7-9), so that their conception of the righteousness of God, which is bound up with a recognizable connection of action and outcome, has proved untenable (Childs). Therefore they have not spoken 'rightly' about God (42.7), whereas Job, who has challenged this, has. This is an expression of the crisis of wisdom (Schmid) by which the whole book of Job is stamped. For Job, the rules of experiential wisdom are shattered on the reality of his suffering (cf. Crüsemann). However, no new rules are put in their place. What we have is a new knowledge (the root yd^c, know, appears four times in Job's answer in 42.2-4, and another four times at the beginning of the divine speech in 38.2-5, also in vv.12,18,21,33; 39.1f.): it is God's business, and not man's, to know the order of the world and the rules of divine action, so man is dependent on God's instruction (42.4).

This is also what is said by ch.28: man does not know (yd^c) where wisdom is to be found (vv.12f.), but God does (v.23). The chapter therefore certainly has a deliberately chosen place in the composition; at the end of the cycle of speeches, before Job's 'challenge'. It also says what is important for man: 'The fear of the Lord, that is wisdom, and remaining aloof from evil is insight' (v.28), precisely what the Job of the narrative fi imework did (1.1, cf. Laurin)! The keyword 'knowledge' (de^a) also appears in the Elihu speeches at the beginning of the first (32.6,10,17) and the fourth (36.3): Job speaks 'without knowledge' (34.33,35; 35.16; cf. 36.12) as in the divine speech (38.2) and in Job's answer (42.3), and towards the end Elihu as it were anticipates the questions in the divine speech about Job's knowledge (36.26; 37.5,7,15,16,19). Thus the speeches of Elihu have two functions in the composition as a whole: they form a bridge between the dialogue and the divine speeches by giving the positive example of a wisdom which is aware of the limitations imposed by God, and at the same time bring out the connection between wisdom and creation (Childs).

The end of the narrative framework shows Job in the role of one who makes a vicarious sacrifice for his friends (42.7-9) – as he did earlier for his sons (1.5). Then there is a brief account of his rehabilitation, which is in fact an improvement on his earlier situation (42.10-17). This conclusion seems remarkably inappropriate given the bitter arguments presented in the speeches. It has no specific importance in the narrative; along with 1.22; 2.11; 42.7 it is probably meant to indicate that Job passed the testing of his piety. (Abraham, too, goes home in Gen.22.19 as though nothing had happened.)

It is hard to define the date and origin of the Job traditions. We know of numerous Near Eastern texts which deal with the problem of the innocent suffering of the righteous in a variety of different forms. The earliest of them comes from Sumeria and was probably composed in 2000 BC; there are comparable Ugaritic texts which are closer to Israel in time and place; others come from Babylon and Egypt and there are also later Arabic and Jewish traditions. There are arguments over individual points of comparison (cf. Müller 1978, Lévêque, Gray, Preuss). However, it is interesting that even the biblical tradition does not designate Job an Israelite, but settles him in the land of Uz (1.1; in

Writings

→36, 175

Lam.4.21 it is identified with Edom). His riches are compared with those of 'the people of the East' (*bᵉne qedem*, 1.3), who also serve as a comparison for Solomon's wisdom (I Kings *5.10*). This clearly brings out the connection between Job and international Near Eastern wisdom.

Time of composition

→7ff., 134ff.

→211

It is impossible to define the date of the composition of the narrative framework. Job's way of life is depicted as that of a rich owner of flocks and herds – he might be called a Bedouin sheikh. There is perhaps also intended to be a parallel to the patriarchs, though this is nowhere spelt out. In Ezek.14.14,20 Job is mentioned along with Noah and Daniel as an example of the model righteous man; this similarly indicates a tradition which puts him among the great figures of the early period.

→125f.

→265ff.

The speeches section presupposes quite different conditions: Job was a well-respected and influential citizen of a city (cf.29.7-10, 1-25). The poem probably also arose in such civic circles of educated wise men (cf. Whybray). Here we might best think of the post-exilic period, in which Koheleth, too, was written as another example of the 'crisis of wisdom' which at the same time represents a crisis of social order (Crüsemann, Albertz, cf. also Lévêque).

Bibliography

Commentaries: Delitzsch (BC) 1864, ²1876; Duhm (KHC) 1897; Budde (HK) 1896, ²1931; Driver/Gray (ICC) 1921 (1951); Dhorme 1926; Hölscher (HAT) 1937, ²1952; Torczyner (Tur-Sinai) 1941; id. 1957; Weiser (ATD) 1951, ⁷1980; Fohrer (KAT) 1963; Horst (BK), chs.1-19, 1968; Pope (AB) 1965, ³1974; Hesse (ZBK) 1978; cf. also Habel (OTL) 1985.

R.Albertz, 'Der sozialgeschichtliche Hintergrund des Hiobbuches und der Babylonischen Theodizee', in *Die Botschaft und die Boten, FS H.W.Wolff*, 1981, 349-72; A.Alt, 'Zur Vorgeschichte des Buches Hiob', *ZAW* 55, 1937, 265-8; F.Crüsemann, 'Hiob und Kohelet. Ein Beitrag zum Verständnis des Hiobbuches', in *Werden und Wirken des Alten Testaments, FS C.Westermann*, 1980, 373-93; G.Fohrer, *Studien zum Buch Hiob*, 1963; H.Gese, *Lehre und Wirklichkeit in der alten Weisheit. Studien zu den Sprüchen Salomos und zu dem Buche Hiob*, 1958; J.Gray, 'The Book of Job in the Context of Near Eastern Literature', *ZAW* 82, 1970, 251-69; Y.Hoffman, 'The Relation between the Prologue and the Speech-cycle in Job', *VT* 3, 1981, 160-70; A.Jepsen, *Das Buch Hiob und seine Deutung*, 1963; O.Keel, *Jahwes Entgegnung an Ijob*, 1978; V.Kubina, *Die Gottesreden im Buche Hiob*, 1979; R.Laurin, 'The Theological Structure of Job', *ZAW* 84, 1972, 86-9; J.Lévêque, *Job et son Dieu*, two vols, 1970; id., 'La datation du livre de Job', *SVT* 32, 1981, 206-19; H.P.Müller, *Hiob und seine Freunde. Traditionsgeschichtliches zum Verständnis des Hiobbuches*, 1970; id, 'Die weisheitliche Lehrerzählung im Alten Testament und seiner Umwelt', *WO* 9, 1977/78, 77-98; id., *Das Hiobproblem. Seine Stellung und Entstehung im Alten Orient und im Alten Testament*, 1978; R.M.Polzin, 'An Attempt at Structural Analysis in the Book of Job', in *Biblical Structuralism*, 1977, 54-125; H.D.Preuss, 'Jahwes Antwort an Hiob und die sogenannte Hiobliteratur des alten Vorderen Orients', in *Beiträge zur alttestamentliche Theologie, FS W.Zimmerli*, 1977, 323-43; G.von Rad, *Wisdom in Israel*, ET 1972; H.H.Schmid, *Wesen und Geschichte der Weisheit*, 1966; C.Westermann,

Der Aufbau des Buches Hiob, 1956, ³1978; R.N.Whybray, *The Intellectual Tradition in the Old Testament*, 1974; E.Würthwein, 'Gott und Mensch in Dialog und Gottesreden des Buches Hiob' (1938), in *Wort und Existenz*, 1970, 217-95.

Steuernagel, §145-148; Eissfeldt, §64; Fohrer, §50; Soggin, 5.IV; Kaiser, §34; Smend, §41; Schmidt, §29; Childs, XXXIV.

4.3 Proverbs

The book of Proverbs proves to be a collection of independent parts each with its own title:

Collections

1-9	'Sayings of Solomon, son of David, king of Israel'
10.1-22.16	'Sayings of Solomon'
22.17-24.22	('Words of the wise')
24.23-34	'These sayings also (are) of the wise'
25-29	'These, too, are sayings of Solomon which the men of Hezekiah the king of Judah copied'
30	'Words of Agur, the son of Jakeh (from Massa?)'
31	'Words of Lemuel, king (of Massa?)'

The three major collections 1-9; 10.1-22.16; 25-29 are the easiest to identify because they all have the title 'Sayings of Solomon'. This fact puts its stamp on the whole book, which the title in 1.1 clearly attributes as a whole to Solomon.

→36, 175

In the introductory collection chs.1-9 the wisdom sayings have been collected into ten larger units which can be described as didactic discourses. The first important figure to be introduced in them is the wisdom teacher, who always begins his discourses with the words 'My son' (1.8 etc.). The second figure to appear alongside him is Wisdom herself. She gives public teaching (1.20-33): along with the second major wisdom discourse (ch.8) her discourse forms a framework around the discourses of the wisdom teacher in chs.2-7 (cf. Plöger, Commentary). This makes the first collection a programme for the whole book. This also applies particularly to the introduction (1.1-7), in which the central concepts of wisdom terminology are produced as the aim of the collection: wisdom (*ḥokma*), insight (*bina*), knowledge (*da'at*), discipline (*musar*) and, in a final climax, the fear of God (*yir'at yhwh*). The programmatic statement about the 'beginning of wisdom' (1.7) is repeated towards the end of the collection in a rather different form (9.10). It is preceded by Wisdom's invitation to a meal in her house (9.1-6); this is contrasted with the invitation of 'Lady Folly' (9.13-18).

Didactic discourses
→110
→110f.
→110f.

Lang divides up the didactic discourses as follows: 1.8-19; 2; 3.1-12; 3.21-35; 4.1-9; 4.10-19; 4.20-27; 5; 6.20-35; 7 (similarly Scott, Whybray diverges more markedly). Otherwise chs. 1-9 are often regarded as the latest part of the book, especially as Wisdom is personified (or even hypostatized in 8.22-31), a development which is supposed to indicate Greek influence. However, Whybray, Kayatz and others have pointed out the Egyptian background to this collection and have assumed that it was taken over and transformed in pre-exilic Israel.

The extensive collection of 'Sayings of Solomon' in 10.1-22.16 consists of a large number of independent individual sayings (375 in all). It proves very difficult to recognize rules or principles here by which the sayings have been arranged. In many instances there are, of course, echoes of keywords, or similarities of theme between adjacent sayings, but at most this extends over only a few verses, and it is almost impossible to recognize a comprehensive principle (cf. Hermisson, 174ff., on chs.10-15; Plöger 1971). However, Whybray (1979) has taken a decisive step towards clarifying the associations. He recognized that, in their present context, sayings which explicitly speak of YHWH often have the function of reinterpreting earlier sayings. Moreover, this means that the section 15.33-16.9, in which the YHWH sayings are concentrated, forms the centre of the collection 10.1-22.16. Here we have what
amounts to an exposition of a 'wisdom theology' in its briefest form. At the same time links with the context are clear: 15.33 forms the conclusion of a small group of texts which speak of instruction and discipline (vv.31-33). By contrast, 16.10-15 are concerned with the king, who thus appears as the exemplary 'man' (v.7) with whose ways God is well pleased. So 15.31-16.15 form a deliberately planned unit in the centre of the collection consisting of 10.1-22.16.

Here are some further examples of the process of the reinterpretation of earlier wisdom sayings by YHWH sayings: 15.17 is given a 'religious' interpretation by being prefaced with v.16: the fear of God is more important than human approval. (Perhaps v.16 also at the same time interprets v.15, thus forming a small group.) 18.10 not only interprets the following v.11 but contradicts it: not wealth, but only the name of YHWH, offers security. 19.20: human counsel ('eza) only endures when it is based on YHWH's counsel ('eza) (v.21). 'Wisdom' (14.1) is interpreted by 'fear of God' (v.2); saving righteousness (10.2) comes from YHWH (v.3). The formation of groups through YHWH sayings is shown in 16.33-17.3; 20.8-12 etc.

The collection of 'Words of the wise' in 22.17-24.22 contains to a large degree verbal parallels to the Egyptian teaching of Amenemope, above all in 22.17-23.11 (cf. Gressmann, text in *AOT*, 38-63; *RTAT*, 75-85; *ANET*, 421-4). However, the Hebrew text is shorter, and the sequence of individual sayings is much changed; nevertheless there can be no doubt of its dependence on the Egyptian model, so that here we can see the international interweaving of the wisdom traditions. At the same time, however, the interpretative revision by means of YHWH sayings is also clear: 22.2 has an almost verbatim parallel in the Egyptian text; v.23 adds a Yahwistic motivation (cf. also 24.17, 18 without an Egyptian model). A YHWH saying appears in the introduction (22.19), one in the closing section (24.21), and an invitation to fear God in the middle of the collection (23.17).

The third collection of the 'Sayings of Solomon', chs.25-29, which according to the title was made in the time of Hezekiah, again contains
exclusively individual sayings. Often, because of the different themes
and forms of the sayings, this is sub-divided into two parts (chs.25-27
and 28ff., cf. Skladny), but the reasons for this are not compelling (cf.
Hermisson, 76ff.; McKane, 10ff.), so that it is worth keeping the division
given by the title. In contrast to 10.1-22.16, the number of YHWH
sayings is far smaller. In 25.22 a reason for the preceding saying is added
which is reminiscent of 22.22f.; 24.17f. (see above); 28.5 looks like a
programmatic summary of vv.1-14; 28.25 interprets the verses before
and after; 29.25f. stand in the concluding part of the collection. (I
cannot find a place for 29.13.)

In the 'Sayings of Agur' (ch.30), in addition to the numerical sayings (vv.15-31)
there is a remarkable lament over vain striving for wisdom and a question about
the name of the creator of the world (vv.1b-4) which echoes Job. Verses 5f.
answer this with quotations from other books of the Old Testament (II
Sam.22.31 = Ps.18.31; Deut.4.2), which are here evidently already presupposed
to be sacred writings (cf. Childs). These words are again replied to with a prayer
(vv.7-9). The 'Sayings of Lemuel' in ch.31 contain an instruction of the king by
his mother (vv.1-9) to which the 'Praise of the virtuous housewife' (vv.10-31)
with its alphabetical structure has been added. It is clear that further texts have
been added here after the completion of the collection.

The conclusion of the book is less clear than its beginning. However,
the overall understanding is clearly stamped by chs.1-9, as can also be
seen from the interpretative theological work in the following collections
(especially in 10.1-22.16). We can leave open the question whether
some of the sayings were originally understood in a 'secular' way. They
are now dominated by the leading thought formulated in 1.7, that 'the
fear of God is the beginning of knowledge (i.e. according to 9.10,
wisdom)', and through this have been incorporated into the overall
context of the Old Testament traditions. However, the wisdom
traditions maintain their independence over against the 'law' and the
'prophets'.

It is only possible to give an approximate indication of the age of the
individual collections. The clearest indication is the reference to the
time of Hezekiah (25.1), and there is nothing against putting the
collection chs.25-29 in the time of the monarchy. In principle the same
can be said of 10.1-22.16. It is even evident here that the interpretative
insertion of YHWH sayings still makes use of the figure of the king as
a model (see above on 15.31-16.15); this presupposes the existence of
the monarchy. Given the Egyptian parallels it is also probable that
22.17-24.22 appeared in the monarchy. The arguments which were used
earlier to support a post-exilic origin of chs.1-9 have lost their weight,
so that there are no certain points of reference for this part and thus
for the whole collection. However, as with the majority of the Old
Testament writings we can assume that the final shaping took place in
the post-exilic period. (This seems certain for 30.1-9.) The designation

Proverbs
Hezekiah
collection

Sayings of Agur
→83, 108

Sayings of
Lemuel

Leading ideas

Dating

257

of Solomon as the author of the wisdom sayings collected here is fully in accord with the picture of the wise king that is painted for us by the Deuteronomistic history.

Bibliography

Commentaries: Wildeboer (KHC) 1897; Gemser (HAT) 1937, ²1963; Ringgren (ATD) 1962, ²1980; Scott (AB) 1965; McKane (OTL) 1970; Plöger (BK) 1981ff.
    E.G.Bauckmann, 'Die Proverbien und die Sprüche des Jesus Sirach. Eine Untersuchung zum Strukturwandel der israelitischen Weisheitslehre', *ZAW* 72, 1960, 33-63; H.Gressmann, 'Die neugefundene Lehre des Amen-em-ope und die vorexilische Spruchdichtung Israels', *ZAW* 42, 1924, 272-96; H.-J.Hermisson, *Studien zur israelitischen Spruchweisheit*, 1968; C.Kayatz, *Studien zu Proverbien 1-9*, 1966; B.Lang, *Die weisheitliche Lehrrede. Eine Untersuchung von Sprüche 1-7*, 1972; O.Plöger, 'Zur Auslegung der Sentenzensammlungen des Proverbienbuches', in *Probleme biblischer Theologie, FS G. von Rad*, 1971, 402-16; H.H.Schmid, *Wesen und Geschichte der Weisheit*, 1966; U. Skladny, *Die ältesten Spruchsammlungen in Israel*, 1962; R.N.Whybray, *Wisdom in Proverbs*, 1965; id., 'Yahweh Sayings and their Contexts in Proverbs 10.1-22.16', in M.Gilbert (ed.), *La Sagesse de l'Ancien Testament*, 1979, 153-65.
    Steuernagel, §143-144; Eissfeldt, §65; Fohrer, §49; Soggin, 5.III; Kaiser, §33; Smend, §42; Schmidt, §27; Childs, XXXV.
    Cf. also the bibliography on II.5.

4.4 The Five Megilloth (Festival Scrolls)

In the Jewish tradition the five books Ruth, Song of Songs, Koheleth, Lamentations and Esther are treated as a self-contained group because they are all used as readings on particular festivals. In the course of the festal year this produces the sequence Song of Songs (Passover), Ruth (Feast of Weeks), Lamentations (Commemoration of the Destruction of the Temple on 9 Ab), Koheleth (Tabernacles), Esther (Purim). This sequence is also followed in the usual Jewish editions of the Bible. In some mediaeval manuscripts, however, there is a chronological order. At the beginning is the book of Ruth, which is concerned with the prelude to the story of David, then come Song of Songs and Koheleth, which are attributed to Solomon, and finally Lamentations and Esther. The Leningrad MS, which is the basis for *Biblia Hebraica*, also contains this sequence, so that it has become usual in academic circles.

That the five Megilloth were only collected at a late stage is evident from the fact that the mediaeval manuscripts frequently have Ruth at the head of the Writings (as in the Babylonian Talmud, Baba Bathra 14b), while Esther follows Daniel. In accordance with this, at one point in the Babylonian Talmud (Berakoth 57b), the Song of Songs, Koheleth and Lamentations are named as the 'three minor writings', and Esther is mentioned separately after that. Once they were combined, however, the Megilloth were particularly valued, and in many manuscripts of the Bible and even in early printings they were put immediately after the Pentateuch, undoubtedly because of their use in worship. Hence their designation as *m^egillot*, scrolls: they were probably used in scroll form in the liturgy for a long time, as is still the case with the book of Esther. (Cf. *EJ* 4, 827ff., with tables.)

4.4.1 The Book of Ruth

Now that in modern times the biblical texts have also come to be appreciated as literature, the poetic art and beauty of the book of Ruth has been much praised (beginning, e.g. with Herder and Goethe). More recent exegetes have also recognized that in this apparently 'idyllic' narrative there are many allusions and references to questions and problems of which the contemporary readers or hearers must have been immediately aware (cf. the sensitive retelling by Gunkel). Thus the decisive section of the narrative (chs.3f.) deals with the legal questions of a levirate marriage (i.e. the obligation to marry the widow of a deceased relative, cf. Deut.25.5-10) and the associated claim to land. Another dimension to the story is that the person who is spoken of with such praise here is a foreigner (the Moabitess Ruth). It is also significant that a woman presented as a foreigner (Ruth the Moabitess) is the ancestress of king David (4.17-20). Finally, the narrative can be considered from a variety of ethical or religious aspects: as praise of the faithfulness of a widow (Gunkel, 88) or of faithfulness (*ḥesed*) generally, which is shown by all the main figures in the narrative, Ruth, Boaz and Naomi (Würthwein), or as a prime example of divine guidance (Rudolph, Hertzberg). How one understands the narrative generally depends essentially on the significance one attaches to its individual features.

The structure of the narrative is clear and obvious. According to Gunkel it is divided into four main narrative sections, each of which contains several individual scenes, connected by interludes and framed by an introduction and a conclusion: 1.1-5 introduction, Naomi's situation; 1.6-18 first chapter: Naomi's return, Ruth's decision for Naomi; 1.19-22 interlude: arrival in Bethlehem; 2.1-17 second chapter: encounter between Ruth and Boaz; 2.18-22 (23) interlude: conversation between Ruth and Naomi; 3.1-15 third main section: Naomi's plan and its implementation: 3.16-18 interlude: conversation between Ruth and Naomi; 4.1-12, fourth chapter: legal matters, Boaz inherits the land and Ruth; 4.13-17: conclusion, the birth of the descendant, the end of Naomi's misfortune; 4.18-20 genealogy of David. (Bertman has a rather different division, stressing the symmetrical construction of the story.)

To simplify matters considerably, how we understand the book can be reduced to the question how we understand the reference to David. In the present version this connection is emphatically stressed by the genealogy at the end, and it is made the focal point of the whole narrative. However, it is already made in v.17, so that the narrative would have no conclusion if this aspect were regarded as a later feature. (Consequently many exegetes conjecture that the original conclusion was suppressed by the redactor.) Thus many more recent critical exegetes maintain the originality of this context (e.g. Rudolph, Gerleman, Loretz 1960), albeit drawing different conclusions for their understanding of the whole work. Gerleman's argument that it is hard to understand how a later period could have invented a Moabite great-grandmother for King David, if the tradition knew nothing of it, is an important one.

Relationship to David In my view it is therefore most probable that from the beginning the narrative was focussed on David. The mention of Rachel and Leah (4.11) shows the importance of the context in the history of Israel; these women are not mentioned as the ancestral mothers of Israel anywhere outside Genesis. So does the mention of Judah's son Perez (similarly the offspring of a kind of levirate marriage, v.12, cf. Gen.38). Here the fact that the protagonists are models, and above all the divine guidance (not without human involvement), are important aspects of the narrative, which certainly (like most Old Testament narratives) could be told and heard or read with quite different interests (cf. also Prinsloo).

It is worth considering Gerleman's suggestion that the exemplary portrayal of Ruth and the detailed account of legal matters would have served to counter criticism of the Moabite origin of the Davidic dynasty. Less illuminating is the theory, often put forward, that the narrative set out to be a counterbalance to the prohibition of mixed marriages by Ezra and Nehemiah, because the religious problems standing in the foreground there are here *a priori* ruled out by Ruth's confession in 1.16f.

Genre
→86

→110

In genre, the narrative can be defined as a Novella (Gunkel, Witzenrath). Its didactic purpose is clearly expressed in the account of the exemplary figures and the happy ending, so that it can also be described as a didactic wisdom narrative. The age of the narrative is hard to determine. If the reference to David is an original ingredient of the story, there is much to be said for putting it in time of the monarchy (cf. Rudolph, Gerleman, but Vesco differs). However, the narrative does not offer any firm points of reference for dating.

Bibliography

Commentaries: Bertholet (KHC) 1898; Rudolph (KAT) 1939, 1962; Haller (HAT) 1940; Hertzberg (ATD) 1953, ⁵1974; Gerleman (BK) 1965, ⁴1981; Würthwein (HAT²), 1969; Campbell (AB) 1975.

D.R.G.Beattie, *Jewish Exegesis of the Book of Ruth*, 1977; S.Bertman, 'Symmetrical design in the Book of Ruth', *JBL* 84, 1965, 165-8; H.Gunkel, 'Ruth' (1905), in *Reden und Aufsätze*, 1913, 65-92; O.Loretz, 'The Theme of the Ruth Story', *CBQ* 22, 1960, 391-99; id., 'Das Verhältnis zwischen Rut-Story und David Genealogie im Rut-Buch', *ZAW* 89, 1977, 124-6; J.M.Myers, *The Linguistic and Literary Form of the Book of Ruth*, 1955; W.S.Prinsloo, 'The Theology of the Book of Ruth', *VT* 30, 1980, 33-41; T. and D.Thompson, 'Some Legal Problems in the Book of Ruth', *VT* 18, 1968, 79-99; J.-L.Vesco, 'La date

du livre de Ruth', *RB* 74, 1967, 235-47; H.H.Witzenrath, *Das Buch Ruth*, 1975.
Steuernagel, §92; Eissfeldt, §66; Fohrer, §36; Soggin 5.V; Kaiser, §18;
Smend, §43; Schmidt, §26; Childs, XXXVI.

4.4 2 The Song of Songs

The basic question in the exegesis of the Song of Songs is: How did a
collection of love songs come to be in the canon of holy scripture? A
broad tradition of Jewish and Christian exegesis answers this question
by means of an allegorical interpretation; the texts do not deal with the   Allegorical
love between man and woman but with that between God and Israel or   exegesis
between Christ and the church.

However, it is by no means certain that this allegorical interpretation antedated
the incorporation of the work into the canon. Sharp criticism from Rabbi Akiba
(c.AD 50-135) is reported of those who sing the Song of Songs in the taverns
(Tosephta Sanhedrin XII, 10, cf. Segal), so this evidently happened at that time.
The Mishnah (Tractate Yadayim III.5) hands down a rabbinic discussion about
the sanctity (i.e. the canonicity) of the Song of Songs (and Koheleth); here
again Rabbi Akiba declares against those who challenge them: 'All scripture is
holy, but the Song of Songs is most holy.'

In modern times the view has increasingly become established that   Love songs
these are indeed love songs. However, this view has been held in many   →81f.
varied forms. First it was argued that they are songs sung at a wedding
feast, for which comparative material was produced from Syria
(collected by Wetzstein in the nienteenth century, cf.Budde). Budde
believed the Song of Songs to be 'as it were as the order for a Palestinian
Israelite wedding' (XIX). The cultic mythological interpretation moves
in quite a different direction, seeing the Song of Songs as the reflection
of a *hieros gamos*, a sacred marriage, in which the sexual union of two
gods (according to the Babylonian tradition Ishtar and Tammuz) was
enacted cultically by a priestly couple (Haller, Schmökel). However,
this depends on a particular view of the adoption of Canaanite traditions
in Israel, especially of 'sacral kingship', which has now largely been
given up. Moreover, Schmökel had to transpose the texts of the
Song of Songs arbitrarily, in order to 'reconstruct' the course of the
hypothetical cultic festival. Finally, Müller wanted to emphasize the
mythical dimension of the love songs over against a purely 'natural'
interpretation of their lyricism. (Cf. the accounts of exegesis by Kuhl
and Würthwein.)
The most illuminating view remains that which sees the Song of Songs
as containing a collection of love songs. Here the largely predominant
view is that it is a loose collection without recognizable divisions.
However, it can be demonstrated that in its present form the whole
book is a very well thought out composition.   Composition˙

The framework is formed of 1.2-6 and 8.8-14. It contains the following elements   Framework
in a chiastic construction: 1. a declaration of love by the woman for her beloved   **261**

with the invitation 'Draw me after you, let us make haste' (1.2-4); this is matched by the conversation of the lovers at the end (8.13f.) which in turn leads up to the woman's invitation, 'Make haste, my beloved!'; 2. the metaphor of the vineyard (1.6b; 8.11f.) in which the woman herself is depicted as the vineyard; 3. associated with this, the speech of the brothers (1.6b; 8.8-10) who care for their sister but cannot prevent her welcoming her beloved. This framework is so to speak anchored to the centre of the composition by the invitation of the man to his betrothed, 'Come with me, my bride' (4.8), which corresponds to the invitations of the woman at the beginning and at the end.

One basic dividing line is provided by the woman's appeal to the 'daughters of Jerusalem'. It has a twofold function in the composition. On the one hand the phrase, 'I adjure you, daughters of Jerusalem', used four times (2.7; 3.5; 5.8; 8.4), each time marks a conclusion, so that the whole collection within the

framework is divided into four sections. 1.7-2.7 contain three conversations between the lovers (1.7f., 9-17, 2.1-3) and a final description of the love scene with words of the woman (2.4-7) which ends with the appeal to the 'daughters of Jerusalem'. 2.8-3.5 contain only words or songs of the woman; here 2.8f. and 17 correspond, and in 3.1-5 again, to conclude with, there is the description of a love scene which ends with the appeal to the 'Daughters of Jerusalem'; 3.6-5.1 begin with the description of a splendid procession of king Solomon (3.6-11) and are followed with words of the man: first of all a description of the beloved (4.1-7) and then further discourses and songs to the 'bride' (*kalla* only here in 4.8-12; 5.1), which end with a conversation (4.16-5.). The section 5.2-8 serves as a transition: this time the concluding love scene does not take place, so that the appeal to the 'daughters of Jerusalem' (5.8) is at the same time an introduction to a conversation with a double question-and-answer play (5.9-16; 6.1-3). 6.4-*7.10* contain descriptions of the beloved and love songs by the man (6.4-7, 8-10, 11f. [+ *7.1?*]; 7.[*1*] *2-6, 7-10*); in 7.11 the woman again speaks until the concluding love scene in 8.1-4, which again ends with an appeal to the 'daughters of Jerusalem'.

As well as serving as a dividing line the 'daughters of Jerusalem' appear at important points as conversation partners of the woman. In 1.5f. the woman says of her own beauty, 'Do not gaze at me', in 3.11 'Behold king Solomon!', and in 5.16, as a conclusion to the description of her beloved. 'This is my beloved and this is my friend, O daughters of Jerusalem!' This last comment stands in the context of the conversation which already begins with the evocative address in 5.8 (see above), so that here both functions of the 'daughters of Jerusalem' interlock.

Between the last love scene (8.1-4) and the final part of the framework (8.8-14) there is a concluding conversation between the lovers (vv.5-7) which contains

emphatic, reflective sayings about love ('Love is strong as death, v.6). This forms the climax of the love conversations and songs.

The structure of the Song of Songs can be presented like this:

1.2-6   Invitation to set out, vineyard metaphor, brothers (v.5 'Daughters of Jerusalem')

I   **1.7-2.7**

1.7f.		
9-17	}	Conversation of the lovers
2.1-3		
2.4-7	}	**Love scene** ('I adjure you, daughters of Jerusalem')

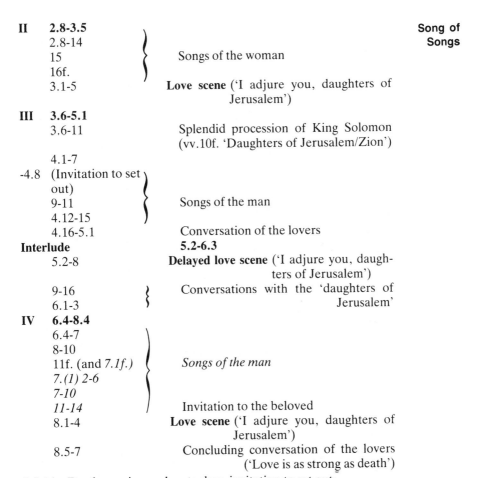

II   **2.8-3.5**
     2.8-14
     15   Songs of the woman
     16f.
     3.1-5   **Love scene** ('I adjure you, daughters of
                 Jerusalem')

III   **3.6-5.1**
     3.6-11   Splendid procession of King Solomon
                 (vv.10f. 'Daughters of Jerusalem/Zion')

     4.1-7
-4.8   (Invitation to set
        out)
     9-11   Songs of the man
     4.12-15
     4.16-5.1   Conversation of the lovers
Interlude   **5.2-6.3**
     5.2-8   **Delayed love scene** ('I adjure you, daugh-
                 ters of Jerusalem')

     9-16   Conversations with the 'daughters of
     6.1-3   Jerusalem'
IV   **6.4-8.4**
     6.4-7
     8-10
     11f. (and *7.1f.*)
     7.(1) 2-6   *Songs of the man*
     7-10
     11-14   Invitation to the beloved
     8.1-4   **Love scene** ('I adjure you, daughters of
                 Jerusalem')
     8.5-7   Concluding conversation of the lovers
                 ('Love is as strong as death')

8.8-14   Brothers, vineyard metaphor, invitation to set out.

There is a similar division on another basis in J.C.Exum, and another proposal in W.H.Shea.

This insight into the plan behind the composition shows that as a   Woman's song whole the Song of Songs is constructed as a woman's song; she has the first and last words and also plays the dominant role in other respects. Her conversation partners are always the 'daughters of Jerusalem'. Her beloved, who also speaks often (mostly indirectly within one of the woman's discourses: 2.10-14; 5.2), is described as a herdsman (1.7; 2.16 etc.) who comes from out on the mountains (2.8,17 etc.). He is contrasted with King Solomon, on whom the woman looks from afar   Solomon as a with the 'daughters of Jerusalem' (3.6-11) and whose many wives (6.8)   contrast figure and rich vineyards (8.11) only serve as a contrast to her one beloved (6.9; 8.12). (In 1.4,12, 'king' is a metaphor for the beloved.)

To begin with, it must remain open whether this composition is to be considered in purely literary terms or whether it was intended for 'performance' (with changing scenes and speakers or singers). It is hardly possible to understand it as 'drama', as used formerly to be argued, because there is no recognizable progress in the action and no inner development.

→108ff.

Finally, it is important to note that the mention of Solomon as its author (1.1) puts the Song of Songs in the context of wisdom literature, which is in fact attributed to Solomon (Audet, Gordis, Childs). How far that would alter the significance of the love songs is hard to see. The reflective conclusion in 8.6f. suggests that the sayings about love have been generalized after the fashion of wisdom. It remains striking that in the Song of Songs the initiative to love largely begins from the woman; this contrasts with the patriarchal structure of Israelite society (Crüsemann).

Origin

Little can be said about the origin and age of the individual songs and about the composition as a whole. Linguistic peculiarities suggest that the final form is post-exilic, but its affinity to pre-Israelite Canaanite traditions has also been stressed (e.g. Loretz). Perhaps we might suppose that the individual songs underwent a long history of tradition before they were finally collected in the post-exilic period and made into a composition. In this final version the Song of Songs cannot be counted as court wisdom (thus e.g. Gerleman), and the content, which largely presupposes a country milieu, also tells against this. However, the 'daughters of Jerusalem' and the description of the city (e.g. 3.2f.; 5.7) show that the final version is related to Jerusalem.

Bibliography

Commentaries: Budde (KHC) 1898; Haller (HAT) 1940; Gordis, 1954, ²1974: Ringgren (ATD) 1958, ³1981; Rudolph (KAT) 1962; Robert/Tournay/Feuillet 1963; Gerleman (BK) 1965, ²1981; Würthwein (HAT²) 1969; Pope (AB) 1977.

J.-P.Audet, 'Le sens du Cantique des Cantiques', *RB* 62, 1955, 197-221; F.Crüsemann/H.Thyen, *Als Mann und Frau geschaffen*, 1978 (esp.81-91); J.C.Exum, 'A Literary and Structural Analysis of the Song of Songs', *ZAW* 85, 1973, 47-79; P.Haupt, *Biblische Liebeslieder. Das sogenannte Hohelied Salomos*, 1907; F.Horst, 'Die Formen des althebräischen Liebesliedes' (1935), in *Gottes Recht*, 1961, 176-87; C.Kuhl, 'Das Hohelied und seine Deutung', in *TR* NF 9, 1937, 137-67 (account of scholarship); O.Loretz, *Das althebräische Liebeslied*, 1971; H.-P. Müller, 'Die lyrische Reproduction des Mythischen im Hohenlied', *ZTK* 73, 1976, 23-41; H.H.Rowley, 'The Interpretation of the Song of Songs' (1937), in *The Servant of the Lord*, ²1965, 195-245; H.Schmökel, *Heilige Hochzeit und Hoheslied*, 1956; M.H.Segal, 'The Song of Songs', *VT* 12, 1962, 470-90; W.H.Shea, 'The Chiastic Structure of the Song of Songs', *ZAW* 92, 1980, 378-90; E.Würthwein, 'Zum Verständnis des Hohenliedes', *TR* NF 32, 1967, 177-212 (account of scholarship).

Steuernagel, §160-161; Eissfeldt, §67; Fohrer, §45; Soggin, 5.VI; Kaiser, §31; Smend, §44; Schmidt, §26; Childs, XXXVII.

4.4.3 Koheleth (Ecclesiastes)

The book of Koheleth (for the name see below) is part of the wisdom literature. It reflects the crisis of wisdom which is evident also in other ways in the book of Job. In contrast to Job, however, Koheleth copes with this crisis exclusively in the form of reflection, without God himself being addressed or speaking.

→252f.

Koheleth comes close to Proverbs in that it contains a large number of individual sayings and there is no obvious progression of thought within the book. This has been particularly stressed by Galling (1932), who initially (1940) divided the book into thirty-seven 'sentences', which he later (1969) reduced to twenty-seven. However, a clear difference from the book of Proverbs lies in the fact that these 'sentences' are more extensive than the short sayings collected in the latter and that they often contain recognizable patterns of argument from which the reflective character of the book becomes clear (cf. also Zimmerli 1974).

→258ff.
Individual
sayings

Many exegetes have tried to mark out larger units and identify a division in the book, but so far no agreement has been reached. (There are tables of conjectures in Ellermeier [131ff.] and Wright [315ff.].) A new approach is evident in Castellino and Wright, who see the regularly recurring, almost stereotyped phrases as dividing lines. The concluding formula 'All (or: This) is vanity and a striving after wind' appears nine times in the section 1.12-6.9 (1.14,15; 2.11,17,26; 4.4,6,16; 6.9), but not again after that. Wright sees the phrase 'Man cannot (or: Who can) discover it' (7.14,24; 8.17; cf. 7.25-29) and the statement that man 'does not know' (9.1.5,10,12; 10.14,15; 11.2,5,6) as dividing lines.

On the basis of the illuminating suggestion by Wright, the book can be divided as follows:

Division

	1.1	Title
	1.2-11	Poems about vain toil
I.	1.12-6.9	Critical investigation of human life. Overriding tenor: 'All is vanity and a striving after wind' Sub-divisions: 1.12-15, 16-18 (double introduction); 2.1-11, 12-17, 18-26; 3.1-4.6; 4.7-16; 4.17-6.9
II.	6.10-11.6	Consequences
	6.10-12	Introduction
A	7.1-8.17	Man cannot discover what it is good for him to do. Sub-divisions: 7.1-14, 15-24, 25-29; 8.1-17.
B	9.1-11.6	Man does not know what will come after him Sub-divisions: 9.1-6, 7-10, 11f.; 9.13-10.15; 10.16-11.2; 11.3-6
	11.7-12.8	Poem on youth and old age
	12.9-14	Epilogue

Certainly other divisions are conceivable (cf. the commentaries). Here a more exact investigation of particular keywords could produce yet further clarification. Thus for example the word *'amal*, 'toil' (noun or verb) occurs only in the first part (noun and verb together twenty-nine times as opposed to five

Keywords

times in the second part), while the word-group *ra'/ra'a*, 'bad, evil', dominates the second part. The words derived from the root *ḥakam*, 'be wise', appear in the first part only in chs.1f. (apart from 6.8), while they are widespread in the second part, etc. The structures of the individual units also need closer investigation (see the tables in Ellermeier, 66ff.).

Crisis of wisdom

In Koheleth as in Job, the crisis of wisdom has its roots above all in the insight that men do not understand the action of God and cannot know the divine plans. However, the reaction here is fundamentally different. Koheleth is not curious, but takes this fact for granted. As compared with traditional wisdom we find here a profound resignation. However, the basic presuppositions are never put in question: the 'omnipotence' of God is fully recognized (3.14), though man may not be able to understand his work (v.11), because God is in heaven and man is on earth (5.1). One can even say that Koheleth draws his **Consequences** conclusions from Job and occupies the position of author of Job as it is **of Job** expressed in the divine speeches (Crüsemann 1980). The consequence **Fear of God** of this is a summons to the fear of God (3.14; 7.18; 8.12f.; 12.13, cf. Gese). To this degree Koheleth is not a sceptic, as is often said (cf. Klopfenstein). The basis for his often-repeated comment that there is nothing better for man to do than enjoy life (2.24; 3.12f., 22; 8.15) is always that this has been given him by God.

However, Koheleth's resignation also has features which could be described as cynical. He speaks from the perspective of a well-to-do class (e.g. 2.4ff.) for whom money is as important as wisdom (7.11f.), indeed for whom having money is everything (10.19). Here we have a **→75** reflection of the situation in the Hellenistic period (Crüsemann 1979, Müller). A late dating for the book follows from the language, which already shows clear echoes of the post-biblical Hebrew of the Mishnah. The influence of Hellenistic philosophy on the author has often been assumed (cf. Hengel, Braun), but so too has Egyptian and Babylonian influence (cf. Loretz); however, this remains disputed. Without doubt **→108ff.** a critical attachment to the traditions of Israelite wisdom is the dominant factor.

Name *qohelet* There is no obvious explanation of the name *qohelet*. We should probably understand it as the designation of a function in an assembly (*qahal*), e.g. leader of the congregation, etc. In 1.12 the author clothes his discourse in the garb of a 'royal testament'; the title has extended **→34ff., 175ff.** this and designated him 'son of David' (1.1), doubtless an allusion to Solomon. This puts the book emphatically in the context of wisdom literature. This is also suggested by the epilogue (12.9-14), in which Koheleth is described as a wise man (*ḥakam*) (v.9), and fear of God and the keeping of the commandments are mentioned in a summary (v.13). Here we have a more comprehensive understanding of wisdom **→75, 110f.** that connects it with the Torah, in a way which then developed in post-biblical wisdom (cf. Sheppard).

Commentaries: Delitzsch (BC) 1875; Wildeboer (KHC) 1898; Siegfried (HK) 1898; Hertzberg (KAT) 1932, 1963; Galling (HAT) 1940, ²1969; Zimmerli (ATD) 1962, ²1980; Scott (AB) 1965; Lautha (BK) 1978.

R.Braun, *Kohelet und die frühhellenistische Popularphilosophie*, 1973; G.R.Castellino, 'Qohelet and his Wisdom', *CBQ* 30, 1968, 15-28; F.Crüsemann, 'Die unveränderbare Welt. Überlegungen zu Krisis der Weisheit beim Prediger (Kohelet)', in W.Schottroff/W.Stegemann (eds.), *Der Gott der kleinen Leute. Sozialgeschichtliche Auslegungen* I, 1979, 80-104; id., 'Hiob und Kohelet', in *Werden und Wirken des Alten Testaments, FS C.Westermann*, 1980, 373-93; F.Ellermeier, *Qohelet I, 1*, 1967; K.Galling, 'Kohelet-Studien', *ZAW* 50, 1932, 276-99; H.Gese, 'Die Krisis der Weisheit bei Kohelet' (1963), in *Vom Sinai zum Zion*, 1974, 168-79; H.L.Ginsberg, 'The Stucture and Contents of the Book of Koheleth', *SVT* 3, 1955, 138-49; M.Hengel, *Judaism and Hellenism*, ET 1974, I, 115-30; M.A.Klopfenstein, 'Die Skepsis des Qohelet', *TZ* 28, 1972, 97-109; O.Loretz, *Qohelet und der Alte Orient*, 1964; H.-P.Müller, 'Neige der althebräische Weisheit. Zum Denken Qohäläts', *ZAW* 90, 1978, 238-64; G.von Rad, *Wisdom in Israel*, ET 1972; H.H.Schmid, *Wesen und Geschichte der Weisheit*, 1966; G.T.Sheppard, 'The Epilogue to Qoheleth as Theological Commentary', *CBQ* 39, 1977, 182-9; A.G.Wright, 'The Riddle of the Sphinx: The Structure of the Book of Qoheleth', *CBQ* 30, 1968, 313-34 (= J.L.Crenshaw [ed.], *Studies in Ancient Israelite Wisdom*, 1976, 245-66); W.Zimmerli, 'Das Buch Kohelet – Traktat oder Sentenzensammlung?', *VT* 24, 1974, 221-30.

Steuernagel, §149-51; Eissfeldt, §68; Fohrer, §51; Soggin, 5.VI; Kaiser, §35; Smend, §45; Schmidt, §28; Childs, XXXVIII.

4.4 Lamentations (Threni)

The book of Lamentations (Threni) contains a collection of five independent songs which are connected by the dominant element of lamentation. The basis of the lamentation is the destruction of Jerusalem and the temple with all its catastrophic effects on the people involved.

Lamentation over Jerusalem

In details there are considerable differences between the five songs (which correspond to the chapter divisions). That is even true of the people who speak in them. In the first, second and fourth songs there is a pictorial, narrative lament over Jerusalem without any indication of the person of the speaker or poet: in the second song Jerusalem is addressed and summoned to lament; in the first, Jerusalem itself speaks in more detail. In the third song we have much more in the first person singular, but there is no indication of identity; in the fifth song the first person plural of the suppliant community is predominant.

By genre, the fifth song is a popular lament and shows a close affinity to similar psalms. The rest of the songs cannot be clearly assigned to a genre which appears anywhere else. The first, second and fourth songs are stamped with elements from the lament for the dead; this is already evident from the 'How' (*'eka*, cf. II Sam. 1.19,25,27; Isa.1.21, etc.) which introduces the lament and from the characteristic *qina* metre.

Popular lament
→101f.
Lament for the dead
→81f.

However, one difference from the lament for the dead is that here Jerusalem/Zion or its inhabitants themselves lament, or are depicted as lamenting and mourning (in contrast to e.g. Amos 5.1f.; but cf. the raising of the general lament for the dead in Amos 5.16). Thus elements of the genres have been used in a derivative way. The third song begins as an individual lament, but it does contain elements of other genres (see below).

→119f.

→101f.

Acrostic form   A characteristic feature of the lamentations is that each of the first four songs has an alphabetical acrostic, i.e. the twenty-two strophes each begin with a letter of the alphabet, and in the third, even all three lines of each strophe do this. (In the second, third and fourth songs the sequence of ʿ and p is transposed.) Perhaps the fifth song, which does not have an acrostic, has twenty-two verses for the same reason. (Bergler wants to see a word-acrostic here in which the initial letters of the lines produce a saying.) However, this peculiarity does not allow us to draw any particular conclusions about the lamentations, as we also find the acrostic form in psalms of quite varied genres.

The five songs form a self-contained group, so that it seems likely that they also have a common Sitz im Leben. One frequent suggestion is the ceremonies of lamentation mentioned in Zech.7.3,5; 8.19, but we know nothing about them. On the basis of a Sumerian parallel Kraus assumes a common genre for all the songs, the 'lament over the destroyed sanctuary' (but cf. McDaniel 1968); however, the marked differences of genre between the individual songs do not support this assumption. Rather, they show that the authors of these lamentations have agonized over the situation after the destruction of Jerusalem and the temple from quite different perspectives (cf. Lanahan). There is nothing against the assumption that these various songs were also sung together within a festival of lamentation.

Ceremonies of
lamentation
→239f.

The first song laments the fate of the city of Jerusalem, which is depicted as a widow; it is permeated by the key phrase 'She has no comforter' (1.2,9,17; vv.16,21 in the first person). In vv.9b, 11b, Zion itself speaks with the petition 'Behold, YHWH' (cf. v.20), and vv.12-16, 18-22 are formulated throughout as a lamentation of Zion. In both parts there is emphatic mention of the sin of Jerusalem as the reason for her fate (vv.5 [cf.12], 8, 14,22). The depiction of the destruction, which is seen as a consequence of the divine wrath (vv.1ff., cf.1.12), dominates the second song; in vv.13-17 Zion is addressed and in vv.18f. called on to lament; this lamentation then follows in vv.20-22 (again beginning with the petition 'Behold, YHWH!', v.20); the saying about the day of wrath (v.22) refers back to the beginning (v.1). The third song depicts the catastrophic situation in the destroyed city and like chs.1f. speaks of the sin of Jerusalem (v.6) and its ministers (v.13) and of the wrath of YHWH (v.11, cf.v.16); in vv.21f. there is an announcement of a change in the fates of Edom and Zion. The whole of the fifth song is a prayer of the people, beginning with 'Remember, YHWH, look and see' (v.1, cf. 1.9,11,20; 2.20). Here too the description of the misery is bound up with the confession of sin (vv.7,16). The prayer ends with the confession of the eternal reign of God (v.19) and a petition for a final restoration (vv.20-22, cf. Gordis).

→57

The third song remains difficult to understand. Here first of all an individual raises a lament (vv.1-18) reminiscent of the Confessions of Jeremiah and Job;

→204, 252
268

this leads, via a summons to 'remember' (vv.19-21), to stereotyped confessions of faith in the unchanging grace and faithfulness of God (vv.22-24). Wisdom statements are attached (vv.25-36) which in turn end in a confession of faith in God the Creator (vv.37-39, cf. Ps.33.9). (Verse 39 echoes the argumentation in the speeches of God in the book of Job, but the text is hard to understand.) In vv.40-47 there follows a lamentation of the people, and in vv.48-66 again the prayer of an individual; it moves from a lament (vv.48-51) to an account of deliverance, so that vv.52-59 are to be regarded as a thanksgiving (with the account of the 'oracle of salvation' in v.57). In vv.59-66 this again turns to lamentation and petition (against the 'enemies', as often in the psalms of lamentation). The chapter looks almost like an independent liturgy; some exegetes, however, regard it as a literary text which makes use of liturgical elements.

The person of the speaker in the third song remains obscure. The alternation between the first person singular and first person plural within the chapter shows that he is to be understood as a representative of the people. Thus the position of this chapter in the centre of the collection is certainly intentional, as is the position of the credal strophes vv.22-24, 37-39, 55-57. At the same time the 'I', who remains anonymous, sounds like a representative (or vicarious) sufferer such as we also find in the suffering servant of Isa.53. Here the tradition has evidently also seen the proximity to Jeremiah (which is also a chronological one); perhaps the author of the chapter even had him in mind (Rudolph), or at least the image of the suffering prophet as depicted in the book of Jeremiah.

Jewish tradition sees Jeremiah as the author of Lamentations (cf. the Babylonian Talmud, Baba bathra 15a; there the Lamentations are called *qinot*, but in later Jewish tradition and in editions of the Bible they are called *'eka* after the first word); the Septuagint also already has a similar introduction. More recent exegetes tend to attribute these songs to different authors. The time of their composition is predominantly put in the years after the destruction of the temple in 586. (According to Rudolph, ch.1 was already written shortly after 597, chs. 2-4 immediately after 586, and chs.3,5 somewhat later.) McDaniel even regards the language of the book as 'pre-exilic' (despite the book's origin in the exile), while Kaiser dates the individual songs in the fifth and fourth centuries. In my view there is everything to suggest a dating before the end of the exile, as there is nowhere any indication of a basic shift (as generally in the prophetic books). It is important to note here that a variety of direct and indirect references to other Old Testament texts can be recognized (Albrektson stresses in particular the references to the Zion tradition); Lamentations is evidence of a reaction to the catastrophe of 586 with the resources of, and against the background of, the religious tradition.

Brunet puts forward quite a different view. He sees Lamentations as the work of nationalistic circles in Jerusalem hostile to Jeremiah during the last twenty-seven days before the final occupation and destruction of Jerusalem (cf. II Kings 25.3,8).

Koheleth

→252

→102

→102f.

'I' and 'We'

195

→206

Author

Date

→243ff.

→99f.

→53

269

Commentaries: Lohr (HK) 1893, ²1906; Budde (KHC) 1898; Rudolph (KAT) 1939, 1962; Haller (HAT) 1940; Gordis 1954, ²1974; Kraus (BK) 1956, ³1968; Weiser (ATD) 1958, ²1967; Plöger (HAT 2) 1969; Hillers (AB) 1972; Kaiser (ATD³) 1981.

A.Albrektson, *Studies in the Text and Theology of the Book of Lamentations*, 1963; S.Bergler, 'Threni V – nur ein alphabetisierendes Lied? Versuch einer Deutung', *VT* 27, 1977, 304-20; G.Brunet, *Les Lamentations contre Jérémie*, 1968; R.Gordis, 'The Conclusion of the Book of Lamentations (5:22)', *JBL* 93, 1974, 41-9; T.F.McDaniel, 'The Alleged Sumerian Influence upon Lamentations', *VT* 18, 1968, 198-209; id., 'Philological Studies in Lamentations', *Bib* 49, 1968, 27-53; 199-220.

Steuernagel, §158-159; Eissfeldt, §69; Fohrer, §44; Soggin, 5.V; Kaiser, §30; Smend, §46; Schmidt, §26; Childs, XXI.

4.4.5 The Book of Esther

Diaspora
tradition

In many respects the book of Esther has a special position in the Old Testament. It is set entirely in the Diaspora, without even a hint at connections with the homeland of Judah. The crucial point of conflict is the special position of the Jews in their Persian environment, but nowhere (outside the general statement in 3.8) is this identified in terms of specifically Jewish religious modes of behaviour (as e.g. the observance of food laws in Dan.1.8ff.). Finally, God is not mentioned anywere in the book (except perhaps in the veiled hint in 4.14, that help will come 'from another place').

→110

Wisdom
traditions

However, on closer inspection it is evident that in many ways the book is bound up with the rest of the Old Testament traditions. The idea of the hidden action of God exercised through human intrigue also stamps other Old Testament narratives (e.g. the Joseph story and the Succession Narrative, cf. also Esther 6.13). There are also agreements even down to phraseology with the Joseph story, which is similarly set in a foreign court (cf. Rosenthal, Gerleman, Meinhold). The book is steeped in wisdom traditions (cf. Talmon). Finally, the two protagonists reflect a hostility which dates back to the traditions about the early period of Israel: Haman, the persecutor of the Jews, is a descendant of Agag (3.1) king of the Amalekites, the deadly enemies of Israel (Ex.17.14, 16; Deut.25.17-19), while the genealogy of Mordecai the Jew goes back to Saul (2.5; cf. I Sam.9.1f.), who wanted to spare Agag (I Sam.15). Moreover, as the book ends with the founding of the festival of Purim (9.20ff.), which is introduced generally as a Jewish fast, we should not overstress the distance of Esther from the other books of the Old Testament, but must understand it in terms of the situation in which it came into being.

→171

Supreme
narrative art

270

The supreme narrative art of the book of Esther is universally praised. The narrative tension is generated above all by the contrast between the protagonists Mordecai (with Esther) and Haman in parallel courses of action; stylistic means are also employed: concealment, building up of tension, and quickening of pace (cf. Striedl, Dommershausen). The exposition (1.1-2.3) relates the earlier developments: how the Persian king Ahasuerus cast off his insubordinate consort Vashti (ch.1) and how the Jewess Esther became queen in her place (2.1-18). Mordecai is already introduced at this point (2.5-7), and we are told of an event which counts in his favour (vv. 19-23); this is initially forgotten, but then occupies a key position in the narrative (6.1ff.). The main part (3.1-9.19) begins immediately with a portrait of the conflict between Haman and Mordecai, which very quickly develops from personal enmity to a large-scale pogrom of Jews throughout the Persian empire (ch.3). Mordecai involves Esther in order to avert disaster (ch.4); after initial hesitations she takes his side in a dangerous undertaking, supported by a three-day fast among all the Jews in the Persian empire (vv.16f.). Her plan is carried out, at a deliberately slow pace, in several stages (chs.5-7). Meanwhile, Haman thinks that his great hour has come and he prepares for the execution of Mordecai (5.9-14). However, he then has to recognize that he has lost the game (ch.6, esp. v.13) and is finally himself hanged on the gallows which he had prepared for Moredecai (7.9f.). Mordecai now occupies Haman's former place of honour (8.1f.) and the Jews successfully defend themselves, with the king's support, against the planned pogrom, which turns into a jubilant festival (8.3-9.19; according to Gordis, 8.11 is a quotation from 3.13, and thus speaks of the murderous plans of the enemy, not of the Jews). The concluding section contains not only a final notice (10.1-3) reminiscent of the frameworks of the books of Kings but also a detailed statement about the date and observances of the feast of Purim and the reason why it is held (9.20-32); here there is repeated stress on the obligatory character of the festival and its regulations (vv.21,23,27,31,32).

The conclusion clearly shows that in its present form Esther is meant to be understood as the festival legend of the feast of Purim. However, many exegetes doubt whether this was also the purpose of the original narrative. In fact the name Purim appears only in the conclusion and is explicitly introduced and explained in 9.26. The word *pur*, though, from which it is derived (9.24,26), already appears in the narrative (3.7) and is explained by the Hebrew world *goral*, lot. (In Akkadian there is evidence of the word *pūru* with the meaning of 'lot'.) Moreover, the festival element is anchored in the narrative (9.17,19). So the regular festival could have developed from the narrative about a single occasion.

The narrative itself can be termed a Novella. Gunkel calls it a 'historical romance', in which the situation of the Jewish minority in the Persian Diaspora is described accurately in historical terms, though the narrative is fictional. Talmon stresses the wisdom elements and speaks of a 'historicizing wisdom narrative'. Common to the various definitions in terms of genre is that they describe the narrative as a historicizing account which does not set out to be the report of a historical event.

Esther becomes queen

Conflict between Haman and Mordecai

Prevention of pogrom

Purim festival

Diaspora Novella

→110f.

Writings The story is often thought to have had a lengthy prehistory. Bickermann conjectures two and Bardtke even three different narratives which the author has worked over; Cazelles sees a historical-political and a liturgical text. Lebram sees the combination of various traditions as an attempt to smooth out differences over the feast of Purim between the eastern Diaspora and Palestine (cf. the 'Mordecai day'in II Macc.15.36). Gerleman understands the Esther narrative as a new interpretation of the Exodus story which perhaps sought to replace Passover by Purim in the Persian Diaspora. However, all exegetes stress the artificial narrative unity of the present final version, so that the assumption of previous stages remains very hypothetical and helps little by way of explanation. The question of the origin of the feast of Purim and a possible Gentile prehistory has also yet to be clarified.

Origin There can hardly be any doubt as to the origin of the narrative in the Persian Diaspora. The author evidently has a very good knowledge of conditions in Persia and in particular of life at the Persian court. Moreover, outside the Diaspora it is hard to imagine any interest in such a narrative or an occasion for it to be produced, given that its central concern is the survival of the Jewish minority at a time of rising hostility to Judaism (cf. 3.8f.)(cf. also Humphreys). There is little to tell us anything about the time of origin; it is generally accepted that the time of Ahasuerus (i.e. Xerxes I, 485-465) is historicizing dressing. There is much to suggest that the narrative arose during the period of Persian rule, but affinity with Hellenistic romances is often pointed out in arguments for a third-century dating.

Septuagint additions The Septuagint translator already felt the often-stressed lack of religious content and added several sections to the narrative: a dream of Mordecai at the beginning and interpretation at the end, prayers of Mordecai and Esther (after 4.17), and so on. Most English Bibles include these passages in the Apocrypha.

Bibliography

Commentaries: Wildeboer (KHC) 1898; Siegfried (HK) 1901; Haller (HAT) 1940; Ringgren (ATD) 1958, ³1981; Bardtke (KAT) 1963; Würthwein (HAT²) 1969; Moore (AB) 1971; Gerleman (BK) 1973, ²1982.

E.Bickerman, *Four Strange Books of the Bible*, 1967; H.Cazelles, 'Note sur la composition du rouleau d'Esther', in *Lex tua veritas, FS H.Junker*, 1962, 17-29; W.Dommershausen, *Die Estherrolle. Stil und Ziel einer alttestamentlichen Schrift*, 1968; R.Gordis, 'Studies in the Esther Narrative', *JBL* 95, 1976, 43-58; H.Gunkel, *Esther*, 1916; W.L.Humphreys, 'A Life-Style for Diaspora. A Study of the Tales of Esther and Daniel', *JBL* 92, 1973, 211-23; J.C.H.Lebram, 'Purimfest und Estherbuch', *VT* 22, 1972, 208-22; A.Meinhold, 'Die Gattung der Josephsgeschichte und des Estherbuches: Diasporanovelle (I.u.II)', *ZAW* 87, 1975, 306-24; 88, 1976, 72-93; L.A.Rosenthal, 'Die Josephsgeschichte mit den Büchern Ester und Daniel verglichen', *ZAW* 15, 1895, 278-84; 17, 1897, 126-8; H.Striedl, 'Untersuchungen zur Syntax und Stilistik des hebräischen Buches Esther', *ZAW* 55, 1937, 73-108; S.Talmon, 'Wisdom in the Book of Esther', *VT* 13, 1963, 419-55.

Steuernagel, §93; Eissfeldt, §70; Fohrer, §37; Soggin, 5.VII; Kaiser, §20; Smend, §47; Schmidt, §26; Childs, XL.

4.5 The Book of Daniel

The book of Daniel is one of the most disputed books in the Old Testament. This is already clear from the different positions in which it appears. In the Hebrew canon the book stands right at the end among the Writings (before Ezra-Nehemiah and the books of Chronicles), whereas in the Septuagint it brings to an end the series of 'Major Prophets'; the Vulgate and most English translations follow the Septuagint. The reason why the Hebrew tradition does not count Daniel among the prophets may well be that at the time when it was composed the collection of the prophetic books had already been closed. However, it has regularly been suggested that the separation of Daniel from the (other) prophets was made deliberately and is the expression of a negative evaluation (cf. Koch 1980, 28f.). *Position in canon*

In the text, too, the Septuagint tradition deviates markedly from the Hebrew version and contains substantial extensions and expansions: two larger additions to ch.3, the 'Prayer of Azariah' and the 'Song of the Three Men in the Fiery Furnace'; also two additional chapters at the end with the story of Susanna and the double story of Bel and the Dragon in Babylon. Protestant Bibles have relegated these passages to the Apocrypha, while in Catholic translations of the Bible (and therefore also in the 'Common Versions') they appear within the book of Daniel. *Septuagint additions*

The book also occupies a special position in terms of genre. At first glance it seems to be divided into two parts, which have quite different characters: chs.1-6 contain narratives about Daniel and his friends, and chs.7-12 visions. However, this division contrasts with another dividing line which represents a further peculiarity of the Book of Daniel, the change in language. The book begins in Hebrew, changes into Aramaic in 2.4 in the middle of the narrative, and returns to Hebrew at the beginning of ch.8. The Aramaic part, 2.4b-7.28, is thus framed by the Hebrew part, but this division does not coincide with the division by genre into narratives and visions. *Change of language*

The best explanation of this apparent contradiction is probably in terms of composition. Chapter 1 forms the introduction in which the main figures are described: four young men deported from Judah, who have been selected for service in the royal court, refuse to eat the 'unclean' food there for religious reasons but nevertheless, with divine help, develop better than the others and stand out especially through their 'wisdom' (vv.17,20). Daniel also has the special gift of the interpretation of visions and dreams (v.17b). The fact that ch.1 is essentially an introduction is also evident from the fact that in what follows Daniel and his three friends never appear acting together (apart from some connecting remarks in 2.13,17f.,49), and while we are told of the fidelity of Daniel's friends to the faith, we are never told of their wisdom (ch.3). *Composition*

The Aramaic part, chs.2-7 (the change of language in 2.4 has a narrative connection with the beginning of the speech of the Chaldaean

advisor to the king) proves to be a well-thought-out concentric composition (cf. Lenglet, partly also already Plöger 1959, 19ff.). The framework is provided by chs. 2 and 7, the two visions of the four world
kingdoms (we would do better to call them 'dreams', cf. 2.1.; 7.1),
between which there are many common features and relationships (see
below). Chapters 3 and 6 also correspond. They are martyr legends (for
the definition of the genre cf. Koch 1980, 88ff.); here in ch.3 the three
friends are the protagonists, as Daniel is in ch.6. The structure is largely
parallel: command to worship the king as god, refusal, denunciation,
enforcement of the penalty, miraculous deliverance (from the fiery
furnace or the lion's den), acknowledgement of the God of the Jews by
the pagan king (cf. Lenglet, 182ff.). Finally, chs.4 and 5 are the centre
(and thus also according to Lenglet the central statement) of the
composition. Both deal with the divine judgment on a king, which is
announced in a mysterious way (in *4.2* by a dream, in 5.5 by the writing
on the wall), but first has to be interpreted by Daniel (*4.5ff.*; 5.13ff.)
and finally is fulfilled (*4.25ff.*; 5.30). The message of these two chapters
is that the 'Most High rules over the kingdom of men and gives it to
whom he will' (*4.14,22,29*; cf. *4.32*; 5.22f.).

It is hardly possible to give a certain answer to the question why this section was
written in Aramaic (for the whole complex of problems see Koch 1980, 34ff.).
In my view the best assumption is that the author of the whole book had more
or less substantial parts of this chapter already written in Aramaic and that he
incorporated them into his work in this form, at the same time giving them an
Aramaic context.

Chapter 7 at the same time forms the connecting link with the
following chapters; for whereas chs.1-6 constantly show Daniel and his
friends in confrontation with the Babylonian or Persian king, in ch.7
Daniel is alone with his vision, as he is in the following chapters.
Terminologically the bridge backwards is formed by the word 'dream'
in 7.1. Otherwise the introductory datings in 2.1; 7.1; 8.1; 9.1; 10.1 also
produce a connection.

Chapters 7-12 are usually described as visions, but they differ very
widely in character. Chapter 8 comes closer to chs. 2 and 7 with its
vision (*ḥason*, 8.1) of the battle between the ram and the goat, while in
chs.9-12 the visionary element consists only in the fact that Daniel sees
angels and other figures through whom a 'word' (9.23;10.1) is revealed
and explained to him. The dramatic historical events of which there is
explicit mention are not presented as visions.

The dreams or visions show a clear trend. In ch.2, the image of the
'colossus with feet of clay' depicts four successive world kingdoms
(probably those of Babylon, Media, Persia and Greece, cf. Koch 1980,
187), the last of which (along with the whole image) is destroyed and
replaced by an 'eternal' kingdom (vv.34f., 44f.). Here the fourth
kingdom is described as iron, i.e. violent (vv.33,40), but this is not
developed further. However, in ch.7, where the world kingdoms are
depicted as four beasts, the main interest is in this fourth kingdom, its

evil acts and its fate (vv.7ff.). Here there is further differentiation;
within this fourth kingdom the last feature is the growth of a horn (v.8),
which symbolizes a king who is worse than all the others and who will
speak and act against God (vv.24ff.). This image is taken up in ch.8
(vv.9ff.) and interpreted in the same way (vv.23ff.). Here there is also
mention of impious intervention in the sacrificial cult (vv.11f., 13).

Here the historical interpretation is obvious: the reference is to Contemporary
Antiochus IV (Epiphanes), who in 168 BC desecrated the altar of interpretation
sacrifice in the temple in Jerusalem and among other things thus sparked 168 BC
off the Maccabaean revolt (cf. Lebram 1975). He is also mentioned at
length in the last great vision (chs.10-12) (cf. Koch 1980, 141ff.), where
he is introduced in 11.21 as the 'contemptible person' who does away
with the daily sacrifice and sets up 'the abomination of desolation' (v.31;
cf. 8.31; 9.27; 12.11).

The dates given for the duration of the tribulation present difficulties. According Duration of
to 7.25 the interventions in the cult are to last 'a time, (two) times and half a tribulation
time'. i.e. probably three and a half years: this is matched by the mention of 'a
half week (of years)' (9.27) and by 12.7: 'a cult time (*mo'ed*), two cult times and
half a cult time.' A similar calculation can probably be made from 7.14, which
mentions '2300 evenings and mornings'; these can be interpreted as 1150 days,
i.e. rather more than three years. but somewhat less than three and a half. 12.11
mentions 1290 days, which is restated in v.12 as 1335 (as a correction?).
According to I Macc.4.52f. (in comparison with 1.59), however, the altar was
reconsecrated just three years after the desecration. So the intervals are too
long. Were they written down before this event? Or is the three and a half years
an indeterminate mythical figure (Gunkel, 266ff., cf. Koch 1980, 145ff.)?
However, in that case the 'correction' in 12.12 is all the harder to understand
(but cf. Burgmann). It is even more difficult to establish what is meant in 9.24ff.
by the seventy weeks (of years) which are given as an interpretation of the
seventy years prophesied by Jeremiah (v.2, cf. Jer.25.11f.; 29.10). Here there
are a variety of models of calculation which attempt to interpret the seventy
times seventy (= 490) in terms of contemporary history (cf. Koch 1980, 149ff.).
However, here too we are left with the basic question whether these are
speculative calculations or a retrospective *vaticinium ex eventu* and whether the
calculation leads up to the restoration of the altar of burnt offering or beyond
that to the end of the world.

The portrayal of the final judgment in heaven in 7.9-14 with its Heavenly final
interpretations in vv.18,22,26f. raises particular exegetical problems. judgment
In a scene of heavenly judgment before the 'ancient of days' (vv.9,13,32)
'one like a son of man' appears with the clouds of heaven (v.13). He is Son of man
given eternal, imperishable rule over all the nations of the world (v.14).
In the attached interpretation, however, rule is given to the saints of Saints of the
the Most High (vv.18,22) or the 'people of the saints of the Most High' Most High
(v.27). All the elements of this picture are without clear parallels in the
Old Testament or in other texts which are earlier than the book
of Daniel, Therefore despite an almost overwhelming amount of
literature, fundamentally all the problems remain unresolved. Who is
the 'son of man' (An individual? A heavenly or earthly figure? A

collective figure?)? Who are the 'saints of the Most High' (or more exactly the 'highest saints')(Israel? A heavenly being?)? How are the two related (does the 'son of man' represent Israel? Are the two identical, or are vv.14 and 18ff. rival traditions?)? Where are the roots of these conceptions (in the Old Testament? in Babylon, Ugarit or Iran?) (for the whole question cf. Colpe; Koch 1980, 214ff.)?

The problems in interpreting ch.7 once again demonstrate the special position of the book of Daniel in the Old Testament. In its final version it undoubtedly comes from the time of the Maccabees and is thus probably the latest book in the Old Testament. It is the only book of

Apocalyptic
→123

the Old Testament to contain apocalyptic material to any extent, so that as a whole it can be assigned to apocalyptic (cf. Lebram 1970, Koch 1982, 1ff.). However, this is not the case with all the traditional material that it has incorporated. In particular the narratives about Daniel and his friends contain no apocalyptic elements and moreover presuppose quite a different situation, namely that of the Jews in the Babylonian and Persian Diaspora (cf. Collins, 1975), whereas the controversies of the Maccabean period emerge increasingly clearly in the visions. (According to Childs chs.7-12 bring up to date the earlier vision in ch.2 from the changed conditions of the Maccabaean period.) Therefore in my view it is quite improbable that the book was written entirely by one author (thus above all Rowley), especially as some of the material has

Prehistory

had a lengthy prehistory (cf. e.g. Meyer and Dommershausen on ch.4 and Gammie 1981). However, the final form can go back to one author who himself wrote in Hebrew but incorporated the parts of the tradition which existed in Aramaic into his book (cf. Bickermann, Gammie 1976). This could also be suggested by the fact that the Hebrew of the book seems to be later than the Aramaic (cf. Koch 1980, 43ff.; Kitchen).

Name
→211

The name Daniel was probably derived from a figure in the tradition who is mentioned in Ezek.14.14,20 alongside Noah and Joab among the exemplary righteous men and in 28.3 as an exemplary wise man. It is uncertain whether there is any connection with the Dn'il mentioned in the texts from Ugarit.

Bibliography

Commentaries: Marti (KHC) 1901; Montgomery (ICC) 1927,(³1964); Bentzen (HAT) 1937, ²1952; Porteous (OTL) 1965; Plöger (KAT) 1965; Delcor 1971.

E.Bickermann, *Four Strange Books of the Bible*, 1967; H.Burgmann, 'Die vier Endzeittermine im Danielbuch', *ZAW* 86, 1974, 543-50; J.C.Collins, 'The Court-Tales in Daniel and the Development of Apocalyptic', *JBL* 94, 1975, 218-34; id., *The Apocalyptic Vision of the Book of Daniel*, 1977; C.Colpe, ὁ υἱὸς τοῦ ἀνθρώπου, *TDNT* 8, 403-81; F.Dexinger, *Das Buch Daniel und seine Probleme*, 1969; W.Dommershausen, *Nabonid im Buche Daniel*, 1964; H.H.P.Dressler, 'The Identification of the Ugaritic Dnil with the Daniel of Ezekiel', *VT* 29, 1979, 152-61; J.G.Gammie, 'The Classification, Stages of Growth and Changing Intentions in the Book of Daniel', *JBL* 95, 1976, 191-204; id., 'On the Intention and Sources of Daniel i-vi', *VT* 31, 1981, 282-92;

H.Gunkel, *Schöpfung und Chaos in Urzeit und Endzeit*, 1895; K.H.Kitchen, 'The Aramaic of Daniel', in D.J.Wiseman et al, *Notes on Some Problems in the Book of Daniel*, 1965, 31-79; K.Koch, *Das Buch Daniel*, 1980 (account of scholarship); id./J.M.Schmidt (eds.), *Apokalyptik*, 1982; J.C.H.Lebram, 'Apokalyptik und Hellenismus im Buche Daniel (review of M.Hengel, *Judentum und Hellenismus*, 1969)', *VT* 20, 1970, 503-24; id., 'Perspektiven der gegenwärtigen Danielforschung', *JSJ* 5, 1974, 1-33; id., 'König Antiochus im Buche Daniel', *VT* 25, 1975, 737-72; A.Lenglet, 'La structure littéraire de Daniel 2-7', *Bib.* 53, 1972, 169-70; R.Meyer, *Das Gebet des Nabonid. Eine in den Qumran Handschriften wiederentdeckte Weisheitserzählung*, 1962; O.Plöger, *Theocracy and Eschatology*, ET 1968; H.H.Rowley, 'The Unity of the Book of Daniel' (1952), in *The Servant of the Lord*, ²1965, 249-80.

Steuernagel, §139, 140; Eissfeldt, §71; Fohrer,§74; Soggin, 5.VIII; Kaiser, §25; Smend, §48; Schmidt, §24; Childs, XLI.

4.6 The Books of Ezra and Nehemiah

The books of Ezra and Nehemiah are the only narrative account of the time after the Babylonian exile to have been handed down in the Old Testament. It is often assumed that along with the books of Chronicles they formed one historical work. However, since, with the exception of the introductory verse (Ezra 1.1-3a is almost synonymous with II Chron.36.22f.), their content is almost independent of the books of Chronicles, it is worth first treating them separately.

The earlier Jewish tradition knows Ezra and Nehemiah as one book under the name Ezra, who is also regarded as its author (Babylonian Talmud, Baba Bathra 14b/15a). Only after the end of the Middle Ages is it divided into two. However, even today in Hebrew editions of the Bible the book of Nehemiah does not have an independent title; there is simply the observation 'The Book of Nehemiah' in the margin alongside Neh.1.1.

The books of Ezra and Nehemiah deal with two periods in post-exilic history: first of all the time immediately after the end of the exile (538 BC) down to the end of the rebuilding of the temple in Jerusalem (515), and then the time of the activity of Ezra and Nehemiah (from 458 or 445). The two periods are not, however, differentiated by an explicit break but are partly even interwoven in the account (see below on Ezra 4-6), so that they appear as consecutive periods: the rebuilding and the reordering of conditions after the exile.

The first major section is dominated by the theme of the return from exile and the rebuilding of the temple (Ezra 1-6). Its most striking feature is the alternation between Hebrew (1.1-4.7; 6.19-22) and Aramaic (4.8-6.18) parts, the content of which partially overlaps.

Chapters 1-3 cover the first phase. First of all there is the report of a public declaration by Cyrus king of Persia that the temple in Jerusalem is to be rebuilt and that all Israelites who are prepared to do so shall return to Jerusalem (1.1-4); this is immediately followed by an account

Two periods

Return and rebuilding

→59ff.

277

of the return (vv.5f.). In connection with that we are told that Cyrus gave the temple vessels which Neuchadnezzar had taken from Jerusalem to a man called Sheshbazzar, who brought them back to Jerusalem (vv.7-11). (For the parallel Aramaic texts in 6.3-5 or e.g. 5.11-16 see below.)

→61f. In ch.2 a list is attached of those who returned (this is repeated in Neh.7). It is headed by the names of Zerubbabel and Joshua (here in the form Jeshua). These two then appear as the protagonists in ch.3, whereas Sheshbazzar is not mentioned again. Ch.3 reports the first steps towards the restoration of the cult in Jerusalem: the beginning of sacrifices on a provisional altar (vv.1-3); the celebration of the feast of tabernacles (v.4) and the continuation of regular sacrifices (v.5); and the preparations for the laying of the foundations for the rebuilding of the temple and its completion (vv.6-13).

Opposition to the building of the temple Here we can see a clear break. 4.1-6.13 deal with opposition to the building of the temple (and of the walls, see below); only after this was overcome could the building be completed and the temple consecrated (6.14-22).

4.1-6.13 contains a variety of problems. First of all, it is striking that 4.8-6.18 **Aramaic documents** are written in Aramaic. The reason for this is probably that letters and documents are quoted here which were written in official language ('Imperial Aramaic'). The fact that the accompanying text is also written in Aramaic shows how bilingual people were at this time, so that there was nothing unusual in fluctuating between the two languages.

Then there are chronological problems. First of all, there is an account of the opposition of 'the enemies of Judah and Benjamin' (4.1; in v.4 'people of the land') during the period of the reigns of the kings from Cyrus to Darius (v.5); then there is mention of an 'accusation' in the time of Xerxes, i.e. the successor of Darius (v.6); finally there is a correspondence with his successor Artaxerxes (vv.7-23); however, its subject-matter is not the rebuilding of the temple but the building of the city walls; with 4.24 the account returns to the time of Darius.

Composition The reasons for this are probably to do with the composition: the opposition to the various building projects in Jerusalem and the inquiries at the Persian court are discussed together; here there is first an account of the successful obstruction to the building (of the walls) and then of the unsuccessful opposition to the building (of the temple), with the result that this whole section can end with jubilation and thanksgiving for the success of the work and the support of the imperial rulers (6.14,22; cf. Japhet 1982, 73f.).

Finally, there are tensions between the content of the Aramaic documents and that of the Hebrew texts in chs.1-3 (e.g. over the question whether Cyrus already gave permission for the return, and over the role of Sheshbazzar in the rebuilding of the temple, cf. also Gunneweg 1982). In general, we may take the Aramaic text to be more reliable. The retreat of Sheshbazzar can perhaps be explained from the fact that the author of the present complex of texts wanted to stress the

basic importance of Zerubbabel and Joshua (as a pair, in parallel to the later Ezra and Nehemiah). Given this, and especially in view of the great gap in time, the figure of Sheshbazzar lost significance (cf. Japhet 1982, 94).

The account of Ezra's activity begins with ch.7. It extends first to ch,10, but in Neh.8 there is again mention of Ezra, though in chs.1-7 the report was exclusively concerned with the activity of Nehemiah. The composition as it now is seems deliberately to have combined the activity of the two (cf. the joint mention of them in Neh.12.26; also 8.9;12.36), although the texts as we now have them give no indication of this.

Chapters 7f. give a detailed account of Ezra's journey from Babylon to Jerusalem. Here another Aramaic text has been inserted in 7.12-26: the credentials given by King Artaxerxes to Ezra, the 'scribe of the law of the God of Heaven' (vv.12,21; cf. vv.6,11; Neh.8.1, etc.). Here those Israelites who are willing to return are allowed to join Ezra (v.13). Ezra himself is charged with an investigation of Judah and Jerusalem on the basis of the 'law of your God which is in your hand' (v.14). Later, instructions are given for implementing this law (v.25) with the threat of penalties for those who do not follow 'the law of your God and the law of the king' (v.26). Moreover, there is detailed information about contributions to the temple in Jerusalem (vv.15-23).

In 7.27f. a eulogy of Ezra is attached to the text of the royal credentials. Here God is praised for 'putting into the heart of the king' the idea of giving generous support to Ezra's mission. We can see the same intent as in 1.1ff.; 6.22; to depict the Persian kings as willing instruments for the implementation of the divine plans with Israel. (The narrative is continued in 7.28b, but now in the first person in contrast to the third person form which dominates from 7.1); there is a dispute as to whether this suggests different sources (cf. Mowinckel 1961, 1965, 75ff.).

The travel account proper in ch.8 begins with a list of those returning (vv.1-14) and an episode concerned with the persuasion of Levites willing to return, who hitherto had been lacking (vv.15-20). Otherwise the account seems very stylized: a three-day stay by a river (v.5) with prayer and fasting (vv.21-23), the commissioning of the priests to bear the temple vessels they had brought with them (vv.24-30) and a solemn handing over in Jerusalem (vv.32-34; the journey itself is mentioned only briefly, v.31). Finally, there is a great sacrificial ceremony 'for all Israel' (v.35). We could see here deliberate parallels to the exodus from Egypt (cf. Ex.14) and the crossing of the Jordan on the occupation of the land (cf. Josh.3f.); however, the question remains whether this is literary stylization or whether one may draw consequences from it for Ezra's own aims (thus Koch).

Next, in chs.9f., a basic problem is tackled, the question of mixed marriages. The responsible leaders (*śarim*) of the people advise Ezra that members of all groups (laity, priests and Levites) have entered into marriages with women from the 'peoples of the land' (9.1f.); thereupon Ezra reacts with agitation (vv.3f.) and utters a long penitential prayer (vv.5-15). Next a spontaneous assembly of the people commits itself to arrange matters in accordance with the Torah (10.1-3) and asks Ezra to take the initiative (vv.4-6); a public assembly is summoned (vv.7ff.), but because of its great size (and the rain) the whole matter is ultimately handed over to a commission (vv.16f.) which produces a list of all those involved (v.18-44). The Hebrew text tells us nothing about the consequences. (The report about the dismissal of wives and children which appears in many translations is based on a textual emendation.)

Thus there is no conclusion here to the account of Ezra's activity. One basic reason for this lies in the fact that in the overall account of the books of Ezra and Nehemiah, Ezra is mentioned later (Neh.8, see below). However, in the context it is doubtless presupposed that the obligation to dissolve the mixed marriages expressed in Ezra 10.3,11f. was fulfilled.

There is a new development in Neh.1.1: 'The words of Nehemiah', i.e. an account of which Nehemiah himself claims to be the author. Accordingly, large parts of the book of Nehemiah are written in the first person (1.1-7.5; 12.31-13.31), so they (or at any rate their basic material) can be assigned to a 'Nehemiah source'.

Nehemiah reports that on the basis of accounts of the disquieting situation in Jerusalem (1.1-3), he was given permission by King Arta-

xerxes, whose cupbearer he was (1.11), to go to Jerusalem to rebuild the city (2.1-8). The first part of the book (chs.1-6) is devoted to this rebuilding and the difficulties which had to be overcome.

In detail Nehemiah reports external opposition which is presented by Sanballat (the governor of Samaria), Tobiah (presumably one of Sanballat's officials) and the 'Arab' Geshem (perhaps the governor of a neighbouring province, cf. Kellermann, 170ff.). These attempt to prevent the rebuilding of the city walls by means of mistrust (2.10), mockery (2.19f.; 3.33-37), military assault plans (*4.1ff.*) and murder plans against Nehemiah (6.1-14). Opposition within is presented by a group which cooperates with these opponents (6.17-19). This opposition comes from the upper class, which is also responsible for serious social injustices leading to disturbances and therefore also to some hindrance to the building activity (5.1-13). But despite all resistance Nehemiah's building plans (2.11-18) are carried through (3.1-32; *4.9-17*) and completed after fifty-two days.

There is a striking break in ch.7. In connection with the problem of the inadequate population of Jerusalem (vv.4f.) we first have a repetition of the list of those who returned, from Ezra 2. To this is attached (as in

Ezra 3) an account of a liturgical action (Neh.8). Here, however, *Ezra* is the one involved; thus the Nehemiah source has evidently broken off. However, this can hardly be attributed to a mistake or redactional thoughtlessness; there is doubtless a purpose behind it. The solemn

liturgical reading and interpretation of the Torah brings to an end the work of rebuilding the city and in a wider context also that of religious reform in the question of mixed marriages (Ezra 9)(Childs). The Jewish

community, its purity restored and its city rebuilt, without aliens (cf.Neh.2.20), hears the words of the Torah (Neh.8.1-12) and goes on to celebrate the feast of Tabernacles (8.13-18). The observance of the fast which follows (9.1-3) and the great penitential psalm (9.6-37) fit into this framework.

Nehemiah 8 (often along with ch.9, and partially also 10) is often considered originally to have been part of an Ezra source which once belonged after Ezra 8 or (thus Mowinckel and others) Ezra 10. Other exegetes (e.g. Noth, Kellermann) regard the chapter as the work of the author of the book as we now have it (whom they identify with the Chronicler). At all events it is worth noting that the account of the reading of the Torah in Neh.8 contains elements of synagogue liturgy: bringing the Torah scroll (v.2), mounting the elevated platform (*bima*) containing the reading desk (v.4), opening the Torah scroll (v.5), the blessing (*beraka*, v.6a), the communal 'Amen' (v.6b), perhaps verse-by-verse translation into Aramaic (v.8, cf. Schaeder, 52f.; for the whole question, Kellermann, 29f.). Here we presumably have a reflection of how the service was held in the synagoge (or its predecessor) at the time when the text was composed.

Chapter 10 poses a special problem. It contains a written 'pledge' (v.*1*) given by those listed in vv.*1b-29*, 'to walk in God's law which was given by Moses, the servant of God' (v.*30*); this is developed further in vv.*31-40*. In a series of points this development corresponds to the reforms later (Neh.13) introduced by Nehemiah: mixed marriages (*10.31*; cf. 13.23-30a), hallowing of the sabbath (*10.32a*; cf. 13.15-22), provision of firewood for the altar (*10.35*, cf. 13.31); provision of firstfruits (*10.36f.*; cf.13.31), tithes for the Levites (*10.38f.*; cf. 13.10-14). So this obligation can hardly have stood before Neh.13. Nevertheless it is regarded by many exegetes as an original document which either stood elsewhere in the Nehemiah source or is an independent document from the temple archives (Rudolph, Mowinckel etc.).

In ch.11 a variety of lists are added, following an account of measures for the resettlement of Jerusalem (v.1f.): inhabitants of Jerusalem →105f. (vv.3-19, additions vv.21-24), of Judah (vv.20, 25-30) and Benjamin (vv.31-35, addition v.36), various lists of priests and Levites (12.1-26, for the lists cf. Mowinckel 1964 I, 62ff.). This is followed by a solemn stylized description of the dedication of the walls (12.27-43). The conclusion is formed by various reports of individual measures of Nehemiah's reform: regulation of offerings (12.44-47), purification of the community from aliens (13.1-3), abolition of the misuse of a room in the temple (vv.4-9), rules for the service of the Levites (vv.10-13), sabbath order (vv.15-22), problems over mixed marriages (vv.23-29), ordinances for the temple liturgy (vv.30f.).

The last sentence of the book of Nehemiah, 'Remember me, O my God, for good' (13.31; cf. 5.19; 13.14,22), gives an indication of the character and purpose of this work. There used to be a tendency to call it 'memoirs' or a 'report', but Mowinckel (1964 II) and von Rad in particular have shown its affinity to texts from the ancient Near East which were brought to or laid up in temples by kings and princes and which are in fact addressed to the deity. (Kellermann stresses the affinity to the 'prayer of the accused' in the Psalms.) The designation 'memorial' (Mowinckel) expresses this aspect of the petition for divine remembrance and also the political function of the justification which this work was also doubtless intended to provide.

The Nehemiah memorial has been incorporated into the wider context of the books of Ezra and Nehemiah. For the first part of this the author had, e.g., some Aramaic documents at his disposal (see above). It is impossible to tell in what form they came down to him. Many exegetes also think here of 'memoirs' (Meyer) or a 'memorial' (Schaeder) from Ezra's own hand. Mowinckel (1965) speaks of an 'edifying church history'; Noth (146f.), however, regards the Chronicler (see below) as the real author, while In der Smitten talks in terms of a Chronistic 'midrash' on the official Aramaic credentials given to Ezra (7.12-26).

Despite many contradictions in matters of detail, the author of the books of Ezra and Nehemiah has brought together his material into a well considered composition (cf. also Gunneweg 1981, 154ff.). God 'arouses the spirit of king Cyrus' (Ezra 1.1) and in so doing makes a new beginning in the history of his people. The first phase, the rebuilding of the temple, has a happy ending despite all the resistance, because God inclined 'the heart of the king of Assyria' to the Israelites (6.22). The second and third phases also begin with divine help in the form of the inclination of the heart of the Persian king to Ezra (Ezra 7.6, 27f.) and Nehemiah (Neh. 1.11; 2.4,8). Over against this we have the constant hostility (Ezra 3.3; 4.1-6.13; Neh.2.10, 19f.; 3.33-37; *4.1f.*; 6.1-14, 17-19), though this is always overcome with divine help.

A further constant theme is the purity of the newly constituted community. This is evident from its separation from outsiders (Ezra 4.1-3; 9f.; Neh.2.20; 13.23-29) and from the emphasis on the fact that members of this community have cut themselves off from the members of other peoples (Ezra. 6.21; 10.11; Neh.9.2; *10.29*; 3.3). This theme can be found in all three spheres, the rebuilding of the temple and the activity of Ezra and Nehemiah.

Finally, the great feast of the reading of the Torah followed by the feast of Tabernacles (Neh.8.) is quite emphatically (despite the disruption to the chronological sequence) put after the successful completion of the building of the walls. This makes the whole period covered by the books of Ezra and Nehemiah one great epoch of return and rebuilding, framed by two celebrations of the feast of Tabernacles, the first at the return (Ezra.3.4) and the second after the rebuilding is complete (Neh.8.13-18). Both times it takes place in accordance with what has been 'written', and 'in order' (Ezra 3.4; Neh.8.14,18).

Most more recent exegetes regard the books of Ezra and Nehemiah as part of the Chronistic History (cf.Noth). However, after Pohlmann (143ff.) and Kaiser (166) questioned whether the Nehemiah memorial is part of the Chronicler's work, Japhet (1968) and Williamson have shown convincingly that the books

of Ezra and Nehemiah as a whole cannot belong with Chronicles (cf. also
Throntveit, though Gunneweg 1981, 47ff., differs). The way in which Ezra and
Nehemiah form a self-contained composition, as described here, also tells
against this. The agreement between the end of Chronicles (II Chron. 36.22f.)
and the beginning of Ezra (1.1-3a), which has often been used as an argument
for holding them together, could also be used to prove the opposite: that two
works which did not originally belong together have been linked in this way.
Moreover the affinity of the two works is based on the common 'language of
the time', which remains unmistakable despite the differences and contrasts
pointed out by Japhet and Williamson.

Bibliography

Commentaries: Siegfried (HK) 1901; Bertholet (KHC) 1902; Rudolph (HAT)
1949; Galling (ATD) 1954 (1958); Myers (AB) 1965.
   A.H.J.Gunneweg, 'Zur Interpretation der Bücher Esra-Nehemia. Zugleich
ein Beitrag zur Methode der Exegese', *SVT* 32, 1981, 146-61; id., 'Die aramäische und die hebräische Erzählung über die nachexilische Restauration – ein
Vergleich', *ZAW* 94, 1982, 299-302; W.T.in der Smitten. *Esra. Quellen,
Überlieferung und Geschichte*, 1973; S.Japhet, 'The Supposed Common Authorship of Chronicles and Ezra-Nehemia Investigated Anew', *VT* 18, 1968, 330-
71; id., 'Sheshbazzar and Zerubbabel – Against the Background of the Historical
and Religious Tendencies of Ezra-Nehemiah', *ZAW* 94, 1982, 66-98; U.Keller-
mann, *Nehemia. Quellen, Überlieferung und Geschichte*, 1967; K.Koch, 'Ezra
and the Origins of Judaism', *JSS* 91, 1974, 173-97; E.Meyer, *Die Entstehung
des Judentums*, 1896 (1965); S.Mowinckel ' "Ich" und "Er" in der Ezrage-
schichte', in *Verbannung und Heimkehr, FS W.Rudolph*, 1961, 211-33; id.,
Studien zu dem Buche Ezra-Nehemiah, I and II, 1964; III, 1965; M.Noth,
Überlieferungsgeschichtliche Studien, 1943 (³1973); G. von Rad, 'Die Nehemia-
Denkschrift', *ZAW* 76, 1964, 176-87; H.H.Schaeder, *Esra der Schreiber*, 1930;
M.A.Throntveit, 'Linguistic Analysis and the Question of Authorship in
Chronicles, Ezra and Nehemia', *VT* 82, 1982, 210-16; H.G.M.Williamson,
Israel in the Books of Chronicles, 1977.
   Steuernagel, §89-91; Eissfeldt, §73; Fohrer, §34; Soggin, 5.X; Kaiser, §17;
Smend, §49; Schmidt, §12b; Childs, XLII.

4.7 The Books of Chronicles

Surprisingly, the last book of the Hebrew canon contains a second
account of the history of the period of the monarchy, beginning with
the death of Saul (I Chron.10) and ending with the Babylonian exile (II
Chron.36.17ff.). However, we can immediately see a fundamental
difference from the account in Samuel and Kings. Chronicles contains
only the history of the Davidic monarchy. All we are told of Saul is the
circumstances of his death (I Chron.10; cf. I Sam.31). After the division
of the northern and southern kingdoms only the history of Judah is
pursued, while the state of Israel and its kings only emerge as opponents

→171
177f.

or allies of Judah; because of this the synchronisms which are characteristic of the books of Kings are also absent (II Chron.13.1 is the only
exception). This is all the more striking, as the author largely had only
Samuel and Kings as his source (see below). So the alterations were
made deliberately. Therefore a comparison of the two accounts gives
us important insights into the purpose of Chronicles.

The Hebrew name of Chronicles is *dibre ha-yamim*, which could be translated
'annals' (the same term is used in I Kings 14.19,29 etc.). Originally there was
only one book. The Septuagint calls it παραλειπόμενα (i.e. what is 'left over'
in the sense of being left out), thus regarding it as a supplement to Samuel and
Kings. It also puts Chronicles after the books of Kings and after that the books
of Ezra and Nehemiah. The Vulgate and most English Bibles have adopted this
order.

The book begins with a large-scale genealogy (I Chron. 1-9), which
in its present form extends from Adam (1.1) to the return from the
Babylonian exile (9.1ff.). There may be evidence of some expansions
in places, but these can hardly be described as a 'hotchpotch of secondary
wild accretions to the text' (Noth, 122). Utilizing the relevant texts from
Genesis, it leads from Adam to Abraham (1.1-27; cf. Gen.5; 10f.) and
his sons and to the twelve sons of 'Israel', i.e. Jacob (1.28-2.2). There
follows a genealogy of Judah down to David and his kin (2.3-17) and
then further branches of the descendants of Judah (2.18-55; 4.1-23); in
between there is a list of the descendants of David. This last also
contains, in addition to David's sons, all the Davidic kings and the
descendants of the last kings leading far into the post-exilic period
(ch.3). This is followed by very different kinds of lists relating to the
rest of the Israelite tribes, in which Levi in particular occupies a great
deal of space (5.27-6.6). They end with the genealogy of Saul (8.33-40),
which is repeated in 9.35-44 after the insertion of a list of those who
returned from exile (9.1b-34). (For details see Rudolph.) Here the
stress on the genealogy of David and the Levites already indicates
particular concerns.

The history of David (I Chron.10-29) begins with the account of the
death of Saul (ch.10). This evidently not only serves as an introduction
but at the same time is an exemplary demonstration of the danger posed
to the kingdom and thus to all Israel by the 'faithlessness' of Saul,
because he did not 'keep' the word of YHWH and did not 'seek' him
(vv.13f.; cf. Mosis, 17ff.; Ackroyd, 3ff.). The beginning of the reign of
David is thus made all the more impressive (chs.11-16). The Chronicler
does not mention David's temporary rule over Judah but, diverging
from his source, simply has 'all Israel' make David king (11.1; cf. II
Sam.1.5); immediately afterwards David captures Jerusalem (v.4; cf.
II Sam.5.6). Before the entry of the ark the author, with no support
from his model, makes David hold a great assembly of the people
(13.1ff.), so that it is with their express consent (v.4) that he brings in
the ark with 'all Israel' (v.5; cf. II Sam.6.1). When it is finally brought
into the city of David (chs.15f.; cf. II Sam.6.12ff.), the ark is borne by

Levites whom David has appointed to this role (15.11-15), and also as **Chronicles**
temple singers (vv.16ff.). For the first time they sing a psalm (16.7-36,
a combination of Pss.105; 96; 106). In between we hear of David's →249
victories over the Philistines (14.8ff.), which first make it possible to
introduce the ark (Welten 1979, 175f.; Mosis, 55ff., differs).

The consistent development of this one line is also evident in the
following section, chs.17-29, which is wholly devoted to the theme of
the future building of the temple and therefore at the same time focussed **Preparations**
on Solomon. Here all the features which might disturb the picture of **for building the**
David and Solomon have been left out. Neither David's adultery with **temple**
Bathsheba and the subsequent judgment of Nathan nor the rebellions →172f.
against David are mentioned (i.e. the whole of the Succession Narrative →33f.
is passed over). Instead of this, by a slight alteration in the basic model,
the mention of a son of David is introduced (v.11; cf. II Sam.7.12) into
the prophet Nathan's speech (17.1-15); here Solomon already comes
into view as the future builder of the temple (cf. Braun 1973, 507; Mosis,
93). The role of Solomon as the one who succeeds David and completes
his life's work is then stressed particularly in chs. 22; 28; 29, which the
Chronicler constructs without any basis in his sources. Here there are
striking (and evidently deliberate) parallels to the account of the
transition from Moses to Joshua (Deut.31/Josh.1, cf. Williamson 1976). →154f., 165

Chapters 23-27 are now usually regarded as a later addition, but cf. Williamson
1979.

The history of Solomon (II Chron.1-9) is now focussed entirely on **Solomon**
the building of the temple prepared for by David, and all the negative →34ff., 175ff.
aspects (the murder of his oppponents including his own brother, I
Kings 2, but also the marriage with the daughter of Pharaoh, I Kings
3.1) are omitted. In the preparations there is an emphatic link with the
cultic traditions from the time of Moses: at the high place in Gibeon **Temple**
there are the tent of meeting and the altar of burnt offering from the **building**
wilderness period (II Chron. 1.3,5f.; cf. I Chron.21.29; cf. Ex.33.7-11; →19f., 142
38.1-7), and in II Chron. 1.4 there is express mention of the ark, which
is already in Jerusalem, but which belongs in the same context in the
tradition (cf. Ex.37.1-9; and Mosis, 127f.). The description of the
splendour and the riches of the temple even surpasses that in I Kings 6- →175f.
8 and takes over numerous elements from the tabernacle of Moses (cf. →142f.
Mosis, 136ff.). When all is complete, after Solomon's prayer fire falls
from heaven and consumes the sacrifice on the altar (II Chron. 7.1),
and the glory (*kabod*) of YHWH fills the temple (vv.1b,2) – as at the
consecration of the tabernacle in Ex.40.34f. Thus Solomon is given a →143
very high position in the history of the religion of Israel; at the same
time there is constant stress that here he reaped the fruits of David's
preparation (II Chron.2.6,13,16; 3.1; 5.1; 6.3-11, cf. Williamson 1976),
so that it is the combined activity of the two which brings the great work
to completion. **Judah**

The next chapters now portray the history of Judah to the Babylonian **285** exile (II Chron. 10.36), so that essential parts of what is reported in the books of Kings are not mentioned. Here too the Chronicler sometimes uses his sources literally and sometimes with varying degrees of alteration (cf. Willi; Mosis, 169ff.). Above all, however, certain sections stand out which have no basis in the books of Kings. There are many

references in this special material to building activities, military and administrative matters which many exegetes regard as valuable historical information from a special source (Noth, 139ff.; Galling, 11f.). However, it is evident that this material has a clearly recognizable function within the Chronistic account of history and therefore is to be seen as being specifically Chronistic (Welten 1973). Therefore (apart from a few individual notes) it cannot be regarded as an independent historical source.

Here three themes above all often appear as a complex: fortifications and buildings, the formation of an army, war reports. In addition there are reports about cultic reform, instruction of the people, and homage and tribute from other peoples. The corresponding sections appear exclusively in connection

→176f.

with kings who are assessed positively or within a phase of their reign which is assessed positively (cf. the tables in Welten 1973, 187f.) Rehoboam's building activity (11.5-12) takes place in the first phase of his reign, whereas later he is punished for his apostasy from the Torah of YHWH by the expedition of

→40

Pharaoh Shishak (12.1ff.). Abijah is assessed positively, in contrast to the earlier source (I Kings 15.3), in the war account (13.3-20) at the centre of which is a long theological address to the apostate inhabitants of the northern kingdom. In the case of Asa, who is already assessed positively in the source (I Kings 15.11-15), we have the whole complex of notes about building, forming an army, war and cultic reform (II Chron. 14.5-15.15); this happens in even more detail in the case of Jehoshaphat (17.6-19; 19.4-1; 20.1-30), so that in contrast to the original source, the history of Judah begins with four kings who are assessed positively. Later there are similar notes in the cases of Uzziah (26.6-15), Jotham (27.3-6), Hezekiah (29.3-31.20 with support from the original, II Kings 18.4; 32.5f.), Manasseh (33.14-17; in contrast to the original, II Kings 27.1-16) and Josiah (24.3-35.19, with the incorporation of the original, II Kings 22.3-23.24).

Thus the Chronicler's account of the monarchy gives an essentially different picture from that in Samuel and Kings. The research on Chronicles which has revived again after about a decade (cf. the books by Willi, Welten, Mosis, Williamson and Japhet, and numerous articles) has been largely agreed in stressing the independent literary and theological work of the Chronicler (as did von Rad earlier). Here it has become evident that the author of Chronicles used his sources, i.e. Samuel and Kings, very carefully and deliberately. Willi calls this revision 'exegesis', for which the existing text already had canonical authority. Other authors put more stress on the Chronicler's own historically conditioned interest in a new interpretation of the history

of the Davidic monarchy.

However, opinions differ widely as to his real purpose. Some see it in the way in which he stresses and vindicates Jerusalem and its temple as the sole legitimate place for the worship of YHWH; here the controversy with the Samaritans and the dispute over the legitimacy of the sanctuary in Samaria is regarded as the real occasion for the composition of the work (Noth, Rudolph, Galling, etc.). However, this view has largely been modified or abandoned, among other reasons because not a single tendency hostile to the north can be seen anywhere (cf. Willi, 190ff.; Mosis, 200ff.). Rather, the north is expressly considered to be part of Israel (Braun 1977). Indeed, the Chronicler continues to see 'Israel' as a unity which embraces all twelve tribes (Williamson 1977). There is also a dispute as to whether the motives of the Chronicler should be regarded as more theological (Mosis and others) or as more political and historical (Welten 1973 and others), though of course these are not to be seen as opposites.

Chronicles

→73f.

A variety of other questions are connected with this. Whether the books of Ezra and Nehemiah (in part or as a whole) are to be regarded as part of a 'Chronistic history' considerably influences interpretation as a whole, because this is bound up with the question whether the author of Chronicles also described and interpreted the post-exilic continuation of the history of Israel. While even recently the existence of a 'Chronistic history' could be taken to be beyond dispute, among most recent authors this view tends to be questioned or rejected. If not on linguistic grounds (see above on the books of Ezra and Nehemiah), the main objections are made on grounds of content (cf. Willi, 179ff.; Newsome; Braun 1979, etc.), which suggest a clear division between the two books. It is, however, obvious that Chronicles and Ezra/Nehemiah came into being at the same time and largely speak the same language. Therefore in my opinion there is much to be said for the view that these are in fact two independent works which have a deliberate relationship and are meant to complement each other. Given the complete anonymity of the author or authors, whether we can speak of two works by the same author (Willi, 180) is another matter. (Some scholars have suggested that the whole work came into existence in stages, in which the subsequent addition of the Nehemiah memorial played an important part, cf. In der Smitten, Cross, etc.)

Chronistic history?

→282f.

Ultimately this is also bound up with the question of the dating of the books of Chronicles. It is generally accepted that they were composed in the post-exilic period. Freedman puts Chronicles, with the inclusion of Ezra 1-3 (though its conclusion remains uncertain), in the time immediately after the rebuilding of the temple in 515 and sees it in connection with the hope for restoration of the Davidic monarchy in Haggai and Zechariah (Newsome has a similar view). Other authors conjecture a much later origin, e.g. only in the Hellenistic period (e.g. Welten 199f.; Williamson 1977, 83ff. is critical). The answer to this question largely depends on our understanding of the purpose of Chronicles; it is made more difficult by the fact that our knowledge of the post-exilic situation is extremely fragmentary, so that for the moment no certain decision will be possible.

Dating

Further 'sources' are often quoted in Chronicles, including various prophetic writings (I Chron.29.29; II Chron.9.29; 12.15; 13.22; 20.34; 26.22; 32.32; 33.19). However, it is evident that the content derives from the relevant places in Samuel or Kings. So these are not independent sources but only a special kind of quotation which seems to be based on the relationship of the Chronicler to his sources (cf. Willi, 229ff.; Childs, 645ff.).

Bibliography

Commentaries: Benzinger (KHC) 1901; Kittel (HK) 1902; Rothstein-Hanel (KAT), *I Chron.* 1927; Galling (ATD) 1954; Rudolph (HAT) 1955; Myers (AB) 1965.

P.R.Ackroyd, 'The Chronicler as Exegete', *JSOT* 2, 1977, 2-32; R.L.Braun, 'Solomonic Apologetic in Chronicles', *JBL* 92, 1973, 503-16; id., 'A Reconsideration of the Chronicler's Attitude towards the North', *JBL* 96, 1977, 59-63; id., 'Chronicles, Ezra and Nehemiah: Theology and Literary History', *SVT* 30, 1979, 52-64; F.M.Cross, 'A Reconstruction of the Judaean Restoration', *JBL* 94, 1975, 4-18; D.N.Freedman, 'The Chronicler's Purpose', *CBQ* 23, 1961, 436-42; W.T.In der Smitten, 'Die Gründe für die Aufnahme der Nehemiaschrift in das chronistische Geschichtswerk', *BZ* NF 16, 1972, 207-21; S.Japhet, *The Ideology of the Book of Chronicles and Its Place in Biblical Thought*, 1977 (in Hebrew); R.Mosis, *Untersuchungen zur Theologie des chronistischen Geschichtswerkes*, 1973; J.D.Newsome, 'Toward a New Understanding of the Chronicler and his Purpose', *JBL* 94, 1975, 201-17; M.Noth, *Überlieferungsgeschichtliche Studien*, 1943 ³1973); G.v.Rad, *Das Geschichtsbild des chronistischen Werkes*, 1930; P.Welten, *Geschichte und Geschichtsdarstellung in den Chronikbüchern*, 1973; id., 'Lade – Tempel – Jerusalem. Zur Theologie der Chronikbücher', in *Textgemass, FS E.Würthwein*, 1979, 169-83; T.Willi, *Die Chronik als Auslegung*, 1972; H.G.M.Williamson, 'The Accession of Solomon in the Books of Chronicles', *VT* 26, 1976, 351-61; id., *Israel in the Books of Chronicles*, 1977; id., 'The Origins of the Twenty-Four Priestly Courses. A Study of I Chronicles XXIII-XXVII', *SVT* 30, 1979, 251-68.

Steuernagel, §82-88; Eissfeldt, §72; Fohrer, §34,35; Soggin, 5.IX; Kaiser, §17; Smend, §50; Schmidt, §12; Childs, XLIII.

Cf. also the bibliography on III. 4.6.

5 The Canon of the Old Testament

The individual books of the Old Testament have had a very varied history, which we have attempted to trace in the previous chapter. This includes the formation of wider complexes like the great collection which comprised the Pentateuch and the historical books which follow,

→242ff.
or the collection of the prophetic books. In this way there came into
→185ff.
being a collection of writings which were recognized as 'canonical'.

Conclusion of
the formation of
the canon

It is impossible to say exactly when the individual stages of the collection and formation of the canon came to a conclusion. However, we have some important indications. Thus the author of Chronicles had access to the books of Samuel and Kings in essentially their present form. Moreover, for the genealogy in I Chron.1-9 he used traditions from Genesis and other books of the Pentateuch. Here, of course it must remain open how far these are later additions and supplements to the work of the Chronicler. The fact that the Samaritans adopted the Pentateuch as canonical scripture clearly shows that at the time when they became independent it had essentially its present form and extent. The work of Jesus Sirach (about 190 BC) gives a further point of reference; in its great 'Praise of the fathers' (chs.44-50) it presupposes basically the whole of the Old Testament traditions in the form in which we have them. About 130 BC, Sirach's nephew speaks in his introduction to the Greek translations of the 'Book of the Law, the Prophets and the other Writings', and thus presupposes the division of the canon into three. Towards the end of the first century AD Josephus speaks of twenty-two books (*Contra Apionem* I, 7f.), and about the same time IV Ezra speaks of twenty-four books (14.44-46); here both represent different ways of counting the books of the Hebrew canon (which are nowadays reckoned to be thirty-nine).

Canon
→287f.
→283

→73f.

The widespread theory that the canon was finally established by a 'synod' in Jamnia (Jabneh) about AD 100 is historically incorrect (cf. Schäfer).

A Greek collection developed alongside the Hebrew canon. On the one hand it consisted of the translation of the writings of the Hebrew canon into Greek. According to the legend in the Letter of Aristeas (about 100 BC), on the orders of king Ptolemy II (285-246) the Torah (i.e. the Pentateuch) is said to have been translated in seventy-two days by seventy-two scholars (six from each of the twelve tribes); hence the name Septuagint (seventy) for the whole of the Greek translation. This legend has a historical point of reference in that the translation of the Pentateuch was probably in fact made by the third century BC. The nephew of Jesus Sirach (see above) then already mentions the translation of all three parts of the canon. Further works were added to these writings, some of which had first been written in Hebrew or Aramaic and then translated into Greek, and some of which had been written in Greek from the start. This collection made by the Greek-speaking Diaspora was taken over by the Christian church and also forms the basis of the official Latin translation (the Vulgate). Since the time of the Reformation the Hebrew canon has been the Bible of Protestant churches, with the other books banished to the Apocrypha (i.e. the hidden books, those not intended for public use in the church).

Septuagint

Vulgate

Apocrypha

Modern biblical scholarship has paid too little attention to the final canonical stage of the individual books and to the canon as a whole. The real and essential task has been seen as a critical analysis of the books of the Bible and the traditions they contain, so that the final forms of the books have not attracted any independent interest. In most recent times, however, we can see a change in the questions asked. It relates both to individual books and to the canon as a whole.

In the previous chapters an attempt has been made, stimulated by

Canon

Final form of the
books

Significance of
the canon

Prophecy and
Torah

Moses
→126f., 155f.,
161f., 185ff.

Eschatology
→243

Jewish and
Christian
understanding

the works of Childs and others, to consider the 'canonical' final form of the individual books and understand them in the light of the history by which each of them came into being, at the same time asking what the final form set out to say. Here in many cases it has transpired that it is only possible fully to understand a book from that perspective, and that many individual points of detail also only become comprehensible in the light of the final form and its intention. One of the most important insights here is that the shaping of the biblical books in their present form is usually not the result of chance or of thoughtless and uncomprehending redaction, as was often supposed by earlier historical-critical exegesis, but that quite deliberate forces of shaping were at work which were often guided by a specific and often very pointed theological purpose. Looked at in this way the biblical books in their final form were often important testimonies to the history of Israelite and Jewish religion.

This indicates a task which must be tackled next. Enquiries into the purpose and significance of the canon must go beyond the consideration of individual books and consider the collection as a whole and the relationship between its individual components. For here too we must take into account the possibility that it was not mere chance which led to the present form of the canon. Rather, the form of the canon is to be understood as an expression of particular religious and theological developments and decisions. Here too there have been important preliminary studies. Thus J.A.Sanders has pointed out that the canon is the form in which particular traditions were laid down as binding and that this expresses the self-understanding of the community which made this assertion. Blenkinsopp took these ideas further and made decisive distinctions. Here he worked out the reciprocal relationship between prophecy and Torah and showed that the authority of the canon depends essentially on its prophetic character, but that here there is a transformation in the understanding of prophecy which makes Moses the central figure. Here the Deuteronomic school (in a very broad sense) plays a vital role. The tension between Torah and prophecy is kept alive by the eschatological shaping of post-exilic prophecy. And it is the awareness of this irremovable tension that is expressed in the last sentences of the prophetic canon, in which there is mention of the tense reciprocal relationship between the Torah of Moses and the imminent 'Day of YHWH' (Mal.*3.22-24*).

These questions lead beyond the tasks and possibilities of an Introduction. However, they do indicate central problems for the new 'Theology of the Old Testament' that has to be worked out. Here, then, we need also to consider again quite thoroughly the relationship between the Jewish and the Christian understanding of the Old Testament. Here, too, the works by Childs and Blenkinsopp have made an important start: Childs stresses the understanding of the Old Testament canon as a part of the Christian Bible, whereas Blenkinsopp is aware of the danger of drawing too narrow-minded conclusions which could rob the Old Testament canon of its present significance within the history of

Jewish religion. (As far as I can see, German-speaking discussion has yet to take up the theological problem of the canon.)

These last considerations remind us once again that work on the individual books of the Bible, especially that leading towards their final form, represents an essential contribution to the theological understanding of the Old Testament and is at the same time the indispensable presupposition for it.

Bibliography

J.Blenkinsopp, *Prophecy and Canon*, 1977; B.S.Childs, *Biblical Theology in Crisis*, 1970; G.W.Coats/B.O.Long (eds.), *Canon and Authority*, 1977; J.A.Sanders, *Torah and Canon*, 1972, ²1974; P.Schäfer, 'Die sogenannte Synode von Jabne. Zur Trennung von Juden und Christen im ersten/zweiten Jh.v.Chr.', *Jud* 31, 1975, 54-64, 116-24 (= *Studien zur Geschichte und Theologie des rabbinischen Judentums*, 1978, 45-64).

Steuernagel, §23-26; Eissfeldt, §74, 75; Fohrer, §75-77, Soggin, 1.II; Kaiser, §36; Smend, §2; Schmidt, §1; Childs, II-IV, XLIV.

Abbreviations in the Bibliography

(*a*) Works cited by author's name only

Alt, *KS*	A.Alt, *Kleine Schriften zur Geschichte des Volkes Israel*, I 1953 (⁴1968); II 1953 (⁴1977); III 1959 (²1968) (Partial ET of I in *Essays in Old Testament History and Religion*, 1966)
Begrich, *GS*	J.Begrich, *Gesammelte Studien zum Alten Testament*, 1964
Ben-Sasson	H.H. Ben-Sasson (ed.), *History of the Jewish People*, 1976ff.
Bright	J.Bright, *History of Israel*, ³1981
Childs	B.S.Childs, *Introduction to the Old Testament as Scripture*, 1979
Eissfeldt	O.Eissfeldt, *The Old Testament. An Introduction*, ET 1965
Eissfeldt, *KS*	O.Eissfeldt, *Kleine Schriften* II, 1963
Fohrer	E.Sellin, *Introduction to the Old Testament*, completely revised by G.Fohrer, ET 1968
Gunneweg	A.H.J.Gunneweg, *Geschichte Israels bis Bar Kokhba*, 1972, ⁴1982
Hayes/Miller	J.H.Hayes/J.M.Miller (eds.), *Israelite and Judaean History*, 1977, including II W.G.Dever/W.M.Clark, 'The Patriarchal Traditions' III T.L.Thompson/D.Irvin, 'The Joseph and Moses Narratives' IV J.M.Miller, 'The Israelite Occupation of Canaan' V A.D.H.Mayes, 'The Period of the Judges and the Rise of the Monarchy' VI J.A.Soggin, 'The Davidic-Solomonic Kingdom' VII H.Donner, 'The Separate States of Israel and Judah' VIII B.Oded, 'Judah and the Exile' IX G.Widengren, 'The Persian Period'
Herrmann	S.Herrmann, *History of Israel in Old Testament Times*, ET ²1981
Kaiser	O.Kaiser, *Introduction to the Old Testament*, ET 1975
Koch	K. Koch, *The Growth of the Biblical Tradition*, ET 1969
Malamat	A.Malamat (ed.), *The World History of the Jewish People IV: The Age of the Monarchies*, 1979
Mazar	B.Mazar (ed.), *The World History of the Jewish People*, *II: Patriarchs*, 1961 (1970), *III: Judges*, 1961 (1971)
M.Noth, *GS*	M.Noth, *Gesammelte Studien zum Alten Testament*, I 1957, II 1969 (partial ET of I in *The Laws in the Pentateuch*, 1966)
Noth	M.Noth, *History of Israel*, ET ²1959
G.von Rad, *GS*	G.von Rad, *Gesammelte Studien zum Alten Testament* I 1958 (⁴1971), II 1973 (partial ET of I in *The Problem of the Hexateuch*, 1966)

R.Rendtorff, *GS*	R.Rendtorff, *Gesammelte Studien zum Alten Testament*, 1975
Schmidt	W.H.Schmidt, *Introduction to the Old Testament*, ET 1984
Smend	R.Smend, *Die Entstehung des Alten Testaments*, 1978, ²1981
Soggin	J.A.Soggin, *Introduction to the Old Testament. From Its Origins to the Closing of the Alexandrian Canon*, ²1980
Steuernagel	C.Steuernagel, *Lehrbuch der Einleitung in das Alte Testament mit einem Anhang über die Apokryphen und Pseudepigraphen*, 1912
de Vaux	R.de Vaux, *The Early History of Israel. I: To the Exodus and Covenant of Sinai, II: To the Period of the Judges*, ET 1978
H.W.Wolff, *GS*	H.W.Wolff, *Gesammelte Studien zum Alten Testament*, 1964 (²1973)

(*b*) Other abbreviations

AB	The Anchor Bible
ABLA	M.Noth, *Aufsätze zur biblischen Landes- und Altertumskunde*, two vols, 1971
ANET	J.B.Pritchard (ed.), *Ancient Near Eastern Texts relating to the Old Testament*, ²1955, Supplement 1969
AOT	H.Gressmann (ed.), *Altorientalische Texte zum Alten Testament*, ²1926
ASTI	*Annual of the Swedish Theological Institute*
ATD	Das Alte Testament Deutsch
BA	*The Biblical Archaeologist*
BAR	*The Biblical Archaeologist Reader*
BCAT	Biblischer Commentar über das Alte Testament
BHH	*Biblisch-Historisches Handwörterbuch*
Bib	*Biblica*
BK	Biblisches Kommentar Altes Testament
BRL	K.Galling (ed.), *Biblisches Reallexikon*, ²1977
BZ	*Biblische Zeitschrift*
CAT	Commentaire de l'Ancien Testament
CBQ	*Catholic Biblical Quarterly*
DBAT	*Dielheimer Blätter zum Alten Testament*
EJ	*Encyclopaedia Judaica*
EvTh	*Evangelische Theologie*
HAT	Handbuch zum Alten Testament
HK	Handkommentar zum Alten Testament
HS	Die Heilige Schrift des Alten Testaments
IB	*The Interpreter's Bible*
ICC	International Critical Commentary
IEJ	*Israel Exploration Journal*
IDB.S	*The Interpreter's Dictionary of the Bible Supplement*
JBL	*Journal of Biblical Literature and Exegesis*
JQR	*Jewish Quarterly Review*
JSS	*Journal of Semitic Studies*

JTS	*Journal of Theological Studies*
Jud	*Judaica. Beiträge zum Verständnis des jüdischen Schicksals in Vergangenheit und Gegenwart*
JSJ	*Journal of the Study of Judaism in the Persian, Hellenistic and Roman Period*
JSOT	*Journal for the Study of the Old Testament*
KAI	H.Donner/W.Röllig, *Kanaanäische und aramäische Inschriften* I-III, 1962-1964 (I ⁴1979, II ³1973; III ³1976)
KAT	Kommentar zum Alten Testament
KeH	Kurzgefasstes exegetisches Handbuch zum Alten Testament
KHC	Kurzer Hand-Commentar zum Alten Testament
KuD	*Kerygma und Dogma*
NERT	W.Beyerlin (ed.), *Near Eastern Religious Texts relating to the Old Testament*
NF, NS	Neue Folge, New Series
OrAnt	*Oriens Antiquus*
OTL	Old Testament Library
OTS	*Oudtestamentische Studiën*
PJB	*Palästinajahrbuch*
POuT	*Die Prediking van het Oude Testament*
RB	*Revue Biblique*
SAT	Die Schriften des Alten Testaments in Auswahl übersetzt und erklärt
STU	*Schweizerische Theologische Umschau*
SVT	*Supplement to Vetus Testamentum*
TDNT	G.Kittel (ed.), *Theological Dictionary of the New Testament*
TDOT	Botterweck and Ringgren, *Theological Dictionary of the Old Testament*
TGI	K.Galling (ed.), *Religionsgeschichtliche Textbuch zum Alten Testament*, 1975
TLZ	*Theologische Literaturzeitung*
TR	*Theologische Rundschau*
ThViat	*Theologia Viatorum. Jahrbuch der Kirchlichen Hochschule*, Berlin
TRE	*Theologische Realenzyklopädie*
TUAT	O.Kaiser (ed.), *Texte aus der Umwelt des Alten Testaments*, 1982ff.
TZ	*Theologische Zeitschrift*
VF	*Verkündigung und Forschung*
VT	*Vetus Testamentum*
WO	*Die Welt des Orients*
WuD	*Wort und Dienst. Jahrbuch der Theologischen Schule (Kirchlichen Hochschule) Bethel*
ZAW	*Zeitschrift für die alttestamentliche Wissenschaft*
ZBK	Zürcher Bibelkommentar
ZDMG	*Zeitschrift des deutschen Morgenländischen Gesellschaft*
ZDPV	*Zeitschrift des Deutschen Palästinavereins*
ZTK	*Zeitschrift für Theologie und Kirche*

Indexes

In each case the index is a select one and is supplemented by the Table of Contents and the marginal references.

Index of Subjects

Reference to sections in which the word in question appears in the title are usually not included: cf. the Table of Contents.

Passover, 10, 12, 19, 95, 97, 99, 140,
147, 162
Patriarchs, patriarchal
narratives, 7, 135, 160
period, 9, 19
religion, 8
sagas, 126
Penuel, 7, 40, 136
Pentateuch as canonical writing, 289
Philistines, 26–34, 49, 50, 87, 132, 171,
172, 212, 215, 284
Phoenicians, 43
Pilgrimage, *see* Zion
Pilgrimage festivals, 96
Pithom and Raamses, 11
Plagues, 10, 97
Pogrom of Jews, 270
Post-exilic, 197, 222, 229, 241, 254, 287
Prayers, 77
Priest(s), 228, 235
Priestly
blessing, 147
tradition, 137, 141
Writing, 158, 159
Primal history, 132, 160
Processions, 99
Prohibitives, 161
Promise
of increase, 136
of land, 136
of return, 195f.
speeches of, 197
Prophecy, 245, 290
against foreign nations, 122, 190, 201,
204, 209, 214, 220, 234, 241
and fulfilment, 181
Prophet(s), 117, 188, 215, 216, 243,
244
disciples of, 44, 112
false, 204, 227
and kings, 113, 116, 179, 204
self-understanding of, 116, 203, 223
as watchmen, 209, 214
Prophetic
books, 117; 188, 215, 216, 243, 244
groups, 111
narratives, 2, 37, 42–44, 88, 114, 178,
225
office, 113, 121
writings, 118
Proverbs, 82, 110
Proverbs, book of, 245, 265
Psalms, 2, 75, 78, 99, 100, 101, 108
acrostic, 230, 246
eschatological, 192
halleluyah, 248
messianic, 75, 249
penitential, 103
pilgrimage, 247

royal, 108, 248
Torah, 104, 110, 246, 248
wisdom, 103, 110, 125
outside the Psalter, 140, 173, 180,
191, 225, 230, 231, 232
Psalter, Elohistic, 248
Purim, feast of, 97, 258, 270
Purity
of Jewish religion/community, 62, 67,
70, 73, 74, 98, 147, 152, 282
regulations for, 98, 145, 147, 181

Rechabites, 121, 205
Recognition, 252
formula, 208, 211, 219
Redaction history, 184
Redactor, 159
Rejection, 29, 41
Remnant
of Jacob, 228
of Joseph, 221
of Zion, 191
Repentance, 221, 226, 239, 243
call to, 239
Reuben, tribe of, 20, 24, 27, 136
Return of exiles, 60, 193, 197, 277, 278
Riddle, 83
Righteousness, 199
of God, 199, 252
Rise of David, 31, 107, 172
Ruth, book of, 110, 164, 245

Sabbath, 97, 162, 197, 281
commandment, 150
year, 153
Sacrifice, 97, 103, 145, 233
calendar of, 97, 149
communion, 19, 95, 98, 101
regulations for, 97, 98
Sagas, 1, 25, 84–88, 131
Salvation, announcement of, 121, 193
conditional words of, 119
eschatological, 237
nationalistic prophets of, 122, 224
oracle of, 58, 103, 122, 193, 268
promise of, 122, 193
words of, 117, 120
see also Judgment and salvation
Samaria, 42, 45, 48, 70, 74, 192, 217,
221, 223, 286
and Jerusalem *see* Jerusalem
province of, 61
Samaria/Samaritans, 48, 62, 74, 229,
287, 288
Sanctuaries
Canaanite, 8, 45
on high places, 96 *see also* Cult
nomadic, 40
Sanctuary, cities of, 107, 150, 165

Index of Names

References to sections in which a name appears in the title are not usually included, cf. the Table of Contents.

Index of Hebrew Words

The sequence follows the Hebrew alphabet.

Differences between Hebrew and English Biblical References

At a number of points in the Old Testament there are differences the numbering of chapters and verses between the Hebrew (or Aramaic) text and most English versions. In the present book, references where there is such a difference have been given to the numbering in Hebrew (Aramaic) text and printed *in italics*; the table below gives the most significant differences between the systems. In every case the Hebrew (Aramaic) reference is given first.

Genesis		*13.1*	12.32	*II Kings*	
32.1	31.55	*13.2–19*	13.1–18	*12.1*	11.21
32.2–33	32.1–32	*23.1*	22.30	*12.2–22*	12.2–21
		23.2–26	23.1–25		
Exodus		*28.69*	29.1	*Isaiah*	
7.26–29	8.1–4	*29.2–28*	29.2–29	*8.23*	9.1
8.1–28	8.5–32			*9.1–20*	9.2–21
21.37	22.1	*Joshua*		*63.19b*	64.1
22.1–30	22.2–31	21.36ff. is lacking in most		*64.1–11*	64.2–12
		Hebrew MSS			
Leviticus				*Jeremiah*	
5.20–26	6.1–7	*I Samuel*		*8.23*	9.1
6.1–23	6.8–30	*21.1*	20.42b	*9.1–23*	9.2–20
		21.2–16	21.1–15		
Numbers		*24.1*	23.29	*Ezekiel*	
17.1–15	16.30–50	*24.2–33*	24.1–22	*21.1–5*	20.45–49
17.16–18	17.1–13			*21.6–37*	21.1–32
25.19	26.1a	*II Samuel*			
30.1	29.40	*19.1*	18.33	*Hosea*	
30.2–17	30.1–16	*19.2–44*	19.1–43	*2.1–2*	1.10–11
				2.3–25	2.1–23
				12.1	11.12
Deuteronomy		*I Kings*		*12.2–15*	12.1–14
5.17	5.17–20	*5.1–14*	4.21–34	*14.1*	13.16
5.18–30	5.21–33	*5.15–32*	5.1–18	*14.2–9*	14.1–8

Index of Biblical References

References to the sections in Part Three in which the book in question is discussed are included only in exceptional cases, cf. the Table of Contents. To simplify matters, the verse numbers have occasionally been left out and several mentions of a chapter have been consolidated.

Index of Biblical References

Index of Modern Scholars

This selection is meant to provide some orientation for the history of Old Testament research; it contains only the names of authors cited in the text who have completed a specific contribution to Old Testament study.